BEANO books
geddes & grosset

Published 2000 by Beano books geddes & grosset,
an imprint of Children's Leisure Products Limited,
David Dale House, New Lanark ML11 9DJ, Scotland



ISBN 1 84205 014 1

Printed and bound in Europe

CLASSIC TOPPER
GHASTLY MANOR
I HOPE SOMEBODY BUYS THIS PLACE SOON—I CAN'T STAND IT MUCH LONGER!
FOR SALE
THIS IS MISTER FEAR, OWNER OF GHASTLY MANOR.

HOUSE FOR SALE, EH? IT COULD BE JUST WHAT I WANT.
FOR SALE
I—I'M SURE IT IS, SIR. COME AND LOOK ROUND. BRING YOUR CHEQUE BOOK.

ERK!
ER—D—DON'T WORRY ABOUT THAT. IT'S—ER—JUST MY DOG.

INTERESTING OLD TREE, THAT. WHAT KIND IS IT?

WAH!
BOO-HOO!
A WEEPING WILLOW!
SOB!
WAIL!

YAAGH!
ER—ER—THAT'S QUITE A LARGE GOLDFISH, I—ISN'T IT?

I—I DON'T THINK I WANT TO BUY—
WAIT! YOU HAVEN'T SEEN INSIDE YET!

YUM! IS HE MY LUNCH?
NO, NO. HE'S COME TO BUY THE HOUSE. MAYBE, PERHAPS.
N—NOT L—LIKELY!

H—HOLD ON, SIR! L—LOOK! THIS HOUSE HAS A WISHING WELL THAT WORKS!

WORKS, EH? I'LL TOSS A COIN IN AND SEE!

GRAAAAH!
ERK! I—I WISH I WAS WELL AWAY FROM THIS PLACE!

YOUR EVERY WISH IS MY COMMAND. GRAAAH!
SEE? I TOLD HIM IT WORKED.

PIG TALES
POPPA
MOMMA
PIGGLES

SNURFLE! SNARFLE!
WHIMPER! The nasty fox is after me.

YOINK! My tail's caught on the fence—I'm de-FENCE-less!
BOUND!
SNAG

CLASSIC NUTTY
HOINK! I'm going straight back towards that fox!
TWANG!
SLURP! CACKLE!

BIFF!
PHEW! I think that fox has had enough of me.
UGH!

I can't always be so lucky. I wish I was something other than a pig—a hound, maybe!

Hounds get to chase foxes.

BUT—
I say! Keep moving, hound. The dashed fox is escaping.
Hmm! Hounds chase foxes ALL day—that's no life.

I wish I was Farmer. He's got a really easy life.
YAWN! It's been a hard day.

What's for tea, wife?

BACON!
HM! GOOD!

HOWEVER—
And there it is! Go and catch it!
BOOT!
EEK!

I think I'll stick to being a pig . . .

. . . at least I'm always popular and in demand!
GRR! Stop that piglet!

NERO
and
ZERO
ZERO
NERO

Caesar's due home from the wars today! We'd better roll out the red carpet to welcome him!
Let's hope we've no trouble this time!

CLASSIC BUZZ
Remember the first time we used the carpet?

It was too long! Knocked him right over!

Into the gutter!

Fools!
He wasn't too happy!

We cut a bit off the carpet after that!

Hail, great Caesar!
That's me!
It fitted
erfectly!
It did!

Pity we noticed specks of dust on the carpet!

We gave it a good shaking!
Don't remind me!

We shook Caesar off into the gutter again!

We're safe this time! The carpet's been rolled up in the cupboard for months!
Here he comes!

Hail, great conquering Caesar!

Moths? Oh, no!

CHOMP!
CHOMP!
CHOMP!

Delicious!
My best toga ruined!

By the stars, you'll pay for this, you fools! Stand and fight!
Ho-ho! Caesar's in the wars again!
Keep going, Nero! We'll be on the carpet if he catches us!

Colonel
CLASSIC BEEZER
BLINK

WELL, I MUST BE GETTING HOME NOW, NEPHEW!
NO NEED TO WALK, AUNTIE! I'LL RUN YOU HOME IN MY CAR! ARF!

GALLOPIN' GUNNERS! IT'S GONE! I'VE BEEN ROBBED!
BACK DOOR!

HELLO! HELLO! POLICE? YOU CADS HAVE BEEN SLEEPING AGAIN! MY CAR'S BEEN STOLEN! SEND A MAN ROUND STRAIGHTAWAY! I WANT MY CAR! AT ONCE!

THAT'LL SHAKE 'EM UP A BIT, EH, AUNTIE? MUST KEEP 'EM ON THEIR TOES, WHAT! ARF! ARF!

BY THUNDER! LOOK, AUNTIE! THAT WAS QUICK WORK! THEY'VE GOT IT BACK ALREADY!

GOOD GRIEF! SOMEONE'S STOLEN THE STEERING WHEEL NOW!
B-BUT—

MEANWHILE
AT LAST! IT'S ARRIVED AT LAST! I'VE ALWAYS WANTED A LAWN-SPRINKLER!
WONDO LAWN SPRINKLER

MY STEERING-WHEEL! CARTWRIGHT! YOU THIEVING BOUNDAH!
?
WONDO LAWN SPRINKLER

WOULD YOU BELIEVE IT! CARTWRIGHT OF ALL PEOPLE! I'LL NEVER TRUST THAT FELLOW AGAIN!
I'LL TEACH THE OLD FOOL A LESSON!
TURN!

HELP! WHAT NEXT? THE BLINKIN' RADIATOR'S SPRUNG A LEAK!

FRIGHTFULLY SORRY, AUNTIE! THE OLD BUS HAS HAD IT! I'LL CALL YOU A TAXI!
TITTER!

TAXI!

MY WORD! THAT'S SERVICE FOR YOU! HERE'S THE TAXI CHAPPIE ALREADY! COME ON IN, SIR!
MUST CHECK UP ON THAT STOLEN CAR!
POLICE

IT'S THIS LADY, SIR! TAKE HER AWAY!
AHA! THE OLD BOY MUST HAVE CAUGHT THE THIEF HIMSELF!

BYE-BYE, AUNTIE! PLEASANT TRIP! ARF! ARF!
B-BUT— B-B-BUT—

B-BUT—
I WARN YOU, MADAM—ANYTHING YOU SAY MAY BE . . .
POLICE

WHY DIDN'T I JUST WALK HOME?

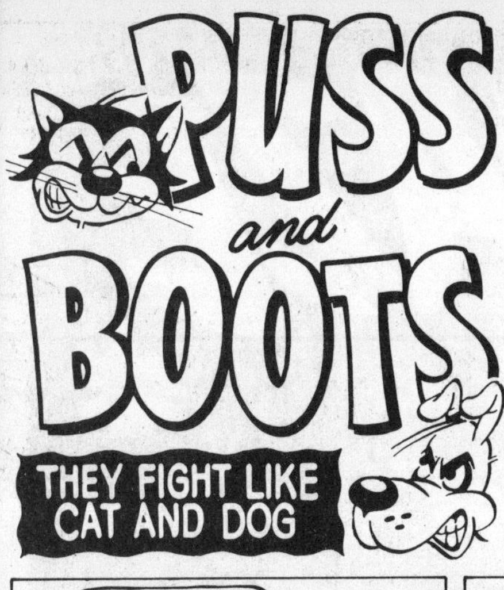
PUSS and BOOTS
THEY FIGHT LIKE CAT AND DOG

EXCUSE ME, LORD LAWDOWN, THERE IS AN UNCOUTH PERSON TO SEE YOU.
SHOW HIM IN, RAISIN, OLD FRUIT!
THE Sparky 1897

I WANT YOU TO CLEAR ALL THE GHOSTS AND SPOOKS OUT OF LAWDOWN HALL! THEY'RE SCARING MY DEAR WIFE, LADY LAWDOWN!
CLASSIC SPARKY
BUT OF COURSE, YOUR LARDSHOP! THEY HAVEN'T A GHOST OF A CHANCE! YUK! YUK!
GHOST HUNTERS LTD.

I'M OFF TO BED, LADDIE! REMEMBER, THEY'LL COME OUT AT MIDNIGHT!
YES, YOUR LOUDSHEEP, I'M SETTING UP MY PUSS PATENT SPOOK-SPLATTERING KIT!

PHEW! WAIT A MINUTE, THAT SOUNDS LIKE ONE OF THEM NOW!
RAPELLA MOONA WASA SHINING-A...

DING!
CLANG!
DONG!
BLAM!
AARGH!
OOH!
OW! EH?
'ERE!?!

DEARIE, DEARIE ME! IT'S NOT A GHOST AT ALL! IT'S JUST A SILLY OLD POOCH WITH A BUCKET ON HIS HEAD!
OOO-OW!
CLANG-DOING!

SEE HERE, MOGGIE, LORD LAWDOWN SENT FOR ME TO GET RID OF THE PIANO AND TUNE THE MICE!
OH, YEAH? LOOK WHAT YOU'VE DONE TO MY GHOST-NOBBLIN' GEAR!

TAKE THAT!
OUCH! NOW YOU TAKE THIS!
WE ARE THE GHOSTS OF LAWDOWN HALL, AND WE... YIKES! WHAT'S THAT?
BOP!
BLAM!
BASH!
BANG!
CRUMBS!
OO-ER!

WHAM!
THIS IS NO PLACE FOR A NICE, PEACEFUL GHOST! LET'S GO AND HAUNT SOMEWHERE ELSE!
YOWL!
OUCH!
BOP!
CRUNCH!
BASH!
WAM!
WAIL!
SCREAM!
BONK!

RATTLE!
BOOM!
EVERYBODY OUT, LADS! THE PLACE IS HAUNTED!
GRRR! OUCH! SNARL!
OOYA! GNASH! OOF!
ZOOM!
ZOOM!
ZOOM!
WOO-OOF!

WHO'S RAISIN' THAT DIN, RAISIN?
SIR! THE GHOSTS HAVE GONE! THOSE TWO REVOLTING ANIMALS HAVE DRIVEN THEM OFF!
HELP! MOTHER!
OW!
GROAN!
OOH!
ERK!

WELL DONE, MY FURRY FRIENDS!
SEE THAT FIST? HAVE A GOOD CLOSE LOOK!
BLAM!
BONK!
IT'S NICE TO GET PAID FOR DUFFIN' YOU UP, MOGGIE, BUT HERE'S A FREE SAMPLE FOR NOTHIN'!

CLASSIC CRACKER

# SKOOLDAZE

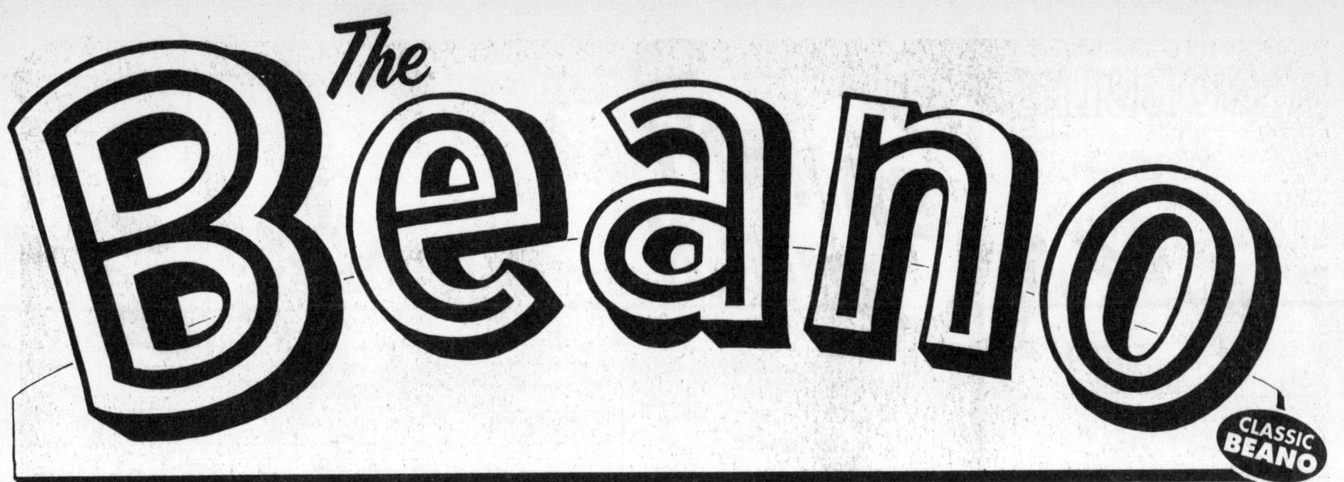
The Beano
CLASSIC BEANO

BIFFO THE BEAR

OH, DEAR! THERE'S BEEN A LOT OF BURGLARIES IN THE DISTRICT!
Daily Blah

LATER IN TOWN—
PET SHOP
WATCH DOG BARGAIN PRICE
SALE TODAY
AH! THE VERY THING!

HE LOOKS CLEVER. I'LL TAKE HIM.
RIGHT YOU ARE, SIR! BUT I MUST WARN YOU THAT DOGS BOUGHT AT A SALE CANNOT BE RETURNED.

THAT NIGHT—
YOU STAY THERE AND BARK AT THE FIRST SIGHT OF A BURGLAR!

WUFF!
YOWF-F!
TH-THERE MUST BE S-SOMEBODY OUT THERE! I'D BETTER GO AND SEE.

SO—
N-NO SIGN OF A BURGLAR—OR THE WATCH DOG!

HEH! HEH! THE DOG MUST BE CHASING THAT BURGLAR OUT OF THE DISTRICT!

SLAM!
CLICK!
WOW! SOMEBODY'S SLAMMED THE DOOR AND LOCKED ME OUT!

GRR! HE'S A CLEVER WATCH DOG ALL RIGHT—ONLY IT'S TV HE LIKES TO WATCH!

MUTTER-MUTTER! MAN IN THE SHOP SAID HE COULDN'T TAKE HIM BACK! OH WELL, THERE'S ONLY ONE THING FOR IT!

SO, IN THE MORNING, AFTER THE LOCKSMITH HAS BEEN—
BIFFO HERE. I WANT ANOTHER WATCH DOG.... YES, YOU HEARD—ANOTHER WATCH DOG—THE BIGGEST ONE YOU'VE GOT!

THAT NIGHT—
BIFFO
HEH! HEH! NOW THAT I'VE A WATCH DOG TO WATCH MY WATCH DOG, I SHOULD GET A PEACEFUL EVENING IN FRONT OF THE TV!

The GOBBLES
GIT A NEW COOKERY BOOK, YUH LAZY OL' BURD!
ERK!
YEAH! THE MICE ARE SO HUNGRY, THEY ATE THAT ONE FOR BREAKFAST!

OH, BOY! A COOKERY BOOK!
GOING— GOING—
MRS EAT-ON'S COOKERY BOOK

GONE! HEH! HEH!
DONK!
EAT-ON'S COOKERY BOOK
SNATCH!

GAWSH! THAT WUZ JUST TOO EASY! NOW THEN, WHAT KIN MAW COOK FER DINNER?

THERE'S A PESKY FINE BUNCH O' RECIPES IN HERE! WE COULD HAVE— ER—SPAGHETTI SOUP, RHUBARB RAVIOLI, BANANA BOLOGNESE, SAUSAGE SUNDAE—

CLASSIC BEEZER
The BANANA BUNCH

Z-ZOOM! OOH! JUST MISSED THAT BIG FACTORY CHIMNEY!
HOW DO WE GET RID OF HIM, BRAINY?

YEAH! WE DON'T WANT HIM TO COME TO THE PICTURES WITH US AND SPOIL EVERYTHING AS USUAL! NOW, LISTEN! WE'LL PLAY AT BLIND MAN'S BUFF...

OOH! THANKS FOR LETTING ME BE THE BLIND MAN FIRST, BRAINY!
THAT'S OKAY, DOPEY! HEH! HEH!
WINK!

THAT'S WHAT HE THINKS! WE'RE AWAY TO THE PICTURES! HEE-HEE! AND HE CAN'T SEE US!
I'M COMING TO GET YOU!

GOT YOU! OH, NO! IT'S JUST THE CHAIR! BUT I'LL FIND YOU! JUST YOU WATCH!

THEY MUST BE IN THE BEDROOM! I'LL TRY IN THERE! THROUGH THE DOOR WE GO! OOH! THIS IS GOOD FUN!

HEE-HEE! I KNOW YOU'RE IN HERE! I'LL GET YOU THIS TIME!

RIGHT, SID! THAT'S THE LOT! LET'S GO!

ROTTERS! THEY'RE NOT BENEATH THE BED!

PLAZA
NOT IN HERE AT ALL! THEY MUST BE HIDING IN THE TV ROOM!
HERE WE ARE, SID! LET'S GET UNLOADED!

PLAZA
HELP! HOW DID HE GET IN THERE?
?

HEH! HEH! YOU MUST ADMIT THAT WAS A BRILLIANT IDEA OF MINE! DOPEY'LL NEVER FIND US IN HERE!

SUDDENLY—
?
BRISTLY HAIR! BIG SPECS! YEP! I KNOW WHO YOU ARE! YOU'RE BRAINY!

YIPPEE! I WAS RIGHT!
DOPEY!

I GOT YOU, BRAINY, SO NOW IT'S YOUR TURN TO BE THE BLIND MAN! OOH! I LIKE THIS GAME!
HO! HO! NOW BRAINY WON'T BE ABLE TO SEE ANY OF THE PICTURE!

—OR MAYBE PEA PIE, MUTTON MASH, AND CARROT CUSTARD! SLURP! SLURP! SLURP!
SCORCH!
LOOK OUT, PAW! THE SUN'S SHINING THROUGH YOUR GLASSES AND BURNING THAT BOOK!

TURNIP TURNOVER, CHEESE CURRY, POTATO PICKLES, SULTANA SALAD, MINCED MELON, BEETROOT BUTTER—

WE TRIED TO TELL YOU, PAW!
AARGH! HELP! NO!

OH, MY GAWSH! AH'S TOO LATE! IT'S BURNED TO A CINDER! GULP!
SSS!

WELL, WHAT'S YER EXCUSE THIS TIME, EH? EH?
OUR DINNER! BURNED!
IT'S A HARD LIFE!

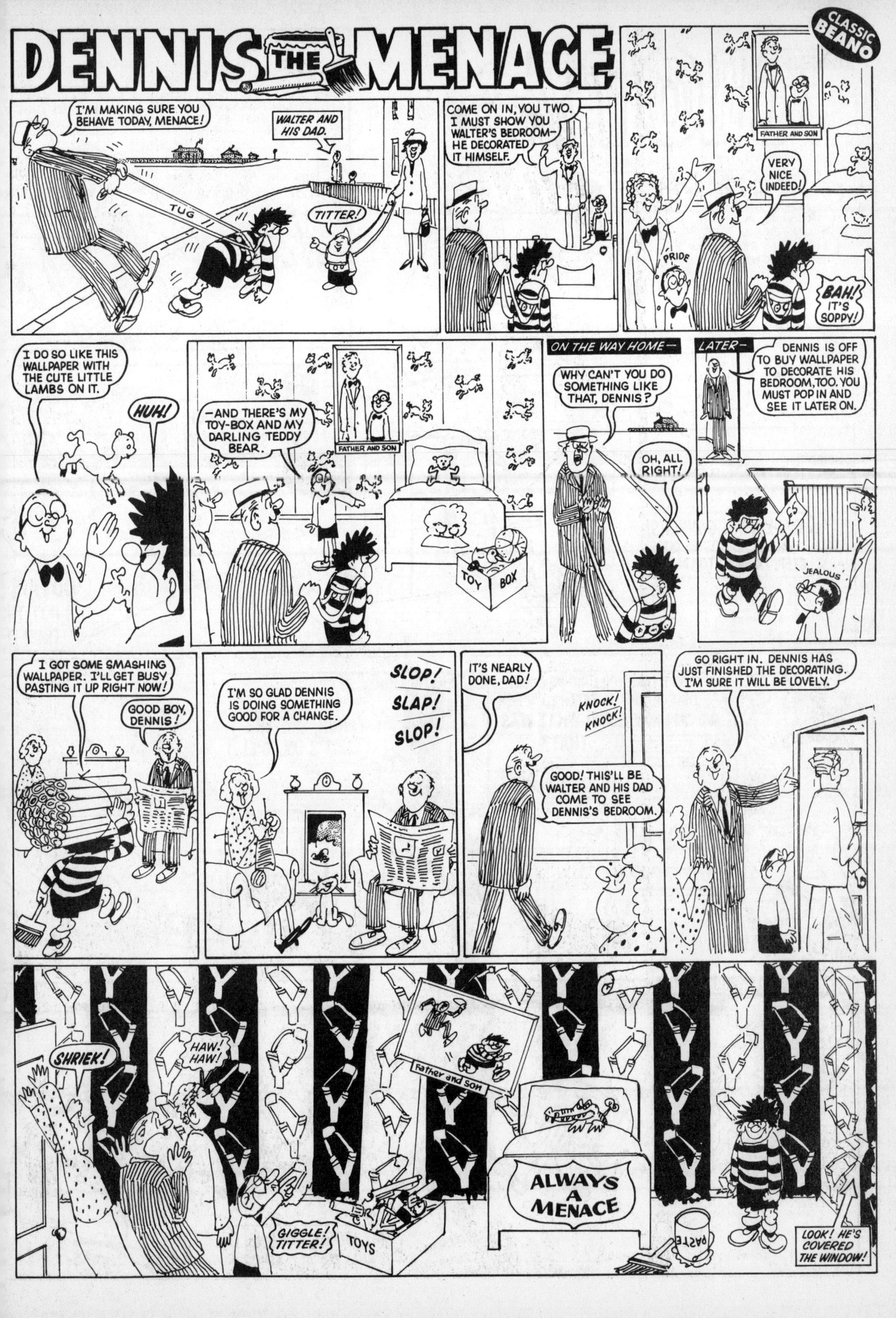
DENNIS THE MENACE
CLASSIC BEANO
I'M MAKING SURE YOU BEHAVE TODAY, MENACE!
WALTER AND HIS DAD.
TUG
TITTER!
COME ON IN, YOU TWO. I MUST SHOW YOU WALTER'S BEDROOM— HE DECORATED IT HIMSELF.
FATHER AND SON
VERY NICE INDEED!
PRIDE
BAH! IT'S SOPPY!
I DO SO LIKE THIS WALLPAPER WITH THE CUTE LITTLE LAMBS ON IT.
HUH!
—AND THERE'S MY TOY-BOX AND MY DARLING TEDDY BEAR.
FATHER AND SON
TOY BOX
ON THE WAY HOME—
WHY CAN'T YOU DO SOMETHING LIKE THAT, DENNIS?
OH, ALL RIGHT!
LATER—
DENNIS IS OFF TO BUY WALLPAPER TO DECORATE HIS BEDROOM, TOO. YOU MUST POP IN AND SEE IT LATER ON.
JEALOUS
I GOT SOME SMASHING WALLPAPER. I'LL GET BUSY PASTING IT UP RIGHT NOW!
GOOD BOY, DENNIS!
I'M SO GLAD DENNIS IS DOING SOMETHING GOOD FOR A CHANGE.
SLOP!
SLAP!
SLOP!
IT'S NEARLY DONE, DAD!
KNOCK! KNOCK!
GOOD! THIS'LL BE WALTER AND HIS DAD COME TO SEE DENNIS'S BEDROOM.
GO RIGHT IN. DENNIS HAS JUST FINISHED THE DECORATING. I'M SURE IT WILL BE LOVELY.
SHRIEK!
HAW! HAW!
Father and Son
ALWAYS A MENACE
GIGGLE! TITTER!
TOYS
PASTE
LOOK! HE'S COVERED THE WINDOW!

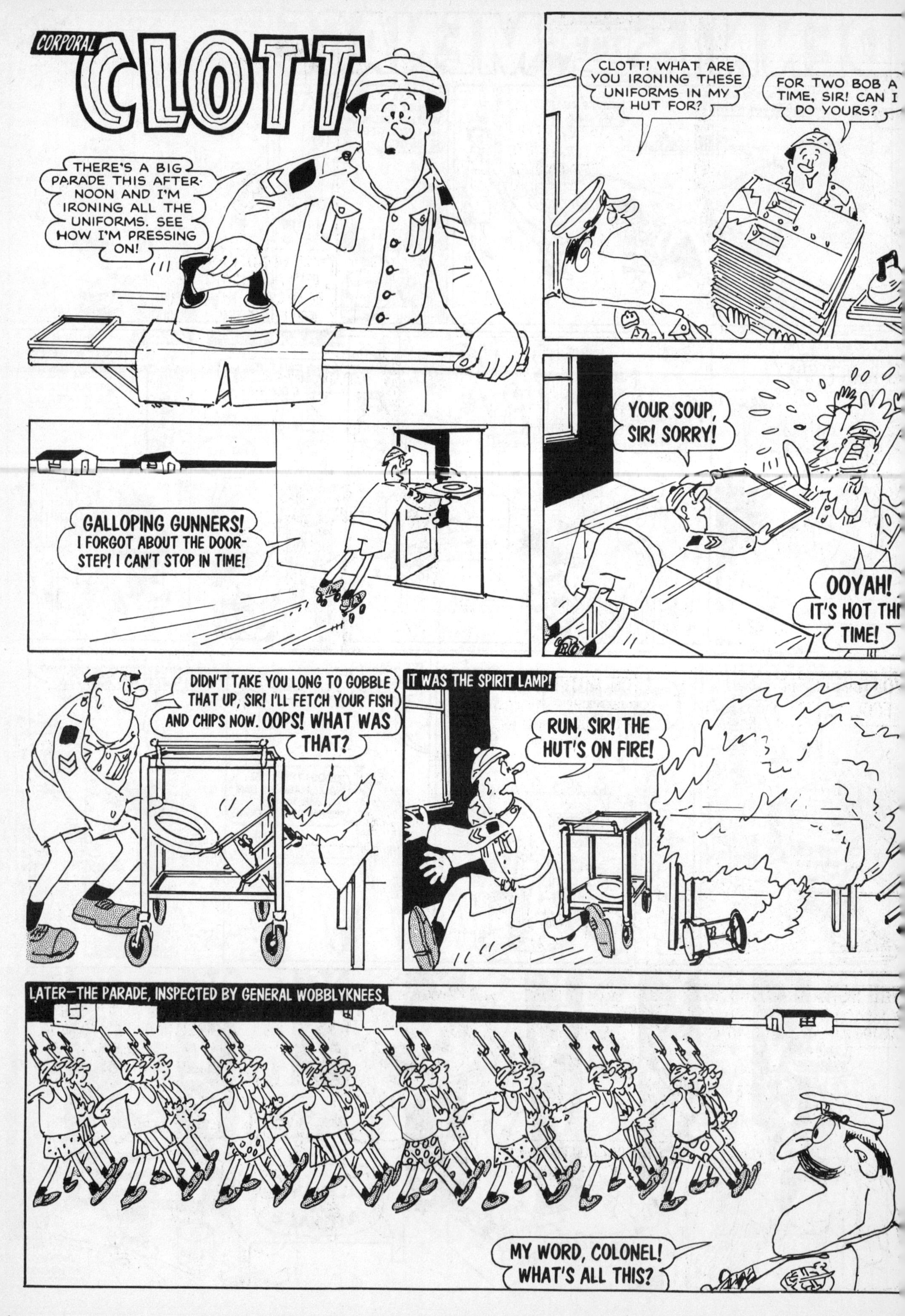
CORPORAL CLOTT
THERE'S A BIG PARADE THIS AFTER-NOON AND I'M IRONING ALL THE UNIFORMS. SEE HOW I'M PRESSING ON!
CLOTT! WHAT ARE YOU IRONING THESE UNIFORMS IN MY HUT FOR?
FOR TWO BOB A TIME, SIR! CAN I DO YOURS?
GALLOPING GUNNERS! I FORGOT ABOUT THE DOOR-STEP! I CAN'T STOP IN TIME!
YOUR SOUP, SIR! SORRY!
OOYAH! IT'S HOT THI TIME!
DIDN'T TAKE YOU LONG TO GOBBLE THAT UP, SIR! I'LL FETCH YOUR FISH AND CHIPS NOW. OOPS! WHAT WAS THAT?
IT WAS THE SPIRIT LAMP!
RUN, SIR! THE HUT'S ON FIRE!
LATER—THE PARADE, INSPECTED BY GENERAL WOBBLYKNEES.
MY WORD, COLONEL! WHAT'S ALL THIS?

CLASSIC DANDY
NO, YOU WON'T! BUT YOU CAN FETCH MY DINNER— NOW! THIS VERY INSTANT!
TEN MINUTES LATER CLOTT RETURNS.
THIS SOUP'S COLD! TAKE IT AWAY AND BRING A HOT LOT!
SORRY, SIR, BUT THE COOK-HOUSE IS SO FAR AWAY IT JUST GETS COLD.
CLEVER CLOTT, THAT'S ME! WITH THESE SKATES ON I'LL BE SO QUICK THAT THE SOUP WON'T HAVE TIME TO COOL!
WHY WEREN'T YOU BORN WITH BRAINS, CLOTT?
TERRIBLY SORRY, SIR! PITY IT WAS TOMATO SOUP, EH?
HERE'S THE ANSWER —A SPIRIT LAMP UNDER THE PLATE OF SOUP TO KEEP IT WARM!
SOUP, SIR, PIPING HOT!
WELL DONE, CLOTT! SERVE IT UP—I'M FAMISHED!
YOU HAM-FISTED FOOL, CLOTT!
OH, MOTHER! ALL THE UNIFORMS I WAS IRONING IN YOUR HUT ARE BEING BURNED!
FOOL! IDIOT! CLOT!
WELL- THE MEN ARE WEARING THEIR NEW TROPICAL KIT, SIR! YOU SEE, IT'S FAR TOO HOT FOR THEM TO WEAR UNIFORMS!
HOPE HE BELIEVES THAT!
TIP TOP TAILORS
WE'VE GOT NEW UNIFORMS OUT OF THE TAILORS!
THE BILL, CORPORAL! YOUR COLONEL SAID YOU'D BE GLAD TO SETTLE THE BILL. IF YOU DIDN'T HE MUTTERED SOMETHING ABOUT LETTING THE MEN SETTLE WITH YOU!
I'LL HAVE TO ROB A BANK!
BILL
£352

CLASSIC NUTTY

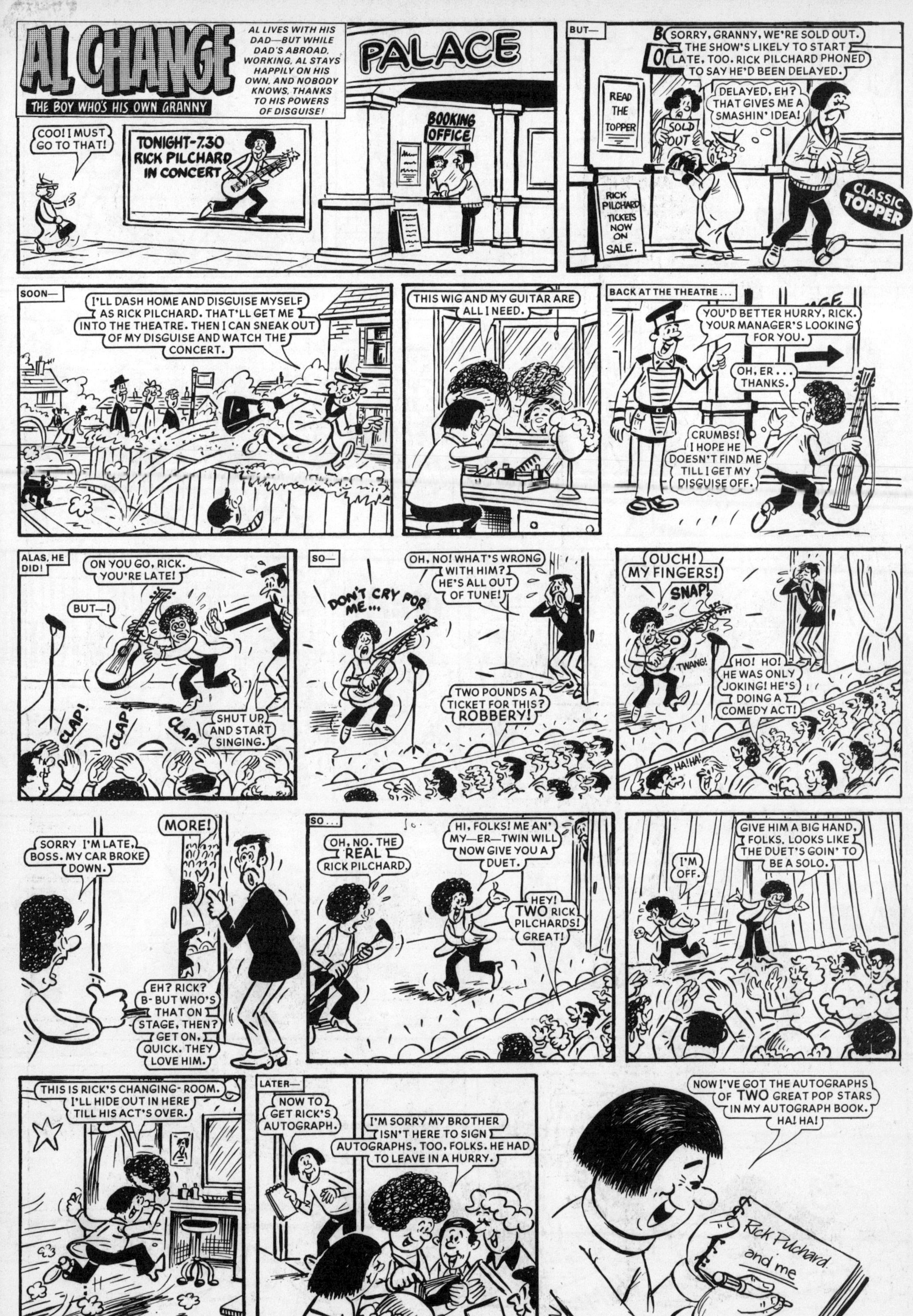
AL CHANGE
THE BOY WHO'S HIS OWN GRANNY
AL LIVES WITH HIS DAD—BUT WHILE DAD'S ABROAD, WORKING, AL STAYS HAPPILY ON HIS OWN, AND NOBODY KNOWS, THANKS TO HIS POWERS OF DISGUISE!
PALACE
BOOKING OFFICE
TONIGHT-7.30 RICK PILCHARD IN CONCERT
COO! I MUST GO TO THAT!
BUT—
SORRY, GRANNY, WE'RE SOLD OUT. THE SHOW'S LIKELY TO START LATE, TOO. RICK PILCHARD PHONED TO SAY HE'D BEEN DELAYED.
DELAYED, EH? THAT GIVES ME A SMASHIN' IDEA!
READ THE TOPPER
SOLD OUT
RICK PILCHARD TICKETS NOW ON SALE.
CLASSIC TOPPER
SOON—
I'LL DASH HOME AND DISGUISE MYSELF AS RICK PILCHARD. THAT'LL GET ME INTO THE THEATRE. THEN I CAN SNEAK OUT OF MY DISGUISE AND WATCH THE CONCERT.
THIS WIG AND MY GUITAR ARE ALL I NEED.
BACK AT THE THEATRE . . .
YOU'D BETTER HURRY, RICK. YOUR MANAGER'S LOOKING FOR YOU.
OH, ER . . . THANKS.
CRUMBS! I HOPE HE DOESN'T FIND ME TILL I GET MY DISGUISE OFF.
ALAS, HE DID!
ON YOU GO, RICK. YOU'RE LATE!
BUT—!
CLAP! CLAP! CLAP!
SHUT UP, AND START SINGING.
SO—
DON'T CRY FOR ME...
OH, NO! WHAT'S WRONG WITH HIM? HE'S ALL OUT OF TUNE!
TWO POUNDS A TICKET FOR THIS? ROBBERY!
OUCH! MY FINGERS!
SNAP!
TWANG!
HO! HO! HE WAS ONLY JOKING! HE'S DOING A COMEDY ACT!
HA! HA!
MORE!
SORRY I'M LATE, BOSS. MY CAR BROKE DOWN.
EH? RICK? B-BUT WHO'S THAT ON STAGE, THEN? GET ON, QUICK. THEY LOVE HIM.
SO . . .
OH, NO. THE REAL RICK PILCHARD.
HI, FOLKS! ME AN' MY—ER—TWIN WILL NOW GIVE YOU A DUET.
HEY! TWO RICK PILCHARDS! GREAT!
I'M OFF.
GIVE HIM A BIG HAND, FOLKS. LOOKS LIKE THE DUET'S GOIN' TO BE A SOLO.
THIS IS RICK'S CHANGING-ROOM. I'LL HIDE OUT IN HERE TILL HIS ACT'S OVER.
LATER—
NOW TO GET RICK'S AUTOGRAPH.
I'M SORRY MY BROTHER ISN'T HERE TO SIGN AUTOGRAPHS, TOO, FOLKS. HE HAD TO LEAVE IN A HURRY.
NOW I'VE GOT THE AUTOGRAPHS OF TWO GREAT POP STARS IN MY AUTOGRAPH BOOK. HA! HA!
Rick Pilchard and me

NOBBY

Nobby, there's a new bully in town—he's huge. Must be this height at least!
Oh!

I'd like to meet him. I'm not scared of anybody!

Nobby! Me just been fumped by a shuge bully. He was twice as big as me! Shuge he was!

I wouldn't have let him get away with that! I'd have smashed him!

Hi, Andy! Have you let this bully thump you, too?
Yeah!

But you should have seen the height of him—he was enormous!
Huh!

It's all very well for you to talk—YOU haven't even seen him yet!
Yeah!

We'll fix up a fight for you so you can show us what a great fighter you are! Be in the park in half an hour!
What am I going to do now?

IDEA!

He's in the park, is he? Wantin' a fight, is he? Well, I'll give him one all right!

Come and get me, you big baboon!
You can't get away from me out there, y'know!

I'm comin' to get you!
I'm waiting!

Come and get me then! Don't just lie there!
SPLOSH!
THUMP!

Look before you leap in future!
Ha-ha! The water was only two inches deep!
Good for Nobby!

CLASSIC BEANO
BABY-FACE FINLAYSON
THE CUTEST BANDIT IN THE WEST!

I'M MOVING TO A NEW TOWN WHERE MY HANDSOME FACE WON'T BE KNOWN!

SO—
WHAT'S THIS?
BRAKE!
LOOK OUT FOR "BABY-FACE" FINLAYSON, THE BANDIT, BELIEVED TO BE IN THIS DISTRICT.
OH, DEAR!

LOOK OUT FOR "BABY-FACE" FINLAYSON, THE BANDIT, BELIEVED TO BE IN THIS DISTRICT.
NOW TO PUT THESE NOTICES UP ALL OVER TOWN.
HOW ANNOYING! I DON'T WANT MY FACE KNOWN IN THESE PARTS!

YUK! YUK! I'LL SOON SOLVE THE PROBLEM. FIRST, I REMOVE THE PICTURE...
LOOK OUT FOR "BABY-FACE" FINLAYSON, THE BANDIT, BELIEVED TO BE IN THIS DISTRICT.

...THEN I STICK IT ON UPSIDE-DOWN—IT STILL LOOKS LIKE A FACE!
LOOK OUT FOR "BABY-FACE" FINLAYSON, THE BANDIT, BELIEVED TO BE IN THIS DISTRICT.

THAT'S ALL THE NOTICES UP.
YUK! YUK! IT'S NOT FAIR THAT ONE PERSON SHOULD BE SO CLEVER!

KEEP FIT AT JIM'S GYM
LOOK OUT FOR "BABY-FACE" FINLAYSON, THE BANDIT, BELIEVED TO BE IN THIS DISTRICT
HM! THAT'S INTERESTING!

MY TUM IS A LITTLE LARGE—PERHAPS SOME EXERCISE WOULD GET RID OF THE FAT.

AT JIM'S—
WELCOME, SMALL SIR! JUST JOIN IN WHAT THE REST OF THE CLASS ARE DOING.

THAT FACE IS FAMILIAR—WHY, IT'S THAT BANDIT I SAW ON THE WANTED NOTICE ON MY WAY HERE!
HE'S RECOGNISED ME!

GRAB HIM! HE'S "BABY-FACE" FINLAYSON, THE BANDIT!
PUFF! I'M GOING TO GET PLENTY OF EXERCISE NOW!

ENOR MOUSE

SCRITCH AND SCRATCH

GORDONZOLA CHEDDAR GEORGE

HIS NIBS

CHISELLER SNIFFLER

# DIRTY DICK

CINEMA
BULL-WHIP DENVER
NOW SHOWING
OH, BOY! THAT WAS SMASHING! I MUST MAKE MYSELF A WHIP!

HOW'S THAT? BULL-WHIP DICK— THAT'S ME!
CRACK!

CLASSIC DANDY
HOI! DIRTY DICK! HOW DO YOU LIKE MY BALLOON?
DIRTY DICK IS A DRIP!
GRR! YOU CHEEKY MONKEY, JIMMY JONES!

CRACK!
THAT'S WHAT I THINK OF YOUR SILLY BALLOON!

HO-HO! I FORGOT TO TELL YOU IT WAS FULL OF WATER, DICK!
WHOOSH!

WHACKO! WHAT A TARGET!
RIGHT, BOYS, NOW WE'LL SEE WHO IS THE NEW MARBLES CHAMP!
OW!
WHO DID THAT?
CRACK!
OWCH!

IT WAS DIRTY DICK! AFTER HIM, BOYS! WE'LL GET HIM THIS SIDE OF THE STREAM!
THAT'S WHAT THEY THINK!

WHEE! THIS IS HOW BULL-WHIP DENVER ESCAPED IN THE FILM!

MADE IT! NOW A GOOD SHARP TUG SHOULD FREE IT FROM THE BRANCH! HEAVE!

PYOING!
WHACKO! AND OFF IT COMES!

CLEVER ME! I'M AS CRAFTY WITH MY WHIP AS BULL-WHIP DENVER!

PLOP!
OOF! I SPOKE TOO SOON! MAYBE BIRDS DON'T MAKE NESTS IN TREES WHERE HE LIVES!

HARUM SCAREM
Carrots here I come!

Oh, boy! Someone's dug up dozens!

I'll take a week's supply!

Lucky this is a high wall! The farmer won't spot me!
BUT HE SURE SPOTS THE BASKET!
CHOKE!

Scarem! That pest's pinching more grub!

So he is—the fiend!
OH NO!

THUMP!
Heh-heh! The end is near!

CRUMP!
Oof! Foiled again!

NEXT MORNING—
I won't be so greedy today! That was my mistake yesterday!

Tch! Scarem's guarding the carrot heap!

Aw, well, I'll just have to dig up some nice fresh ones!

SNARL!
Rasp! Can't catch me, Horror-face! You're tied up!

That's what you think! This is elastic!
Yikes!

Help!
WHEE
Prepare to meet my teeth!

Wow!

Oh, boy! What a bit of luck!

AND SO—
Now, now, Scarem—don't get angry! I'm almost finished!
PYOING!
GNASH! GNASH!

Oh, boy! A whole month's supply! A bee-ootiful sight!
HARUM'S HOUSE

ALI'S
BABA

OH-OH! BABA'S DRAWIN' THAT TREE, AND THERE'S SOMEBODY COME TO CHOP IT DOWN!

CLASSIC TOPPER
TIMBER! ...ERK! IT'S NOT FALLING!
???
GOOD! TREE NOT FALL! BABA CAN FINISH DRAWING!
PUFF! HOPE HE'S QUICK! THIS TREE'S HEAVY!

ALL IT NEEDED WAS A GOOD PUSH!
BABA FINISHED! BABA DRAW SUMP'THIN' ELSE NOW!
OW!

BABA DRAW MOO-COW!

AW! MOO-COW NO SIT DOWN TILL BABA'S DRAWED IT!
I'D BETTER DO SOMETHING!
SIGH...

GOOD MOO-COW! BABA FINISH DRAWIN' YOU NOW!
HURRY UP, THIS THING WEIGHS A TON!
?

THAT'S BETTER! MMM! NICE 'N' SOFT, TOO!
YAAARGH!

OOH-OUCH! GROAN!
BETTER CYCLE INTO THE VILLAGE BEFORE THE SHOPS SHUT!
BABA DRAW BIKE!

S'POSE I'D BETTER DO SOMETHING.. KEEP BABA HAPPY...
AW! MAN TAKE BIKE AWAY TA-TA'S!

NNNGHH!
PUFF! WHAT'S WRONG WITH THIS BIKE?!?
THANKS FOR STAYIN', MISTER! BABA NEARLY DONE!

THAT'S BETTER! THE GEARS MUST'VE BEEN STUCK!
OOF! AARGH!
WHOOSH!
PLOP!
CRUMP!
BABA FINISHED! TA-TA, MISTER!

NOW BABA TAKE LOOK AT WHAT BABA DRAWED!
OOOO... I'LL TAKE A LOOK TOO!

OH, NO! TO THINK WHAT I WENT THROUGH FOR THAT!!
WOW! BABA A GREAT ARTIST, BABA IS!
TREE
COW
BIKE

CLASSIC BEANO

CLASSIC TOPPER

# BIG-HEAD BRANNY

## THE STRONG-ARM JANNY

CLASSIC CRACKER

THAT NIGHT, A FIENDISH FIGURE SNEAKS UP TO THE SCHOOL AQUARIUM...

NEXT MORNING!

CRIKEY! SHE'S GONE STARK RAVING POTTY!

I'D BETTER MAKE MYSELF SCARCE!
GASP! WHEEZE!

CLASSIC CRACKER
OH, NO, YOU DON'T, MATE!

I'LL TEACH YOU TO SET ME UP FOR A BASHING!
NOT LIKE THAT—YOU TENTACLED TWIT! USE ALL EIGHT TENTACLES TO THRASH HIM WITH!
THRASH! WHACK! BASH!
AFTER A SEVERE WHACKING BRANNY COOLS OFF....
SSSS
GASP!
OH, NO! DON'T GO NEAR THAT TANK..!
PIRANHA
...THAT'S WHERE WE KEEP THE PIRANHA FISH!
CHOMP!
SNAP!
SNAP!
ROAR! BELLOW! UGGLE! GLOYCK! GIBBER!
SNIP!
NOSH!
CHOMP!
MUNCH!
FRANTIC LEAP!
CHOMP!
CHOMP!
MUNCH!
* NATURE NOTE:- PIRANHA— SOUTH AMERICAN MAN-EATING FISH!
DON'T WORRY, MATES—WE EXPECT A PHONE CALL FROM JOHN O' GROATS TO SAY BRANNY HAS BEEN SIGHTED UP THERE...SO WE'LL ISSUE HIM WITH A NEW UNIFORM IN TIME FOR NEXT WEEK'S ADVENTURE!
EEK! ARRGH! GERREMOFF ME!
NOSH! MUNCH!
CHOMP! MUNCH!
CHOMP!
FRANTIC 50 MPH MAD DASH!

BADDIE
GOODIE
Jimmy Jinx
AND WHAT HE THINKS

GO ON, JAMES. OFFER TO HELP YOUR FATHER.
DAD...
PUSH OFF, JIMMY. YOU'LL JUST GET IN MY WAY.

OH, WELL, JAMES, YOU MAY GO AND PLAY FOOTBALL, I SUPPOSE.
GOOD IDEA!

CLASSIC TOPPER
BOUNCE
HEH! A GOOD BOOT...

SPINNN!
...A BODY-SWERVE, AND...GULP! A SLICED SHOT!

PHEW! IT'S LUCKY THE WINDOW WAS OPEN.

CRIKEY! LOOK AT THE MESS THE BALL'S MADE! BETTER CLEAN IT UP QUICKLY, JIM!
DAD'S NOT HERE JUST NOW, THANK GOODNESS.

HURRY! HURRY! HURRY!
SHLIP!
SHLOPP!

DAD'S COMING! HIDE!
CLOMP!
CLOMP!
CLOMP!

AAGH! HOW..? WHO..? JIMMY? NO—HE'S OUTSIDE.

WOE IS ME! I'LL HAVE TO DO ALL THAT PAPERING AGAIN!
OO-ER!
SWOON!

YEEK! WHASSAT?
OORF!
LEAP!

SO! IT WAS YOU!
ER...HI, DAD. GULP!

THIS WAS ALL YOUR FAULT! YOU SUGGESTED JIM PLAY FOOTBALL.
BUT I THOUGHT THE...GLUB!
SPLUT!
GRR! WHEN I CATCH YOU, I'LL DECORATE YOUR BEHIND WITH MY SLIPPER!

LORD SNOOTY
AND HIS PALS
I REPRESENT A STICKING PLASTER FIRM. THERE'S 10/- FOR YOU IF YOU DELIVER THIS PILE OF FREE SAMPLES.
LEAVE IT TO US!

WE'LL EACH TAKE AN AREA. WE'LL BE FINISHED QUICKLY THAT WAY.

CLASSIC BEANO
WHERE DOES JONES LIVE?
IN THE TOP FLAT.

ONLY ONE MORE FLOOR TO GO. WE'RE ALMOST THERE.
WHEEZE!
GASP!

SORRY! YOU CAN'T GET PAST. YOU'LL HAVE TO GO DOWN AGAIN!

HALF AN HOUR LATER~
JONES
OO-OH! MY FEET!
PUFF! PUFF!

FAT JOE'S HAVING TROUBLE TOO~
COR! THIS IS STIFF!

YEOW! IT'S A SPRING FLAP BOX, WITH A STRONG SPRING!
SNAP!
NIP!

SCRAPPER ISN'T FARING MUCH BETTER~
GR-R-R!

NEITHER IS THOMAS~
GR-R! STICKING PLASTER, EH? TRYING TO BE FUNNY JUST BECAUSE I TOOK A LICKING IN MY LAST FIGHT! GET OFF!
I. SLUGGEM

AS FOR SNOOTY~
.....AND THIS SUPERB CLEANER BLOWS AS WELL AS SUCKS, MADAM!

LET ME DEMONSTRATE!
MY SAMPLES!
WOOSH!

WD TRAINING GROUND

CHARGE. MEN!
SNOOTY DOESN'T KNOW THE ARMY IS ON EXERCISE–AND HE'S IN THE WAY

....CRUMP!

AT LAST THEY FINISH~
D-O-OH-H! THAT WAS TERRIBLE! WE'RE ALL INJURED! LET'S GO TO THE CHEMIST AND GET FIXED UP.

BAH! WE EARNED 10/- DELIVERING THE SAMPLES BUT IT COST US 12/6 FOR STICKING PLASTER FOR OUR CUTS AND BRUISES!

KEYHOLE KATE

CLASSIC SPARKY
ALL THOSE LOVELY KEYHOLES, AND ME STUCK IN A CHAIR WITH THIS LEG IN PLASTER!

I'LL LEAVE YOU HERE. THE DOCTOR WILL SEE YOU SOON.

PHEW! THIS IS AWKWARD. I CAN'T GET DOWN LOW ENOUGH TO PEEP!

I'LL HAVE TO MOVE MY LEG.

WOW! I'M NOT STOPPIN' HERE FOR THAT SORT OF TREATMENT!

WHAT KATE SAW—
A-ARGH!!

WE'LL HAVE TO CUT THREE MORE INCHES OFF.
OH, NO! OW—HELP!
CRASH!

—NOW I'LL START ON THE NEXT ONE!
NOT IF I CAN HELP IT!

NO—LET'S HAVE A CUPPA BEFORE WE START ON THE SECOND CUPBOARD!
NEXT!
I'M OFF!

LET ME OUTA HERE!
WATCH IT!
WHAT'S SHE SCARED OF?

HOSPITAL
OH, WELL—ALL THAT EXERCISE SHOULD BE GOOD FOR HER.
BUMP!
HOP!

BIG HEAD AND THICK HEAD ARE OFF ON A PICNIC TO HERON ISLAND—
IT'S A SMASHING DAY FOR IT, BIG HEAD—AND THIS WATERPROOF TUCK-BOX YOU'VE MADE FOR OUR GRUB IN CASE IT RAINS, IS YOUR BRAINIEST EFFORT SINCE THAT TRANSPARENT UMBRELLA YOU INVENTED—IN CASE IT TURNED OUT SUNNY!
G-GOSH! DON'T EMBARRASS ME, PAL! I KNOW I'M MARVELLOUS!
RAINPROOF TUCK-BOX PATENT APPLIED FOR

BIG HEAD AND THICK HEAD
CLASSIC DANDY
ARRIVING AT THE LAKE, THE PALS CLIMB ABOARD THE MOTOR BOAT THEY'VE HIRED FOR THE DAY—
ALL SET, BIG HEAD? RIGHT! I'LL START THE OUTBOARD MOTOR!
ERK! NO, WAIT!
BOATS FOR HIRE
PUT-PUT-
WE HAVEN'T UNTIED THE BOAT YET—EE-E-E-YOW-W-W!
EEK!
ROAR-R-R-R-R
BRM-M
TUG

AGH-H!
GLUB!

AFTER THE DOUBLE-DUCKING—
RIGHT! WE'LL TRY AGAIN AND THIS TIME, UNTIE THE PESKY ROPE FIRST!
OKAY! HOW'S THAT?
PUT PUT

AGH-H-H-H! YOU BLOATED, BULBOUS BABOON!
YOU SHOULD HAVE STOPPED THE ENGINE FIRST!
WOW! GRAB SOMETHING, QUICK!

WITH GREAT PRESENCE OF MIND, BIG HEAD GRABS AT THE TRAILING MOORING-ROPE—AND, BY SHEER ROTTEN LUCK, HE SUCCEEDS IN DOING SO!
YAR-RAGH-H!
HOLD IT—SPLUTTER! TURN THE MOTOR OFF—QUICK!
ER—OKAY!
?
BRM-M-M
WHIZZ
SPLAT!
HANG ON, WHILE I FIND OUT HOW TO DO IT!

BIG HEAD HANGS ON UNTIL, AT THE 48th TIME ROUND THE LAKE, THICK HEAD MANAGES TO GET THE ENGINE STOPPED—BY RUNNING OUT OF PETROL!
YOU GREAT PHLABBY, PHUDDLE-BRAINED PHATHEAD! GULP! PHROM NOW ON, I'LL TAKE THE CONTROLS! GLUGGLE!

SO, AFTER RE-FUELING—
YOU SEE, PAL, IT'S SIMPLE! JUST HOLD THE TILLER NICE AND STEADY!
OKAY! I GOTTA ADMIT IT! I'M A GREAT, BLUNDERING OAF AND YOU'RE A—

ERK!—BOSS-EYED, CLUE-LESS CLOT!
YOU NIT! THAT'S THROUGH DISTRACTING MY ATTENTION, BY HAVING TO EXPLAIN TO YOU!
CRASH

THE END OF THEIR PATHETIC ATTEMPT TO HAVE A PICNIC ON HERON ISLAND—
WHAT DO YOU MEAN—IT'S A GOOD JOB YOU MADE THE TUCK-BOX WATERPROOF? WE HAD TO CHUCK ALL OUR GRUB INTO THE WATER TO GET INTO THE TUCK-BOX, DIDN'T WE?
(DISCREET SILENCE)

PUNCH and JIMMY

I'm a better climber than you!
Oh, yeah? I'll race you to the top of the wardrobe!
CLASSIC BEANO

I'll be up first!
Rot! I will!

I won!
No, you didn't!

Did!
BOP!
Didn't!
Shriek! Stop! You're damaging my beloved hats!

So you're keen on climbing, eh? Well, you can go out and do some hill climbing. Maybe that'll stop you fighting.

SO—
I'll race you to the top of that hill!
Right! I'll beat you easily!

Puff! Bet I'm winning!
Gasp! I'm beating him easily!

Tough luck, Jimmy! I got here first!
What do you mean? I was here first!

I was!
No— I was!

Anyway, I'll beat you to the bottom of the hill!
Not if I can help it!

I was down first!
Nonsense! I was!
Grr! They're fighting again!

Come back, you two!
Bet Mum catches you first!
Rubbish! She'll catch YOU first, slow-coach!

WOO-AAH-OOO-EEEEE!
You don't frighten me!
PETER PIPER
CLASSIC TOPPER
PETER AND HIS PAL TOMMY ARE VISITING A HAUNTED CASTLE—
HEY! LOOK, PETER! IT SAYS HE HAUNTS THE CASTLE! WOW!
SIR BAZIL, WHOSE GHOST STILL HAUNTS THE CASTLE
HUH! I DON'T BELIEVE IT, TOMMY!
SIR BAZIL, WHOSE GHOST STILL HAUNTS THE CASTLE
THERE'S NO SUCH THING AS GHOSTS!
WOOOOOOO!
P-P-P-P-P-P-P-P PETER-
WOOOOOOOOO!
BOOO!
WOOOOOO!
HELP!
YEEK! I TAKE IT ALL BACK, TOMMY!
HAR! HAR! HAR! GET A FRIGHT, BOYS?
HEE-HEE!
WHEW! IT WAS ONLY THOSE TWO WITH SHEETS ON!
I'LL TEACH THEM A LESSON! I'LL PLAY MY PIPES TO THIS SUIT OF ARMOUR!
C'MON, CLIVE! LET'S SCARE SOMEONE ELSE!
GRRR!
CLANK!
CLANK!
HAW! HAW! CAN'T FRIGHTEN US...WE KNOW THERE'S SOMEONE INSIDE....
OH, NO THERE'S NOT!
YAGH! IT'S EMPTY!
HELP!
CLANK!
CREAK!
HA!-HA!-HA!
NOW TO BRING THAT SKELETON TO LIFE...
RATTLE!
ARRRGH!
TWITCH!
CLINK!
RATTLE!
QUICK, BERT! UP HERE!
RATTLE!
HO!-HO!-HO!
HA!-HA!-HA!
CLANK!
HO! HO!
HA! HA!
RATTLE
HO-HO! WE REALLY SCARED THEM THAT TIME!
YES! YOU DID, DIDN'T YOU?
?
?
HAR! HAR! HAR!
MUMMY!
HELP!
WAH!
YAH! IT'S SIR BAZIL ... THE REAL GHOST... RUN FOR IT!

THE BASH STREET KIDS
CLASSIC BEANO

MORNING BREAK—
TUT! TUT! LOOK AT THAT COLLECTION OF EMPTY-HEADED CLOWNS! I MUST GET TEACHER TO GIVE THEM SOMETHING TO OCCUPY THEIR MINDS.
SHUFFLE

THEN PROFESSOR MOULD, THE HISTORY EXPERT—
MY BEAUTIFUL COLLECTION OF FOSSILS AND RELICS IS ONE OF THE FINEST IN THE LAND!
NEVER BE WITHOUT A FOSSIL
HOW INTERESTING!
DINOSAUR'S FUNNY BONE
MAMMOTH'S TOE-NAIL
SAUSAGE ROLL STONE AGE
CAVE MAN'S TIN OPENER
JELLY BABIES
THE MISSING LINK
PTERODACTYL'S FEATHER

THEN—
I WANT YOU ALL TO GO OUT AND START MAKING COLLECTIONS. THE HEADMASTER WILL INSPECT THEM TOMORROW.
CLASS IIB OR NOT IIB
TIMBER!

SOME OF THE KIDS ARE DIGGING FOR FOSSILS—
WE'RE GETTING SOME GOOD FOSSILS HERE!
HUM
TUG
YE OLD HUMBUGS
ERK!
HERE STOOD BASH STREET RUBBISH DUMP 1642

MEANWHILE—
I CAN'T THINK OF ANYTHING TO COLLECT!
SCRATCH
SCRATCH

OOPS! I'VE GOT A SPLINTER IN MY FINGER

NEXT MORNING IN CLASS IIB—
AH, HEADMASTER! I THINK THE CHILDREN ARE ARRIVING WITH THEIR COLLECTIONS NOW!
RUMBLE!
CRUNCH!
RATTLE!

HOW DO YOU LIKE MY "STUMP-COLLECTION", TEACHER?
CLASS IIB
I THINK MY FLOWER-COLLECTION IS LOVELY.
STRANGE AROMA
TEN YEAR OLD CAULIFLOWERS
TEE-HEE! I'M A TACKS-COLLECTOR!
TACKS
TINK
WHAT DO YOU THINK OF OUR FOSSIL COLLECTION?
FOSSILS
MORE FOSSILS

EAD TALKS TO TEACHER—
I'VE AN IDEA, HEADMASTER. WHY DON'T WE GET THEM TO START MAKING COLLECTIONS? I'LL INVITE SEVERAL WELL-KNOWN COLLECTORS TO GIVE THEM LECTURES.
EXCELLENT!

THE FIRST LECTURE IS GIVEN BY MISS PENNY BLACK, THE WELL-KNOWN STAMP-COLLECTOR—
IT HAS TAKEN ME TWENTY YEARS TO COLLECT THESE STAMPS —EEK!
ACHOO!

NEXT, A LECTURE ON FLOWER-COLLECTING BY MISS PRIMROSE PLANT—
AREN'T THESE PRESSED FLOWERS LOVELY, CHILDREN?
PAH! I'D RATHER HAVE A NICE BIT OF PRESSED HAM ANY DAY!
PRANG!

I KNOW WHAT I'LL COLLECT!

YES, THROW THEM OUT. THEY'RE NO USE TO US NOW!
Q. CUMBER GREEN-GROCER BACK DOOR

WOW! JUST WHAT I NEED FOR MY COLLECTION!

GRR! THERE GOES THE TAX-COLLECTOR!
CASH

THESE NICE LADIES HAVE GIVEN ME A GREAT IDEA!

LATER, IN SMIFFY'S HOUSE—
ERK! WHAT'S HAPPENED TO MY LINO?
SMIFFY
PYONG!
PYONG!
PYONG!

AH! THERE'S ONLY ONE COLLECTOR WHO'D BE INTERESTED IN THESE COLLECTIONS—

—AND THAT'S THE REFUSE-COLLECTOR!
PRANG
SWEEP
CORPORATION RUBBISH BARROW
STOP ME AND BUY SOME

GUESS WHAT THE KIDS ARE GOING TO COLLECT NOW, READERS!

SOON—

ETHEL'S IN THE SOUP AGAIN!

# KORKY the cat

DENNIS the MENACE
CLASSIC BEANO
HELLO, READERS! I'M OFF FOR SOME THRILLS AND SPILLS IN THE PARK.
2
HEH! HEH! THRILLS FOR ME! SPILLS FOR THEM!
THEN—
HALT, LADDIE! I'LL SOON PUT A STOP TO THIS CARTIE NONSENSE.
SCRAPE
NO MORE RECKLESS DRIVING FOR YOU, BOY.
LATER—
WHAT'S FOR TEA, MY DEAR?
IT'S YOUR FAVOURITE, DAD—PANCAKES!
YUGH! I DON'T LIKE PANCAKES! WAIT A MINUTE THOUGH—!
SNIGGER! THIS'LL GIVE DAD SOMETHING TO GET HIS TEETH INTO.
QUICK-SETTING CEMENT
PANCAKE MIXTURE
SLURP! NOW TO SINK MY TEETH INTO THIS TASTY MORSEL!
AGH-H!
CRACK!
SPLINTER!
GNASH!
I CAN'T THINK WHAT WENT WRONG!
JUST AS I PLANNED, READERS! I HAVE A USE FOR THESE HARD PANCAKES.
ERK! IT'S THAT MENACE AGAIN!
LOOK, CHUMS—PANCAKES! WHO'S FOR A FREE FEED?
YIPPEE! THEY MAKE SMASHING WHEELS!
RUMBLE!
WOW!
GOOD! THAT SAVES ME A JOB!
WHIZZ-Z-Z!
OOOYAH!
GRATE
SCRAPE

# The Beano

CLASSIC BEANO

## BIFFO

STILL HAS THAT CRAFTY DOG HE BOUGHT LAST WEEK.

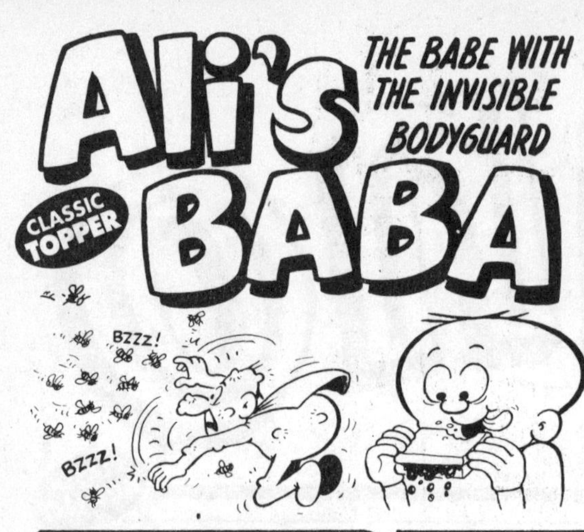
Ali's BABA
THE BABE WITH THE INVISIBLE BODYGUARD
CLASSIC TOPPER
BZZZ!
BZZZ!

COO! THIS A GREAT STORY ABOUT MAJI THE HYPNOTIST—BET BABA COULD BE A HYPNOTIST!
OH, SURE! CHUCKLE!
THE GREAT MAJI

THEN—
ON YOUR OWN, EH, KID? YOU WON'T MIND ME NICKIN' A FEW VALUABLES, THEN!
A BURGLAR! BABA NOT AFRAID! BABA HYPNOTISE HIM!
OH-OH!

YOU UNDER BABA'S POWER. YOU DO WHAT BABA TELL YOU.
ARF! THE KID'S A NUT!
GRR! I'LL SHOW HIM!

BURGLAR DO SPLITS!
RIGHT, MATE!
PUSH!
PUSH!

BURGLAR STAND ON HEAD!
HUP!
YIKE!

BURGLAR BUMP HEAD ON FLOOR!
THUD!
THUD!
THUD!
OOH! OW! OUCH! EEK! WAAH!

BURGLAR PUNCH HIMSELF ON CHIN!
BONK!

'BYE-EE!
HEAVE!
BURGLAR JUMP OUT OF WINDOW!

GROAN! LET ME AWAY FROM THAT KID!
HA!
HA!
WHERE THE BURGLAR'S CHIN CONNECTED!
TEETH

LATER—
HEH! BABA HYPNOTISE MUM AN' DAD—HAVE FUN! HEE! HEE!
HMM! I THINK YOUR HYPNOTISING DAYS ARE OVER, CHUM.

YOU BOTH UNDER BABA'S SPELL. DAD, ACT LIKE MONKEY. MUM, POUR MILK OVER DAD!
WHAT'S HE ON ABOUT?
BABA! DON'T BE DAFT! COME AND HAVE YOUR TEA!

HUH! IT NOT WORK! MAYBE BABA ONLY HYPNOTISE BURGLARS. PITY.
HO! HO! WHAT A KID!

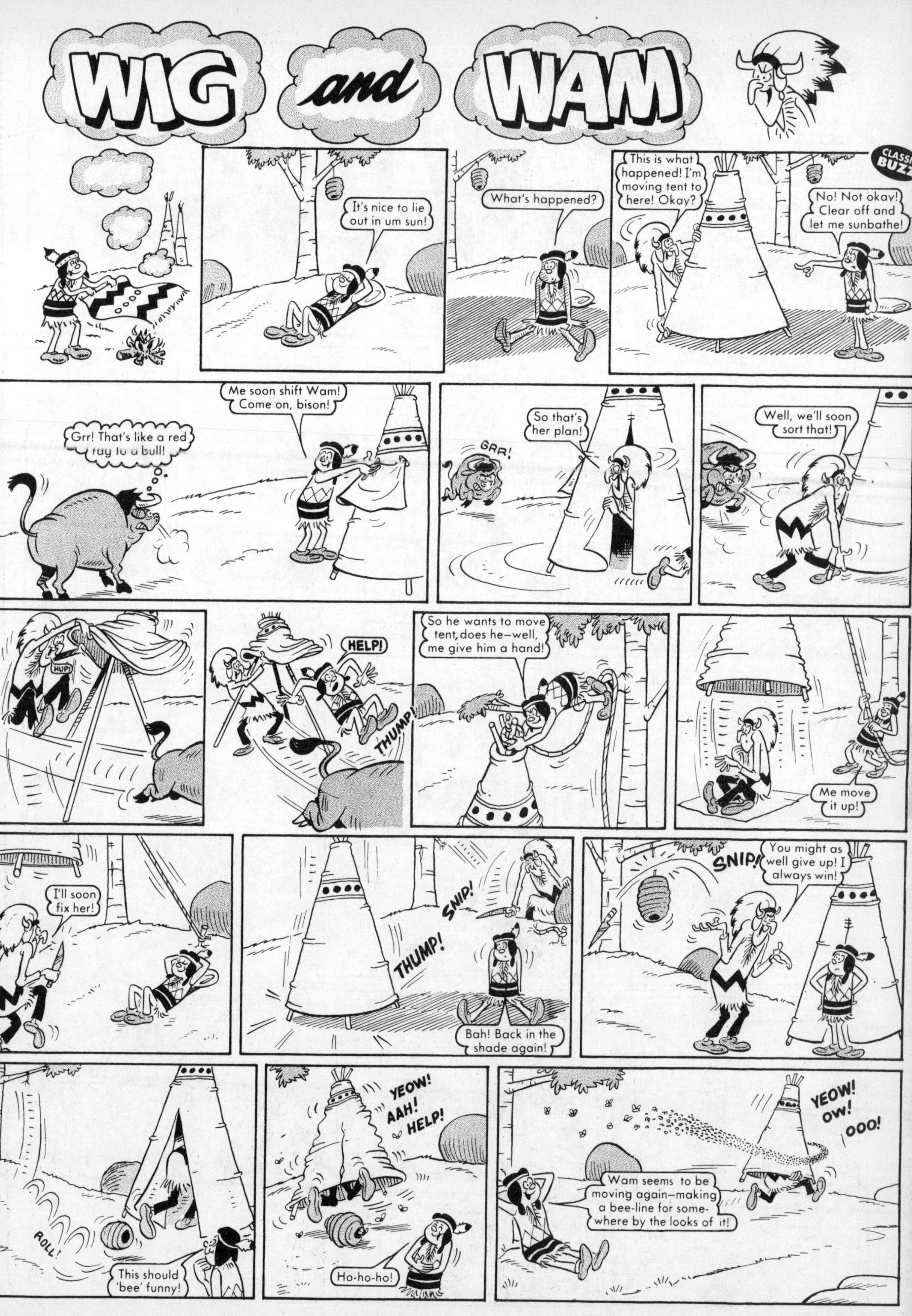
WIG and WAM
CLASSIC BUZZ
It's nice to lie out in um sun!
What's happened?
This is what happened! I'm moving tent to here! Okay?
No! Not okay! Clear off and let me sunbathe!
Grr! That's like a red rag to a bull!
Me soon shift Wam! Come on, bison!
So that's her plan!
GRR!
Well, we'll soon sort that!
HUP!
HELP!
THUMP!
So he wants to move tent, does he—well, me give him a hand!
Me move it up!
I'll soon fix her!
SNIP!
THUMP!
Bah! Back in the shade again!
SNIP!
You might as well give up! I always win!
ROLL!
This should 'bee' funny!
YEOW! AAH! HELP!
Ho-ho-ho!
Wam seems to be moving again—making a bee-line for somewhere by the looks of it!
YEOW! OW! OOO!

CLASSIC DANDY
DINAH MO
In school—
I'LL TEACH YOU NOT TO CALL ME SOFT, WIMPO!
SOCK!
STOP THAT AT ONCE!
SWISH!
THERE IS TO BE A HISTORICAL PAGEANT THIS AFTERNOON AND YOU, PEST, WILL PLAY THE PART OF A GENTLE HANDMAIDEN.
HUMPH!
That afternoon—
BAH! I'M BORED. I WISH I WAS PLAYING A KNIGHT INSTEAD.
OH, NO, YOU'RE NOT!
IN FACT, I THINK I WILL. I'M GOING TO BORROW YOUR PIKE AND HELMET, TOMMY!
OH, YES I AM—NOW TO GET MY MOUNT.
GIDDUP, FAITHFUL STEED!
SWIPE!
THIS IS MORE LIKE IT—CHARGE!
THUNDER!
CRASH!
RUMBLE!
YIELD, WEAKLINGS!
ULP! THE HEADMASTER!
DISMOUNT AT ONCE, GIRL.
AS YOU DON'T FIND BEING A HANDMAIDEN SUITABLE, I'M GOING TO GIVE YOU A NEW ROLE TO PLAY.
DUCK YE VILLAGE WITCH
BAH! HE PUT ME IN THE DUCKING STOOL!
3

CLASSIC BEANO
JONAH
!
A NEW TYPE OF HOVERCRAFT IS ABOUT TO BE PUT THROUGH ITS INITIAL TESTS, ON LAKE LINDENMERE—
I HOPE YOUR NEW DESIGN MERITS THE MONEY WE'VE PUT INTO THE PROJECT, PROFESSOR PRANKWORTHY!
HAVE NO FEAR, SIR FRUMPSBY—
FLIGHT LIEUTENANT KITE CAN REST ASSURED THAT ALL MY THEORIES WILL WORK OUT IN PRACTICE, MY DEAR CHAP!
HAW-HAW! WHIZZ-HO! BANG-ON AN' ALL THAT!
BUT NO ONE NOTICES JONAH BOARDING THE HOVERCRAFT FROM THE OTHER SIDE.
HEH-HEH! I FANCY A TRIP IN ONE OF THESE!
UNTIL—
HUM-M-M-M!
GOODNESS! THE ENGINE HAS STARTED!
SHE'S COMING AT US!
NO! STOP!
CAN'T!
BLIMEY!
!
ARGH!!
CRASH
IT CAN'T BE TRUE! IT'S ONE OF THOSE THINGS YOU READ ABOUT IN THE PAPERS—THAT ALWAYS HAPPENS TO SOMEBODY ELSE!
HOW-D'YOU-STOPPIT?
GOOD! MY CALCULATIONS WERE CORRECT! MY HOVERCRAFT CAN STAND A TERRIFIC IMPACT!
WHAT A PRANG!
AND SO, UNDER THE CLOTTISH CONTROL OF THE WORLD'S BIGGEST AQUATIC CRACKPOT, THE HUMMING HOVERCRAFT HEADS TOWARDS THE FAR END OF LAKE LINDENMERE—WHERE SCORES OF HAPPY HOLIDAY-MAKERS ARE LOLLING ON LUXURIOUS LAUNCHES.
ERK! WHICH KNOB STOPS IT?
LOOK! IT'S THAT NEWFANGLED THING-M'BOB I READ ABOUT IN THE 'WHAT'S-ITS-NAME' WEEKLY!
HO! HO! WE'RE JUST IN TIME TO SEE THAT JOLLY OLD HOVERCRAFT PUT THROUGH ITS PACES, OLD BOY!
WATER SPRITE
THESE SCIENTIST CHAPS HAVE MADE TREMENDOUS STRIDES, RECENTLY!
EEK!
?
THEY DESERVE A JOLLY OLD PAT ON THE BACK!
OI!
CRASH
AGH-H!
HOWLING HORRORS!
DAD!
CRUMP
COURAGE, LAD! DADDY'S WITH YOU!
CRASH
THERE'S A KNOB TO STOP IT SOMEWHERE—BUT WHERE?
S.O.S!
ZOOM-M-M
LADY
SHATTER!!
ER-R-R-R-R-RK!!
LAUNCH THAT DINGHY!!
WHERE'S THAT KNOB?
ERK!
AWLK!
CRASH!
IT'S A NATIONAL CATASTROPHE!
HEH-HEH! FANTASTIC! MY HOVERCRAFT IS EVEN BETTER THAN I THOUGHT!
GANGWAY!
AGH-H!
CRASH!
GLUG!
WHAT A SHAMBLES!
THE "QUEEN OF LINDENMERE," THE "SILVER CLOUD," THE "WATER SPRITE," THE "WHITE SWIFT," AND THE "LADY OF THE LAKE" LATER.
SUFFERIN' CATS! IT'S GOING TO SMACK INTO THAT MOUNTAIN! TEN THOUSAND QUIDS WORTH OF UN-TESTED HOVERCRAFT GONE UP IN SMOKE!
IF IT SURVIVES THIS LOT—IT'LL PROVE WHAT I'VE ALWAYS SAID—I'M A GENIUS!
CRUNCH!
ERK!
GLURK! IT'S GOTTA STOP NOW!
BUT, AS YOU KNOW, JONAH STOPS AT NOTHING!—AND NOTHING STOPS JONAH!

SOUPER BOY
CLASSIC TOPPER
SB
SIDNEY BRAITHWAITE.
ARR! IT BE GOIN' TO RAIN CATS AND DOGS TODAY.
HO! HO! I'D BETTER TAKE SOME SOUP TO PROTECT MYSELF WHILE I TAKE A STROLL, THEN!
I'M REALLY TAKING THE SOUP 'COS THESE GROCERIES ARE BECOMIN' HEAVY.

THERE! MUM'S GROCERIES FEEL REALLY LIGHT NOW! RAINING CATS AND DOGS, INDEED! HAR! HAR!
OH-OH! SILLY SID! NO LID!
SPLASH!
BLUB.

TA-TA, BUG!
YIPPEE!
100 M.P.H.
SCRATCH!
VAROOM!
OOYAH! YOU BIG BULLY!
SPLASH!
SID'S SOUP

WOW! I FEEL LIKE SOUPER-FLEA NOW— REALLY TOUGH!
YELP!
POW!

GRR! TAKE THAT, HOUND!
UGH!
SPLATT!

TOSS!
HAR!
YAROOP! A FLYING DOG—AND THERE ISN'T A CLOUD IN THE SKY!

MEANWHILE, SID'S SOUP KEEPS SPLASHING!
OUCH! WHASSAT? ROTTEN MOGGIES POURIN' WATER DOWN ME MOUSEHOLE, I BET!
SPLASH!

'S FUNNY! I FEEL REALLY STRONG— JUST CALL ME SOUPER-MOUSE!
ZAPPO!
POP!

RIGHT, MOGGIES, THIS IS WHERE I GET YOU BACK!
MEOWL!
CATS HOME
R-RIP!
CRASH!

SCRREECH!
MEW-YIKES!
WAIL!
RAIN!
RAIN!
BIFF!
BASH!
THUMP!
SPLATT!
OH, NO! IT'S RAINING CATS!

THANKS FOR THE WARNING, OLD-TIMER! IT IS RAINING CATS AND DOGS! I'M OFF HOME!
WHAT'S HE ON ABOUT? IT ISN'T EVEN DRIZZLING YET!

# DREAMY DANIEL

THE WORLD'S BIGGEST DOG

PUNCH and JIMMY
GLOOM

CLASSIC BEANO
Groan!
SCREECH!
LOVE-BIRDS
CHATTER!

Bah! There's nothing but fighting in this house!

BUT-
Ah! Peace-perfect peace!

Hm! Those fish have given me an idea to stop the kids fighting.

WHOOSH!
SPORTS SHOP

I want two small skin-diving outfits, please.
AIR
AIR

Follow me, you two.
SWIMMING BATHS

OK, get into the water!

SPLASH!
Tee-hee! I'll bet they won't fight now.

Peace-perfect peace!
BLUB!
GLUB!

BUT-
Blub! I'm a better diver than you!
Blewp! Rot! I'm best!

Oh, no! I've failed again!
SPLOOSH!

I can think of a good use for this when I get home!
GLOOMY
GLOOMIER

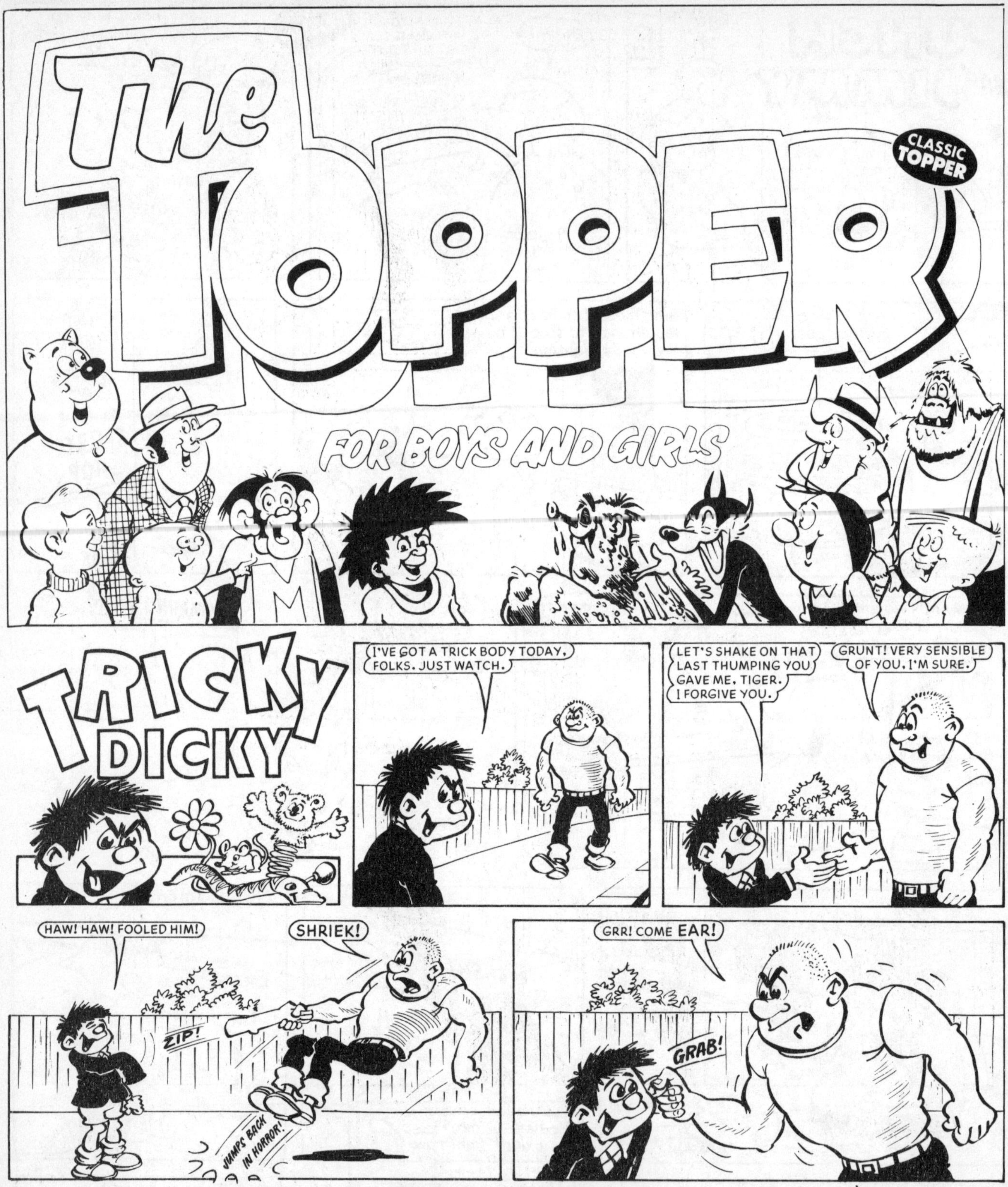

# The TOPPER

CLASSIC TOPPER

FOR BOYS AND GIRLS

MORE FUN ON THE BACK PAGE—

**H**i, tricksters! Here's a great gag to pull on all your pals. Tell them that you can hold your breath for five minutes! But when they don't believe you, and get all set to time you, just blow up a balloon and hold it for five minutes! Your breath's in the balloon, and you're holding it, aren't you? Ho! Ho!

# Dirty DICK

KEEP YOUR THIEVING HANDS OFF, DICK — THOSE ARE FOR TEA!
AW, MUM! YOU WOULDN'T MISS ONE!
SLAP!

WE'LL PUT THE TARTS IN THE PANTRY WHILE WE GO OUT, DAD.
YES, AND I KNOW A SMART PLACE TO HIDE THE KEY SO THAT DICK DOESN'T FIND IT!
?

WE'LL BE OUT ABOUT AN HOUR, DICK. BE A GOOD LAD AND DO YOUR PIANO PRACTICE WHILE WE'RE AWAY!
CLASSIC DANDY
OH YEAH? SOME HOPES!

HO-HO! DAD THINKS HE'S EVER SO CLEVER — BUT I BET I KNOW WHERE HE'S HIDDEN THE PANTRY KEY!

SURE ENOUGH! DAD WILL HAVE TO THINK OF A SMARTER PLACE THAN THAT TO FOOL ME!

I'LL JUST HAVE ONE JAM TART, THEN PUT THE KEY BACK AND MUM WILL NEVER KNOW!

FIVE MINUTES LATER ~~
OO-ER, I'VE SCOFFED THE LOT! THERE'S SOMETHING ABOUT JAM TARTS — ONCE I START, I CAN'T STOP!

.....I'LL PUT THE KEY BACK IN THE PIANO AND HOPE FOR THE BEST!

I HOPE DICK DID HIS PIANO PRACTICE WHILE WE'VE BEEN OUT!
I DOUBT IT — BUT I'LL CHECK UP ON THE PANTRY JUST IN CASE!

ALL GONE! OUCH!
DAD! YOU GREEDY THING! WE'RE HARDLY HOME BEFORE YOU'VE EATEN ALL THE JAM TARTS!
BONK!

GRR! I'LL TAKE MY SLIPPER TO DICK WHEN I FIND HIM!

DICK! WHERE ARE YOU?
HA-HA! I'M IN A GOOD HIDING PLACE! DAD KEEPS HIS SLIPPERS IN HERE, SO IT'S THE LAST PLACE HE'LL THINK OF LOOKING FOR ME!

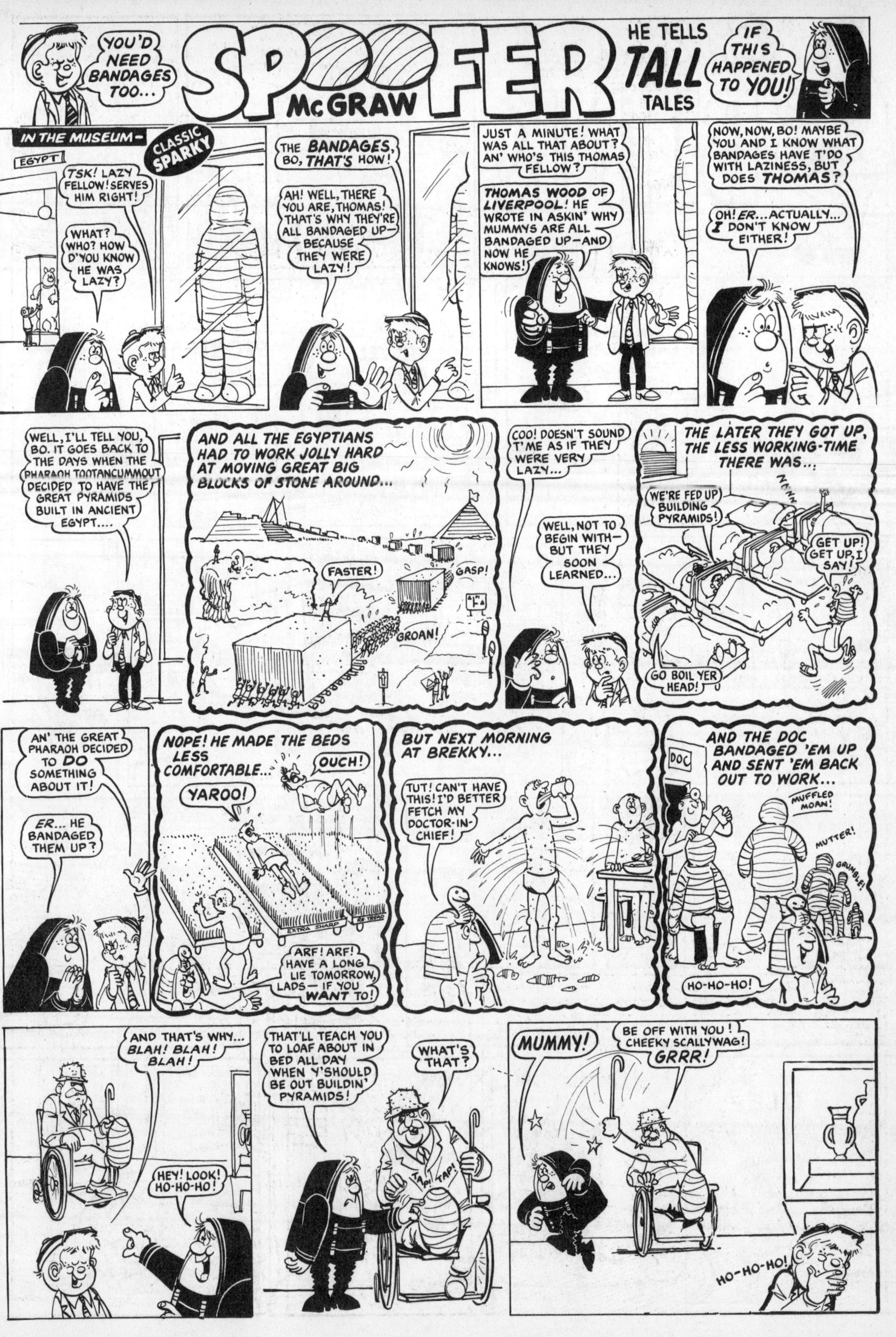

YOU'D NEED BANDAGES TOO...
SPOOFER McGRAW
HE TELLS TALL TALES
IF THIS HAPPENED TO YOU!
IN THE MUSEUM—
CLASSIC SPARKY
EGYPT
TSK! LAZY FELLOW! SERVES HIM RIGHT!
WHAT? WHO? HOW D'YOU KNOW HE WAS LAZY?
THE BANDAGES, BO, THAT'S HOW!
AH! WELL, THERE YOU ARE, THOMAS! THAT'S WHY THEY'RE ALL BANDAGED UP— BECAUSE THEY WERE LAZY!
JUST A MINUTE! WHAT WAS ALL THAT ABOUT? AN' WHO'S THIS THOMAS FELLOW?
THOMAS WOOD OF LIVERPOOL! HE WROTE IN ASKIN' WHY MUMMYS ARE ALL BANDAGED UP—AND NOW HE KNOWS!
NOW, NOW, BO! MAYBE YOU AND I KNOW WHAT BANDAGES HAVE T'DO WITH LAZINESS, BUT DOES THOMAS?
OH! ER... ACTUALLY... I DON'T KNOW EITHER!
WELL, I'LL TELL YOU, BO. IT GOES BACK TO THE DAYS WHEN THE PHARAOH TOOTANCUMMOUT DECIDED TO HAVE THE GREAT PYRAMIDS BUILT IN ANCIENT EGYPT....
AND ALL THE EGYPTIANS HAD TO WORK JOLLY HARD AT MOVING GREAT BIG BLOCKS OF STONE AROUND...
FASTER!
GASP!
GROAN!
COO! DOESN'T SOUND T'ME AS IF THEY WERE VERY LAZY...
WELL, NOT TO BEGIN WITH— BUT THEY SOON LEARNED...
THE LATER THEY GOT UP, THE LESS WORKING-TIME THERE WAS...
WE'RE FED UP BUILDING PYRAMIDS!
GET UP! GET UP, I SAY!
GO BOIL YER HEAD!
AN' THE GREAT PHARAOH DECIDED TO DO SOMETHING ABOUT IT!
ER... HE BANDAGED THEM UP?
NOPE! HE MADE THE BEDS LESS COMFORTABLE...
OUCH!
YAROO!
EXTRA SHARP
ARF! ARF! HAVE A LONG LIE TOMORROW, LADS— IF YOU WANT TO!
BUT NEXT MORNING AT BREKKY...
TUT! CAN'T HAVE THIS! I'D BETTER FETCH MY DOCTOR-IN-CHIEF!
AND THE DOC BANDAGED 'EM UP AND SENT 'EM BACK OUT TO WORK...
DOC
MUFFLED MOAN!
MUTTER!
GRUMBLE!
HO-HO-HO!
AND THAT'S WHY... BLAH! BLAH! BLAH!
HEY! LOOK! HO-HO-HO!
THAT'LL TEACH YOU TO LOAF ABOUT IN BED ALL DAY WHEN Y'SHOULD BE OUT BUILDIN' PYRAMIDS!
WHAT'S THAT?
TAP! TAP!
MUMMY!
BE OFF WITH YOU! CHEEKY SCALLYWAG! GRRR!
HO-HO-HO!

Colonel
BLINK

MUST GET MYSELF SOME PETROL!
AUTOMATIC CAR WASH
CLOSE ALL WINDOWS
OIL, SIR?

HELP! A THUNDERSTORM!

BLINKIN' WEATHER! DAREN'T GO OUT WITHOUT A COAT! THERE'S AN IDEA, THOUGH. SUNNY SPAIN, EH? YES WHY NOT! OFF YOU GO, BLINKY LAD!
VISIT SUNNY SPAIN BY CAR FERRY
BOOK AT YOUR LOCAL AGENCY

I'LL GET A TICKET FROM THIS TRAVEL AGENCY.
TRAVEL AGENCY
SPORTS SHOP
TONIGHT— GRAND FOOTBALL MATCH— STANCHESTER v. MADRID

TICKET FOR MADRID, PLEASE.
CERTAINLY, SIR. STAND?

STAND? OF COURSE I'M NOT STANDING!
GET YOUR BIG MATCH TICKETS HERE
ER-THAT'LL BE SEVEN-AND-SIX, THEN, SIR!

SEVEN-AND-SIX! MUST BE AN EXCURSION TICKET. NOW, THEN, WHERE'S THAT AIRPORT...?
AIRPORT

AH, HERE WE ARE— AND THE CAR FERRY'S WAITING!

IN WE GO! ARF!
RIGHT, BERT—LET'S GET GOING!

HUP!

BY JINGO! WE'RE OFF ALREADY!
AGRICULTURAL SHOW

AN HOUR LATER.
WE'VE STOPPED! THAT WAS QUICK—MUST BE ONE OF THESE SUPER JETS!
SHOW RING
OKAY, BERT, LET'S GET THE OLD BULL ABOARD.

THANK YOU, CAPTAIN—A SPLENDID FLIGHT! A TRIFLE BUMPY, PERHAPS, BUT FAST, VERY FAST!
?

GALLOPIN' GUNNERS— THE FOOL'S LANDED IN A BULL RING!

OLÉ!

AAARGH!
BOOMF!

GARDEN EQUIPMENT

SUNNY SPAIN? BAH! JUST WAIT TILL I GET BACK TO THAT TRAVEL AGENCY! THE RAIN HERE'S WORSE THAN IT IS AT HOME!

# Jinx

I'M OFF TO WATCH MY SCHOOL, WEST STREET, COMPETE IN A SPORTS CONTEST AGAINST CLOBBER ACADEMY. THERE'S A BIG TUCK HAMPER FOR THE WINNING SCHOOL!

SCHOOL SPORTS

AT THE SPORTS GROUND—

HA-HA! LOOK AT THAT USELESS CLOBBER BUNCH! THE HAMPER'S AS GOOD AS OURS!

HEH-HEH! I'LL JUST GRAB MYSELF A CUP OF TEA AND A JAM TART TO WORK UP AN APPETITE FOR THAT HAMPER!

CLOBBER FOR EVER

TEAS Snacks

JUST AS JINX IS LEAVING THE TEA-TENT, WILHELMINA WEED OF CLOBBER ACADEMY IS ABOUT TO TRY THE LONG JUMP.

OOPS! I'VE SLIPPED!

HOT TEA

EEK!

TEAS Snacks

LONG JUMP

CLASSIC BEANO

EE-YOW-W!

G-GOSH!

WHIZZ-Z-Z!

SWISH-H-H!

CLOBBER FOR EVER

WOW! WHAT A LEAP!

GIRLS! BELIEVE IT OR NOT, THE COMPETITOR FOR CLOBBER ACADEMY HAS JUST JUMPED 40 FEET!

CRUMBS! I'M THE BEST JUMPER IN WEST ST. SCHOOL — BUT I'LL NEVER BEAT THAT!

AND SHE DOESN'T.

BAH! THAT WAS ALL JINX'S FAULT!

OH, WELL! BETTER LUCK IN THE NEXT EVENT! I'LL JUST LEAVE MY JAM TART HERE WHILE I GO AND GET ANOTHER CUP OF TEA.

CLASSIC TOPPER
JIMMY JINX
AND WHAT HIS RABBIT THINKS
I'D BETTER FEED PERCY.
HIGH TIME, TOO! HE'LL BE STARVING!

HOI, PERCE! HERE'S YOUR CHANCE TO ESCAPE!
I DO NOT APPROVE, PERCIVAL.

LOOK OUT, JIM! PERCY'S GETTING OUT!
HEH!
BUMP!
ZOOM!

NET HIM, JIM! HURRY!
THAT'S NOT NICE!
GRAB!

BAH! I'VE BROKEN THE HANDLE.
RRRASP!
TALK TO HIM NICELY, JAMES.
SNAP!

WHAT A STUPID IDEA! I KNOW WHAT'LL HAPPEN.
PRRRP!
SWEET LITTLE PERCY—COME TO JAMES!
HE'S GOTTA BE KIDDIN'!

LISSEN! C'MERE, YOU STOOPID LONG-EARED OBJECT!
YIKE!

I'M OFF!
GRAB HIM, QUICK!
BOUND!

GRR! I'LL GET . . .
TWIST!
NOTE:— SLIPPERY VEG.

. . . EEARGH!
FLIP!

DOOH!
DONK!

PERCIVAL, YOU'D BEST BE BACK IN YOUR HUTCH SOON BEFORE JAMES'S FATHER FINDS OUT THAT YOU'RE EATING HIS WINTER CROP!
CLOMP!
SLOBBER!
MUNCH!

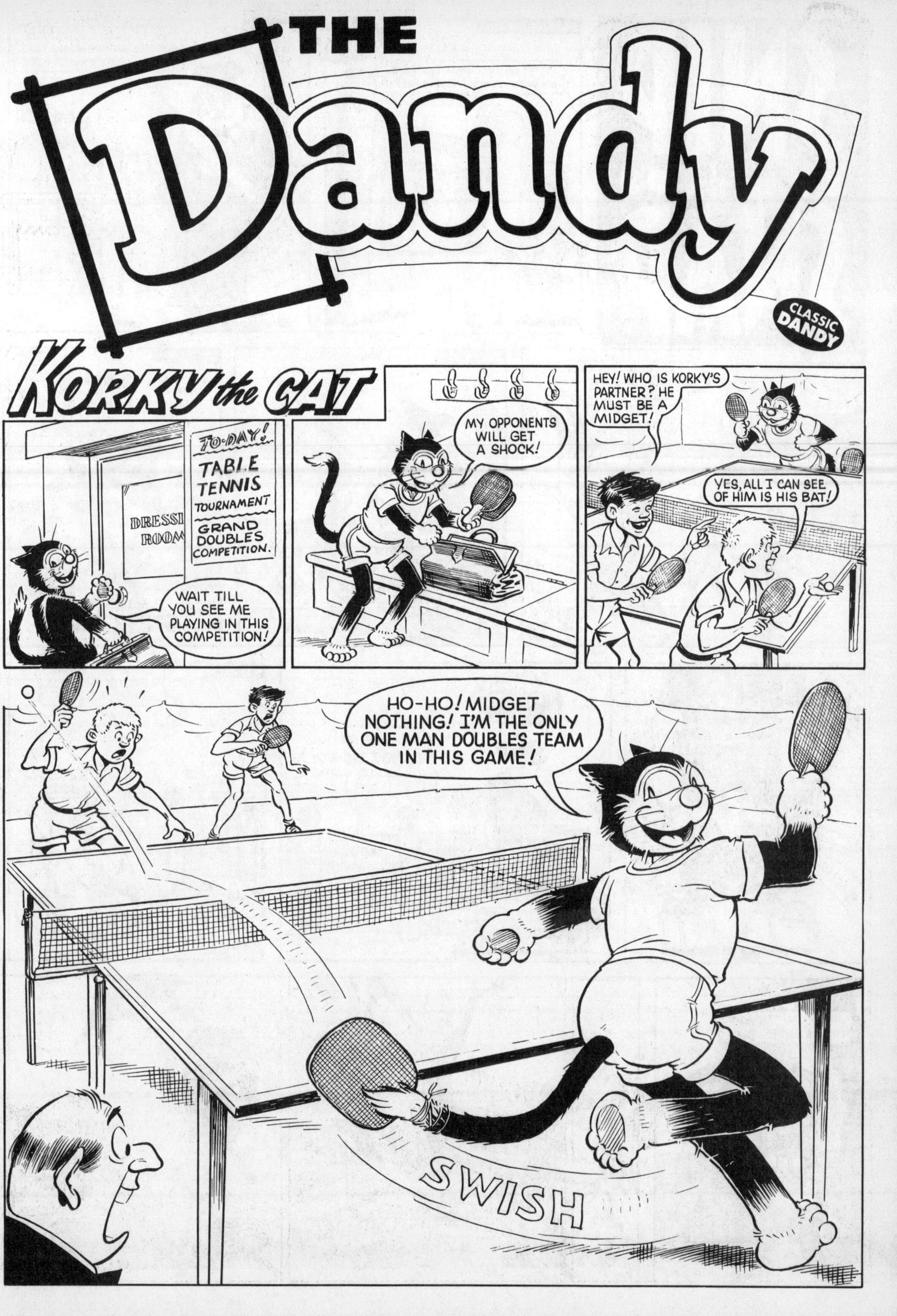

# KORKY the CAT

HO-HO! MIDGET NOTHING! I'M THE ONLY ONE MAN DOUBLES TEAM IN THIS GAME!

SWISH

SNIP and SNAP

EARLY ONE MORNING—
CLASSIC SPARKY
YIPPEE! THIS MUST BE ONE OF MY MOST FIENDISH PLANS EVER! RIZZLE! RIZZLE!
BEWARE OF THE

SOON AFTER—
TUM-TE-TUM! I DUNNO WHY, BUT I'VE GOT A FEELING THAT THIS COULD BE MY LUCKY DAY!
P.O.
SNIGGER!

MEANWHILE—
HE'S COMING, SNAP— AND HE LOOKS HAPPY!
ZZZ! HE'LL LOOK EVEN HAPPIER WHEN HE SEES MY "SPECIAL" POSTER!

SURE ENOUGH—
WHOOPEE! THEY'VE GONE! HOORAY! IT IS MY LUCKY DAY!
BEW
GONE ON HOLLADAY
OGS

BUT INSIDE—
OH-OH! HOLLADAY? HOLIDAY?
GULP!

AAAA!
SNIP!
SNAP!

GLOOM
HAR-HAR! ZZZ! RIZZLE-HO!
BEWARE OF THE DOGS

NEXT DAY—
HO-HO! TRIP WIRES! JUST THE THING FOR A RAINY DAY! ZZZ!
OH- HO!
KER-SQUISH! RIZZLE!

A LITTLE LATER—
LA-DEE-DA! IT'S GOING TO BE A SUPER DAY...

P.O.
...THANKS TO MY POGO STICK! HO-HO-HO!
BOING!
BOING!

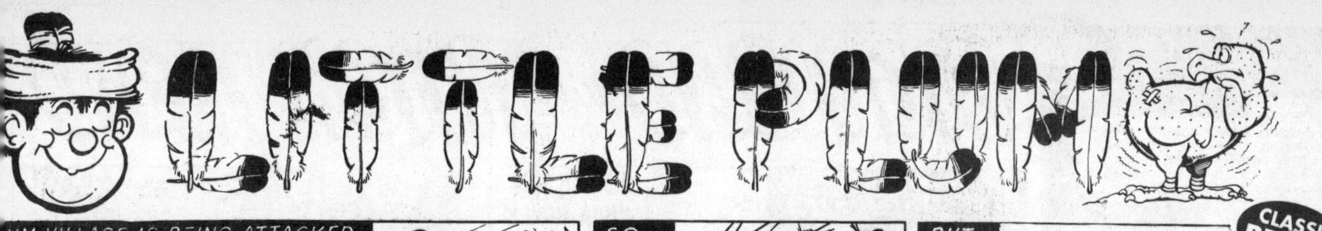

UM VILLAGE IS BEING ATTACKED BY UM PUTTYFOOT TRIBE.
FETCH UM CAVALRY, PLUM! CAMOUFLAGE YOURSELF WITH UM LONG GRASS!

SO—
HEH! HEH! THIS IS UM EASY!

BUT—
CLASSIC BEANO
WAIL!
SPOTTER CORPS
CHEW
MUNCH
GULP! UM MUSTANGS HAVE EATEN UM CAMOUFLAGE!

ZOOM!
HELP!
SMELLY-FOOT VILLAGE

PLUM TRIES AGAIN—

I'LL CARVE MY NAME ON THIS TREE.
PUTTY-FOOT LINES

EEK!
UM SPY!

GRR! I DON'T LIKE UM SPIES!
HOME

LATER—
WE'LL TRY SHOOTING YOU OVER THEIR HEADS THIS TIME, PLUM!

BUT UM HUMAN CANNONBALL FALLS SHORT
ZOOM!

THUD!
CHIEF

HE'S KNOCKED OUT UM CHIEF! WE CAN'T FIGHT WITHOUT UM LEADER! RUN FOR IT, MEN!

CHEERS!
NO NEED TO FETCH UM CAVALRY NOW, CHIEFY!

# BIG HEAD and THICK HEAD

Little
MO

HO-HO! THE MUNCHERS ARE REALLY FUNNY THIS WEEK!
BEEZER

CLASSIC BEEZER
LET ME TEST MY SCISSORS ON YOUR 'BEEZER', GIRLS!
EEK!

MUGSY! YOU PEST!

Later, in Mo's garden —
MUGSY WON'T ANNOY US HERE.

But—
YOU WERE SAYING, MO?

Then—
WOW! LOOK AT THE TIME! I'D BETTER HURRY IF I'M NOT GOING TO BE LATE FOR WORK!
WE KNOW WHERE HE WORKS, EH, MIRABELLE? I'VE AN IDEA!

So—
SURE YOU CAN PLAY WITH MY PUPPY, MO. HERE YOU ARE.
THANKS, MISTER GRANT.

Later—
NEWSAGENT
HI, FATSO!
GRR! I'LL SEE YOU AFTER MY PAPER ROUND!

Then—
WHASSAT?
MUNCH! TEAR!

EH? WHERE DID THAT PUPPY COME FROM?
COME ON, BOBBY!

OH, NO! IT'S CHEWED UP ALL MY PAPERS!
HO-HO! THAT'LL TEACH YOU NOT TO CUT UP OUR 'BEEZERS'!
YES! BOBBY IS A LITTLE 'TEARAWAY'! HO-HO!

# BULLY BEEF AND CHIPS

CLASSIC DANDY

WHIZZ!
GOSH! ISN'T THAT CLEVER? I WONDER IF WE COULD MAKE A PYRAMID?
JUMP!

LATER, IN CHIPS' GARDEN–
UP YOU GO ON TOP, TICH– OW!
AARGH! GET YOUR FOOT OFF BY DOSE!
HO-HO! THIS IS TOO GOOD A CHANCE TO MISS!
WATCH IT!
OUCH! MY NECK!

THERE! WE'VE MADE IT!

HEY! WHAT'S THAT?
HOOK!

WOW!
EEK!
HELP!
YANK!

AARGH!
OOYAH!
YEOW!
OUCH!
THUD!
DONG!
OOF!
BIFF!

COME HERE! I'LL SHOW YOU LOT HOW TO BUILD PYRAMIDS!
ERK!
OOYAH!

MOAN!
GROAN!
HO-HO! NOW THAT'S WHAT I CALL A PYRAMID!
OOH!
AAH!

LATER–
HO-HO! NOT INTERESTED IN PYRAMIDS ANY MORE, CHIPS?
OH, YES! I'VE BEEN READING ABOUT THE PYRAMIDS OF EGYPT. THEY'RE MADE OF STONE, Y'KNOW!

–JUST LIKE THIS LUMP HERE!
OOYAH! MY TOES!
CRUNCH!

ROGER the DODGER
CLASSIC BEANO
THE ART OF DODGING By ROGER VOL. I
DODGES GALORE
THE SCIENCE OF DODG
Dodger's Diary
1001 DODGES BY ROGER
THE DODGER'S COMPANION By GER
ROGER'S DICTIONARY OF DODGES

GOLLY! WHAT'S THIS—ROGER CHASING DAD? IT CAN'T BE!
NO, IT ISN'T! DAD'S CHASING ROGER ROUND AND ROUND THE HOUSE — AND ROGER'S GOING SO FAST HE'S ALMOST LAPPED DAD!

BUT—
AH, GOT YOU, YOU LITTLE PEST!
TWISS-S-T
EEK! H-HOW DID YOU KNOW I WAS BEHIND YOU?

HEH-HEH! SIMPLY BY KEEPING MY EYE FIXED ON THIS LITTLE DRIVING MIRROR — NOT A BAD DODGE FOR AN OLD CHAP, EH? AND NOW WE'LL GET ON WITH THE LITTLE EXERCISE WE WERE ENJOYING WHEN YOU BOLTED— BEND DOWN!
GULP! W-WHY NOT THINK ABOUT IT FOR A YEAR — OR TWO? YOU WOULDN'T HIT A LITTLE FELLOW—

—WOULD YOU, DAD? WOULD YOU—
OUCH!
WE WON'T GO INTO THE DETAILS OF WHAT ROGER DID TO DESERVE THIS READERS, BUT DESERVE IT HE DID!

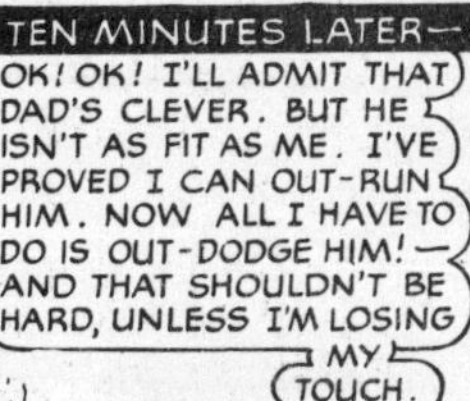

TEN MINUTES LATER—
OK! OK! I'LL ADMIT THAT DAD'S CLEVER. BUT HE ISN'T AS FIT AS ME. I'VE PROVED I CAN OUT-RUN HIM. NOW ALL I HAVE TO DO IS OUT-DODGE HIM! — AND THAT SHOULDN'T BE HARD, UNLESS I'M LOSING MY TOUCH.

AND SO—
ROGER! I WANT YOU!
OH-OH! THIS IS THE TEST. I'VE GOT THE SPEED. ALL I MUST WATCH OUT FOR IS DAD'S DODGER-TRAPS.

FIRST STOP — THE GARDEN —
A -HAH! THAT LONG GRASS UNDER THE TREE COULD BE HIDING A TRAP. I'LL SEND COUSIN WILLIE'S TOY HORSE TO FIND OUT.

JERK
HO-HO! WHAT DID I TELL YOU?

HUH! I CAN GUESS WHAT DAD'S NEXT TRICK'LL BE.

A FEW YARDS FURTHER ON —
I THOUGHT SO — A CONCEALED PIT!

I'D BETTER VAULT OVER THE HOLE — JUST IN CASE IT'S WIDER THAN THE EYE CAN SEE —
— AND NOW DOWN ON TO THE OLD SPRINGY MATTRESS I PUT THERE IN CASE I EVER NEEDED TO MAKE A QUICK GET-A-WAY.

SEE? IT'LL BOUNCE ME OVER THE WALL — HEE-HEE!
— WELL CLEAR OF THE BROKEN GLASS DAD CEMENTED ON TOP —
—YA-HOO! I'VE OUT-DODGERED DAD — ERK! NO! SOMEBODY STOP ME—

—AGH-H! OUCH! EEK! YAH-H! OO-YAH! ERK!
AH, SO YOU'VE TURNED UP AT LAST, ROGER! I WANTED YOU TO HELP ME CLEAR ALL THESE NETTLES AWAY BEFORE SOME SILLY ASS FALLS IN THEM!

LATER — GOODNESS! WHAT'S WRONG WITH ROGER? HE SEEMS "NETTLED" ABOUT SOMETHING!
GR-R-R! ALL RIGHT, LAUGH! BUT I STILL SAY I'M A BETTER DODGER THAN DAD. IT'S JUST THAT HE HAS ALL THE PESKY LUCK!

CLASSIC BUZZ
SKOOKUM SKOOL
←TEECHER
DING-A-LING-A LING!
YAHOO!
QUIET!
RAT-TAT-TAT!
Don't forget to bring your cricket gear tomorrow, pals!
Cricket? Oh, no!
PETROL
GEAR BOX
CHUG
CHUG
BOWLING MACHINE MARK I
Last year they built a bowling machine, but . . .
VEROOOM!
VEROOOM!
. . . it ran amok!
Then they borrowed a cannon from the museum . . .
. . . and that was another window broken!
I know how to stop them—I'll confiscate their cricket gear!
NEXT DAY—
Leave all your cricket gear here!
WHOOSH!
Aw!
That's right—empty your pockets! There won't be any broken windows this year!
TAP! TAP!
Boo!
The sack, too, Streaky.
Aw . . .
PROD!
HOWL!
. . . okay, sir!
JAB!
YEEOW!
POW!
CRASH!
WHEEEEEE!
CRASH!
CRASH!
CRASH!
CRASH!
Oh, no—I'll have to close the school until the windows are repaired!
Heh-heh! What a "smashing" teacher he is!
DRUM

THE THREE BEARS
CLASSIC BEANO

H'M! I'VE SAVED TEN CENTS—BUT I WON'T GET MUCH GRUB FOR THAT.
YOU'RE LUCKY. MA, TED AND I HAVE ONLY GOT FIVE CENTS EACH.
NEVER BE WITHOUT A "BEANO"

BUT—
HANK'S FOOD STORE
DO YOU REALLY MEAN THIS, HANK?
ALL YOU CAN EAT FOR TEN CENTS
SURE THING, PA. I'M SELLING OFF ALL THE GRUB CHEAP AND STARTING A HARDWARE STORE.

HANK'S FOOD STORE
YOU GIVE ME YOUR FIVE CENTS, TED!
NO, PA! YOU GIVE ME YOUR FIVE CENTS!

RIGHT! WE'LL TOSS FOR IT. "HEADS" I WIN—"TAILS" YOU LOSE.
SOUNDS FAIR ENOUGH, PA.

TOUGH LUCK, TED! "TAILS"—YOU LOSE!
TINKLE

BUT WAIT A MINUTE—"HEADS" HE WINS—"TAILS" I LOSE. HE FOOLED ME!
CHORTLE!

FRAUD!
BONK!
BONK!
BONK!
ZIPPPPP!

WE'LL BOTH GUESS WHAT'S GOING TO COME ROUND THE CORNER FIRST. WHOEVER'S RIGHT GETS THE CASH!
HANK'
OK, TED!

I SAY IT'LL BE A MONKEY RIDING AN ELEPHANT!
NOT A CHANCE! I SAY IT'LL BE A COWBOY ON A HORSE!
FOOD STOR

GULP! TED WAS RIGHT ENOUGH!
MY TEN CENTS I THINK!
HANK'S FOOD STOR
VISIT BINGO'S CIRCUS
CHINK!

HOLD IT! THAT'S NOT A MONKEY—IT'S A MAN DRESSED UP!
WHEW! IT'S HOT IN THIS SUIT!

LOOK, PA—HANK'S CUTTING HIS PRICES. WE CAN BOTH GET A FEED NOW!
HANK'S FOOD STOR
ALL YOU CAN EAT FOR FIVE CENTS

HANK'S FOOD STORE
ALL YOU CAN EAT FOR FIVE CENTS
WHOOOSHH!
WHOOSH!

AGH! WE'RE TOO LATE! SHE'S SCOFFED THE LOT!
APPLES

Dick Turban
DESERT HIGHWAYMAN
and his camel, CARAMEL
CLASSIC NUTTY

AHA! Now for some rich plunderings.
G-goodness m-me!
CREAK!
TOTTER!
WOW!
WHEEEEEEEE!
ERK! A desert rat—I'm scared.
SQUEAK!
SCREECH!

You're too late, my friend. I have already been robbed this morning.
WH-WHAT?

CARAMEL! Come down, you cowardly camel!
WHIMPER! WHINE!
SLASH!
HACK! HACK! HACK!

Be brave! I must find this other bandit or we'll be out of business.
Y-yes, D-Dick!

LATER—
HAH! So you're the nasty bandit who's robbing on MY territory?
Yes! El-p-Misself's the name.

And this is my little brother, El-p-Hisself!
I'm off!
GULP! Er, nice to meet you.

HEY! Come back!
EEK! My turban!

GOODNESS GRACIOUS US!?!
YIKES!
WHIRRR!

H-he's vanished into thin air!
I don't believe it!

SCRATCH!
PROUD!
I vanished into thin SAND. Sometimes a cowardly camel's a bandit's best friend!

CLASSIC DANDY
The SMASHER
NO FISHING
TUM -TE-TUM -TE-TUM!

CAN'T YOU READ, SMASHER? IT SAYS NO FISHING!
GLOOG!
SHOVE
SPLOOSH!

NO FISHING
AND IT ALSO SAYS NO SWIMMING—CLEAR OFF BEFORE I TELL MY DAD—HE'S THE WATER BAILIFF!
GRR!

I'LL FIX THE BULLY WHEN HE COMES BACK!

LATER
HE'S AT IT AGAIN—I'LL JUST HAVE TO TEACH HIM ANOTHER LESSON!

JERK
HO-HO! IT'S ONLY MY STUFFED JERSEY AND TROUSERS!

HO! HO! HO!
GLUG!
SPLOOSH!

HAD A NICE SWIM?
I'LL BE BACK—AND I'LL REALLY TELL MY DAD THIS TIME!
NUTS!

MY CLOTHES ARE DRY—NOW I CAN GET ON WITH MY FISHING AGAIN!

THERE HE IS!
OOER! THE BULLY IS BACK—WITH A PAL!

LET HIM GO—WE'LL HELP OURSELVES TO HIS FISH!

BUT
HEY, PETE! HELP ME! THERE'S GLUE ON THESE FISH—THEY'VE STUCK TO MY HANDS!

I'VE GOT ONE OFF YOUR HAND, BUT NOW IT'S STUCK TO MINE!
OOER! HERE COMES DAD!
HOI!

WELL, CYRIL, I'VE CAUGHT YOU RED-HANDED, EH?
B-BUT, DAD—
SMASHER PUT THE GLUE ON THE FISH TO TRAP US, I BET!

I'LL DEAL WITH THE PAIR OF YOU AT HOME!
HO-HO! NEXT TIME PICK ON SOMEONE WHO ISN'T AS CLEVER AS ME!
BUT, DAD, LET ME EXPLAIN--

DENNIS THE MENACE
CLASSIC BEANO
DENNIS ENJOYS PLAYING GAMES—LIKE ROUNDERS—
CORKS!
BOP!
CRASH!
—AND FOOTBALL—
TINKLE!
THUD!
OOPS!
—AND "HEADERS".
I WON'T BREAK ANYTHING NOW!
OH, NO?
SHATTER!
LATER—
YOUR SON BROKE A LAMP-POST PLAYING "HEADERS".
—AND MY GREENHOUSE, PLAYING FOOTBALL!
—AND MY WINDOW, PLAYING ROUNDERS!
GRR!
SO—
YOUR POCKET MONEY IS STOPPED FOR FIVE YEARS AND YOU'RE BANNED FROM PLAYING FOOTBALL, ROUNDERS AND "HEADERS"!
BUT WHAT GAME CAN I PLAY, DAD?
DOWN AT WALTER'S—
YOU CAN PLAY CROQUET WITH WALTER. THAT'S A NICE, GENTLE GAME.
TITTER! WHAT AN EXCITING GAME!
TAP!
UGH!
DAD DEPARTS—
DAD DIDN'T SAY ANYTHING ABOUT NOT PLAYING GOLF—BUT FIRST I NEED A TEE!
COME HERE, WALTER!
EEK! OUCH! LEAVE ME ALONE, YOU NASTY BOY! WHIMPER!
HEH! HEH! WALTER MAKES A SUPER TEE! NOW FOR A MIGHTY SWIPE!
SOB!
CRUMBS! WHAT IS IT DAD SHOUTS IF HIS GOLF BALL'S HEADING FOR SOMEBODY?—OH, YES—
ZIP-P-P-P!
WHACK!
TUM-TEE-TUM!
FORE!
CRASH!
TINKLE!
TINKLE!
TINKLE!
TINKLE!
TINKLE!
THEN—
THIS BOY SMASHED FIVE PANES OF GLASS!
BUT I DISTINCTLY SHOUTED FORE!
SO—
NO ROUNDERS
NO FOOTBALL
NO "HEADERS"
NO CROQUET
NO GOLF
NO SUPPER
NO POCKET MONEY
LUDO ONLY!
GROAN! WHAT A LIFE!

# KORKY THE CAT

Korky was broke and starving,
But did he mope?—Not a bit!
He built up a booming brush business
By putting his back into it!

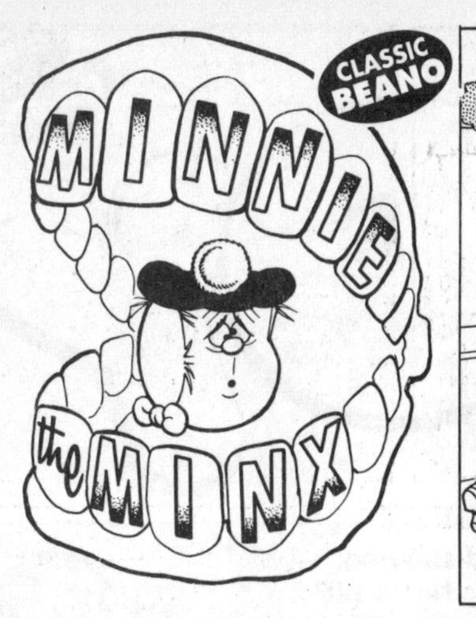
CLASSIC BEANO
MINNIE the MINX

COO! A PARCEL. WONDER WHAT'S INSIDE?
BEWARE OF DOG

HAW! HAW! IT'S A SET OF FALSE TEETH. I COULD HAVE SOME SMASHIN' FUN WITH THEM!

LATER—
AND HOW IS DEAR BABY, MRS ENTWHISTLE?
SHE'S DOING VERY WELL, MRS CLUTTERBUCK. WE EXPECT TO SEE HER FIRST TOOTH ANY DAY NOW!

EEK! L-LOOK-TEETH GALORE!

MINNIE GRABS THE TEETH AND FLEES.
GROCER
RIP!
HEH! HEH! JOLLY GOOD LAUGH, WHAT?

LATER—
HELLO, THERE, MINNIE! I HAVEN'T SEEN YOU FOR AGES. SHAKE HANDS, GIRL!
COO! IT'S UNCLE ERNIE—

CRUNCH!
—THE LAST TIME HE SHOOK MY HAND, I COULDN'T HOLD A LOLLIPOP FOR WEEKS! I MUST GET MY OWN BACK!

THEY SHAKE HANDS—
OOYAH!

SNAP!

HEH! HEH! THAT SHOOK OLD UNCLE ERNIE!
SNAP!
POLICE NOTICE
ALL ARTICLES FOUND IN THE STREET SHOULD BE HANDED IN TO THE POLICE STATION
COO! I'D BETTER DO AS IT SAYS. MAYBE I'LL GET A REWARD!

AT THE POLICE STATION—
I FOUND THESE TEETH IN THE STREET. SOME SILLY OL' SO-AND-SO MUST HAVE DROPPED 'EM!
WANTED
CELLS
SNAP!
ENQUIRIES

GRR! I'M THE SHILLY OL' SHO-AND-SHO WHO DROPPED 'EM! THEY'RE MY FALSH TEESH!
ER-IS THERE A REWARD FOR FINDIN' 'EM?

YES, THERE IS— ONE POUND—
WANTED
WANTED
ENQUIR
OH, TA!

—WHICH WILL PAY FOR THE DAMAGE THAT I'M SURE YOU'VE DONE WITH MY TEETH TODAY!
WANTED
WANTED
SNATCH!

LATER—
YOU CAN JOLLY WELL STAY THERE, PARCEL! I'M NOT PICKIN' YOU UP!

NERO and ZERO

Hurry down to the harbour, guards! Queen Cleopatra has sent me a needle!

AND SO—
Why has she sent Caesar a needle?
We'll soon see . . .
CLASSIC BUZZ

Wow! Look at the size of it!
e won't be able o sew any holes n his socks with that!

LATER—
What a weight! There must be an easier way of carrying it than this!
PALACE 10 MILES

THERE IS—
This old tree makes a super catapult!
TWANG!
Away it goes!

Wow! Some rotter is needling me!

You two! I might have guessed! Get my needle dug out at once!

Mutter! Mutter!
It's coming free!

Wow! IT IS free!

Great trembling togas! My favourite grub—fruit salad!

CRASH!
Aw no! Fruit squash!

Idiots! Vandals! Scoundrels! You'll top the bill at the Coliseum for this! The lions will love you even if I don't!
Gulp!

Quick, Nero—in here!
SLAM!
WHOOSH!
I'm right behind you, Zero—and we'll lock the door from the inside!

THUD!
BANG!
No, sire! Don't break down the door!
CRASH!
Spare us, o great one!
Now do you get the point of my needle? It's just the thing to sort out you 'sew-and-sews'!

Dick Turban
DESERT HIGHWAYMAN
CLASSIC NUTTY
and his camel, CARAMEL

OH, NO! Not again!

Stop zat! You are ze soldiers—remember!
Zere's not much else we can do out here!

Er, what about a game of ze hide-and-seek, mes amis?
Goody!
SWEETNESS

SQUAWK!
Dick Turban's doing ze HIDING—so SEEK heem out!
BLAST!
Y-yes, mon C-Capitaine!

Tee-hee!
Right! We'll go East—OOF!
No, I say West! Get off!
TANGLE!
Ooyah!

Tell you what—I'll begin. You lot hide first.
Doh?!?
UM!?!

SO—
. . . 51 . . . 52 . . . 53 . . .
WINK!
You can COUNT on my master for a crafty plan.
Mm! Lovely grub!
SNIFF! SNIFF!
WHISPER
. . . 99 . . . 100! Coming, ready or not!

THEN—
CAPITAINE! We 'ave found ze bandeet, Dick Turban!
WHAT????

CHUCKLE! Fooled you, Capitaine! Enjoy your trip?
TRIP!
NYUNK!
PHATOOMF!

Yum! Yum! Dee-licious!
CHOMP! CHOMP! CHOMP!
SLURP!

LATER—
Ho! Ho! Looks like the legionnaires are playing at building sandcastles again!
Playing?—no, this is for real!
CLAW!
Keep building!
SCRAMBLE!

THE BADD LADS
CLASSIC BEEZER
THIS IS P.C. DIM, THE MOST ABSENT-MINDED COP IN THE FORCE. HE CAN NEVER REMEMBER A THING
THE BADD LADS ARE HIDING IN CEDAR WOODS. TAKE P.C. BLOGGS WITH YOU AND GO AND ARREST 'EM!
RIGHT, CAP'N OR IS IT CORPORAL? OR, AH, SARGE.
RIGHT, BLOGGS! KEEP IN STEP—LEFT—RIGHT—
OOPS! I FORGOT TO BRING P.C. WHAT'S HIS NAME WITH ME—S'POSE I'LL HAVE TO ARREST THOSE GOOD LADS M'SELF.
RIGHT! OR IS IT LEFT, YOU THREE, I'VE COME TO...
...NOW, WHAT HAVE I COME FOR???
GOSH! I CAN'T REMEMBER! I'D BETTER GO BACK AND ASK SERGEANT WHAT'S-HIS-NAME?
HO-HO! WE WERE LUCKY THERE!
YEAH! BUT WE'D BETTER LEAVE THIS HIDEOUT BEFORE HE GETS BACK FROM THE COP-SHOP!
WE'LL PULL ONE MORE JOB BEFORE WE GO TO OUR OTHER HIDEOUT!
LATER
SNIFF! I'M SUSPENDED FROM DUTY FOR BUNGLING THAT WHAT-D'YOU-CALL-'EM JOB? I'M SURE GLAD I CAN'T REMEMBER THE NAMES THE SERGEANT CALLED ME!
RESENTLY
I'LL GO FOR A RUN IN MY CAR. IT'LL HELP CHEER ME UP!
NOW, THERE WAS SOMETHING I SHOULD'VE DONE WHEN I GOT INTO THE CAR...???
WOW! I JUST MISSED THAT CAT-OR WAS IT A DOG?
I REMEMBER NOW! I SHOULD'VE PUT ON MY SAFETY BELT!
SCREECH!
BRAKE!
WOW! NEARLY ONE OF MY NINE LIVES AWAY THERE.
CLUNK!
THUD!
CRUMP!
HELP! POL...WELL, THAT'S WHAT I CALL QUICK SERVICE!
JEWELLER
GREAT WORK, DIM! HOW DID YOU MANAGE TO NAB 'EM IN THE ACT?
ER, I FORGET!

SPOOKUM SKOOL

CLASSIC CRACKER
It's a nice day for this time of year, so I'm taking you all to the beach!

AT THE BEACH—

Wow! Look at the crowds! Scare some of them away, class!

SO—
Stuck are you, sonny? I'll dig you out!
No, mister...
...there's my body over there!

SEVERAL FRIGHTS LATER—
Well done, spooks! You've cleared a nice big space for us!

Let's knock down that sandcastle!

AAARGH! GHOSTIES!
Don't you dare knock down my sandcastle!

Come along, class! The water's lovely!

Ho-ho! Even the crabs are too frightened to come near us!

Time to go home! We've had a lovely day!

Oh, no! We've scared EVERYONE away! There's not a bus left to get home in!
COACH PARK

Only five miles to go! Puff! What a rotten day! It's enough to make you wish you were human!

# THE TOPPER

CLASSIC TOPPER

MICKEY THE MONKEY
I MUST PHONE THE PLUMBER!

HELLO! TAPP THE PLUMBER HERE!

THIS IS MICKEY! COME ROUND AT ONCE! THE HOUSE IS BEING FLOODED!

EH? WHAT'S THAT?

HURRY! THERE'S A BURST PIPE UPSTAIRS IN THE BATHROOM!

I'LL COME ROUND TOMORROW. IT ISN'T URGENT IS IT?

URGENT? OF COURSE IT'S URGENT!

CAN'T IT WAIT? I'M VERY BUSY TODAY!

LISTEN! CAN'T YOU HEAR IT?
SPLASH!
GURGLE!
TOPPER

NO!

WELL... CAN YOU HEAR IT NOW?

SPLASH!

# Little Plum

CLASSIC BEANO
HAVEN'T HAD UM PESKY CUSTOMER FOR DAYS!
LITTLE PLUM-TOURIST GUIDE
PLUM

HEY, REDSKIN! I WANT YOU TO GUIDE ME UP BOULDER MOUNTAIN!
CRUMP

HUH! ONLY ONE MEASLY DOLLAR FOR GUIDIN' YOU UP A 15,000 FOOT MOUNTAIN!
PURSE

STOP GRUMBLING! YOU'LL GUIDE ME UP AND LIKE IT!

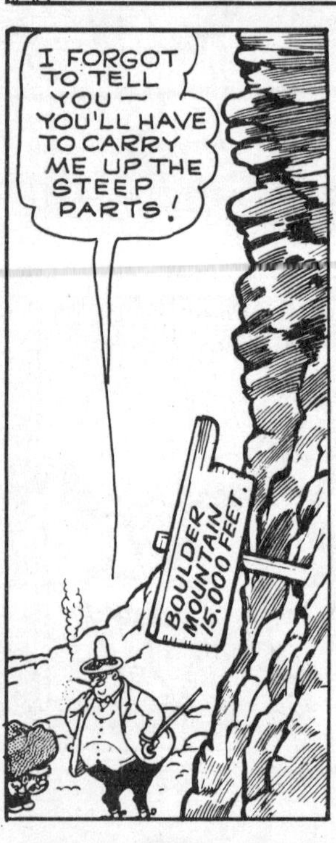
I FORGOT TO TELL YOU— YOU'LL HAVE TO CARRY ME UP THE STEEP PARTS!
BOULDER MOUNTAIN 15,000 FEET.

WHAT LOVELY SCENERY!

WHAT UM BULLY!

I CAN'T WADE ACROSS THIS TORRENT~IT MIGHT SHRINK MY SOCKS!

I'LL USE YOU AS A STEPPING STONE!

CRACK..
HEY! THERE'S A HUNDRED-TON SLIVER OF ROCK BREAKING AWAY~ IT'LL BLOCK THE PATH!

OKAY, I'M PAST! YOU CAN LET GO THE ROCK NOW, PLUM!
IF EVER A GUIDE SUFFERED!

WELL, HERE WE ARE AT UM TOP! HERE'S YOUR PESKY PACK!
AREN'T YOU TAKING YOUR LITTLE PACK OFF?

NO! I'M TAKING UM SHORT CUT DOWN!~AND THIS LITTLE PACK IS MY PARACHUTE!
TUG

HEY! YOU CAN'T LEAVE ME STUCK UP HERE!
OH, YES I CAN! YOU HIRED ME TO GUIDE YOU UP UM MOUNTAIN ~YOU DIDN'T HIRE ME TO GUIDE YOU DOWN!

# THE TRICKS OF SCREWY DRIVER

PUSS and BOOTS
THEY FIGHT LIKE CAT AND DOG

A-WATER-SKI-ING I WILL GO-OH.......

SEE HOW GRACEFULLY I LAUNCH MYSELF INTO THE GREAT BLUE UNKNOWN ABOVE ME!
SNIGGER....

CLASSIC SPARKY
SEE HOW AWKWARDLY HE LANDS IN THE GREAT WET UNKNOWN BENEATH HIM!
SNIP!

ZOOM!
AH-WEY-HEY-HOOO! ME BOAT'S GONE TA-TA'S!
WHEEE!
WELL, WELL, A RARE FLYING, CRYING, SOARING, ROARING, STEAMING, SCREAMING DOGFISH!

DONG!
BUOY OH-BUOY!

LATER-
LITTLE DOES THAT MOGGIE KNOW THAT HE'S ABOUT TO COME UP AGAINST BOOTMAN THE WONDER DOG!

THERE HE IS! THERE'S THAT FLIPPER-FACED, FURRY-FINNED, FEEBLE-FANGED CATFISH!

OI! YOU WITH THE FANCY DRESS—THAT REALLY IMPROVES YOUR LOOKS—YOU'RE ONLY REVOLTING NOW!
WHAT'S THAT? SOMEBODY'S WOKEN ME UP!
URK?
STAMP!

NOW LISTEN TO ME, YOU TWO HORRIBLE LITTLE FURRY BLOTS! ANY MORE TROUBLE AND YOU CAN SPEND THE REST OF YOUR LIVES CLEANING MY BOOTS!

GRRRR! YOU'VE NO RIGHT TO KEEP US HERE!
YOU HAVEN'T A LEG TO STAND ON! SNARL!
OO-ER!

OOOH!
SO TAKE THAT!
AND THAT!
BASH!

AND NOW, YOU GROGGY SOGGY MOGGIE—GET READY FOR THE BIGGEST BEATING YOU'VE HAD SINCE PANSY POTTER MISTOOK YOU FOR A RUG!
LISTEN, YOU HALF-DROWNED UNSOUND HOUND—YOU COULDN'T BEAT A ONE-LEGGED TORTOISE IN A TEN MILE RACE!

WHAT'S THAT? IS THE NAVY FIRING TORPEDOES, OR IS IT A SEA-MONSTER?
NEITHER! IT'S A PUSS AND BOOTS AQUA-THUMP! THEY'VE BEEN AT IT FOR THREE DAYS NOW!
ABANDON SHIP!
FULL AHEAD BACKWARDS!
HOWL! YOW! OUCH! BASH! BOP! BANG! THUMP! CRUMP! WHAM!
COME ON, PUSS! BASH HIM, BOOTS!
← A TROUBLEMAKER

# DESPERATE DAN

CLASSIC DANDY

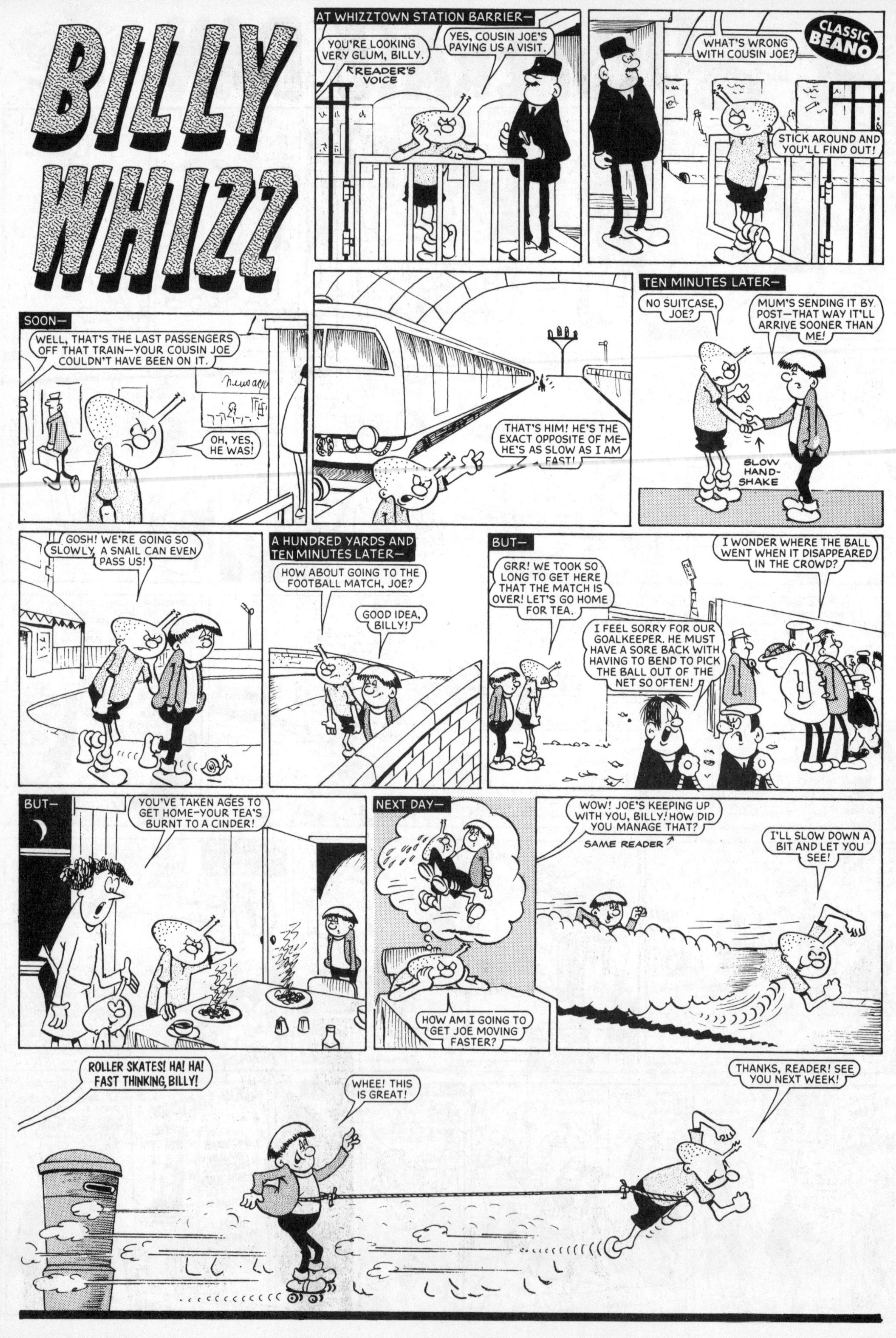
BILLY WHIZZ
CLASSIC BEANO
AT WHIZZTOWN STATION BARRIER—
YOU'RE LOOKING VERY GLUM, BILLY.
READER'S VOICE
YES, COUSIN JOE'S PAYING US A VISIT.
WHAT'S WRONG WITH COUSIN JOE?
STICK AROUND AND YOU'LL FIND OUT!
SOON—
WELL, THAT'S THE LAST PASSENGERS OFF THAT TRAIN—YOUR COUSIN JOE COULDN'T HAVE BEEN ON IT.
OH, YES, HE WAS!
THAT'S HIM! HE'S THE EXACT OPPOSITE OF ME—HE'S AS SLOW AS I AM FAST!
TEN MINUTES LATER—
NO SUITCASE, JOE?
MUM'S SENDING IT BY POST—THAT WAY IT'LL ARRIVE SOONER THAN ME!
SLOW HAND-SHAKE
GOSH! WE'RE GOING SO SLOWLY, A SNAIL CAN EVEN PASS US!
A HUNDRED YARDS AND TEN MINUTES LATER—
HOW ABOUT GOING TO THE FOOTBALL MATCH, JOE?
GOOD IDEA, BILLY!
BUT—
GRR! WE TOOK SO LONG TO GET HERE THAT THE MATCH IS OVER! LET'S GO HOME FOR TEA.
I WONDER WHERE THE BALL WENT WHEN IT DISAPPEARED IN THE CROWD?
I FEEL SORRY FOR OUR GOALKEEPER. HE MUST HAVE A SORE BACK WITH HAVING TO BEND TO PICK THE BALL OUT OF THE NET SO OFTEN!
BUT—
YOU'VE TAKEN AGES TO GET HOME—YOUR TEA'S BURNT TO A CINDER!
NEXT DAY—
HOW AM I GOING TO GET JOE MOVING FASTER?
WOW! JOE'S KEEPING UP WITH YOU, BILLY! HOW DID YOU MANAGE THAT?
SAME READER
I'LL SLOW DOWN A BIT AND LET YOU SEE!
ROLLER SKATES! HA! HA! FAST THINKING, BILLY!
WHEE! THIS IS GREAT!
THANKS, READER! SEE YOU NEXT WEEK!

DREAMY DANIEL
CLASSIC SPARKY
...SO THE FAIRY QUEEN GAVE THE LITTLE BOY HER MAGIC FOOD, AND HE WAS ABLE TO SEE THINGS THAT WERE INVISIBLE TO MORTAL EYES!
COO, FANCY THAT EH, FRED?
HUH! FAIRY STORIES!
LATER–
'BYE, DANIEL– WATCH OUT FOR FAIRIES...HA-HA-HA!
WELL, YOU NEVER KNOW, FRED...
I BET THEY'RE ALL AROUND ME. IF ONLY I COULD SEE THEM!
IMP
IMP MARGARINE TEST
AH! THERE'S SOME-ONE WE CAN USE FOR OUR TV COMMERCIAL!
EXCUSE ME, SONNY, BUT WOULD YOU LIKE TO STEP INSIDE AND TRY THE "IMP" TEST?
WOW! IT'S THE FAIRY QUEEN! I'D BE DELIGHTED TO ENTER YOUR PALACE, YOUR MAJESTY!
ALL YOU DO IS TRY TO TELL THE DIFFERENCE BETWEEN "IMP" MARGARINE AND BUTTER.
THIS IS A GREAT HONOUR. THEY'RE OFFERING ME THE MAGIC FOOD THAT TEACHER TOLD US ABOUT.
AFTER HIS 'MAGIC' MEAL–
JUST A MINUTE– CAN YOU TELL THE DIFFERENCE...?
NO, YOUR MAJESTY, I DON'T FEEL ANY DIFFERENT, BUT I'LL GO INTO THE WOODS AND SEE IF I CAN SEE ANYTHING I COULDN'T BEFORE!
DANIEL CAME UPON A GROUP OF POT-HOLERS–
AHA! THE SEVEN DWARFS GOING INTO THEIR DIAMOND MINE. I'LL FOLLOW THEM AND HAVE A PEEP!
BUT–
HEY! YOU CAN'T COME IN HERE–IT'S TOO DANGEROUS!
TSK! I KNOW WHICH DWARF THIS IS–IT MUST BE GRUMPY!
FARTHER ON–
SURE, AN' WE'LL HIDE IT IN THIS HOLLOW TREE, MICK!
ROIGHT, PADDY!
HA! TWO LEPRECHAUNS HIDING THEIR SECRET CROCK OF GOLD!
ANYONE WHO FINDS A LEPRECHAUN'S CROCK IS ENTITLED TO KEEP IT. I'M RICH!
BACK HOME–
LOOK–I FOUND A LEPRECHAUN'S CROCK–IT SEEMS TO BE EMPTY, THOUGH!
THAT'S ODD, I'M SURE THAT VASE MUST BE VALUABLE!
HMM!
COME ALONG, DANIEL–YOU CAN TELL THE POLICE ABOUT THESE "LEPRECHAUNS" OF YOURS!
POLICE STATION
LATER–
THIS IS FOR YOU, DANIEL! THANKS TO YOUR DESCRIPTION WE'VE MANAGED TO CATCH THE TWO CROOKS WHO STOLE THAT VASE FROM LADY FITZAMATTER'S MANSION!
WHY, HOW KIND OF THE FAIRY QUEEN TO SEND THESE DARK, MYSTERIOUS MESSENGERS WITH A GIFT FOR ME!

CLASSIC BEANO
Dennis the Menace

GRAND CINEMA
WILD WEST STORY
I HOPE I LOOK LIKE HANDSOME HANK WHEN I GROW UP!
STARRING
HANDSOME HANK O'WOOL.

NITZ HOTEL
OH, BOY! I MUST GET HANDSOME HANK'S AUTOGRAPH!
HANDSOME HANK O'WOOL WILL MAKE A PERSONAL APPEARANCE HERE AT 7 P.M. TO SIGN AUTOGRAPHS.

BACK HOME—
DAD, WHY ARE YOU TOOTHLESS, BALD-HEADED AND NOT HANDSOME LIKE HANK O'WOOL, MY HERO?
LATER—
SURELY I'M NOT SO BAD AS ALL THAT!
ONLY MY HEROES CAN GET TO SIGN THIS BOOK.
Autograph Book

AT THE NITZ—
STAND BACK, FANS. HANDSOME HANK ISN'T READY TO SEE YOU YET.

?
STEP ASIDE, FATSO. NOBODY TELLS THE MENACE WHAT TO DO!

CRASH!
HOTEL KITCHEN
AGH!
SPLATCH!
Autograph Book
CHOMP! DELICIOUS!
SWIPE

OOPS! PARDON ME, WAITER!
AGH!

HANK O'WOOL PRIVATE KEEP OUT
HEY, SKINNY! WHERE'S HANDSOME HANK GOT TO?
Autograph Book

WAIT TILL I FIT MY CURLY WIG AND FALSE TEETH—

—AND MY PADDED JACKET! I'M HANDSOME HANK! WHAT DO YOU WANT, SMALL BOY?
AW, FORGET IT!

BACK HOME—
SIGN HERE, DAD. YOU'RE NOT SO BAD AFTER ALL!
WHY, THANK YOU, DENNIS!
DAD'S PLEASED JUST NOW, BUT WAIT TILL HE GETS THE HOTEL DAMAGES BILL!

CLAUDE HOPPER
I CAN'T GET INTO TROUBLE HERE. THERE'S PLENTY OF ROOM ON THIS HEATH FOR MY BIG FEET!
BEWARE OF HEATH FIRES

GOSH! THAT BUSH IS ON FIRE.

CLASSIC DANDY
BIG BOOTS ARE SOMETIMES USEFUL— THEY HOLD PLENTY OF WATER!

THE SMELL OF THIS SAUSAGE IS MAKING MY TEETH WATER!

THAT'S THE WAY TO PUT OUT A DANGEROUS FIRE!
!
HISSS

GURR! YOU'VE RUINED MY LUNCH!
OO-ER!

I'LL TRY AND CATCH A FISH INSTEAD. AH! I'VE GOT A BITE ALREADY.

OOPS! IT HAS COME OFF THE HOOK.

HEY! DON'T STEP ON THAT FISH!

TOO LATE! THE FISH IS SQUEEZED OUT FROM UNDER CLAUDE'S BOOT.
SQUELCH!

GLUB!

BAH! YOU AND YOUR BIG FEET!
I'M OFF!

YOU'D BETTER PUT THE JAMPOT LID BACK ON, JIM. THERE ARE WASPS ABOUT.
JAM

COME BACK!
WHEEE!
TIP!

PLOP!
JAM

COME HERE, YOU! I'VE GOT A USE FOR THOSE BIG BOOTS OF YOURS!

I NEED THEM TO SWAT ALL THESE WASPS!
!
SWIPE!
SWIPE!

# JULIUS CHEESER

CLASSIC TOPPER

# DESERT ISLAND DICK

BURP!
THE THREE BEARS
CLASSIC BEANO

I MUST GET A FAST HORSE AND TRY TO WIN THAT BIG FEED!
BEAR TERRITORY DERBY
BIG FEED FOR THE WINNER

AT THE STABLES—
I LIKE THE LOOK OF THIS RACEHORSE.
RACING STABLES
TICKLE
YOU CAN HAVE A TRIAL GALLOP IF YOU WANT, PA.

DOWN AT THE TRACK—
ARE YOU SURE HE'S FAST?
FAST? WHY, ALL I HAVE TO DO IS SAY—

—GO—AND HE'S OFF LIKE A ROCKET—

—AND HE WON'T STOP TILL HE GETS TO THE WINNING POST!
WINNING POST
SKID

PA TAKES THE HORSE—
OOPS! I'D BETTER MAKE SURE THAT THEY DON'T GET MY HORSE!
BEWARE OF HORSE THIEVES

SO—
BLACKSMITH
I WANT A LENGTH OF STRONG CHAIN.

NO PESKY HORSE THIEVES WILL GET MY HORSE NOW! WHAT'S FOR TEA, MA?
BEARS' CAVE

IT'S YOUR FAVOURITE, PA. SAGO!
SAY—GO? I'M OFF!
BEARS CAVE

WOW! HELP! WHOA!
NOW WHERE'S THAT WINNING POST?
BEARS' CAVE
SNATCH

AVE
WELL, WELL, THAT'S THE FIRST TIME I'VE EVER KNOWN PA BEAR RUN AWAY FROM FOOD!
IS PA OUT OF THE TERRITORY DERBY?—FIND OUT NEXT WEEK!

# the Three Bears

PA
TEDDY
MA

CLASSIC BEANO

LAST WEEK, PA BOUGHT A RACEHORSE TO TRY AND WIN THE TERRITORY DERBY, BUT THE HORSE RAN AWAY, TOWING PA BEHIND IT!

OOYAH! ERK! WHOA!—OH!

I'VE BEEN TRAINED NOT TO STOP RUNNING TILL I'VE PASSED THE WINNING POST!

STOP! BLUB!

THEN—

AH!—GASP!—THE WINNING POST AT LAST!

GIANT LOLLY

SLURP!

HELLO, PA! WHAT ARE YOU DOING HERE?

GIANT LOLLY

SCREECH!

GROAN! I'M TRAINING MY HORSE TO WIN THE BEAR TERRITORY DERBY. THERE'S A BIG FEED FOR THE WINNER!

A BIG FEED, EH?

NEXT DAY, AT THE RACES—

YAH! YOU DON'T STAND A CHANCE, PA!

PA'S PRIDE

GRIZZLY GUS

JUST WAIT AND SEE, GUS! JUST WAIT AND SEE!

SNIGGER! AS SOON AS MY HORSE HEARS THE WORD "GO," HE'S OFF LIKE A SHOT!

READY—STEADY—

STARTER'S BOX

—GO!

ZIPP!

YAHOO! KEEP GOING, PA! YOU'RE WELL IN FRONT!

FLASH

# P.C. BIG EARS

CLASSIC DANDY

HA-HA! WHAT A LAUGH! BIG EARS HAS BEEN PICKED FOR THE POLICE FOOTBALL TEAM. HE LOOKS A PROPER CHARLIE IN SHORTS!

HUH! YOU WON'T BE LAUGHING WHEN I WIN THE PRIZE FOR THE MAN OF THE MATCH.

HAW-HAW! IF BIG EARS WINS THAT, I'LL EAT MY HAT!

THE GAME BEGINS

THERE'S ONLY ME BETWEEN THAT CENTRE FORWARD AND THE GOALKEEPER. I'VE GOT TO STOP HIM.

PEEEP!

HEY! COME BACK! DIDN'T YOU HEAR THE WHISTLE?

YOU IDIOT, BIG EARS! WHY DIDN'T YOU TACKLE HIM?

BUT I THOUGHT THE REF BLEW HIS WHISTLE!

BAH! YOU MUST BE HEARING THINGS, YOU BIG-EARED TWIT!

LATER

ONLY THE KEEPER TO BEAT! I'LL SOON MAKE UP FOR THAT SILLY GOAL I GAVE AWAY!

PEEEP!

BAH! THE REF'S WHISTLE! I MUST BE OFFSIDE!

FRED the FLOP

J. BLOGG'S JEWELLER
I'll show Butch who's the best crook in town!
I'll show Fred who's the best crook in town!
H. BINKS. JEWELLER

CLASSIC BUZZ
Oof!
THUD!
Ooyah!

I'll take back my jewels!

LATER—
There goes Butch in the other direction. He'll not get in my way when I rob the bank in the High Street!

SO—
HIGH ST.
BANK
MEANWHILE
LOW ST
BANK

CRASH!

Look here, Butch! As we keep getting in each other's way, it might be better if we worked together.
I think you're right, Fred!

SOON—
BANK.
Get ready to drive off quickly, Butch.
Sure thing, Fred.

Ooer! I drove off too quickly.
ZOOM
DONK!

THEY TRY AGAIN—
I don't want to miss the car like Fred did, so I'll jump in real hard!
BANK

BUT—
Eek! I jumped too hard!
THUMP!

Bah! This time we'll rob the man who takes the wages to the factory! We won't need a car . . .

Here he comes! Get ready, Butch!

BIFF!
BOP!
Five pence!

These crooks tried to rob me!
They'll get hard labour for this!

Start breaking those rocks, you two!

Ho-ho! They're at it again!
CRUNCH!
CRUNCH!

# THE SMASHER

CLASSIC DANDY

PUP PARADE
with THE BASH STREET DOGS
CLASSIC BEANO
Phew! I'm thirsty— think I'll go and get a drink of water.
SO—
GASP! PUFF! PANT! GASP!
MUCH LATER—
Water—Croak!— water...

STILL LATER—
Ahhhhh! At last!

It would be nice if we had running water at the bin. Then I wouldn't have to come all this distance for a drink!

MEANWHILE—
I do like a game of leap-dog!

THEN—
SPLUDGE!

ERK! Tubby's stuck fast and he's blocked the stream!

LATER—
PLOP!
Out you come!
ROAR!

SOON—
I know I said it would be nice if we had running water at the bin...

...but this is RIDICULOUS!

CLASSIC TOPPER
GHASTLY MANOR
I HOPE SOMEBODY BUYS THIS PLACE SOON—I CAN'T STAND IT MUCH LONGER!
FOR SALE
THIS IS MISTER FEAR, OWNER OF GHASTLY MANOR.

I'M OFF TO TOWN TO GET A HOUSE AGENT TO SELL THE MANOR.
LET'S FOLLOW MR FEAR. I FANCY A TRIP TO TOWN.

INTERESTING PLACE, A TOWN IS.

CAN YOU GIVE ME SOMETHING FOR MY HEAD? I'VE HAD IT OFF AND ON ALL DAY.
CHEMIST

WOOH! DO YOU DO INVISIBLE MENDING?
DRY CLEANING

RESTAURANT
YUM! IS IT LUNCH-TIME YET?

SWOP YOU A GREAT HORRIBLE THING FOR A GOLDFISH!
PETS

ALLOW ME!

A GIANT BAT!
SORRY, MADAM. WE ONLY SEEM TO HAVE THE NORMAL SIZE.

GOOD MORNING. I'D LIKE YOU TO SELL MY HOUSE FOR ME.
ESTATE AGENTS
CERTAINLY, SIR. HAS IT ANY SPECIAL FEATURES?

WELL, IT HAS—ER—

GHOSTS! OGRES! AND HORRIBLE CREATURES!
OH, YOU KNOW THE PLACE, DO YOU?

STEEVIE STAR
AS
006
IN
"Goldthumb"
Enemy agent at large, 006. Bring him in!
Roger and out, F!
TWO-WAY RADIO
READ NUTTY EVERY WEEK!
LEAP!
006
Now, let me see—how d'you start this thing again?
CLASSIC NUTTY
TEA
COFFEE
CHOKE
SUGAR
OOPS! Wrong button!
FLOOOSH!
006
WHIRRRR!
Just as well I'm equipped for every emergency!
THEN—
HOI! Watchski itski!
GOLDTHUMB! So you're the enemy spy!
WHUMP!
Prepare to meet your doomski, 006ski!
We'll see about that!
PRESS!
WAAAski!
Oh-oh! He's still coming at me! I'd better act fast!
SLIP!
CLICK!
SO—
Yah-boo! Missed me!
SHOOOOT
HELPski!
SLIDE!
These spy gadgets are amazing!
CLICK!
SPALOOOSH!
One click of my pen and I've got an instant fishing rod!
CLIK!
CLIK!
CLIK!
It's amazing what modern science can do for us secret agents!
BUT—
Hmph! Someone's nicked my car!
TO SECRET H.Q.

THE BEANO
CLASSIC BEANO

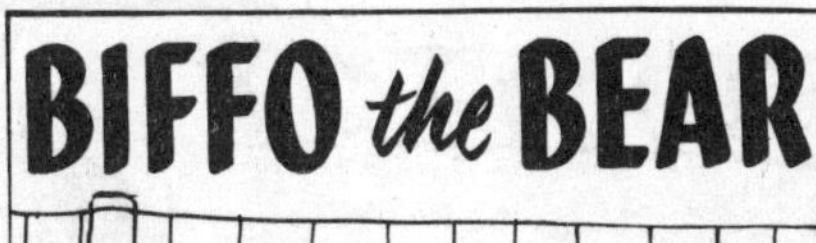
BIFFO the BEAR

BIFFO AND BUSTER ARE HAVING A DISAGREEMENT

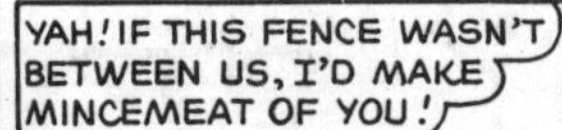
YAH! IF THIS FENCE WASN'T BETWEEN US, I'D MAKE MINCEMEAT OF YOU!

WHAT?

WHY, IF THAT FENCE WASN'T THERE I'D USE YOU AS A HUMAN PUNCH-BAG!

LUCKY FOR YOU THIS FENCE IS BETWEEN US~OR I'D BE KNOCKING THE FUR OFF YOU, YOU HAIRY OAF!

LUCKY FOR ME? IT'S LUCKY FOR YOU THAT THIS FENCE IS PROTECTING YOU FROM MY FISTS, YOU LITTLE WORM.

SUDDENLY
LOOK OUT! MY ROAD THUMPER'S RUNNING AWAY WITH ME!
THUMP!
THUMP!

?
?
THUMP!
THUMP!

!
!

YOUNG FOO
THE KUNG FU KID

LOOK OUT, YOUNG FOO! BASHER'S UP TO HIS TRICKS AGAIN!
Ha! Ha! I just feel like bashing someone today . . . and who better than Young Foo!
HE POUNCES . . .
CLASSIC CRACKER
GOTCHA!
(TRANSLATION)
OH, YES?

YOUNG FOO REACTS WITH TYPICAL EFFICIENCY.
ZAP
VAROOOOOM!
THREE GUESSES WHERE BASHER'S GOING TO LAND!
I like Young Basher . . . he keeps me in training!

RIGHT FIRST TIME!
Oh, dear I do believe we're in for a spot of rain . . .
Gulp! I'm in for a 'Head'-on collision!

THWUMP!
OOOPH!

AFTERWARDS, IN THE HEAD'S STUDY.
Now listen to me, Basher! It's bad enough you always landing in trouble, but when you start landing on me, something's got to be done . . .

. . . so I've decided that you are going to be an artist! You can hardly do any damage with a brush! In any case, Young Foo will be there to keep an eye on you! Now, go and paint me something nice!

LATER, IN THE ART ROOM, THE ART MASTER, MR BRUSHUP, IS GIVING SOME EXPERT ADVICE!
Now, boys! You are going to paint anything you like, but I want you to use bright and pretty colours!
What a twit!
Most nice!

BASHER AND YOUNG FOO ARE LEFT ON THEIR OWN . . .
Mmmmm! Now, what shall I paint?
TICKLE!
TICKLE!
Grrr! Watch where you're putting your brush, you little pest!

Hee-hee! Take a squirt of that, squirt!
SQUEEZE!
SWOOOOOSH!
OUR ART DEPARTMENT INFORMS US THAT PAINT, SQUEEZED VIOLENTLY FROM A TUBE, TRAVELS AT APPROXIMATELY 106.5 M.P.H!

WITH LIGHTNING REFLEXES, YOUNG FOO DUCKS . . .
SPLAT!
What a lovely red!
BASHER TRIES YELLOW AND GREEN . . .
CLASSIC CRACKER
How's that for two at once?
SQUEEZE!
ZIP!
ZIP!
SWOP!
SHLAP!
I think Young Basher is enjoying himself!
SQUEEZE!
BASHER TRIES THE LARGE, ECONOMY SIZE . . .
Ha! Ha! I think I'm going to like art after all!
SQUEEZE!
PHOOOM!
SQUEEZE!
THE HEAD ENTERS . . .
SPLAT!
GULP!
SPEECHLESS!
THIS IS A UNIQUE PICTURE OF UNCONTROLLABLE RAGE . . .
. . . BASHER FLEES— WOULDN'T YOU?
WRETCHED BOY!
HELP!
SNARL! SNORT!
PAINT
AACH!
SHWUP!
YOUNG FOO SPEEDS TO THE RESCUE!
This canvas, on which Basher squirted paint should help to break his fall!
ZOOM!
ART MASTER
PHEW! Got him!
Headmaster! What a FANTASTIC work of art! You MUST do me another!
. . . You must really enjoy painting, judging by the way you throw yourself into it!
Oh! . . . Er! Yes! I do love painting—so . . . er . . . relaxing. Don't you think?
I agree!

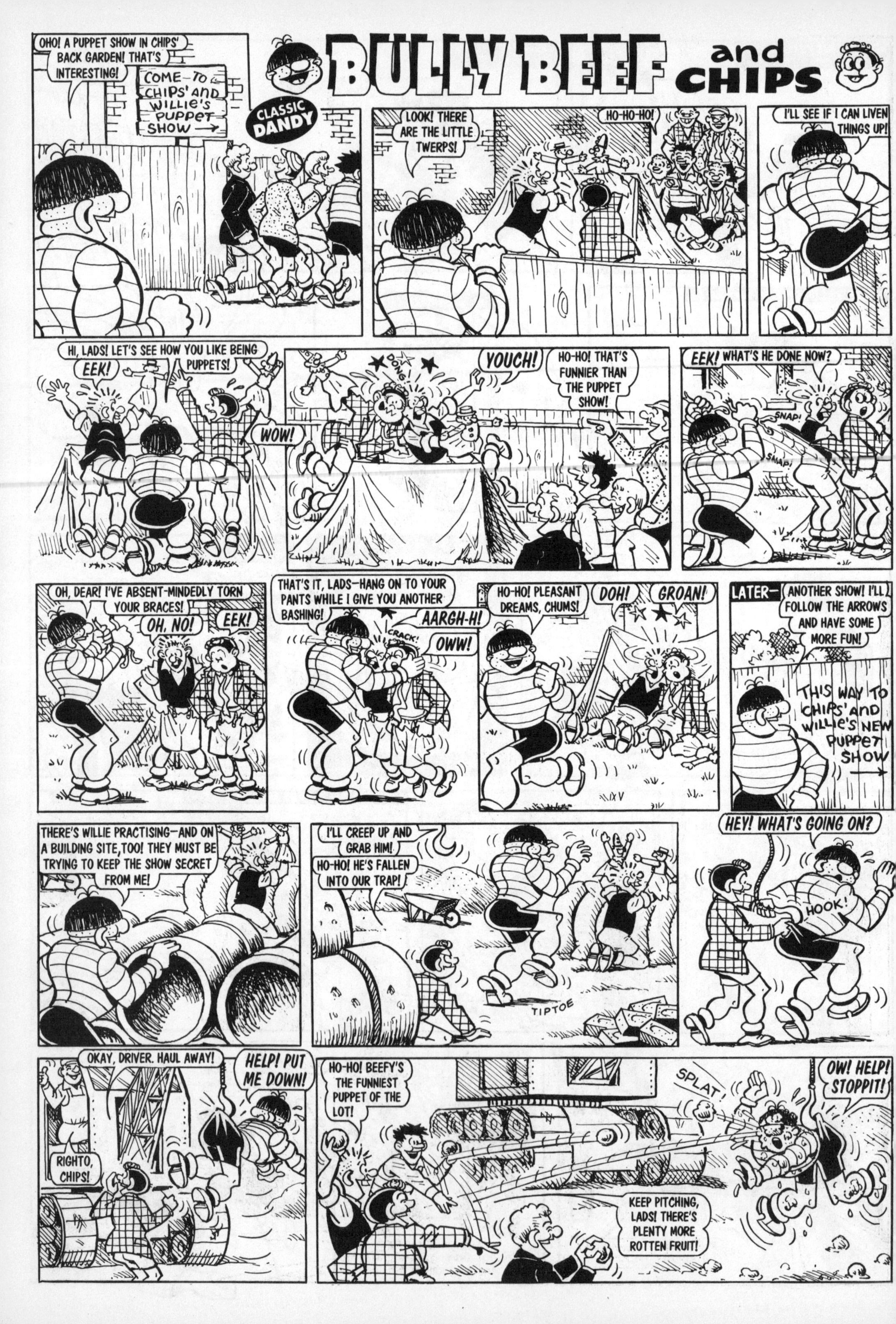
BULLY BEEF and CHIPS
CLASSIC DANDY
OHO! A PUPPET SHOW IN CHIPS' BACK GARDEN! THAT'S INTERESTING!
COME TO CHIPS' AND WILLIE'S PUPPET SHOW →
LOOK! THERE ARE THE LITTLE TWERPS!
HO-HO-HO!
I'LL SEE IF I CAN LIVEN THINGS UP!
HI, LADS! LET'S SEE HOW YOU LIKE BEING PUPPETS!
EEK!
WOW!
DONG!
YOUCH!
HO-HO! THAT'S FUNNIER THAN THE PUPPET SHOW!
EEK!
WHAT'S HE DONE NOW?
SNAP!
SNAP!
OH, DEAR! I'VE ABSENT-MINDEDLY TORN YOUR BRACES!
OH, NO!
EEK!
THAT'S IT, LADS—HANG ON TO YOUR PANTS WHILE I GIVE YOU ANOTHER BASHING!
CRACK!
AARGH-H!
OWW!
HO-HO! PLEASANT DREAMS, CHUMS!
DOH!
GROAN!
LATER—
ANOTHER SHOW! I'LL FOLLOW THE ARROWS AND HAVE SOME MORE FUN!
THIS WAY TO CHIPS' AND WILLIE'S NEW PUPPET SHOW →
THERE'S WILLIE PRACTISING—AND ON A BUILDING SITE, TOO! THEY MUST BE TRYING TO KEEP THE SHOW SECRET FROM ME!
I'LL CREEP UP AND GRAB HIM!
HO-HO! HE'S FALLEN INTO OUR TRAP!
TIPTOE
HEY! WHAT'S GOING ON?
HOOK!
OKAY, DRIVER. HAUL AWAY!
HELP! PUT ME DOWN!
RIGHTO, CHIPS!
HO-HO! BEEFY'S THE FUNNIEST PUPPET OF THE LOT!
SPLAT!
OW! HELP! STOPPIT!
KEEP PITCHING, LADS! THERE'S PLENTY MORE ROTTEN FRUIT!

# THE Beezer

CLASSIC BEEZER

FOR BOYS and GIRLS

## Ginger

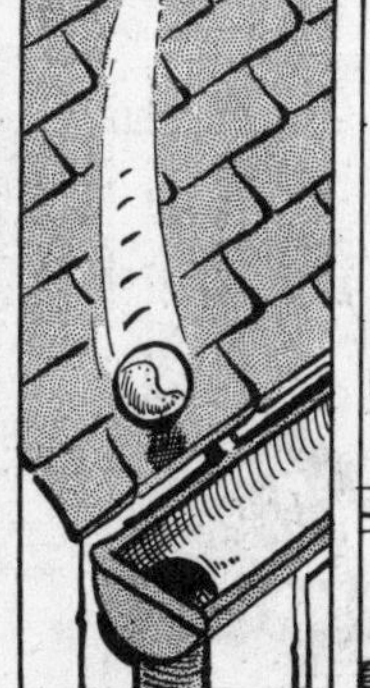

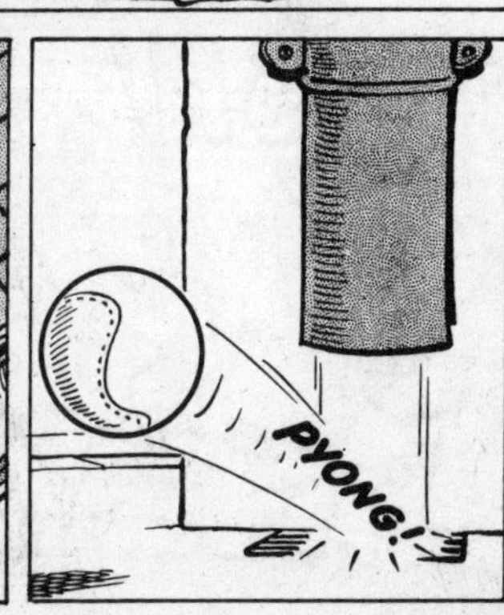

HARUM SCAREM
This should move Scarem!
CREAK

CLASSIC BUZZ
WHACK!

YEOWL!
Now for some carrots!

Oooh!
SIZZLE!

Grr! Where is that Harum? I'm going to have revenge!
Tee-hee! That silly dog will never think of looking for me in his own kennel!

Hmm...listen to this. 'Dog's noses are very sensitive and can be used for tracking down other animals...' Very interesting!
WHAT EVERY GOOD DOG KNOWS

I'm on his trail!
SNIFF!
SNUFFL

Got him! The cunning, long-eared muncher's hiding in MY kennel!
MUNCH!

I'll flatten him!

Bombs away... Here, wait a minute! What am I doing? I'll flatten my kennel too!
CHOMP!
MUNCH!

STOP!
What's all the noise?

CRASH!
Yikes! Good job someone shouted! That was too close!

Boo-hoo! My beautiful kennel! It's ruined! My home—wrecked for ever!
Don't worry, Scarem!
SOB! SOB!

I'll help you build a super-duper, new kennel!
You will? Thanks, pal!

LATER
Now, then, I'll hold the door while you fit the nice strong hinges!
Roo-too-too!

Just a second, Harum.... kennels don't have doors!
This one does! Ho-ho!
SLAM!
SLOT!

Now I can enjoy my dinner in peace! He really is an awfully stupid dog, that one! Aah...
CHOMP! CHOMP!
Grr! This is war! You'll be sorry!

BERYL
THE PERIL
CLASSIC TOPPER
DAD'S GONE INTO TRAINING TO KEEP FIT.
OO! THAT SILLY LAUNDRY MAN'S GONE OFF WITHOUT MY SHEETS.
DON'T FRET, MUM. I'LL CATCH HIM.
SWISHY LAUNDRY Co
GRAB
GOSH! JUST LOOK AT DAD GO! GULP! NEXT TIME I DO SOMETHING WRONG HE'LL CATCH ME EASILY. TIME I WAS GOING INTO TRAINING, TOO.
SWOOSH!
THESE THINGS ARE PART OF DAD'S KEEP-FIT STUFF. BEST START RIGHT AWAY!
PHEW! I'M IN A LATHER. I'LL GO UPSTAIRS FOR A SHOWER.
HRRMPH!
ZOK!
SLIP
TWANG!
SILLY OL' DAD, WALKING INTO TROUBLE LIKE THAT.
YOU HEARTLESS GIRL! JUST LOOK WHAT YOU'VE DONE TO YOUR POOR FATHER.
BLAH-HAH!
LATER-
I BELIEVE THIS STUFF'S GOOD FOR KEEPING YOU FIT. AND BESIDES, I LOVE IT— YUMMY! YUMMY!
PEANUT BUTTER
NOW I'LL DO A SPOT OF TRAINING WITH DAD'S DUMB-BELLS—HUP!—
—AN' HUP!—OOO! I LET 'EM SLIP! MY FINGERS WERE GREASY FROM THAT PEANUT BUTTER.
EH? OH, NO!
YAA-ARGH!
CRUNCH!
SO-
CASUALTY DEPT.
SORRY, DAD. THEY'LL FIX YOU UP IN HERE.
OO! OO!
LATER-
PAH! WHAT'S SHE BROKEN NOW?
CRASH! TINKLE!
MY GLASSHOUSE! JUST WAIT TILL I LAY HANDS ON YOU, YOU PEST!
HOBBLE
O NEED TO E FIT TO SCAPE DAD OW. I CAN UST AMBLE WAY FROM IM.
LOOK OUT, BERYL.
HA! HA! YOU CAN'T FOOL ME INTO STOPPING, DAD!
THIS IS WHAT DAD HAS SPOTTED - THE LOCAL RUGBY CLUB OUT FOR A TRAINING RUN!
COR! STOOD ON SOMEONE, HAVE WE?
OOYAH!
OW!
LATER-
PUT A FROG IN MY MILK, WOULD YOU?
HOBBLE
ULP! AND I DO BELIEVE HE'S GAINING. HOBBLE FASTER, CAN'T YOU, FEET?
HOBBLE

Minnie the Minx
HI, READERS—I JUST GOT A LETTER FROM "THE BEANO" OFFICE INVITING ME TO GRAY'S FARM FOR THE DAY...
BUS STOP

CLASSIC BEANO
..WHY DON'T YOU COME WITH ME, READERS? IT SHOULD BE LOTS OF FUN!
SOSSY'S SUPER SAUSAGES

MEANWHILE, AT BASH ST.—
HEH! HEH! SOMEONE'S INVITED US TO GRAY'S FARM FOR THE DAY—WITHOUT TEACHER!
COUNTRY BUS

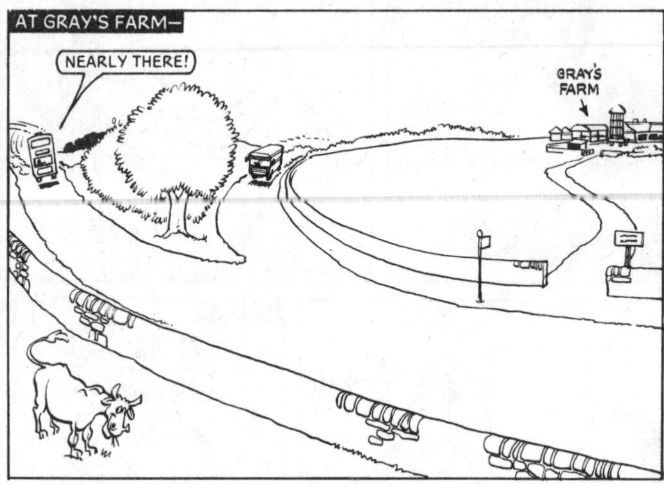
AT GRAY'S FARM—
NEARLY THERE!
GRAY'S FARM

MINNIE THE MINX?
COUNTRY BUS
COUNTRY BUS
BUS STOP
THE BASH ST. KIDS? WHAT ARE YOU LOT DOING HERE?

GRR! I'LL TEACH THE BASH ST. KIDS TO STAY AWAY FROM MY PAGES IN FUTURE!
WHIRR!

IN THE HEN-HOUSE—
SLURP! THINK I'LL HAVE SOME BOILED EGGS.
HM!

NOW, SHOULD I JUST HAVE A DOZEN, OR SHOULD I EAT THE LOT? DROOL!
WHIRR!

HEH! HEH! HEH! THAT'LL TEACH FATTY NOT TO TRESPASS ON MY PAGES! MAYBE I'LL PUT HIM OFF EGGS, TOO!
SPLAT!

CACKLE! CACKLE! YOU'LL HAVE TO HAVE THOSE EGGS SCRAMBLED, FATTY!

SOON—
STAY AWAY FROM US—YOU'RE ALL COVERED IN EGG!
I WAS MINXED!

THEN—
SHRIEK! MOAN! WAIL-L-L!
WAH! THE FARMER'S SCARECROW'S COME TO LIFE!
RUN!

HEH! HEH! STRAIGHT INTO THE DUCK POND—JUST AS I PLANNED!
CLASSIC BEANO
SPLUNGE!

BUT—
OOPS!
THAT'S NO SCARE-CROW! IT'S MINNIE THE MINX . . .

. . . AFTER HER!
CRUMBS! I'D BETTER FIND A PLACE TO HIDE!

THIS HAY TROUGH WILL DO!

SOON—
THINK I'LL HAVE A MUNCH OF MY LUNCH.
SHE'S NOT HERE, PALS!
WHIRR!

YEEOW!
WHIRR!
NIP
SPLUDGE!

GOSH! WHAT A FRIGHT YOU GAVE US, MINNIE!
WHEEEE!

THEN—
HOLD IT, PALS—I'LL LET YOU IN ON MY SECRET NOW—I INVITED YOU ALL TO GRAY'S FARM...
BUT WHY, BIFFO?
WHIRR!

...I'VE FILMED ALL YOUR PRANKS TO BE SHOWN AS A COMEDY FILM FOR CHARITY AT THE PALLODEON CINEMA!
GOSH! ME? A FILM STAR?

LATER—
DEON
MINNIE the MINX
- MEETS -
THE BASH ST. KIDS
SUPER FILM THAT!
WELL, THE FILM WAS A GREAT SUCCESS, PALS!
YES, BUT YOU'VE FORGOTTEN ONE THING...

...WE OWE YOU A DIP IN THE PIGSTY!
BEANO
AW, BUT, PALS...

# JONAH

CLASSIC BEANO

!

INTRODUCING—PROFESSOR HERMAN SCHMIDT—HISTORIAN AND ARCHAEOLOGIST—WHO, AFTER YEARS OF RESEARCH—BELIEVES HE HAS DISCOVERED THE WHEREABOUTS OF A SUNKEN SPANISH TREASURE SHIP!—

HEH-HEH! TOPERMARY BAY—IN SCOTLAND.

SO—AT THE HARBOUR OF TOPERMARY BAY, HE TRIES TO RECRUIT A CREW FOR HIS NEWLY-CHARTERED SALVAGE SHIP.

I HAFF ACCURATE KNOWLEDGE DAT DER GALLEON LIES SUBMERGED IN TOPERMARY BAY—UND DAT SHE ISS LOADED MIT SILVER UND GOLD!

ACH! RUBBISH, MAN!

—WE'VE HEARD YON TALE BEFORE! AULD JOCK, HERE, HAS BEEN DOOKIN' IN YON BAY SINCE HE WAS TWA YEARS OLD AND HE'S NEVER FOUND A BRASS FARTHIN'!

AYE, THAT'S RIGHT!

BUT IT ISS TRUE, I SAY! I HAFF PUT ALL MINE LIFE'S SAVINGS INTO DIS VENTURE! I NEED DER CREW—DESPERATELY!

AH!—

—THAT'LL BE HIM!

AHEM! I'M PROFESSOR SEBASTIAN SMOOCH. I BELIEVE YOUR THEORY—

ISS DAT SO?

YES, INDEED!—

—AND WOULD BE HONOURED TO JOIN YOUR CREW!

MOST KIND OF YOU, MINE FRIEND!

PSSST!! JOCK! IF TWA O' THESE BRAINY CHAPS ARE CONVINCED ABOOT YON GALLEON, IT MAK'S YE THINK! MAYBE YE'VE BEEN SEARCHIN' IN THE WRANG PLACES A' THESE YEARS!

AYE!

AND SO—

ER—DINNA WORRY, PROFESSOR! WE'LL ROUND YE UP A CREW AND YE CAN COUNT US TWA IN AS WEEL!

GOOT!

CAPITAL!

SIMPER

HEH-HEH! MY DISGUISE DID THE TRICK! I'VE GOT ME A SHIP!

THE FOLLOWING MORNING, THE SALVAGE-SHIP "RECOVERY" SETS SAIL—AND MEETS WITH STARTLING SUCCESS, IN TOPERMARY BAY—

WE HAFF FOUND HER!

COO!—

LOOK AT THAT! EVERYTHING INTACT! CANNON! ARMOUR!—THE LOT! JUST AS SHE WAS WHEN SHE WENT DOWN IN 1588!

JINGS!

COO! IMAGINE THE DRAMA OF HER LAST MOMENTS! WITH THE CAPTAIN STANDING PROUDLY ON HER STORM-LASHED POOP, MAKING HIS FAREWELL SPEECH TO HIS DOOMED CREW!

DOUBTS—AS TO HIS COLLEAGUE'S SANITY.

HERE! PUT THESE TIN TOGS ON, MATES! WE'LL RE-ENACT THOSE FINAL MOMENTS—AS A LAST TRIBUTE TO A PROUD AND NOBLE SHIP.

SOLDIERS AND SAILORS OF SPAIN! OUR GALLANT SHIP IS LOST—NEVER TO RETURN TO OUR HOMELAND!

!

CREAK

GROAN

BUT—THOUGH THE END IS AT HAND—WE SHALL ALL GO DOWN HEROICALLY—LIKE SPANIARDS!

CLANG

OOH!

AWK!

JINGS!

AGH-H-H!

HERE WE SEE ORDINARY SCHOOLBOY, ERIC WIMP, ON HIS WAY TO SCHOOL . . .
Groan! I slept in—I'll be late . . .
. . . BUT ERIC IS REALLY NOT SO ORDINARY! YOU SEE, HE COMES FROM THE MOON, WHICH IS REALLY THE BIGGEST BANANA IN THE SKY . . .
. . . Unless! . . .
. . . AND WHEN ERIC EATS ONE OF HIS SPECIAL BIG BANANAS, HE BECOMES NONE OTHER THAN . . .
CLASSIC NUTTY
BANANAMAN
. . . FASTER THAN THE SPEED OF SOUND . . .
Oh-oh!
I won't be late now!
RUBBISH
ZUMP
. . . STRONGER THAN TWENTY MEN . . .
Phew! Stronger than twenty pounds of Gorgonzola cheese, more like!
NIFF
PONG
. . . HE SOARS THROUGH THE AIR LIKE A BIRD . . .
It'll be quicker by air.
. . . ER . . . UM—AN OSTRICH, PERHAPS!
BLOOF-F!
CRUMP!
CRASH!
CRUMP!
CONDEMNED
HE PERFORMS HELPFUL DEEDS WHEREVER HE GOES!
Ooh! My head!
He saved us a week's demolition work by knocking down that old building!
And we didn't even get a chance to thank him!
AND ONCE HIS GOOD DEEDS ARE DONE, HE CHANGES BACK ONCE MORE . . .
. . . TO ERIC WIMP, ORDINARY SCHOOLBOY, ON HIS WAY TO SCHOOL!
Groan! Sigh! Tomorrow I'm taking the BUS!

CLASSIC SPARKY
L
CARS

STONE THE CROWS! AN ARMOURED CAR!
G-GOSH! IT'S A BANK RAID! AFTER 'EM, FREDERIC!
HIGH STREET
SAVINGS BANK

INSIDE THE ARMOURED CAR—
THERE'S A COP CAR AFTER US, OPERATE LEVER ONE, LEFTY!
TEE-HEE!
RIGHTO, BOSS!

LOOK OUT, FRED!
TACKS!
BANG!

HAW-HAW-HAW!
BURST OUR TYRES, WOULD YOU? GRR!
BAH!

LATER, AT THE POLICE STATION—
COUGH! INSPECTOR! THE SMOKE FROM YOUR PIPE! IT'S EVERYWHERE!
PUFF! PUFF!
WHAT'S THAT? YOU'RE GOING TO ROB THE BANK IN CASTLE STREET? WHO'S THAT SPEAKING?
CHOKE! GULP! WE'RE ON OUR WAY, SIR!

IN CASTLE STREET—
IT'S THE ARMOURED CAR GANG, FREDERIC!
GRR!
WE'D BETTER WATCH OUT FOR THEM TACKS, CEDRIC!
BANK

COPS AFTER US AGAIN, BOYS! OPERATE LEVER TWO, LEFTY!
CERTAINLY, BOSS!
TEE-HEE-HEE!

HAW-HAW! WHAT A GIGGLE!
WE'RE SKIDDING! H-HELP!
YEOW! OIL!
SPLOOSH!
SPLURK!
WHOOM!

CRASH!
TINKLE!
SMASH!
YEEK!
YOW!

NEXT DAY—
HI, YOU SUCKERS! THIS IS THE ARMOURED CAR GANG BOSS HERE! WE'RE HITTIN' THE QUEEN STREET BANK TODAY! AND NOTHIN' IS GONNA STOP US! ARF-ARF!
HEAR THAT, LADS?
PUFF! PUFF!
COUGH!
WE'RE JUST GOIN', INSPECTOR! COUGH! ANYTHING T' GET AWAY FROM THIS SMOKE!

HEH-HEH! HERE COME THE COPPERS AS USUAL!
GET AFTER 'EM!
OPERATE LEVER THREE, LEFTY!
BUT OF COURSE!

WH-WHAT? IT CAN'T BE!
IT IS, Y' KNOW!
GRAB!
LIFT
POLICE
ARF-ARF! GOTTEM!

GAGH!
SID'S SCRAP-YARD
WHEE!
YEEE-OW!
UP AN' OVER! HEE-HEE!

BACK AT THE STATION–
DEEP IN THOUGHT.
I WISH YOU'D PUT THAT PIPE AWAY, INSPECTOR! COUGH! SPLUTTER!
PUFF! PUFF!
NOW LET ME THINK!

I'VE GOT IT!
PUFF! PUFF!

NOW THIS IS THE PLAN! WE... AN' THEN... WHISPER... AND THEN... WHISPER... INTO THE CELLS WITH 'EM!
BRILLIANT, CEDRIC! BRILLIANT, M'BOY!
BRR! RING! DING!

IT'S THEM!
IT'S THE BANK STREET BANK THIS TIME, COPPERS! HO-HO! CHORTLE! CHORTLE!
RIGHT! LET'S GO!

OKAY LADS! I'LL OPEN THE SUN-ROOF!

HEE-HEE! THEY NEVER LEARN!
UNFASTEN YOUR SAFETY BELTS! I'M PUTTING ON THE BRAKES–

-NOW!
WHEEE!
PERFECT LANDING, CEDRIC!
ARF-ARF!

THAT'S RIGHT! LIGHT UP, INSPECTOR! I'M ALMOST THROUGH!
PUFF! PUFF!

C-COUGH!
MIGHTY PUFF.

GOTCHA!
BET THEY'RE PROPER CHOKED OFF NOW, INSPECTOR! HA-HA-HA!
CHOKE! GAGH! MY THROAT! IT'S ON FIRE!
COUGH!
GRR! OOCH!

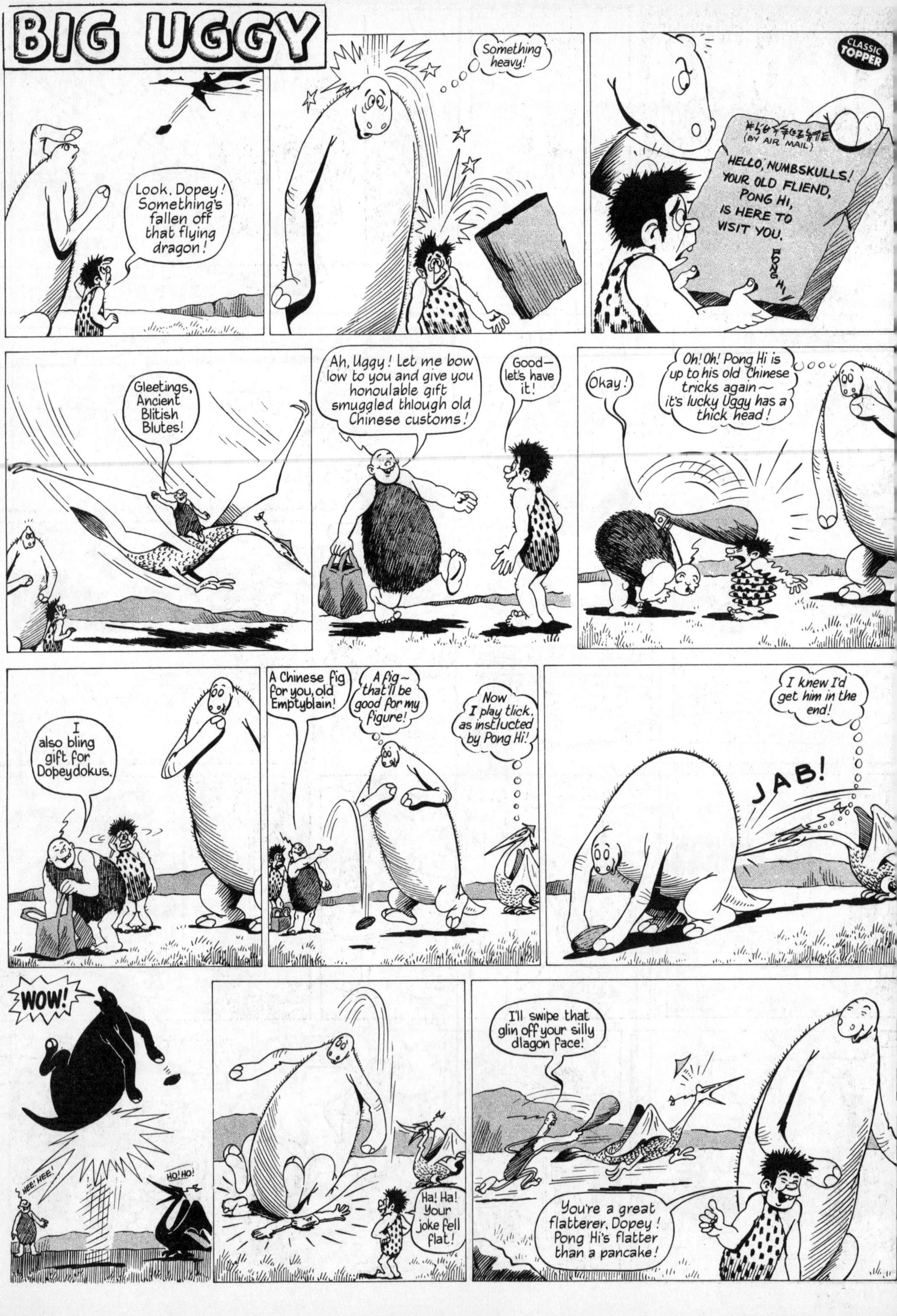

# BIG UGGY

CLASSIC TOPPER

Look, Dopey! Something's fallen off that flying dragon!

Something heavy!

(BY AIR MAIL)
HELLO, NUMBSKULLS! YOUR OLD FLIEND, PONG HI, IS HERE TO VISIT YOU.
PONG HI

Gleetings, Ancient Blitish Blutes!

Ah, Uggy! Let me bow low to you and give you honoulable gift smuggled thlough old Chinese customs!

Good— let's have it!

Okay!

Oh! Oh! Pong Hi is up to his old Chinese tricks again~ it's lucky Uggy has a thick head!

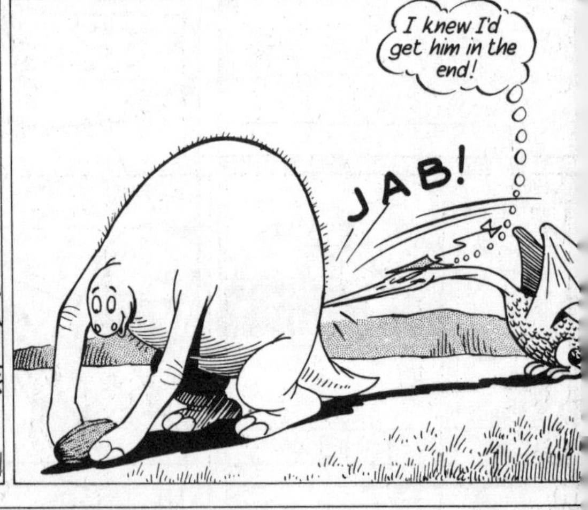

SKOOKUM SKOOL
←TEECHER

Come on, you dozy lot— it's time for gym!
Aw, boo!

CLASSIC BUZZ
We do games at gym, don't we, sir?
Yes, of course, boy!

Here are our games, then.
Get rid of them, and get the vaulting horse out.
SNAKES N' LADDERS
LUDO
MARBLES
TIDDLY WINKS

GYM STORE
Huh! No sense of humour!
TIDDLY WINKS

Right, Pudding—I want you to vault over the horse!
Who, m-m-me?

Oops! Who put castors on this thing?
ZOOM!

Yeeow! My tootsies!
You need some medicine, sir!
ZOOM!

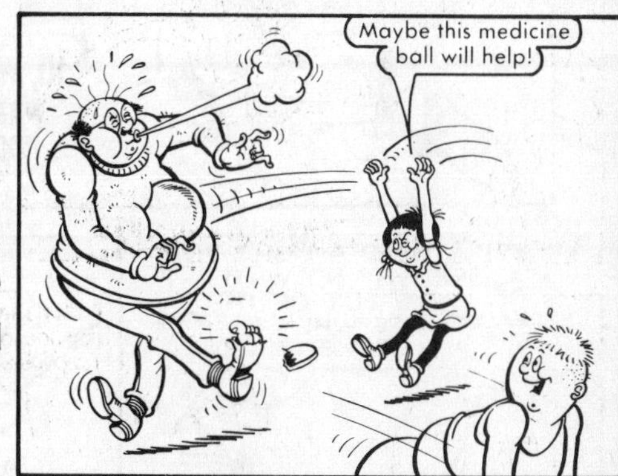
Maybe this medicine ball will help!

Keeping fit is hard work, isn't it, sir?
Bah! I give up . . .

. . . but my friend won't—I'll 'phone him.

Heh-heh! You're just the lad I need, Charlie!
STUDY
GYM INSTRUCTOR

I've got a surprise for you, pupils!
Goody!

I've never seen such an unfit bunch!
I agree—I'll leave you to sort them out!
GYM INSTRUCTOR

SLAM!
Leave? And where do you think YOU are going?
Eh?

Faster, you lazy lot!
GYM INSTRUCTOR
I can't win—I just can't win!
TROPHY CASE
5th 1904

CORPORAL CLOTT
CLASSIC DANDY
GALLOPING GOLDFISH! ALL THE TAPS IN THE CAMP ARE DRY, AND I'VE TO MAKE THE COLONEL'S AFTERNOON TEA! WHERE AM I TO GET WATER?
I'LL GO TO THE CITY WATERWORKS AND COMPLAIN!
CLOTT RUSHES BACK TO CAMP.
HI, WILLIE. I GOT SOME WATER! MUST SHOW THE COLONEL! HE'S GASPING FOR HIS TEA!
LOOK, SIR! YOU SHALL HAVE YOUR TEA AFTER ALL!
I'LL NEED A LIGHT TO SEE WHY NO WATER CAME OUT OF THE PIPE WHEN I BROKE IT.
BOOM
HELLO, CLOTT! WHAT HAVE YOU BEEN UP TO?
FIVE MINUTES LATER.
WAKEY-WAKEY! HERE'S YOUR AFTERNOON TEA!
EH? OH! ER-TEA? GOOD MAN, CLOTT!
ANYONE IN HERE? THE CAMP'S ON FIRE. COME OUT BEFORE YOU'RE GRILLED!
WATER TANKER

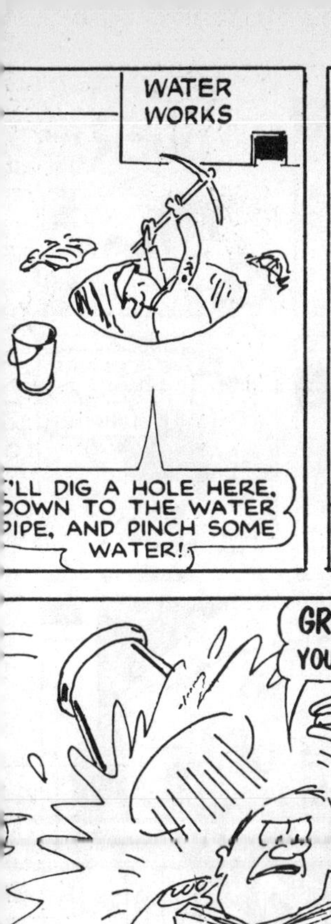
WATER WORKS
I'LL DIG A HOLE HERE, DOWN TO THE WATER PIPE, AND PINCH SOME WATER!

CLASSIC DANDY
YIPPEE! I'VE STRUCK WATER!

THAT ELEPHANT WILL PLUG THE LEAK WITH ITS FOOT TILL TOMORROW!

GROO! YOU DID!

GET OUT OF MY SIGHT, CLOTT, AND DON'T COME BACK UNTIL YOU'VE MADE MY TEA!

I'LL DIG A HOLE IN THE CAMP. THE WATER PIPE MUST BE HEREABOUTS.

I WAS RIGHT! THAT'S FUNNY, THOUGH—THERE DOESN'T SEEM TO BE ANY WATER IN IT!

WHO? ME? ER, NOTHING, SERGEANT!

THAT WAS A GAS PIPE I BROKE, AND THE ESCAPING GAS EXPLODED.
NOW HERE'S THE FIRE BRIGADE TO PUT OUT THE FIRE—AND THEY'VE BROUGHT A WATER TANKER. WHOOPEE! I'LL GET WATER FOR THE TEA NOW!

I'M SORRY, COLONEL, BUT IF SOME STUPID CLOT HADN'T TURNED ON OUR TANKER TAP THEN GONE AWAY AND LEFT IT WE COULD HAVE SAVED YOUR CAMP!
IF I FIND THE CULPRIT I'LL TEAR HIM TO BITS!
ER—GULP! THINK I'LL GO FOR A WALK! BETTER MAKE IT A LONG ONE!

DENNIS the Menace
CLASSIC BEANO

BAH! MENACES DON'T HAVE TO STAND IN QUEUES!
THE SWEET SHOP

LOOK OUT! THE MENACE! DUCK!

THE SWEET SHOP

THE SWEET SHOP
HOW WAS THAT FOR QUEUE JUMPING?

DOESN'T LOOK AS IF I'LL GET ON THIS BUS UNLESS....
BUS STOP

... I WORK MY ROPE TRICK.

BUS STOP

BUS STOP
ONE ONLY!

LATER
WATCH ME JUMP THIS QUEUE, TOO!

STOP HIM, SOMEBODY!
—STOP THAT BOY!
I'LL STOP HIM!

CAUGHT— BY A "Q"!
?

# The TOPPER

MICKEY
THE MONKEY

NOW TO WATCH TELEVISION!

THERE HE GOES! HE'S TELEVISION CRAZY!
CLICK!

BANG!
CLASSIC TOPPER

IT'S BROKEN!

IT'S NO USE! I'LL HAVE TO 'PHONE THE REPAIR MAN!
THUMP

THE TV REPAIR MAN ARRIVES...
H'M! YES! I SEE WHAT'S WRONG, BUT...

...IT'LL BE A FEW DAYS BEFORE I GET THE PART YOU NEED!
BUT, BUT—

AH, WELL! THIS IS ALMOST AS GOOD!

TWO MINUTES LATER...
BUT I WASN'T SPYING ON YOU, MR SMITH! I WAS ONLY WATCHING YOUR TV SET!
MICKEY

HUH! NOW WHAT CAN I WATCH?

I KNOW!

H'MM! NOT BAD! IT'S JUST LIKE 'CORPORATION STREET'!
AH, WELL! IT KEEPS HIM HAPPY!

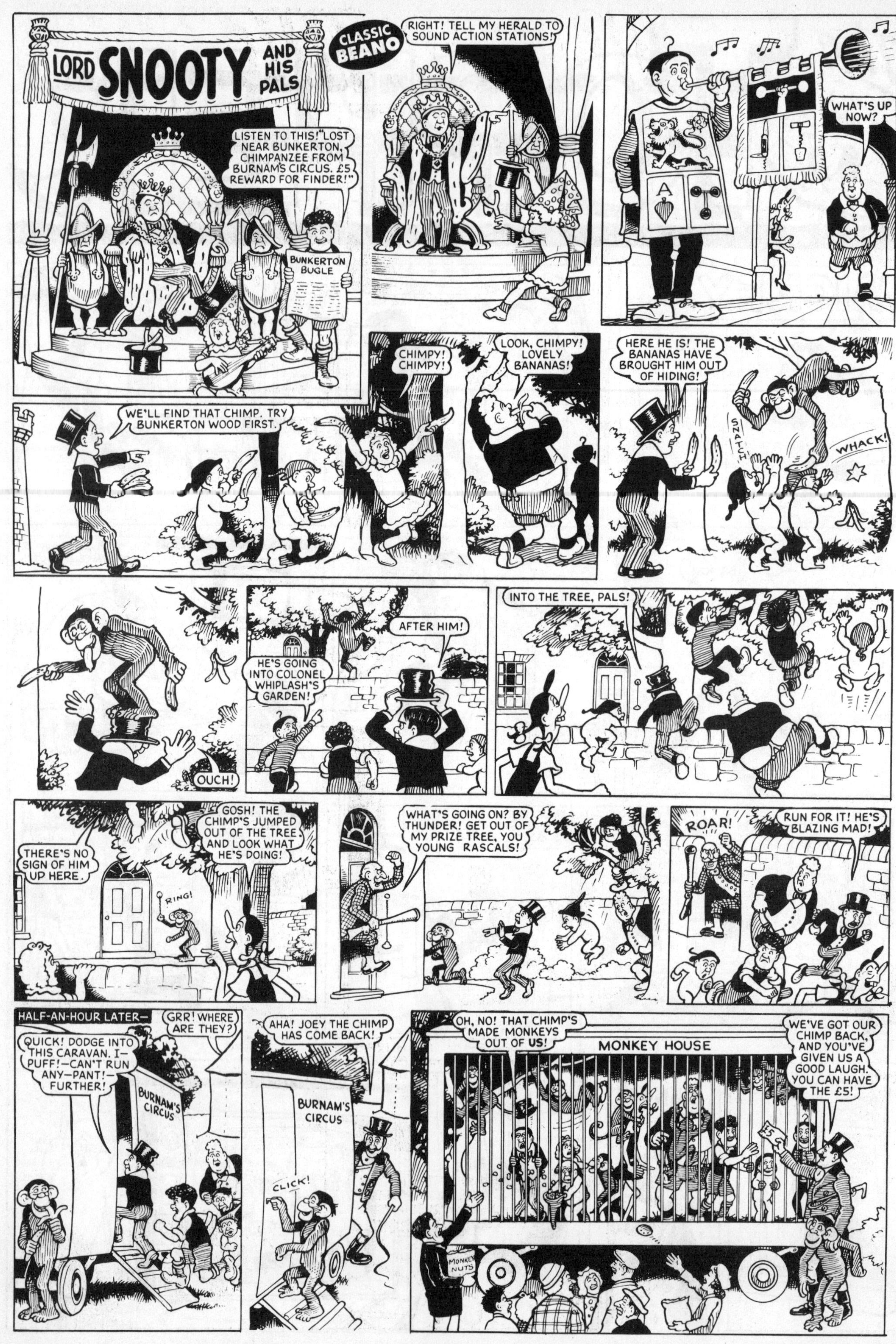
LORD SNOOTY AND HIS PALS
CLASSIC BEANO
LISTEN TO THIS! "LOST NEAR BUNKERTON, CHIMPANZEE FROM BURNAM'S CIRCUS. £5 REWARD FOR FINDER!"
BUNKERTON BUGLE
RIGHT! TELL MY HERALD TO SOUND ACTION STATIONS!
WHAT'S UP NOW?
WE'LL FIND THAT CHIMP. TRY BUNKERTON WOOD FIRST.
CHIMPY! CHIMPY!
LOOK, CHIMPY! LOVELY BANANAS!
HERE HE IS! THE BANANAS HAVE BROUGHT HIM OUT OF HIDING!
SNATCH
WHACK!
OUCH!
AFTER HIM!
HE'S GOING INTO COLONEL WHIPLASH'S GARDEN!
INTO THE TREE, PALS!
THERE'S NO SIGN OF HIM UP HERE.
GOSH! THE CHIMP'S JUMPED OUT OF THE TREE AND LOOK WHAT HE'S DOING!
RING!
WHAT'S GOING ON? BY THUNDER! GET OUT OF MY PRIZE TREE, YOU YOUNG RASCALS!
ROAR!
RUN FOR IT! HE'S BLAZING MAD!
HALF-AN-HOUR LATER—
GRR! WHERE ARE THEY?
QUICK! DODGE INTO THIS CARAVAN. I—PUFF!—CAN'T RUN ANY—PANT!—FURTHER!
BURNAM'S CIRCUS
AHA! JOEY THE CHIMP HAS COME BACK!
BURNAM'S CIRCUS
CLICK!
OH, NO! THAT CHIMP'S MADE MONKEYS OUT OF US!
MONKEY HOUSE
WE'VE GOT OUR CHIMP BACK, AND YOU'VE GIVEN US A GOOD LAUGH. YOU CAN HAVE THE £5!
£5
MONKEY NUTS

BIG HEAD AND THICK HEAD ARE TRYING TO EARN A BIT OF EXTRA SPENDING MONEY, DECORATING AN OFFICE.
BIG HEAD AND THICK HEAD
CLASSIC DANDY
I'LL NEED A LADDER TO DO THE TOP OF THE DOOR.
OKAY, GRAB ONE!
THANKS, PAL. I'LL BORROW YOURS FOR A MINUTE!
WHEE-E-E
SNATCH
ZIP
WHISTLE WHILE YOU WORK—TRA-LA-LA-LA—
AGH-H!
CRASH

YOU FAT, BRAINLESS NOODLE-HEADED NIT!
GOSH!
WHY DID YOU HAVE TO TAKE THAT LADDER?
30 FEET TO GROUND LEVEL

AFTER THICK HEAD HAS MANAGED TO HAUL HIS PAL UP WITHOUT CRASHING TO THE PAVEMENT—
I'VE SENT THE FAT FOOL OUT TO BUY A LEFT-HANDED PAINT BRUSH!
—BY THE TIME HE GETS BACK FROM HIS WILD GOOSE CHASE I SHOULD HAVE THIS CEILING FINISHED!

BUT 10 SECONDS AFTER THINKING OF THIS INGENIOUS PLAN—
AGH-H-H!
EXCUSE ME! WHAT WAS IT YOU SAID, BIG HEAD? A LEFT-HANDED PAINT-BRUSH OR A LEFT-PAINTED HAND-BRUSH?
CRASH
ZIP
SWISH

GR-R! THAT'S DONE IT!
I WOULDN'T GO BACK IN THERE WITH THAT CLOT FOR A THOUSAND POUNDS!

SO BIG HEAD (POOR SAP) DECIDES ON A BRILLIANT SOLUTION—
I'LL PAINT THE OUTSIDE WOOD-WORK! HE CAN'T KNOCK ME THROUGH THE WINDOW WHEN I'M ALREADY THROUGH IT!
SPLAT

AH! THERE'S A BIT MISSED, HERE!
I'LL JUST TOUCH IT UP!
TEE-TUM-TI-TEE!
WOBBLE

YOWLK! PUT THAT LADDER BACK QUICK, YOU CLOT!
ERK! GRAB THIS LADDER QUICK!
BUMP
TIP

GRR! YOU FROG-FACED, LITTLE SQUIRT! THAT'S THE LAST PAINTING JOB YOU'LL GET ME TO DO!
OH, YEAH? WHEN I GET MY MITTS ON YOU, FAT FIEND, THE NEXT PAINTING YOU'LL BE DOING WILL BE ON YOUR FLABBY SELF— WITH IODINE!

# DOODLEBUG

CLASSIC NUTTY

# GRANDPA

WHOOPEE! IT'S RAINING! I LOVE THE RAIN!

HEH! IT GIVES ME A CHANCE TO SAIL MY NEW TOY BOAT!

CLASSIC BEANO
CHUCKLE! THIS IS GREAT!

THEN—
SPLOOSH!

GLUBBLE! IT'S TOO DANGEROUS AT THE SIDE OF THE ROAD! I'LL HAVE TO FIND SOMEWHERE ELSE.

AH! THIS'LL BE SAFER.
HORSE TROUGH

BUT—
CHEEK!
H-HEY! PUT ME DOWN!
HORSE TROUGH

OK, GRANDPA!
GLUB!
SPLOOSH!

SNIFFLE! I'LL HAVE TO GO HOME NOW—I THINK I'VE CAUGHT A COLD!

AND SO—
SNIFFLE! AH, WELL, I CAN SAIL MY BOAT IN PEACE NOW!
SHAKE
SHIVER

HE'S GOT NO TROUSERS, SEE...
SPOOFER McGRAW
HE TELLS TALL TALES
IS HE KIDDING ME?

TICKETS, PLEASE!
TSK! EVERY TIME WE GET THE BUS HE WANTS TO SEE OUR TICKETS. YOU'D THINK IT WAS IMPORTANT!

AN' YOU'D THINK IT WAS IMPORTANT TOO IF YOU HAD T'GO AROUND WITHOUT ANY TROUSERS!
EH? YOU MEAN HE'S GOT NO TROUSERS, SPOOFER?

'S RIGHT, BO. WHY DO YOU THINK HE WEARS THAT LONG COAT?
COO! BUT WHAT DOES HAVING NO TROUSERS HAVE T'DO WITH LOOKIN' AT TICKETS?
CLASSIC SPARKY

AH, SAD STORY, THAT- IT ALL STARTED A LONG TIME AGO WHEN HE WAS JUST A YOUNG FELLOW. IT WAS HIS FIRST DAY AT WORK...

...AND HE'D JUST GOT HIS LOVELY, BRAND NEW UNIFORM...
BUS GARAGE
5 M.P.H.
OOH, I AM SMART!

...BUT HE DIDN'T SEE A BUS COMING OUT OF THE GARAGE, AND...
BRRRRM! BRRRM!
SPLOSH!

YES, BUT WHAT'S ALL THIS GOT T'DO WITH...?
PATIENCE, BO, I'M COMING TO THAT! ANYWAY...
HIS TROUSERS WERE SOAKING, SO HE POPPED THEM INTO THE DRY-CLEANERS...
EEZI-KLEEN
HALF HOUR SERVICE
THEY'LL BE READY IN HALF AN HOUR!
ER... RIGHT! I'LL... ER... CALL BACK!

SO, TO PASS THE TIME, HE POPPED IN TO SEE HIS MATES IN THE BUS-TICKET-MAKING FACTORY...
THERE I WAS, MINDING MY OWN BUSINESS, WHEN...
BUS-TICKET-MAKING MACHINE

...THIS HUGE BUS CAME AN'... ERK!
LAUNDRY TICKET
BUS-TICKET-MAKING MACHINE

GROAN! MY LAUNDRY TICKET!
YOU'VE HAD IT MATE - IT'S IN AMONG THAT LOT... SOMEWHERE!
WELL, HE WENT TO TRY AN' GET HIS TROUSERS BACK, BUT...
NO TICKET, NO TROUSERS!
MOAN!

AN' FOR FORTY YEARS HE'S BEEN SEARCHING FOR THAT TICKET-JUST SO'S HE CAN GET HIS TROUSERS BACK!
HMM?

I'LL JUST HAVE A QUICK PEEK T'MAKE SURE SPOOFER'S NOT KIDDING ME ON...
?

CHEEKY YOUNG RIP - GERROFF!
HO-HO! POOR OL' BO!
OOW!
BOOT!
THUD!

Colonel
CLASSIC BEEZER
BLINK
YOOHOO, AUNTIE!
OOH! WHAT A FRIGHT YOU GAVE ME, NEPHEW!
ES, I CAN SEE HAT! YOUR HAIR'S TANDING ON END! ETTER GET SOME URLERS IN. EMEMBER, WE'RE OING TO THE ICTURES TONIGHT! ARF!
HMM — I WONDER WHAT'S ON AT THE REGAL THIS WEEK? BAH — TYPE'S ALL FUZZY! CAN'T READ A WORD!
BLINKING NUISANCE — I'LL HAVE TO RING UP THE CINEMA.
BUT TRUST OLD BLINKY TO GET THE WRONG NUMBER!
GOOD AFTERNOON, MADAM. COULD YOU TELL ME WHAT'S ON TODAY?
SURE — THERE'S CORNED BEEF AND CABBAGE, AND PRUNES AND CUSTARD!
FRED'S CAFE
UMPH! NOTHING BUT KITCHEN SINK DRAMAS THESE DAYS! I'LL TRY THE ROXY!
SLAM!
BUT YET AGAIN!
HELLO! WHAT'S SHOWING TODAY, MY GOOD MAN?
WELL, THERE'S GARRY THE GHOUL AND HARRY THE HORRIBLE FOR A START....
WHACKO WRESTLING PROMOTIONS
TCH! BLINKING HORROR FILMS NOW! THERE HASN'T BEEN A DECENT FILM ON FOR WEEKS!
MIGHT AS WELL STAY IN AND WATCH THE TELLY!
UGH!
SPLOSH!
MY! YOUR HAIR'S NICE AND CURLY NOW, AUNTIE. BUT YOU SHOULDN'T HAVE BOTHERED. WE'RE STAYING AT HOME. CUTE LITTLE HAT YOU'VE GOT THERE TOO! ARF! ARF!
FUME
SILLY OLD FOOL! TAKE THAT!
WHACK!
WELL, WELL! BLINK'S SEEING STARS AFTER ALL — BUT THEY'RE NOT FILM STARS!
YOU CAN'T WIN!

# Dandy

CLASSIC
DANDY

KORKY the CAT
BAKERY
DELIVER THESE DOUGHNUTS RIGHT AWAY, KORKY.

THEY DON'T CALL ME THE FASTEST DELIVERY SERVICE IN TOWN FOR NOTHING!
VROOM

LATER—
I THINK I'LL ENTER FOR THIS!
Grand MOTOR-CYCLE RALLY! INCLUDING SIDE-CAR RACE

FIT ON A SIDE-CAR AND LET ME RIDE IN IT, UNCLE KORKY!
AND ME!
ME TOO!
HEY! YOU CAN'T ALL RIDE IN IT!

BUT WAIT—I KNOW WHAT TO DO! I'LL JUST POP ALONG TO THE BAKERY!

AT THE RALLY—
GET READY—GET SET—
BANG
SIDE-CAR RACE START

WE WIN IN UNCLE KORKY'S CAKE-STAND CAR!

# MINNIE the MINX

FOXY
CLASSIC TOPPER
CAN'T GET NEAR THE CHICKS LATELY... THAT FARMER'S GETTIN' TOO SMART... WONDER WHAT HE KEEPS IN HERE ?

BAH.... ONLY VEGETABLES — POTATOES, ONIONS, CARROTS.....

CARROTS ? THAT'S IT !

AN'Y' KNOW WHO LIKES CARROTS, FOLKS ?

WHY, RABBITS DO - YOO-HOO !

THERE YOU ARE, SON... HELP YOURSELF TO A NICE, JUICY CARROT !
GOSH ! THANKS !

HEH ! HEH ! AND IT'S RABBIT FOR SUPPER !

OUCH !
THUD
TWANGG

GRR ! NO BLOOMING BUNNY RABBIT IS GONNA MAKE A FOOL O' ME !
TINGLE

LATER.
MY DYNAMITE RABBIT EJECTOR WILL DO THE TRICK !

THIS'LL FIX 'EM !

YEOW ! DYNAMITE !
IT'S THAT FOXY AGAIN !
FSSS

KEEP CLEAR, EVERYBODY ! THIS IS AN EMERGENCY !
FSSSS

SHOWERS OF STUNNED RABBITS WILL COME SHOOTIN' OUT !
THERE HE IS—QUIETLY, NOW !

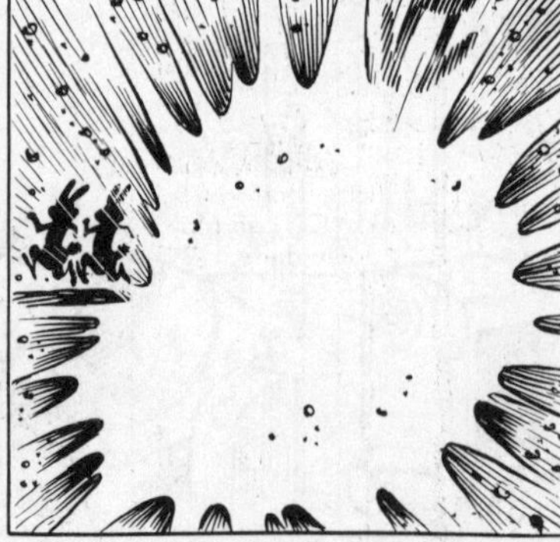

WHAT WENT WRONG ?

NOBBY

I think I'll build myself a tree house!
ZZZ

CLASSIC BUZZ
Oops!
BUMP!

Sorry, Dad!
AAH!
CRASH!

Up we go!
Pest!

Crumbs! I've left the hammer down there!

I'll jump down and get it!

Oh, no!
WHEE!
THUD!

CLUNK!
OOF!

Thanks, Dad! It was good of you to stop it going over the fence!

Soon have it finished now!

I'll just trim this bit up!

HACK!

It's taking a long time!
NO WONDER! YOU'RE SAWING THROUGH THE BRANCH NOW, NOBBY!

CRASH!
HELP!

You stay there, son! I've got work to do.

BANG!
BANG!
Thanks, Dad! I'll be able to play up there sooner than I thought!

?
That's what you think! YOU can play down there..

...I'll stay up HERE! It's the only place I'll get any peace!

THE McTICKLES
CLASSIC BEANO
TIME YOU LADS GOT THE VEGETABLE PATCH DUG– I WANT TO MAKE SCOTCH BROTH!
VEGETABLE PATCH
CROAK!
PUT YOUR BACKS INTO IT!
THUD!
OOYAH! MY BACK'S KILLING ME. THERE MUST BE AN EASIER WAY!
THEN–
AHA! MOLE-HAGGISES! THE VERY THING!
SNAP!
I'M OFF!
ALRIGHT, YOU TWO–START DIGGING!
VEGETABLE PATCH
HOI!
TRUST OLD CHIEF JOCK TO GET THINGS DONE!
VEGETABLE PATCH
GRAND!
BUT–
OH, NO! THEY'RE UNDERMINING CASTLE TICKLE! QUICK! SEND FOR ABERDEEN ANGUS, THE CABER-TOSSING CHAMP!
RUMBLE! RUMBLE!
HEE-HEE! WE'LL TEACH HIM!
TREMBLE!
ZOOM!
QUICK, ANGUS– WE CAN'T HOLD ON MUCH LONGER!
ARGH! CASTLE TICKLE LOOKS MORE LIKE THE LEANING TOWER OF TICKLE! YOU'LL PAY FOR THIS!
McCHORTLE!
WHAT?–ARE THE Mc TICKLES DIGGING THE GARDEN AT LAST?
NO–IT'S A TRENCH TO HIDE FROM MORAG'S MISSILES!
WHIZZ!
ZIP!
CLANG!

CLASSIC NUTTY
ETHEL RED
Here, Ethel! Sew my torn tunic for me. And make a neat job of mending it.
Right, Dad!
I'd better check that there are no rocks around that could hole the ship!
BUT THEN—
YEEE-OWCH!
Oops!
JAB!
YIKES! Dad will hole the ship with his helmet, unless . . .
Phew! I whipped it off just in time!
WHAM!
I'll leave Dad's helmet here till he wants it!
Ooh! Aah!
I still feel groggy! I'll have a seat!
OH, NO! He sat on his helmet!
YAHOOO!
UMFF!
CRACK!
NEXT INSTANT—
CRASH!
Not your day, Ethel! How are you feeling?
EDITOR'S VOICE.
Oh! Sew-sew!
SNARRRL!

THE PAPER WITH THE
ALL-STAR FUN-FOLK!
CLASSIC TOPPER
The TOPPER
FOR BOYS AND GIRLS
TRICKY DICKY
HEH! I'VE MADE THIS WISHING WELL TO GRANT SOME PEOPLE THEIR WISHES.
AHA! A WISHING WELL! I WISH I COULD TRAVEL THE WORLD.
NUMBER ONE VICTIM.
EH, WHASSAT?
WOO-HOO! NOW FOR YOUR TRAVELLING, PAL.
ERK!
SWELL!
POP!
GLOOM! DOOM! I WISH I COULD BE HAPPY.
HOWL! LET ME DOWN! I DON'T WANT TO GO ANYWHERE NOW!
MOURNFUL MORTIMER
PHRRIP!
WOW! A "TOPPER BOOK!" I FEEL BETTER ALREADY!
DROP!
TOPPER BOOK
DING!
BATTER!
TOPPER BOOK
HAR! HAR! THAT'S MY SPECIAL EDITION!

## GAG of the WEEK

**Hi, tricksters! Here's a quick-fire gag to pull. Ask any of your chums if they know who's the silly ass who keeps going about saying, "No!" Without thinking, your pal will probably say, "No!" Success is yours! Get ready to run as you say, "Oh, so YOU'RE the silly ass!"**

CLASSIC BEEZER

# Black BUN

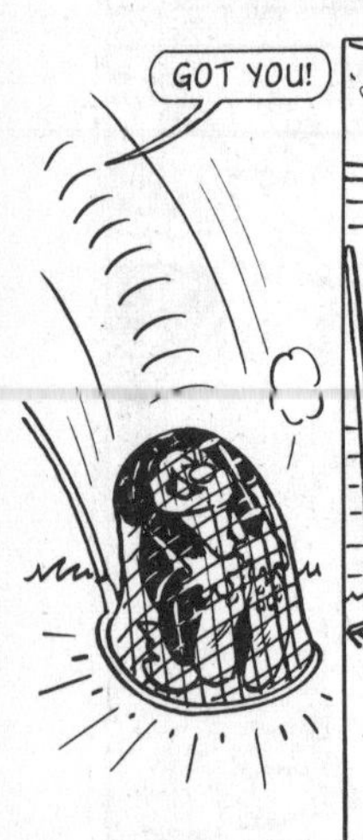

# The Bash Street Kids

# CURLY'S COMMANDOS

OH, OH! HERE COMES THE REAL NESSIE...

COO! WHAT A LOVELY LOCH NESS MONSTERESS!

CLASSIC CRACKER

AHEM... ALLOW ME TO INTRODUCE MYSELF, MADAM...

'ELP!

YEEARGH!

ERK!

ARGH!

I NEED UM NEW WIGWAM BUT I'VE NO CASH.
WISH WE COULD HELP PLUM.
PLUM'S PETS
WIGWAM CATALOGUE

STOP MOPING, PLUM! YOU PROMISED TO CLEAR UM VILLAGE OF LITTER AND DIG HOLES FOR MY APPLE TREES!

WHEN UM RAIN STOPS—
MY BACK'S SORE, PICKING UP THIS LITTER!
CLASSIC BEANO
ACHE
FEAR NOT— I'LL HELP!

LITTLE PLUM

SO—
GOOD WORK, HUBERT! YOU'LL SOON CLEAR ALL UM LITTER AT THIS RATE!
ZOOM-M!

I SAY, LOOK AT THIS— UM 100-DOLLAR NOTE!
HEY!

I'VE BEEN LOOKING EVERYWHERE FOR THAT—KINDLY ACCEPT THIS REWARD!
HOW NICE!

SHORTLY—
OH, MY BACK! DIGGING HOLES IS WORSE THAN PICKING UP LITTER!
CAN I BE OF ASSISTANCE?
ACHE

SO—
RODNEY'S UM FASTEST DIGGER IN UM WEST—HEY! WHAT'S THIS?

WHAT A FINE EXAMPLE OF ANCIENT POTTERY! I'LL GIVE YOU 20 DOLLARS FOR IT!
IT'S UM DEAL!

SOON—
YOU WANT ME TO THROW THIS STONE FOR YOU TO FETCH, EH, AL?
DROP-P

AFTER IT, BOY!
WOOF!

HEY! THIS ISN'T UM STONE I THREW! GASP! IT'S UM GOLD NUGGET! YAHOO! WE'RE RICH!

SEE WHAT I BOUGHT, READERS!

# I Fly

PHEW! IT'S HOT AND I'M THIRSTY!

THERE SHOULD BE A FEW DROPS OF LEMONADE LEFT IN HERE

TRAPPED YOU, I FLY!
OH, NO! IT'S SPIDER!

I'VE SPUN A WEB ACROSS THE GLASS—HE CAN'T ESCAPE!

HO-HO! THAT'S WHAT HE THINKS!

BAH! THIS IS THE LAST STRAW!
HA-HA! HE KEEPS SLIPPING BACK! HE'S TRAPPED HIMSELF!

BARNEY BULLDOG
IN A STICKY SITUATION

Menu
TUM-TE TUM! A WAITER'S LIFE FOR ME!

WOO-OOPS!
TRIP!
PHEW!
YEEK!
GANGWAY!
GULP!
OOF!
POKE!
OOH-OUCH!

HAH! DIDN'T DROP A THING...
...THANKS TO STICKFAST GLUE! SO, TAKE MY TIP, VIEWERS~ FOR TRICKY STICKING JOBS~ STICK TO STICKFAST!
STICKFAST
RIGHT~STOP CAMERA! FADE OUT SOUND. PRINT IT. GREAT, BARNEY~ JUST GREAT!
STICKFAST AD. TAKE 1

THE
Dandy
CLASSIC DANDY

KORKY THE CAT
KORKY'S BARBER-SHOP
KORKY HIGH CLASS HAIRDRESSER
THIS SHOULD BRING IN THE CUSTOMERS.
GET A FABULOUS AMERICAN CREW-CUT HERE!
THIS WAY, SIR— YOU'RE FIRST.

CLICK
NOW WATCH MY QUICK WAY OF TURNING A BEATLE GROWTH INTO A CREW-CUT!

YOW!
QUICKEST HAIRCUT I'VE EVER HAD!
SNIP
SNIP

# DREAMY DANIEL

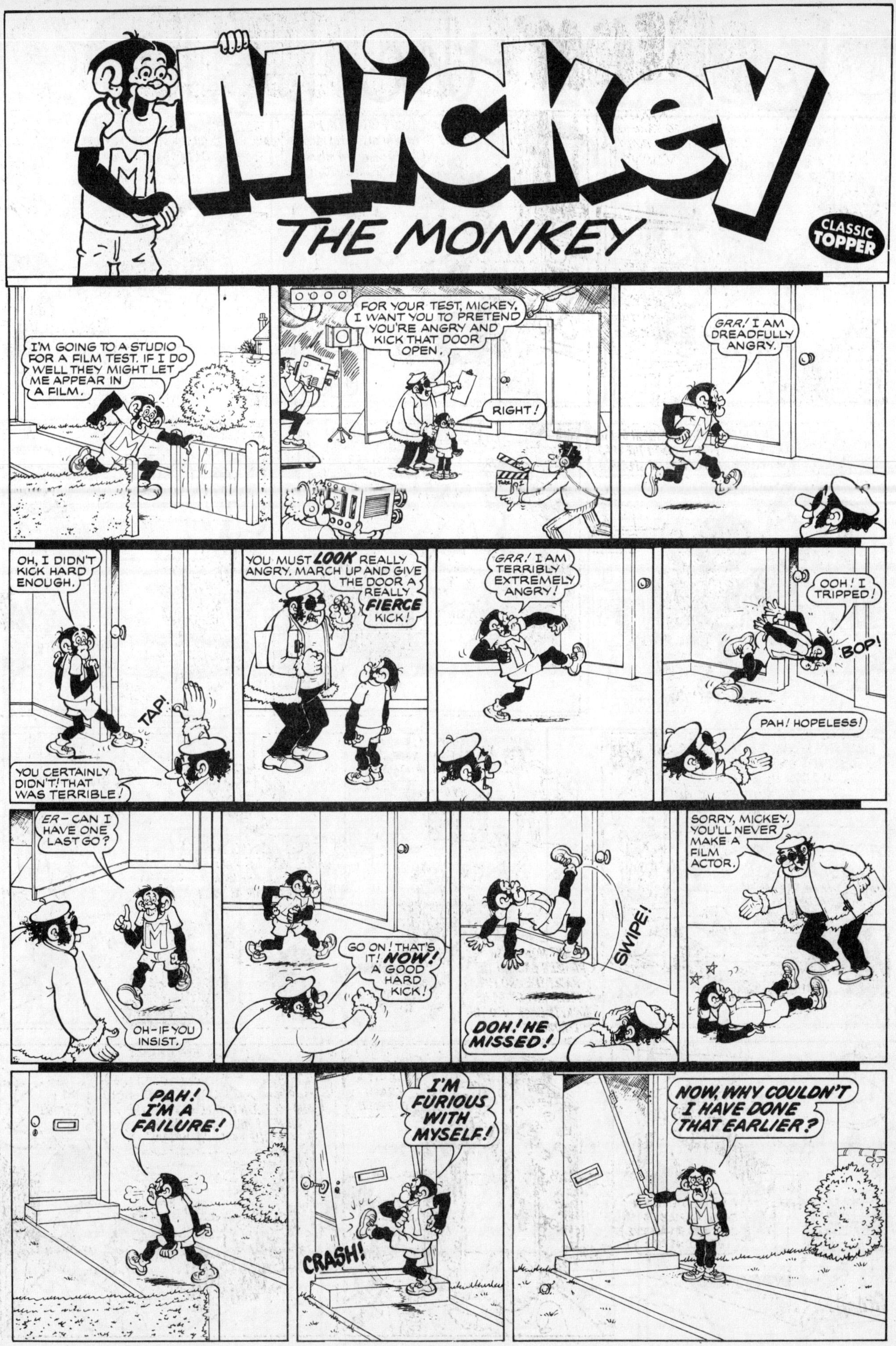

# Mickey THE MONKEY

CLASSIC TOPPER

I'M GOING TO A STUDIO FOR A FILM TEST. IF I DO WELL THEY MIGHT LET ME APPEAR IN A FILM.

FOR YOUR TEST, MICKEY, I WANT YOU TO PRETEND YOU'RE ANGRY AND KICK THAT DOOR OPEN.

RIGHT!

GRR! I AM DREADFULLY ANGRY.

OH, I DIDN'T KICK HARD ENOUGH.

TAP!

YOU CERTAINLY DIDN'T! THAT WAS TERRIBLE!

YOU MUST **LOOK** REALLY ANGRY. MARCH UP AND GIVE THE DOOR A REALLY **FIERCE** KICK!

GRR! I AM TERRIBLY EXTREMELY ANGRY!

OOH! I TRIPPED!

BOP!

PAH! HOPELESS!

# BILLY the KID

AND PONGO

# the BASH STREET KIDS

Jimmy Jinx
and WHAT HE THINKS
CLASSIC BUZZ

My hair's getting nice and long, eh, readers?

Yes—too long—you're going to the barber's!
Aw, no!

Hey, Jim!
No, James—don't do it!
CLIP!
CLIP!

You're next, son!

With any luck he won't notice my change of head!

What a mop of hair—it's just like string!

It is string—it's my mop!
Boo! He noticed!

I know you're in there!

No more nonsense!
Tee-hee!

I've got another plan, Jim!

That's it!
CRANK
WRRRRRR

You've won, Jim!
Oh, no! This is the last straw!

I'm not cutting his hair till he promises to behave!

Pssst! I know what to do!

THAT NIGHT
He'll be sleeping now!
JIMMY'S ROOM
ZZZZZZ

NEXT DAY
Aw, no! Mum must have permed my hair during the night!

Cut these horrible curls off—please!
Mum's too clever for me, readers!

Schoolboy, Eric Wimp, hides an amazing secret. Every time he eats one of his special bananas, he becomes . . .
BANANAMAN
ONE TYPICAL BANANADAY—
WOW! It's Bananaman! He's so dishy!
CLASSIC NUTTY
I have lots of admirers, you know, readers!
BANANAMAN! GET HIM!
ERK! See what I mean!
I'M BANANAS ABOUT BANANAMAN
I WANNA SOUVENIR! GRAB HIS CLOAK!
GULP! Must run!
BUT—
BANANAMAN! OUR HERO! LET'S PULL HIS MASK OFF.
ZOINKS! More of them!
IT'S HIM
OUR HERO!
AND SO—
PHEW! I'll be safe up here at least!
AW!
COME BACK
BUT—
LOOK! IT'S BANANAMAN!
LET'S GET HIS AUTOGRAPH!
Oh, no! Is there no escape?
AFTER HIM!
YIKES! Only one thing left to do . . .
. . . Change back to ordinary school kid, Eric Wimp!
No-one will recognise me now!
OOYAH! I should've landed first!
HO! HO!
SIGH! It may not be as exciting a life being Eric Wimp, but it's a whole lot safer!
BUT—
BANANAMAN CAME ROUND THIS WAY!
YAAARGH!
AND—
AFTER HIM!
GROAN! Sometimes you just can't win!

CLASSIC BEEZER
CAP'N HAND
and his
MERRY MUTINEERS

SHIP OFF THE STARBOARD BOW, CAPTING!

HOIST THE SAILS, SWABS! WE'LL ATTACK!

AARGH! THE MOTHS HAVE BEEN AT 'EM!
HIC!

AND SO, LATER, ASHORE . . .
HERE YOU ARE, CAP'N! FIFTY YARDS O' SAIL MATERIAL! CHEAP, TOO!
I'LL TAKE THE LOT!
SAILMAKER
50 YARDS OF YE BEST SAIL— 30 PIECES OF EIGHT.

GET YOUR BACKS INTO IT, DOGS! I WANT THOSE SAILS MADE TODAY!
THUD!
WE'LL BE DARNIN' SOCKS NEXT!
SEW, SEW, SEW! HE'S GOT T' GO!

OH, CAPTING, SIR! THERE'S A TEAR HERE! COME AN' SEE THIS TEAR HERE, CAPTING, SIR! COME AN' SEE!

WHAT TEAR? WHERE?
CREEP!

AN'— HUP! —HE GOES! HAR! HAR!
HELP!
BOING!

MUTINOUS DOGS!
TOP MAST

AN'— HUP! —HE GOES AGAIN! HAR! HAR!
BOING!

DROP THE SAIL NOW, LADS, AN' HE'LL HIT THE DECK! HAR! HAR!

TWO MINUTES LATER
I'M UP HERE, YE SWABS!
?
?
?
?

SNICK!
SWISH!
YARDARM Nº IIIB

HAR! HAR!
AAAIEEEOOOYAH!
THUD!

GET THESE NEEDLES GOING, DOGS, OR I'LL PRICK YOU WITH MY BODKIN! I'M CAP'N O' THIS SHIP, AN' YE'D BETTER NOT F'RGET IT!
ACHE!

# DENNIS THE Menace

CLASSIC BEANO

HO-HO! I'M GONNA STIR UP TROUBLE WITH THIS EGG-BEATER, FOLKS!

IN A CAFE.

WAITER! BRING ME A TEA-SPOON PLEASE.

DON'T BOTHER, WAITER. I'LL STIR HIS TEA FOR HIM!

IT'S THE MENACE! AFTER HIM!

GET HIM OUT OF HERE!

THE MENACE!

HO-HO! I'LL LAY A SMOKE-SCREEN WITH THIS.

FLOUR

THEY WON'T SEE ME MAKE MY GETAWAY!

HO-HO! THIS EGG-BEATER'S GREAT FUN!

*NOW DENNIS HOPES THAT HE'S FAST ENOUGH TO BE AN EGG-BEATER HIMSELF!*

# BERYL the Peril

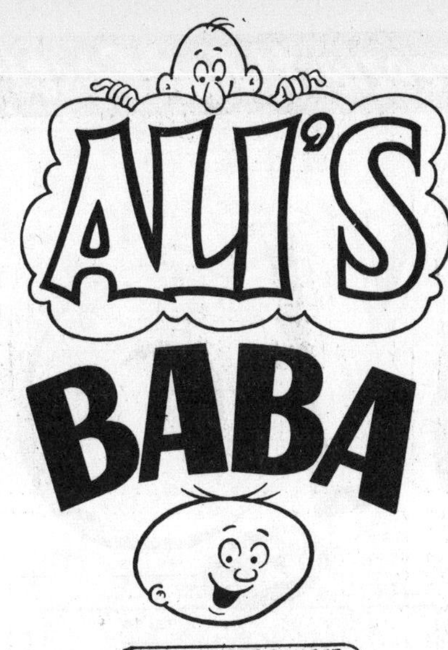
ALI'S
BABA

CLASSIC SPARKY
EVEN BABA CAN'T COME TO ANY HARM PLAYING WITH OLD CARDBOARD BOXES! I'LL HAVE FORTY WINKS!
TUM-TE TUM!

THIRTY-NINE WINKS LATER—
BABA'S A MOUNTAINEER! BABA'S GONNA PUT FLAG ON TOP OF MOUNTAIN!
ZZZZZ

BABA'S FIRST CLIMBER TO REACH TOP OF OLD SMOKEY! WOOPS! BABA WOBBLIN'!
YIKE! OH, NO!

HE'LL FALL DOWN THE CHIMNEY! I'VE GOT TO BE QUICK!
ZOOM!

PHEW! WHAT A DRAUGHT!
SWOOSH!

GOSH! JUST IN TIME! I'D BETTER HELP THE PEST DOWN NOW!
!

I WANT A TON OF COAL AT ONCE! IT WON'T GO IN THE BUNKER, SO JUST TIP IT OVER THE FENCE!
S'FUNNY! BABA MUST'VE FALLEN DOWN, BUT BABA NOT SORE!
??
PUFF!
PANT!

VERY SOON—
PHEW! THESE SUDDEN FRIGHTS AREN'T GOOD FOR ME!
COAL MERCHANT

COAL MERCHANTS
WAAH!

HOORAY! BABA'S GOT A REAL MOUNTAIN NOW!
AAH . . . PHOOEY! YOU JUST CAN'T WIN!

Smiles ahead of all the rest—Brightest! Breeziest! And Best!

MY AUNT HAS REMOVED FROM THIS HOUSE, BUT SHE LEFT A FEW THINGS BEHIND, AND THICK HEAD AND I ARE FOLLOWING ON WITH THEM.
BIG HEAD and THICK HEAD
GASP! WHEEZE! WHEW! I'LL NEVER GET THIS HEAVY CABINET DOWNSTAIRS!
CLASSIC DANDY
HUH! IT WOULDN'T EVEN GO THROUGH THE BEDROOM DOOR! BUT THAT OLD BED-STEAD ON THE PATHWAY MIGHT SOLVE THE PROBLEM!
WITH A MIGHTY HEAVE, THICK HEAD LAUNCHES THE CABINET OVER THE WINDOW-SILL—
HEE-HEE! I WONDER HOW THAT FAT SAP'S GETTING ON UP THERE WITH THAT HEAVY CABINET? IT'S MADE OF SOLID—
ZOO-OOM
BOUNCE
THUD
POIN-NG
WHEE-EE
—MAHOGANY!
BLAH-H!
SHATTERING CRASH

HALF AN HOUR LATER—WHEN BIG HEAD HAS REGAINED CONSCIOUSNESS—
BAH! HE'S MAKING ME WORK DOWN HERE TO KEEP ME OUT OF TROUBLE! CALLED ME A FAT NIT! BUT I'LL SHOW HIM! I'LL SHIFT THE STAIR CARPET ALL BY MYSELF! HERE GOES!

—AGH-H-H-H H!
WHIZZ
TUG

YOU BLITHERING, HALF-BAKED, BRAINLESS BLOCKHEAD! DIDN'T YOU SEE ME UP THERE?
—NO!
EE-YULK!

TWO HOURS LATER—WHEN THICK HEAD HAS RECOVERED HIS MEAGRE SUPPLY OF SCATTERED WITS—
PHEW! I CAN'T BUDGE THE CART AN INCH, AND THE PIANO HAS TO GO ON YET!
POOH! MY SUPERIOR INTELLIGENCE WORKED OUT THAT PROBLEM HOURS AGO! LEAVE IT TO ME!

10 MINUTES LATER—
HERE WE ARE! I'VE BORROWED THE MILKMAN'S HORSE. WE'LL BACK IT INTO THE SHAFTS, AND IT'LL PULL THE LOAD EASILY—PIANO AND ALL!
GOSH! WHAT BRAINS!

AND SO, AFTER REMOVING THE UPSTAIRS WINDOW-FRAME—
THAT'S THE HORSE HARNESSED! NOW TO LOWER THE PIANO ON TO THE CART WITH THIS INGENIOUS PULLEY SYSTEM I'VE INVENTED!
LOWER AWAY!

WOW! THE ROPES HAVE SNAPPED!

AGH-H! WHAT'S HAPPENED?
WHOOSH

15 MINUTES LATER, PASSERS-BY SEE A FANTASTIC SIGHT—
OKAY, BRAINY-BONCE! SO, YOU GOT THE PERISHING PIANO ON WHAT'S LEFT OF THE CART! ALL I WANT TO KNOW NOW IS, HOW DO WE GET THE BLITHERING HORSE OFF THE BLOOMING ROOF?
!

L
CARS
CLASSIC SPARKY

LOOK AT YOUR BOOTS! THEY'RE FILTHY! GO AND CLEAN THEM! I WANT TO BE ABLE TO SEE MY FACE IN THEM— UNDERSTAND?
ER... YES, SIR!
SIR!

AND SO, IN THE CLOAKROOM—
WHOOEE!
PHEW!

FIVE MINUTES LATER—
THEY'RE STILL FILTHY! I CAN'T SEE MY FACE YET! GO AND POLISH THEM AGAIN!

ONE FREDERIC BRAINWAVE LATER—
HO-HO-HO! THAT'LL FOOL HIM, FREDERIC!
HA-HA! NOT HALF!

JOLLY GOOD! I CAN SEE MY FACE PERFECTLY NOW! WELL DONE, BOYS!
THANK YOU SIR!
DRRING! DRRING!

WHAT'S THAT? WANTED MAN JINKY SPINKS SEEN IN EAST STREET! GET GOING!
SIR!

EAST STREET
THERE HE GOES! OOPS! WATCH THESE PUDDLES! WE DON'T WANT TO GET OUR BOOTS DIRTY!
TOO TRUE!
HOP!
HOP!
HOP!
HOP!

SORRY, INSPECTOR—I'M AFRAID JINKY SPINKS GOT AWAY, SIR— BUT YOU'LL BE GLAD TO KNOW OUR BOOTS ARE STILL LOVELY AND CLEAN!
YES, SIR!
GRRRR!

LATER—
JINKY SPINKS SEEN NEAR PLANTER'S PARK—L CAR NUMBER ONE INVESTIGATE!
SIR!
SIR!

AHA! THAT'S HIM!
HE'S RUNNING AWAY OVER THE RUGBY PITCH!
PESKY COPS!
SPLUDGE!
SPLODGE!

CLASSIC SPARKY
WHAT'LL WE DO? WE CAN'T GO ACROSS ALL THAT MUD WITH OUR GOOD CLEAN BOOTS ON, CEDRIC!
RIGHT ENOUGH!
HO-HO, CLEAN AWAY!
WE'D BETTER GO BACK AND TELL THE INSPECTOR!
SO SORRY, SIR! HE GOT AWAY— BUT AREN'T OUR BOOTS NICE AND CLEAN?
SEE? HAVE A LOOK AT YOUR FACE IN THEM, SIR!
OW!
AAH!
WHUMP!
NO—I WILL NOT! GO AND GET HIM!
THEN—
JINKY SPINKS SEEN ON MID-MUD FARM! GO THERE NOW!
AT ONCE, SIR!
SIR!
BRROOM!
BRRROOM!
VAROOOOM!
HE'S RUNNING AWAY OVER THAT MUDDY FIELD! ONLY ONE THING FOR IT! OFF WITH OUR GOOD, CLEAN BOOTS—
YES INDEEDY!
HEY—! THIS IS GREAT! I CAN GO TWICE AS FAST WITHOUT THOSE BIG HEAVY BOOTS!
ME TOO!
SPLURGE!
SPLOTCH!
GOT HIM!
EASY!
URK!
SPLAT!
WE'VE GOT JINKY SPINKS, SIR—AND YOU SHOULD SEE OUR BOOTS—THEY'RE SPOTLESS, SIR!
REALLY CLEAN, SIR!
GARGH! I WISH I'D NEVER SAID ANYTHING ABOUT BOOTS! THEY'RE ALWAYS ON ABOUT HOW CLEAN THEY ARE! ALWAYS SHOWING ME MY FACE IN THEM!
OH, REALLY?
HERE HE IS, SIR—NOW WOULD YOU LIKE TO SEE YOUR FACE IN MY BOOTS, INSPECTOR?
OR MINE, SIR?
NO!
WELL, I WOULD, BOYS! LET'S SEE MY FACE!
WHAT'S THIS? THE INSPECTOR'S FACE—? I SAY—IT'S PAINT!
SO!
GULP!
I'VE GOT MY BOOTS OFF BUT THEY'RE STILL GAINING, CEDRIC!
I KNOW! HELP!
GAGH!
GRRR!
COME BACK HERE SO I CAN BOOT YOU—YOU, YOU TWO-FACED SCOUNDRELS!

# THE TRICKS of SCREWY DRIVER

# BING-BANG BENNY

Dick Turban
DESERT HIGHWAYMAN
and his camel, CARAMEL

CLASSIC NUTTY
Zese are Dick Turban's camel's tracks—after heem, men!
GASP! We sure are HOT on his trail.
THIS WAY FROM THE OASIS!
THIS WAY TO THE OASIS!
TRAMP! TRAMP! TRAMP! TRAMP! TRAMP!

AHA! So he eez loitering within tent.

Come out and face me like a man.
TAB!

How dare you, you nasty little soldier.
WOW! A big, big woman.
BLAST!
THROB! THROB! THROB! THROB! THROB!

Attack a weak, defenceless woman, would you? Take that!
BIFF! THUMP!
AAH! A nice refreshing dip that.

THERE HE GOES, MEN—after heem!
Best hoof forward, Caramel.

Whoa, Caramel—we'll hide around here.
Good thinking, Dick.
SCREECH!

SOON, THE LEGION TRACKS DICK DOWN—
Zis must be ze fiendish bandit's hideout where he hides ze loot—forward, men, into ze cave!

Tut! Tut! He shouldn't have done that. I suppose I should have warned him that . . .

. . . The 2.15 camel train is always bang on time coming out of that tunnel!
AARGH!
THUNDERING HOOVES!

MINNIE the MINX

GRR! LOOK AT THESE BILLS! I'M FED UP PAYING FOR THE DAMAGE YOU CAUSE! YOU'D BETTER WATCH YOUR STEP IN FUTURE, OR I'LL BE GOING OFF THE DEEP END!

LATER-
CLASSIC BEANO
ALL SET FOR A GAME OF CRICKET, PALS? GOOD! I'LL BOWL.

NOW FOR MY SPECIAL DELIVERY-

-A BOUNCER!
DONK!
THUD!

ER... EXCUSE ME, CAN I HAVE OUR BALL BACK?

GRR! HERE YOU ARE, MINX!
THANKS!

GOODY! IT'S MY TURN TO BAT. I'LL SHOW THEM HOW TO HIT A BALL!

KERRACK!
THAT'S SIX RUNS FOR SURE!

MINNIE IS SENT TO FETCH THE BALL BACK.
I MIGHT HAVE KNOWN IT WOULD BE YOUR FAULT, GIRL! HERE!
THANKS!

LATER-
HEH! HEH! IT'S MY TURN TO KEEP WICKET NOW, READERS!

THIS IS AN EASY CATCH!

HOWZAT?
BAWL!
HOWL!
WAIL!

YOU LITTLE PEST! YOU'VE WAKENED OUR BABIES FROM THEIR AFTERNOON NAPS!

LATER-
SLOW AT MAJOR ROAD AHEAD
HUH! I'D BETTER GIVE UP CRICKET FOR A SPELL. I'LL TRY SWIMMING INSTEAD.

AT THE SWIMMING BATHS-
CRASH!
YIPPEE! WATER, HERE I COME!

CLASSIC BEANO
OUT OF THE WAY, SMALL FRY!

OOPS! MY HAND SLIPPED!
DONK!

SHE CAN HAVE THE WATER ALL TO HERSELF! WE'RE NOT STAYING IN WHILE SHE RUNS RIOT!

THE BATHMASTER TELEPHONES DAD.
EXCUSE ME SIR, BUT I'M AFRAID YOUR DAUGHTER'S CREATING A DISTURBANCE.

GRR! JUST WAIT TILL I GET MY HANDS ON HER!

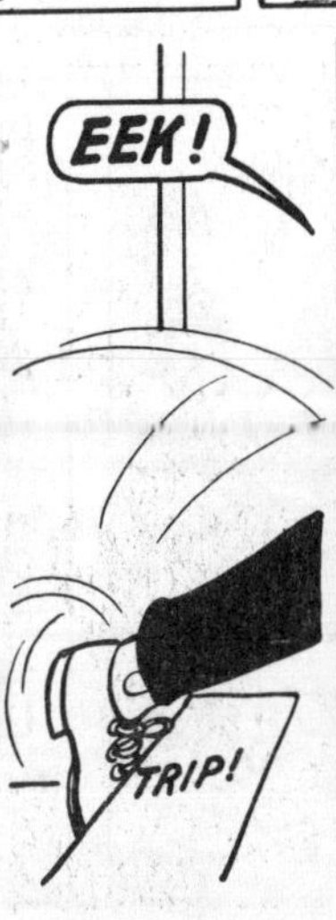
EEK!
TRIP!

SPLASH!

TUT-TUT! IF YOU'D WATCHED YOUR STEP, DAD, YOU WOULDN'T HAVE GONE OFF THE "DEEP END"!

BUT NOW DAD REALLY IS GOING OFF THE DEEP END!
GRR! NO POCKET MONEY FOR FIFTY YEARS! GRR! BREAD AND WATER FOR SUPPER!
GRR! KEPT IN EVERY SATURDAY!
WOW!

CLASSIC TOPPER
FOXY

GOSH! AM I HUNGRY! I'LL HAVE TO TRY RAIDIN' THE FARM!
WHAT A WONDERFUL THOUGHT!
MMM! I'M A FAST THINKER.

OUCH!
ALAS! THIS IS WHAT ALWAYS HAPPENS WHEN I TRY T'GET CHICKS!
OUCH!
OH, BOY! IF ONLY THIS COULD HAPPEN INSTEAD!

MUSEUM
AN' IT CAN HAPPEN!
TA-TUM TE-TUM!
WOW! IT'S FOXY... WITH A CANNON!

QUICK... FARMER HAS A BONFIRE!

TOUCH IT OFF, SO....
HO! HO! POOR, OLD FARMER! HE'LL NEVER KNOW WHAT HIT HIM!
FSSS
TO THE FARM

OOYAH!
BOOM!

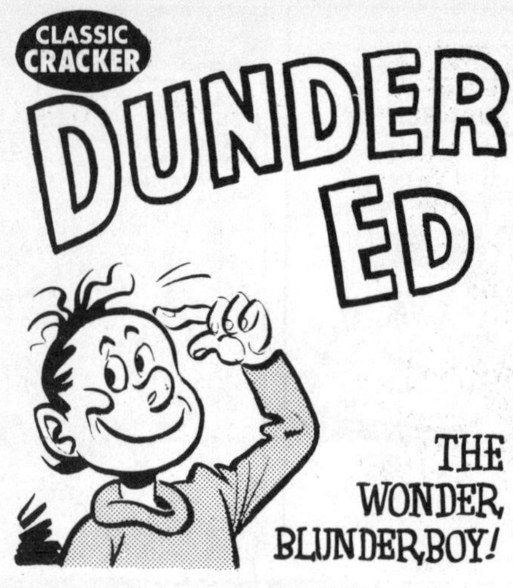
CLASSIC CRACKER
DUNDER ED
THE WONDER, BLUNDER, BOY!

SUPER-MART
AH! THIS IS THE PLACE!

THERE'S THE MANAGER. I MUST SPEAK TO HIM!
ON OFFER

OO-ER!
BUMP!
ON OFFER
KERRASH!

NOW, WHERE'S THE MANAGER GONE?
OOCH!
EEEK!
HELP!
OWK!

FRESH-MADE SAUSAGES
AH! I CAN SEE HIM OVER THERE.
SAUSAGE MACHINE
SWITCH. CLICK!
SLOW
FAST

OOPS! WHAT HAPPENED THEN? — CAN'T STOP!
WHIZZZZZZZ!
GULP!
BONK!
FAST

CHEESE COUNTER
THERE HE IS- HEY, SIR!
CHEDDAR
BOMP!

EEOWK! AAARGH!
WELL, NOW I CAN CATCH HIM UP!
BONK!

YOU'RE THE BOY WHO'S CAUSING ALL THESE DISASTERS! WHAT DO YOU WANT?

I'VE COME TO SEE YOU ABOUT THIS JOB, SIR.
SIGG'S SUPERMART
BOY WANTED
MUST BE NEAT & CAREFUL
APPLY MANAGER

RIP!
SPLUTTER!
I DIDN'T GET IT!
WOMP!

# PUSS and BOOTS

THEY FIGHT LIKE CAT AND DOG

CLASSIC SPARKY

# HARUM SCAREM

COLONEL BLINK
CLASSIC TOPPER
YOOHOO, ROVER! TIME FOR DIN-DINS! WHERE ARE YOU, BOY? YOOHOO!
THERE YOU ARE, YOU OLD RASCAL! WHAT ON EARTH ARE YOU DOIN' UP THERE? ARF!
GRRR!
COME DOWN AT ONCE, YOU SILLY DOGGY! OUR DINNER'S GETTING COLD! ARF! ARF!
ATTENTION, CITIZENS OF PUDDLEWICK! A DANGEROUS ORANG-UTANG HAS ESCAPED FROM THE ZOO! THIS WILD APE SHOULD BE SHOT ON SIGHT! ATTENTION, CITIZENS OF.......
ZOO
SO THAT'S WHY YOU'RE UP THERE, ROVER! COME DOWN AT ONCE AN' STOP THAT SNUFFLIN'!
SNUFFLE!
ALL RIGHT, YOU OL' COWARD! ARF! I'M COMIN' UP TO GET YOU—AN' IT'S THE COLLAR AN' LEAD FOR YOU, M'LAD!
SWOON!
KEEP STILL NOW, YOU SILLY DOG!
?
MUST SAVE TH' COLONEL!
GRRR!
GROWL!
GRRR!
OH! MERCY ME! TH' ESCAPED APE! AN' IT'S TRYIN' TO CLIMB THE TREE!
GRRR!
SNAP!
GRRR!
GROWL!
MUST GET HELP! QUICK!
ARF! GOOD! IT'S GONE!
WHAT'S WRONG, ROVER? THE OLD COLONEL IN TROUBLE AGAIN?
WHIMPER! SNUFFLE! SNUFFLE!
ARF! WE'RE READY FOR IT IF IT DARES TO COME BACK!
THERE IT IS! AN' CARTWRIGHT'S IN ITS CLUTCHES! UNHAND HIM, YOU BRUTE!
IT'S THE ESCAPED APE! GULP!
HELP!
GOOD! SPLENDID! CARTWRIGHT'S GOT AWAY! TAKE THAT, YOU BRUTE!
BOOM!
FLOP!
GOT IT, BY JOVE! IT'S AS DEAD AS A DOORNAIL! BETTER INFORM TH' ZOO! COME ALONG, ROVER!
ZOO KEEPERS' CANTEEN
NO ANIMALS ALLOWED.
GRRR!
JUST POPPED IN TO TELL YOU I BAGGED THAT APE, CHAPS! ARF! YES! DEAD AS MUTTON! WORTH A FREE CUP OF TEA, EH? WHAT? ARF!

# DESPERATE DAN

FIRE OUT—AND CAN'T GET HOME? ALL RIGHT, I'LL PUSH YOU.

BAKER

WHY ARE YOU DRINKING PETROL, DAN?

YOU'LL SEE.

PETROL

MY LIGHTED BREATH WILL START YOUR COAL BURNING QUICKLY.

OVEN

SMASHING!

ROAR

PLOP

PIG TALES
POPPA
MOMMA
PIGGLES

PHEW! It's hot today. Fetch me some chilled swill, Piggles.
Right, Poppa!

BUT—
CLASSIC NUTTY
OH, NO! We've none left.

Let's see if we can borrow a cup of water from Farmer's well.

AAH! This is the life.
SUCKITTY-SUCK!
SLURP! Look at that lemonade.

FARMER'S WIFE
STARCH
I'll just borrow this.

GASP! It sure is hot today.
CHORTLE! Now to mix the starch with water.
STARCH
That's my boy!

Allow us to cool you down, Farmer.
WAAGH!
SPLOOSH!

Come back here, you thieving porkers.
HOP!
HOP!
Aw! Don't be such a STIFF, Farmer.

Oh, no! Corks!
GROAN! We don't have a corkscrew!

Hmm! Never mind!
HEY! What are you up to, Poppa?
STARCH
The heat must be affecting him.

There! Piggles' tail makes a perfect corkscrew.
W-WOW!
TWIRL

BILLY
WHIZZ

OOPS! SORRY, DAD!
CRACK!
BUMP!
WHIZZZ!

CLASSIC BEANO
BILLY! GO AND FETCH THE SCISSORS FROM THE SITTING ROOM.
SURE, MUM!
OH, OH! HERE HE COMES AGAIN. I'LL SIT DOWN HERE OUT OF HIS WAY.

BUT—
GOSH! SORRY, DAD!
ZIP!
BUMP!
WHOOSH!
THUD!

GRR! YOU SHOULD TAKE A LESSON FROM YOUR PET TORTOISE—

—YOU NEVER SEE HIM RUNNING ABOUT CREATING HAVOC!
LIKE TO GO FOR A LITTLE RIDE, TIMOTHY?

A GOOD HARD PUSH— AND OFF YOU GO!

EEK!
EGGS

AARGH! I'M SEEING THINGS— A TORTOISE ON WHEELS!
SCREECH!

OW!
BUMP!

YOWL!

GRR! WHY CAN'T YOU KEEP YOUR TORTOISE UNDER CONTROL INSTEAD OF LETTING IT RUSH ABOUT THE STREETS CAUSING ACCIDENTS?
YOU WERE SAYING, DAD?

THE SMASHER
CLASSIC DANDY
I'LL HAVE TO PLAY TRUANT IF I WANT TO SEE THAT!
ROYAL
FILM FESTIVAL
3
TERRIFIC FILMS
SPECIAL HALF-PRICE MATINEE THIS AFTERNOON.

COME, LITTLE MAN—DON'T BE TEMPTED!
ROYA
OW! IT'S THE HEAD!

IN THE SCHOOL GYM
PHEW! TIME I WAS SNEAKING OFF!

THAT BOY'S FAINTED—TAKE HIM OUTSIDE INTO FRESH AIR!
YES, SIR!
FLOP!

THANKS, LADS! I'M FEELING GREAT NOW!
GYM

GRR! THE JANITOR IS AT THE GATE, I'LL HAVE TO THINK OF SOMETHING!
SCHOOL
GOT IT! I'LL HIDE IN A DUST BIN!

SO
I'M OUT! PHEW! AM I GLAD!

NOW FULL STEAM AHEAD TO THE CINEMA!

WOW! THE HEAD! I'LL HAVE TO TURN BACK!

GOSH! HERE'S THE JANITOR! THEY MUST BE LOOKING FOR ME! I'LL HAVE TO HIDE!

I'LL OPEN THIS VAN AND HIDE IN IT!

WOW! IT'S A PET SHOP VAN!
WOOF!
BARKING PET SHOP
WOOF!

HELP!
HELP!
HO-HO! THE DOGS ARE CHASING THE HEAD AND THE JANITOR!

PRESENTLY
ROYAL
NOBODY ABOUT TO SPY ON ME? GOOD! THEN IN I GO!

INSIDE
HO-HO! WHAT A SMASHING FILM!

SUDDENLY, WHEN THE LIGHTS GO ON
GOSH! I'VE BEEN SITTING BETWEEN THE HEAD AND THE JANITOR!

HO-HO! THEY CAN'T SAY ANYTHING BECAUSE THEY'VE BEEN PLAYING TRUANT TOO!
ROYAL

WANTED!
WILLIE GETAWAY
£1,000 REWARD!
MISSING HEIR TO THE VAST ESTATE OF THE LATE LORD GETAWAY
WANTED—AND I HAVEN'T DONE A THING!
HE'S HEIR TO A FORTUNE—BUT HE CAN'T READ THE SMALL PRINT.

In his pursuit of the local Schoolboys' Boxing Championship, Scrapper is encouraged and trained by his own headmaster, Mr Belcher, who was a boxing champion in his youth.

# FIGARO!

I'M PEDRO DON KEY, FIGARO'S MULE.
AN' WE'RE FIGARO'S GANG!
AND ME - I'M THE GREAT FIGARO HIMSELF!

CLASSIC TOPPER
WOW!
GRAND HORSE RACE TODAY
RACE STARTS AT BOUNCING SPRINGS AND ENDS AT PESO CITY.
ENTER NOW
NOTE - RIDERS FALLING OFF WILL BE DISQUALIFIED

HEY! I'LL ENTER THIS RACE ON PEDRO AND WIN!
HO-HO! WIN? ON THAT OLD SLOWCOACH MULE? ANYWAY YOU ALWAYS FALL OFF HIM!

HUH! YOU THINK I HAVEN'T THOUGHT OF THAT! I WILL GLUE MYSELF TO THE SADDLE!
GOOD IDEA! BUT HOW DO YOU MAKE PEDRO RUN FASTER?

THAT IS EASY! THE ROAD FROM BOUNCING SPRINGS TO PESO CITY IS DOWNHILL ALL THE WAY... WE PUT ROLLER SKATES ON PEDRO'S HOOFS...

GOOD! WHEN I AM STUCK TO THE SADDLE I WILL LEAD YOU TO A PLACE NEAR THE STARTING POINT OF THE RACE.

...AND YOU LOT WILL HIDE THERE WITH THE SKATES WHILE I GO TO THE STARTING POINT.

BOUNCING SPRINGS

WHEN THE RACE STARTS, I'LL RIDE VERY SLOWLY, SO I WILL BE THE LAST RIDER TO REACH HERE. THEN YOU CAN FIT THE SKATES ON PEDRO.
PESO CITY

THEY'RE OFF!
START

HERE COMES FIGARO! GET THE SKATES READY!
PESO CITY

HURRY, PANCHO!

GOOD LUCK, FIGARO!

VERY SOON FIGARO STREAKS PAST EVERYBODY AND GAINS A BIG LEAD
HO! HO! SEE YOU IN PESO!

THE SPEED IS TOO FAST! OOOH! I AM SCARED STIFF! STOP, PEDRO, STOP!
IDIOT! HOW CAN I STOP?

I'LL LASSO THAT ROCK — THAT'LL STOP US!

OH, NO! LIKE A CORK OUT OF A BOTTLES!

THAT HORSE IS DISQUALIFIED - THE RIDER'S FALLEN OFF!
FINISH
?
JUDGE

SO POOR PEDRO HAS TO ROLLER-SKATE ALL THE WAY HOME.
THAT STUPID FIGARO! IF I PASS HIM ON THE WAY, HE WON'T GET ANY LIFT FROM ME!
FIGARO'S SHACK 10 MILES

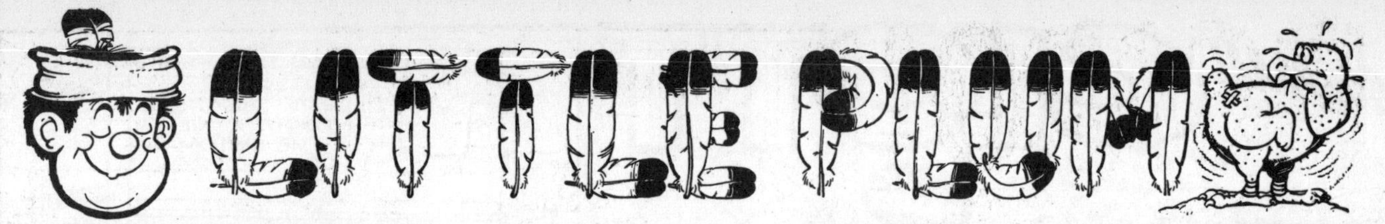
LITTLE PLUM

PHEW! WHAT UM HEATWAVE! I'D JUST LOVE TO HAVE UM NICE, COOL BATHE.

OH, BOY! – A COOL POOL! JUST WHAT I NEED!

CLASSIC BEANO
EEK!-

– UM WATER'S BOILING!
HOT SPRINGS

LATER-
AH! UM RAIN CLOUD!

I'LL TRY TO GET UNDER IT BEFORE UM RAIN STOPS.

TOO LATE! THAT'S UM LAST RAINDROP!
PLOP!
SCREECH!

LATER-
AT LAST! UM POOL OF WATER ALL TO MYSELF!

WHOOPEE!

SLURP!
SLURP!
SLURP!

HUH! UM THIRSTY BUFFALO HAVE DRUNK UM POOL DRY!

LATER-
WHAT UM LOT OF JUICY WILD PEARS!

CAN I BORROW YOUR GUN FOR UM MOMENT, PLEASE?
SURE, PLUM!

BOOM!

AHA! UM LOVELY COLD SHOWER!

CORPORAL CLOTT
CLASSIC DANDY
OUCH! THESE MOSQUITOES ARE PESTS. OOYAH!
LEAVE THEM TO ME, SIR! I'LL GET RID OF THEM!
I'LL MIX THIS DRUM OF MOSQUITO KILLER INTO THE SWIMMING POOL WATER–
BUT
HO-HO! CLOTT'S BOOBED AGAIN!
YOU CLOWN! THE HOSE IS SWELLING UP! YOU SHOULD HAVE TURNED THE PUMP OFF!
SORRY, SIR!
SUDDENLY THE HOSE BURSTS–
GROO!
HELP! MY WATCH!
MY MONEY!
HOWLING HURRICANES! THE VACUUM'S SUCKED EVERYTHING OUT OF THE OFFICERS' POCKETS! WHAT A WINDFALL!
HELP!
HELP!
IT'S NOT A WAR! IT'S A STICK-UP! CLOTT'S LEFT HIS FLY PAPERS WHERE MY SOLDIERS COULD BLUNDER INTO THEM IN THE DARK!
LATER THE GENERAL VISITS
THESE MOSQUITO
THEY DON'T SEEM
COLO

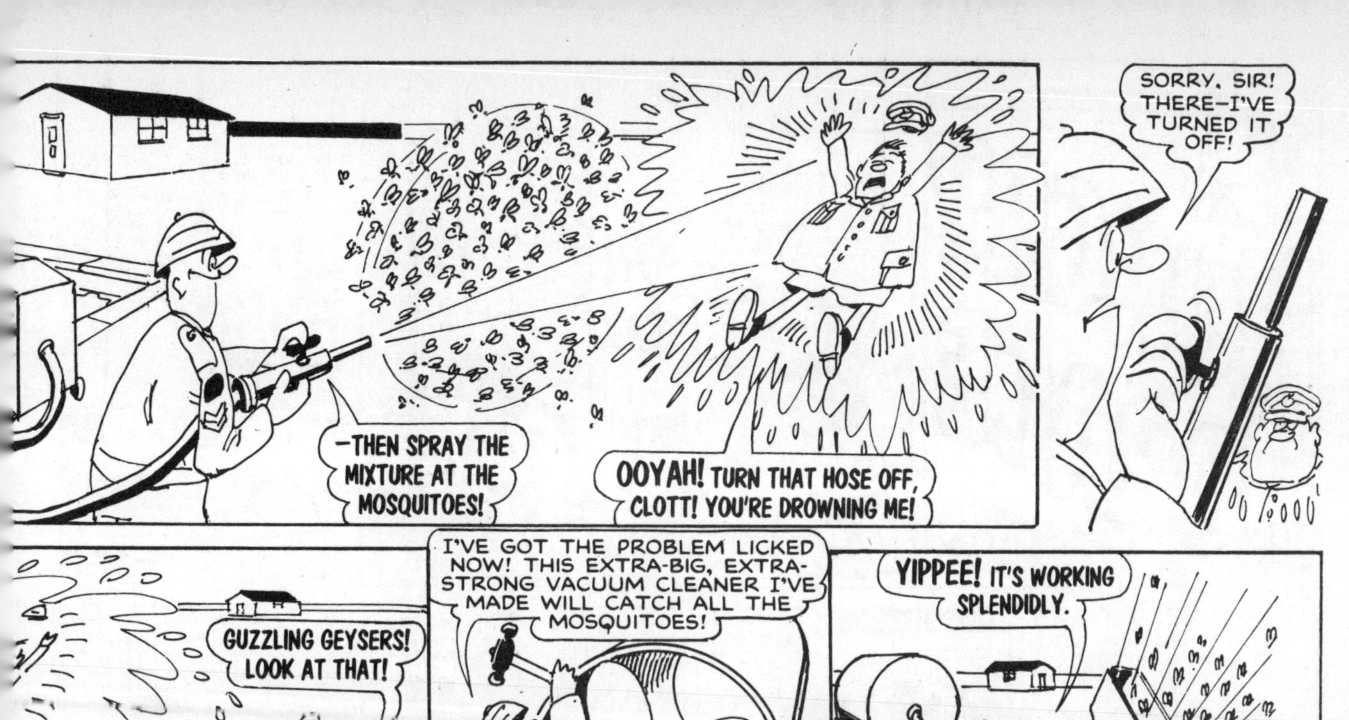
–THEN SPRAY THE MIXTURE AT THE MOSQUITOES!
OOYAH! TURN THAT HOSE OFF, CLOTT! YOU'RE DROWNING ME!
SORRY, SIR! THERE–I'VE TURNED IT OFF!

GUZZLING GEYSERS! LOOK AT THAT!
GLUG!

I'VE GOT THE PROBLEM LICKED NOW! THIS EXTRA-BIG, EXTRA-STRONG VACUUM CLEANER I'VE MADE WILL CATCH ALL THE MOSQUITOES!

YIPPEE! IT'S WORKING SPLENDIDLY.
THE MOSQUITOES ARE BEING SUCKED UP.

T RID OF THAT CONTRAPTION, LOTT! IT'S THE MOSQUITOES YOU'RE TRYING TO KILL— NOT US!

I'LL MAKE FLY PAPERS AND USE A STRONG STICKY GLUE TO CATCH THE MOSQUITOES. HEE-HEE! THEY'LL COME TO A STICKY END!

LATER THAT NIGHT
GALLOPING GUNNERS! WAR'S BROKEN OUT!
OOYAH!
HELP!

AMP.
PROPER PESTS! OTHERING YOU, Y?
BECAUSE WE'VE GOT A BIGGER PEST TO ANNOY US!

AND THERE HE IS—CORPORAL CLOTT! OPEN FIRE MEN WITH THE PEST DESTROYER! AND DON'T MISS!
GROO!

HUNGRY HORACE
CLASSIC SPARKY

GOSH! A CIRCUS! MUST GO AN' HAVE A LOOK AROUND.

SNIFF! SNIFF! WHAT'S THAT DEE-LICIOUS SMELL?

YUMMY! A HUGE POT OF STEW, 'AN' THERE'S NOBODY ABOUT! SLURP! SLOBBER!

NOBODY WOULD KNOW IF I JUS' TASTED A LITTLE BIT...

TEN MINUTES LATER—
HEY! WHAT'S GOING ON? THAT'S OUR LUNCH!
SLURP! MUNCH! OO-ER!

YOW!
WAIT A MINUTE, KOKO— COME OVER HERE. I'VE GOT AN IDEA!

RIGHT—ONE OF OUR PALS IS ILL, SO YOU CAN TAKE HIS PLACE IN THE RING!
THE AFTERNOON PERFORMANCE IS JUST STARTING.
M-ME—A CLOWN?!

REMEMBER—RUN IN WHEN YOU HEAR THE HORN. YOU'LL GET A COUPLE OF PIES ALL TO YOURSELF.
ER...OKAY!

PAR'RP!

CUSTARD PIES—! GLUG!

DON'T GO AWAY, HORACE! HAVE A BIT OF A SAUSAGE!
AW! SHAME! YOU'VE GOT FOOD ALL OVER YOU!
HA-HA-HA!
HO-HO-HO!
YOW! STOPPIT!

HO-HO-HO!
HERE, LET ME WASH IT ALL OFF FOR YOU! HAR! HAR!
HA-HA!
WAH!

HO-HO! HORACE DOESN'T SEEM TO LIKE THE WAY WE SERVE FOOD HERE! CHORTLE!

FRED the FLOP

CLASSIC BUZZ
I'm going to rob the jeweller's on these stilts. They'll never recognise me. You wait in the car for the getaway, Lefty.
Sure thing, Fred.

SO-
Yippee! What a haul! And the cops will be looking for a seven-foot tall crook!
Stop, thief!
JEWELLER

EEEK!
CRASH!

So it was you after all, Fred!
Bah!

LATER
This time I'll rob the jeweller's, looking fat! I can't fall off cushions!
Great plan, Fred.

ND SO-
Ho-ho! Not a hitch —and this time the cops will be looking for a fat thief!
JEWELLER

BUT
Time you went on a diet, mate!
Grr!
STUCK FAST!

LATER-
This time I've got the perfect disguise—I'll rob that house dressed as a coalman. You wait round the corner.
Okay, Fred!

INSIDE-
This makes a fair exchange for my coal.

A burglar!
Time I was going!
OUTSIDE-
Now for my masterstroke— to turn my clothes and the sack inside out.

Clever, eh?
MILLER FLOUR MERCHANT

Funny! There's no sign of that thieving coalman anywhere.
Here comes Fred!

Better start the car—drat that exhaust!
!
BANG!

There he is!
Grr! My disguise is ruined!

Off we go, Fred!
Grr!
There'll be a reward for helping us catch him, sir!
Hm! I think Fred's plan-er-backfired!

CLASSIC BEANO
THE BASH STREET KIDS

THE BASH STREET KIDS TORE UP MY LAWN!
-AND BROKE MY WINDOWS!
ER-TAKE THIS, DEAR LADY-IT WILL HELP TO MAKE UP FOR BEING PUSHED INTO YOUR COMPOST HEAP!
SCHOOL

SO-
YES, SOME OF YOU CAN FILL THE COAL BUCKET AND THE OTHERS CAN WASH THE WINDOWS.

LATER-
IDLE URCHINS! THAT'S NOT THE WAY TO GET THE JOB DONE.
TIRED
WEARY

I'LL SHOW YOU HOW TO WASH WINDOWS!

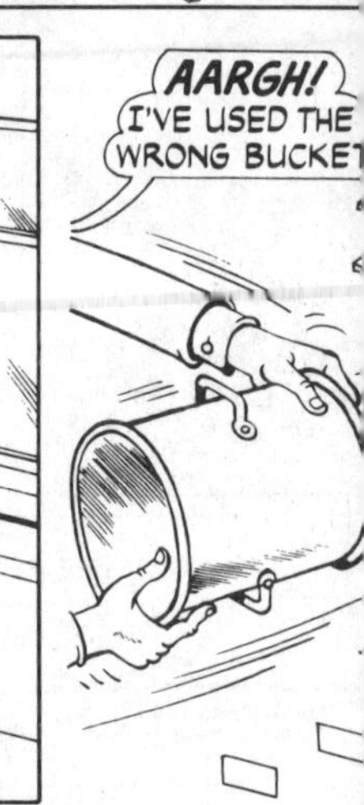
AARGH! I'VE USED THE WRONG BUCKET

LET'S GET STARTED THEN.
PRIZE DAHLIAS

HERE! THAT'S NO WAY TO GET A LAWN CUT!
TIRED
WEARY

PUT YOUR BACK INTO IT—LIKE THIS!

MUCH LATER-
AH! HERE COME THE NEIGHBOURS. NO DOUBT THEY WISH TO THANK ME FOR THE ODD-JOB SCHEME.

BUT-
RUINED MY CARPET!
THAT TEACHER FELLOW WAS THE WORST OF THE LOT!
BROKE MY WINDOWS!
TEACHER SHALL PAY FOR THIS!

TEACHER'S WAGES WILL PAY FOR THE DAMAGE!

TER–
THAT'S THE SCHOOL BANKIE EMPTY, TEACHER. SOMETHING MUST BE DONE TO RAISE MORE SCHOOL FUNDS.
WHY NOT MAKE THE KIDS DO ODD-JOBS FOR THE NEIGHBOURS? IN THAT WAY, WE'LL GET ON GOOD TERMS WITH THE DEAR FOLK AND MAKE SOME MONEY FOR THE FUNDS.

AN EXCELLENT IDEA, TEACHER, BUT CAN YOU GET THE KIDS TO WORK?
FEAR NOT, HEADMASTER. I WILL PERSONALLY SUPERVISE THE WORK.

IN CLASS II B–
CLASSIC BEANO
....AND YOU WILL WORK YOUR FINGERS TO THE BONE, OR ELSE!

CRASH!
TINKLE!

GRR! TRY TO WASH MY WINDOWS WITH COAL, WOULD YOU?

LATER–
YOU CAN BEAT MY GREEN LIVING-ROOM CARPET AND TAKE MY LAWN-MOWER DOWN TO THE IRONMONGER'S TO BE SHARPENED.

BUT–

HOW ARE YOU GETTING ON WITH MY–
SHRIEK!

GRR! YOU'VE RUINED MY CARPET!

HERE'S WHAT'S LEFT– FOURPENCE-HALFPENNY!
TEACHER'S PAY PACKET

LATER–
ANY ODD-JOBS NEEDING DONE, SIR?
COME ON, KIDS– LET'S HELP POOR TEACHER!

# SPOOFER McGRAW

HE TELLS TALL TALES

ELEPHANTS THAT FLY?

SUNNY BOY
HE'S A BRIGHT SPARK!
CLASSIC DANDY
MISS PYM AT THE KINDERGARDEN WILL KEEP SUNNY BOY OUT OF MISCHIEF WHILE WE'RE OUT SHOPPING.
HERE'S SUNNY BOY, MISS PYM.
KINDERGARTE
DEAR LITTLE BOY!
NOW, CHILDREN, YOU CAN HAVE SOME FUN WITH YOUR MODELLING CLAY.
HMM! WHY ARE THEY ALL GIGGLING AROUND SUNNY BOY?
CHUCKLE! GIGGLE!
HEE-HEE! SUNNY BOY HAS MADE A NOSE JUST LIKE YOURS, MISS PYM!
DREADFUL BOY!
SUCH IMPUDENCE! NOW YOU CAN STAND IN THE CORNER!
BAH!
THE REST OF YOU CAN DRAW PRETTY PICTURES ON YOUR BOARDS WITH THESE CRAYONS.
GOODY! SHE'S LEFT THE BOX OF CRAYONS ON THE DESK! NOW ME CAN DRAW TOO.
THIS WALL MAKES A SMASHING BIG DRAWING BOARD!
HOW DARE YOU DRAW A NASTY PICTURE OF ME ON THE WALL? YOU HORRID BOY!
BAH! SHE'S MADE ME RUB IT OUT!
HERE, CHILDREN, YOU CAN PLAY WITH THIS BOX OF TOYS.
TOYS
ME MAKE A FISHING ROD OUT OF THIS LONG RULER AND CATCH A TOY.
NOW THEN, CHILDREN— NO SQUABBLING OVER THE TOYS!
TOYS
MY WIG!
GIVE ME MY WIG BACK!
OOF!
WHOOSH!
WHAM!
I'VE HAD ENOUGH OF THIS— I'M CLEARING OUT!
EXIT
LATER
IT WAS NICE OF MISS PYM TO KEEP SUNNY BOY OUT OF MISCHIEF!
DERG
HULLO MUM! WE'RE HAVING A SMASHING TIME!
WOW!
CRASH!
PLOP!

# DOODLEBUG

CLASSIC NUTTY

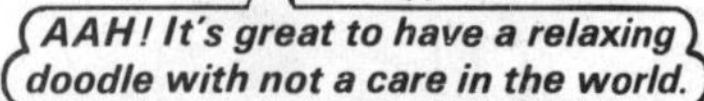
AAH! It's great to have a relaxing doodle with not a care in the world.

SUDDENLY—
BLUGH! DATES!
BLATTER!

AARGH! The DATE —I've forgotten Deedlebug's birthday. She'll be very upset.

I promised her a birthday cake. Where can I get some dough to bake it?

PSST! Dough, huh? Here, I've got a stack of the stuff.
No! You don't understand—not that kind of dough!

Er, thanks, Bugsy—I've no time to bake one now anyway. I'll buy one.
Don't mention it, Doodle. See ya later.

PRESENTLY—
Thanks, Baker Bug. This'll make a fine present.
SHUCKS! It was a piece of cake.

Deedlebug should be along soon—she WILL get a surprise!
SLURP! A CAKE!

OOYAH! You idiot, Tummy Bug!
Oo-er!
GNASH!

OUCH! Sorry, madam!
CRUMPH!
SAY IT WITH FLOWERS

Er, Happy Birthday, my sweet!
SQUEAL! You remembered, Doodlebug. How lovely!
SAY IT WITH FLOWERS
AH!
OUCH!

Little
MO

It's sports day.
WE SHOULD WIN THIS EGG AND SPOON RACE, MIRABELLE.
CLASSIC BEEZER

Just then—
YOU'RE NOT GOING IN FOR THAT RACE, ARE YOU?
YES, MUGSY. WHY?

BECAUSE I FANCY THESE BOILED EGGS, THAT'S WHY!

YOU ROTTER! NOW WE'VE MISSED THE RACE!
PEEP!

Soon after—
WE'LL ENTER FOR THE SACK RACE INSTEAD.
FIRE

But—
IT'S HOT TODAY, BUT THIS'LL HELP YOU COOL DOWN.
FIRE
SHRIEK!

GROOH! WE CAN'T USE THESE WET SACKS! WE'LL GET OTHER ONES.

HM! I'VE AN IDEA!

I'LL COLLECT SOME ANTS.

AND EMPTY THEM IN HERE!

The race starts.
HEH! I'M WINNING!

Then—
OW! WHAT'S BITING ME? AARGH! ANTS!

HELP! GET THEM OFF ME!

Mo goes on to win.
HO-HO! THAT RACE WAS A BIT OF AN "ANTI"-CLIMAX FOR MUGSY!
1ST. PRIZE.

CAPTAIN CUTLER AND HIS BUTLER
CLASSIC SPARKY

CAPTAIN CUTLER ONCE INVENTED A SYSTEM FOR SENDING ELECTRIC LIGHTS BY MAIL. HE CALLED IT A LAMP-POST! HE AND THE AMAZING CRUMBS STILL HAVEN'T FOUND THE SOURCE OF THE RIVER BUNGO—
H'MM...LOOKS LIKE A SHOWER, CRUMBS...
PERHAPS, SIR... OR PERHAPS NOT. ONE CAN NEVER BE TOO CAREFUL.

DON'T BE AN OLD WOMAN, CRUMBS! IT'S JUST A PASSING SHOWER!
WE SHALL SEE, SIR.

ER...WELL... PERHAPS YOU'RE RIGHT, CRUMBS... HARUMPH!
YES, SIR. I FREQUENTLY AM, SIR.

THEN—
CRUMBS?!? NOW WHAT ARE YOU DOING?
OUR CASES ARE UNDERWATER AND I HAVE TO GET YOUR WELLY-BOOTS, SIR.

THAT'S ALL VERY WELLY, CRUMBS, BUT MY FEET ARE UNDERWATER! THEY'RE SOAKED!
NOT TO WORRY, SIR. I SHALL LEND YOU MY SNORKEL.

THERE, SIR. YOUR FEET WILL SOON BE DRY, NOW.
GRUBBLE! CRUMBS! THERE ARE TIMES WHEN I WONDER ABOUT YOU!

WHAT DO YOU WISH TO DO NOW, SIR?
FOLLOW ME, CRUMBS! IF THESE FLOODS GET ANY DEEPER, THE RIVER BUNGO WILL BE UNDER WATER AND WE'LL NEVER FIND THE SOURCE!

BUT BE CAREFUL, CRUMBS! IT'S GETTING DEEPER!
MIGHT I SUGGEST WE WALK TO THE LEFT, SIR?
OH? WHY?

YOU HAD US WALKING DOWN THE RIVER BUNGO, SIR. IT MIGHT BE A LITTLE DRIER ON LAND?
OH, CRUMBS, CRUMBS!

AND ANOTHER THING, CRUMBS— I'M HUNGRY—BUT HOW ARE WE GOING TO EAT?
NOT TO WORRY, SIR. I HAVE THOUGHT OF THAT, TOO.

WATER-MELON, SIR? WITH A LITTLE WATER-CRESS AND SOME WATER CHESTNUTS?
FANTASTIC! WAT-ER BUTLER!

BUT, OUTSIDE-

IS IT GOING OFF? NO, IT'S NOT...CRUMBS, REMIND ME AGAIN WHAT THE SUN LOOKS LIKE?

I SEEM TO RECALL A LARGE YELLOW ROUND THING, SIR. IT GAVE WARMTH, SIR, AND HELPED LIGHT THE DAY...

TEDDY
the Three Bears
PA
MA
CLASSIC BEANO

HURRY UP WITH THE SOUP, MA! SLURP!
ALMOST READY, PA!

SOUP IS SERVED, SIR!
AHH!—SLOOP!

BUT—
YUGH! IT TASTES LIKE DISH WATER!

I'M OFF TO HANK HUCKLEBERRY'S VEGETABLE PATCH TO GET SOME LEEKS. I'LL HAVE SOME TASTY SOUP LIKE MY MOTHER USED TO MAKE.
BEARS' CAVE

BUT—
GRRR!
GOOD! THERE'S NO SIGN OF HANK!

HEH! HEH! MY CAMOUFLAGE FOOLED HIM!
NOW TO HELP MYSELF TO A LOAD OF LEEKS!

HANDS UP, PA!
ERK! HANK! I'M OFF!

SNIGGER! THIS SOUP POT MAKES SUPER ARMOUR!
BAH!
BAM!

BACK AT THE CAVE—
TO MAKE REALLY TASTY SOUP—

—YOU MUST HAVE PLENTY OF LEEKS, TED!
SPLASH!

HAW! HAW! IT SHOULD BE GOOD SOUP, PA—THERE ARE PLENTY OF LEAKS IN IT!
GRR! YOU'VE RUINED MY GOOD SOUP POT!

LATER, WHEN THICK HEAD HAS RECOVERED HIS DIGNITY—

GR-R-R! THE LITTLE MONSTER! BUT I'M NOT LICKED YET! I'LL STEAM THE BRUTE OUT WITH THIS ELECTRIC KETTLE!

TINGLE

HISS-S-S

COUGH! COUGH!

MEANWHILE THICK HEAD'S NEXT DOOR NEIGHBOUR, MR GRUMP, IS JUST ADMIRING THE NEW WALLPAPER HE'S HAD PUT UP AT ENORMOUS COST.

THFRF WILL NOW BE A FORTNIGHT'S INTERVAL, WHILE THICK HEAD HAS HIS BUSTED BONCE ATTENDED TO IN THE ACCIDENT HOSPITAL, BY A BONCE-FIXER!

WHILE FIVE MILES BACK—

FOXY
CLASSIC TOPPER
Y'KNOW, FOLKS, IF YOU ASKED ME TO NAME THE GREATEST OF ALL INVENTIONS, I'D SAY...
THE BALLOON!
BUT THERE ARE BALLOONS...
AND BALLOONS! I NEED A GIANT ONE.
AN' WITH IT I CAN PICK UP A CHICK OR TWO!
FIRST, OF COURSE, I'VE GOT TO GET IT BLOWN UP. BUT IN THESE DAYS OF AUTOMATION, YOU DON'T DO IT YOURSELF...
YOU USE A CYLINDER OF COMPRESSED AIR...
F-SSSS
F-SSSS
AN' JUST SIT BACK AN' WATCH!
F-SSSS
BUT...
BAH! THERE'S NOT ENOUGH AIR TO BLOW IT UP!
I'LL JUST HAVE TO FINISH IT MYSELF!
DEEP BREATH!
ONE GOOD BLOW...
F-S-S-S
GASP
WHAT STUPID CLOWN INVENTED BALLOONS?
W
S
N
E

DENNIS THE MENACE
CLASSIC BEANO
DAD, IT'S MY BIRTHDAY NEXT WEEK. CAN I HAVE A PARTY?
NO!
AW, WHY NOT?
BECAUSE YOU RUIN EVERY PARTY YOU GO TO!
I LIKE PLAYING BLIND-MAN'S "BIFF"!
BIFF!
BIFF!
REMEMBER SPOTTY PERKINS' PARTY?—
TRIFLE
—AND WALTER'S PARTY?
DAD, PLEASE LET ME HAVE A PARTY! I PROMISE TO BE GOOD!
NO, I SAID! NO! NO! NO! NO!
DAD, AREN'T YOU BEING TOO STRICT? LET HIM HAVE HIS PARTY!
OH, VERY WELL THEN!
THE DAY OF THE PARTY—
OH, BOY! WHAT A FEED I'M GOING TO HAVE!
WILL YOU HAVE SOME TRIFLE, DENNIS?
I WILL, WALTER, BOY!
AND HE DOES!
OOOH! I'VE SLIPPED!
PLONK!
AFTER "EATS"—BLIND MAN'S BUFF—
SKINNY JONES
AH! SKINNY JONES—
—GOT YOU!
CRACK!
SOON THE PARTY'S OVER—
BYE-BYE, BOYS.
TA-TA, DENNIS! THANKS FOR INVITING US.
WHEN DENNIS RECOVERS—
DAD, PROMISE NEVER TO GIVE ME A PARTY AGAIN!
EH?

NERO and ZERO

Where will we go for our holidays this year?

CLASSIC BUZZ
What about going back to Pisa-on-Sea?
PISA-ON-SEA
Not on your life! Remember what happened when we went there two years ago . . .

Come back with my royal candy floss, you rotters!

WOW!

YEOW!
THUD!
SLIDE

I bent their lovely tower and ended up in hospital!

Let's go abroad again! The Palace Hotel at Stonehenge is a nice place!

PALACE HOTEL
We can't go back there! Remember when we were last there . . .

BOYNGGGGG
Ooh! I love to ring the dinner gong!

RUMBLE!
CRASH!
PALACE HOTEL
Look out!
Help!

There's only a ruin there now. We all ended up in hospital that year!

Ah, well! We'll just go down to Pudsea-on-the-Tiber. It's quiet there!
Not on your life, Caesar!
We want a proper holiday!

Pudsea-on-the-Tiber and like it!
No! No!

PUDSEA-ON-THE-TIBER!
No! No! Thrice no!

WHUMP!
WALLOP!
CLONK!
WHACK!

GROAN!

Bah! We should have guessed! It's the usual holiday—in bed, in bandages, in hospital!

Billy Whizz
AH, YES, I REMEMBER WHEN I WAS A BOY I USED TO GO DOWN TO THE DOCKS TO WATCH THE SHIPS—IT'S SO RESTFUL THERE.

WHY DON'T YOU DO THAT, BIL...?
GOOD IDEA!

MINUTES LATER—
DAD WAS RIGHT—IT IS RESTFUL HERE.
CLASSIC BEANO

AND THE SEA BREEZE MUST BE DOING ME GOOD—I FEEL AS IF I'M WALKING ON AIR!

ULP! I AM WALKING ON AIR!

I CAN'T CLIMB BACK ON TO THE PIER—I'LL SWIM FOR THAT WARSHIP.

TORPEDO OFF THE STARBOARD BEAM!
GUESS WHO!
NONSENSE!—EEK! HE'S RIGHT! HARD TO PORT!

HARD TO PORT IT IS, SIR!
HEY! WHERE ARE THEY OFF TO?

HELP! THE TORPEDO'S FOLLOWING US!

TREMENDOUS CRUNCH!

HUH! I'M NOT GOING ABOARD A SHIP WITH A CRAZY CAPTAIN—I'LL HEAD FOR ONE OF THE SHIPS MOORED IN THE HARBOUR.
GOOD! A LADDER!

WHIZZ

OUCH! I CLIMBED TOO FAST!
FOR EMERGENCY ONLY—BREAK GLASS TO SOUND ALARM
CRASH!
ZIP!

IT'S THE ALARM! ABANDON SHIP!
OVER THE SIDE, LADS!
EVERYBODY OUT!
HOOT! HOOT! HOOT!

LATER—
WELL, DID YOU FIND THE DOCKS RESTFUL, BILLY?
YES, DAD—

—BUT THESE GENTLEMEN DIDN'T!
GRR!
FUME
MUTTER!

Pansy Potter
THE STRONGMAN'S DAUGHTER

CLASSIC SPARKY
COO! GREAT SHOW, THIS, EH, PANSY?
NOT HALF, PA! I LIKE "STARS ON TUESDAY"!

HEY! WHY DID YOU SWITCH OFF, MA?
YOU WON'T HAVE TIME TO WATCH IT — THAT'S WHY!
CLICK!

I'M GOING TO SPRING-CLEAN THIS ROOM, STARTING WITH THE CARPET— SO I WANT EVERYTHING OUT!
AW, BUT WE'LL MISS "STARS ON TUESDAY!"
HUMPH!

I'LL SOON FIX THIS!

PANSY! WH-WHAT ARE YOU GOING TO D-DO?
DON'T WORRY, PA—JUST LEAVE THIS TO ME!

A-ONE, A-TWO, A...

...THREE!
TUG!
OOH! I DAREN'T LOOK!

HERE Y'ARE, MA — ONE CARPET!

NOW THEN...

HUH! HE'S NOT A PATCH ON YOU, PANSY!
AW, SHUCKS!

# The Beano

CLASSIC BEANO

## BIFFO THE BEAR

# THE SMASHER

CLASSIC DANDY

OH, GOSH! MUM'S GONE OFF WITHOUT THE WHITE ELEPHANT SHE WAS TO TAKE TO HER WHITE ELEPHANT STALL AT THE BAZAAR! I'LL RUN AFTER HER WITH IT.

MUM! MUM! YOU'VE LEFT YOUR WHITE ELEPHANT BEHIND!

OH, SMASHER! YOU CLUMSY FOOL! NOW I'VE NO WHITE ELEPHANT!
CRASH
OOPS!
TRIP

LATER
WHAT ARE YOU LOOKING FOR, SMASHER?
A WHITE ELEPHANT! WHAT D'YOU THINK?

AH! THERE'S ONE IN THAT PRAM! I'LL BORROW IT!

OUCH!
GRR!

HEY, SMASHER! I'VE GOT A WHITE ELEPHANT!

MA SAYS THIS WOODEN LEG IS A PROPER WHITE ELEPHANT—IT'S NO USE TO HER!
THAT'S NOT A REAL WHITE ELEPHANT, IDIOT! IT'S NO USE TO ME EITHER!

I'LL NEVER GET A WHITE ELEPHANT!

ZONK

YIPPEE! AN ELEPHANT ALL ON ITS OWN!
DAZED

JUMBLE
BAZAAR
ODDMENTS
YOO-HOO, MUM! —I'VE GOT YOU A WHITE ELEPHANT! ISN'T IT A SMASHER?
OH, NO!
FRUIT
CAKE STALL

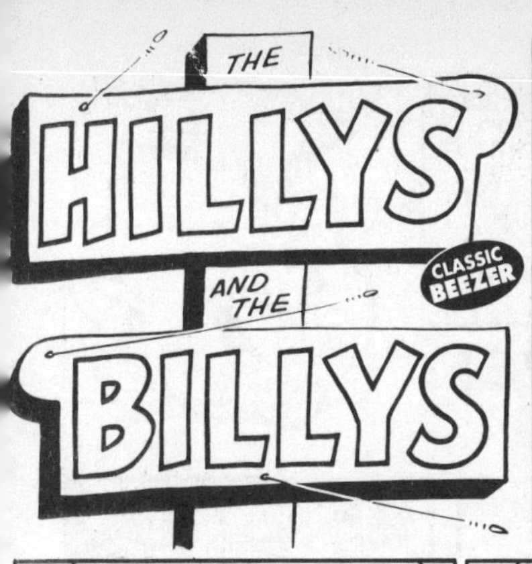
THE
HILLYS
AND THE
BILLYS
CLASSIC BEEZER

PAW HILLY—ARMED TO THE TOOTH—IS LEADING HIS BAND ON A SURPRISE RAID AGAINST THE BILLYS.
QUIET, LADS! WE'RE GOIN' T'GIVE THEM THAR BILLYS A NASTY SHOCK!

HOLD IT RIGHT THERE, YOU HILLYS! I'M THE NEW SHERIFF O' DEADVILLE AN' I'M GOIN' T'CUT OUT THIS FEUDIN'!

THE BILLYS ARE ALSO UP IN ARMS.
SSH, LADS! WE'LL SOON BE GIVIN' THEM HILLYS A TOUCH O' LEAD POISONIN'!

DROP THEM SHOOTIN' IRONS, YOU BILLYS! I'M THE NEW DEPITTY!
OH, NO!

BAH!
THAT'S WHAT I CALL A GOOD HAUL, DEPITTY!
'TAIN'T FAIR!

THEY'VE TOOK ALL OUR SHOOTIN' IRONS AN' WE CAN'T EVEN RUSTLE UP A PEA-SHOOTER BETWEEN US!

THE BILLYS ARE IN THE SAME PLIGHT.
BAH! NOT EVEN A CAP GUN LEFT!

A CRISIS LIKE THIS BRINGS THE HILLYS AND THE BILLYS TOGETHER
FEUDIN'S THE ONLY FUN WE GET OUTA LIFE! LET'S GO AN' BUY MORE GUNS!
YEAH!

LATER—IN DEADVILLE
GUNSMITH
HOPE YOU FOLKS AIN'T CONSIDERIN' BUYIN' MORE GUNS, COS THIS GUNSMITH IS OUTA BOUNDS TO YOU HILLYS AN' BILLYS! YOU'LL HAVE T'THINK O' SOME OTHER GAME!
SPOILSPORTS!

ANOTHER GAME? WHY, OF COURSE! C'MON! LET'S GO TO TH' SPORTS STORE!
?

WE'RE GOIN' T' TAKE YORE ADVICE, SHERIFF—WE'RE GOIN' T'PLAY A NICE FRIEN'LY GAME O' TENNIS!
YEAH—NICE AN' FRIEN'LY!
WELL! WELL! MY LITTLE SCHEME WORKED!

BACK IN HAPPY VALLEY . . .
LUCKY WE STILL HAD THIS KEG O' GUNPOWDER T' FILL THE BALLS WITH! HEH! HEH!

HULLO? WHAT'S ALL THAT BANGIN' COMIN' FROM HAPPY VALLEY?
SURE IS A NOISY GAME O' TENNIS!
BANG!
BANG!
BANG!
BANG!

BANG!
BANG!
BANG!
BANG!
BANG!

FASTER! FASTER!

YOU'VE JES' MISSED A WUNNERFUL GAME O' POWER TENNIS, SHERIFF! HEH! HEH!
YEAH! REAL LOV'LY!

# BIG-HEAD BRANNY

CLASSIC CRACKER

...HE CRASHES THROUGH THE MUSIC ROOM DOOR...

...AND, WITH A GOGGLE-EYED GURGLE, CONTINUES ON THROUGH THE SCHOOL WALL!

CRASH!

ARRGH! GIBBER! GURGLE!

MUSIC LOVERS WILL NOTE THAT THE SPECIALLY REINFORCED GRAND PIANO IS COMPLETELY UNHARMED...

SORRY WE CAN'T SAY THE SAME FOR BRANNY!

I BET SOME OF YOU 'ORRIBLE READERS ARE HOPING TO SEE BRANNY SPIFLICATE HIMSELF ON THE ROCKS BELOW!

ZOOOM!

ARGH! IT'S GOING TOO FAST! I'M FRIGHTENED TO JUMP OFF!

DANGER 200ft. DROP

HARD LUCK, MATES! THE TIDE'S IN!

ARGH! GLOOP!

SPLOSH!

Dirty DICK
I'VE ALWAYS WANTED TO BE ON THE TELLY, SO I'LL GET A NICE TAN AND APPLY FOR THE JOB!
WANTED
SUN-TANNED BOY TO TAKE PART IN T.V. FILM
APPLY:
CLASSIC DANDY
Z-Z-Z!
OHO! SO DIRTY DICK IS TRYING TO GET SUNBURNT AND GET ON THE TELLY SAME AS US, JIMMY!
HUH, WE'LL MAKE SURE HE DOESN'T. LET'S SET FIRE TO HIS DAD'S GARDEN RUBBISH!
LUCKY THE WIND'S IN THE RIGHT DIRECTION! HO-HO!
COUGH! COUGH! SPLUTTER!
HEY! LOOK, JIMMY! DICK'S STILL TRYING TO GET SUNBURNT!
SEE HIM OFF, TOWSER!
GROWL!
HO HO HO!
SNARL!
IF I DON'T MAKE THE FENCE IN TIME, I'LL GET BITTEN INSTEAD OF TANNED!
GRR-R!
PHEW! I GOT CLEAN AWAY-ER, MORE OR LESS!
THEY'LL NEVER FIND ME IN THE GREENHOUSE!
WHAT DO WE DO NOW, JIMMY?
WELL, WE CAN'T SEEM TO STOP DICK SUNBATHING, BUT WE CAN MAKE SURE HE DOESN'T GET A GOOD TAN. LISTEN, AS SOON AS HE FALLS ASLEEP WE'LL SLIP THIS OLD MEAT DISH COVER OVER HIS BONCE!
LATER ~
DICK! WHATEVER HAS HAPPENED TO YOUR FACE? I'D BETTER TAKE YOU TO THE HOSPITAL AT ONCE!
I WAS ONLY TRYING TO GET NICELY SUN-TANNED, DOCTOR, WHEN SOMEBODY PLAYED A TRICK ON ME!
WELL, IF ALL YOU WANT IS A PERFECT TAN, MY LAD, JUST FOLLOW ME!
YOU'LL SOON HAVE THE FINEST TAN IN TOWN, DICK!
SUN-RAY LAMP ROOM
LATER ~
AW, NO! JUST LOOK AT DIRTY DICK, JIMMY!
UGH! GREETINGS, PALEFACES! — I GOT THE JOB!
GRR!

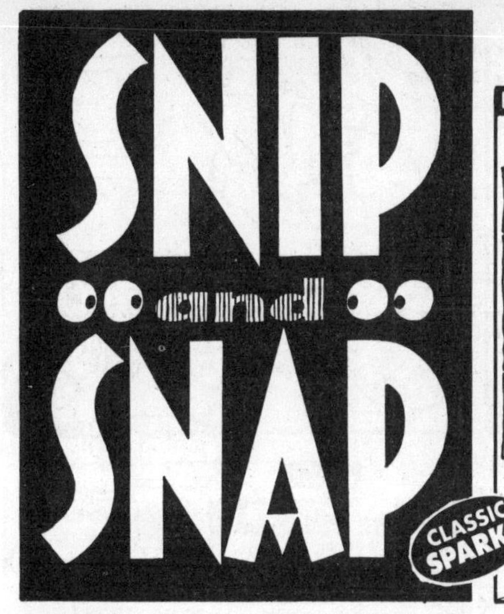
SNIP and SNAP
CLASSIC SPARKY

POSTIE'S AFTERNOON OFF—
PLAZA
TODAY
TEX FRITTER AS THE LONE STRANGER
PONY EXPRESS
BOYSOBOYS! THAT FILM'S GIVEN ME A GREAT IDEA!

NEXT DAY—
IS HE COMING YET, SNAP? RIZZLE!
ANY MINUTE NOW— ZZZ!

SUDDENLY—
YIP! YIP! HEIGH-HO DOBBIN, AWA-A-A-Y! YIPPEE!
LOOK OUT!
YEEK!

HO-HO! THAT SURE FIXED THOSE VARMINTS! THE LONE STRANGER NEVER FAILS!
MOAN!

LATER—
OOH! WHOSE IDEA WAS IT TO JUMP IN A ROSE-BUSH? RIZZLE!
YOURS! RIZZLE!
MOAN! POSTIE WILL PAY DEARLY FOR THIS!

AND SO—
WHERE ARE WE GOING, SNAP?
TO GET THAT OLD HAMMOCK OUT OF THE ATTIC!
MMM! GOOD THINKING, SNAP!

THAT WAS A GOOD IDEA, SNAP! THIS IS MOST COMFORTABLE—I FEEL BETTER ALREADY. ZZZZZ!
FOR GOODNESS SAKE...
GET OUT OF IT!
HEY...!

THAT HAMMOCK IS A CUNNING POSTIE-TRAP, SNIP!
HMM! I DON'T SEE HOW...

SECOND DELIVERY!
YIP! YIP! HUP AND OVER, DOBBIN!

GULP!
!
CHARGE!

MOAN! ANOTHER GOOD IDEA BITES TH' DUST! GROAN! MOAN!
GLOOM!
THROB! THROB!
ACHE! ACHE!

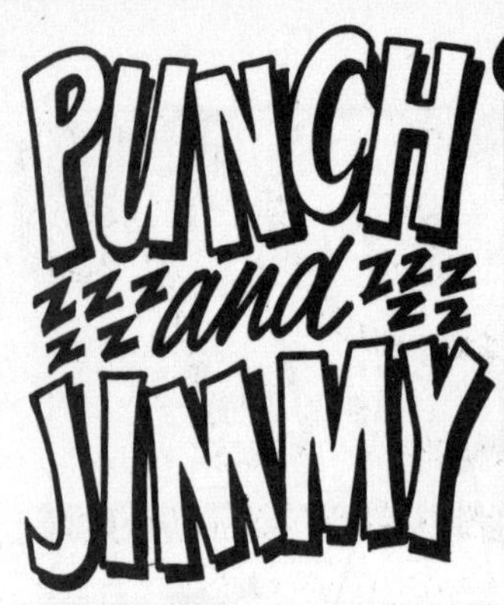
PUNCH
ZZZ and ZZZ
JIMMY

CLASSIC BEANO
They've been fighting all day, but I'm going to put a stop to it ~ NOW!

TIME FOR BED! Off you go, both of you!

15 MINUTES LATER ~
Slumber gently, boys ~ good night!

They're both sound asleep.

BUT ~
Bet I was sounder than you!
Never! I was soundest!

BIFF!
THUMP!
THUD!
WALLOP!

What's going on? Why aren't you asleep?
We're not sleepy!

Well, try counting sheep.
OK, Mum. We'll try it.

Baaa! I can jump higher than you!
Rubbish! I'm the best jumper! Baaa!
ONE!
TWO!
THREE!
FOUR!

My sheep was jumping higher than yours!
Rot! My sheep jumped the best!

3 a.m.
Your more tired than me!
No, I'm not! Your the tiredest!

NEXT MORNING ~
Boys! Boys! Wake up! It's time for school!
SNORE!

What a life! First I couldn't get them to sleep! Now I can't get them to waken!
Z Z Z Z Z Z

# The Topper

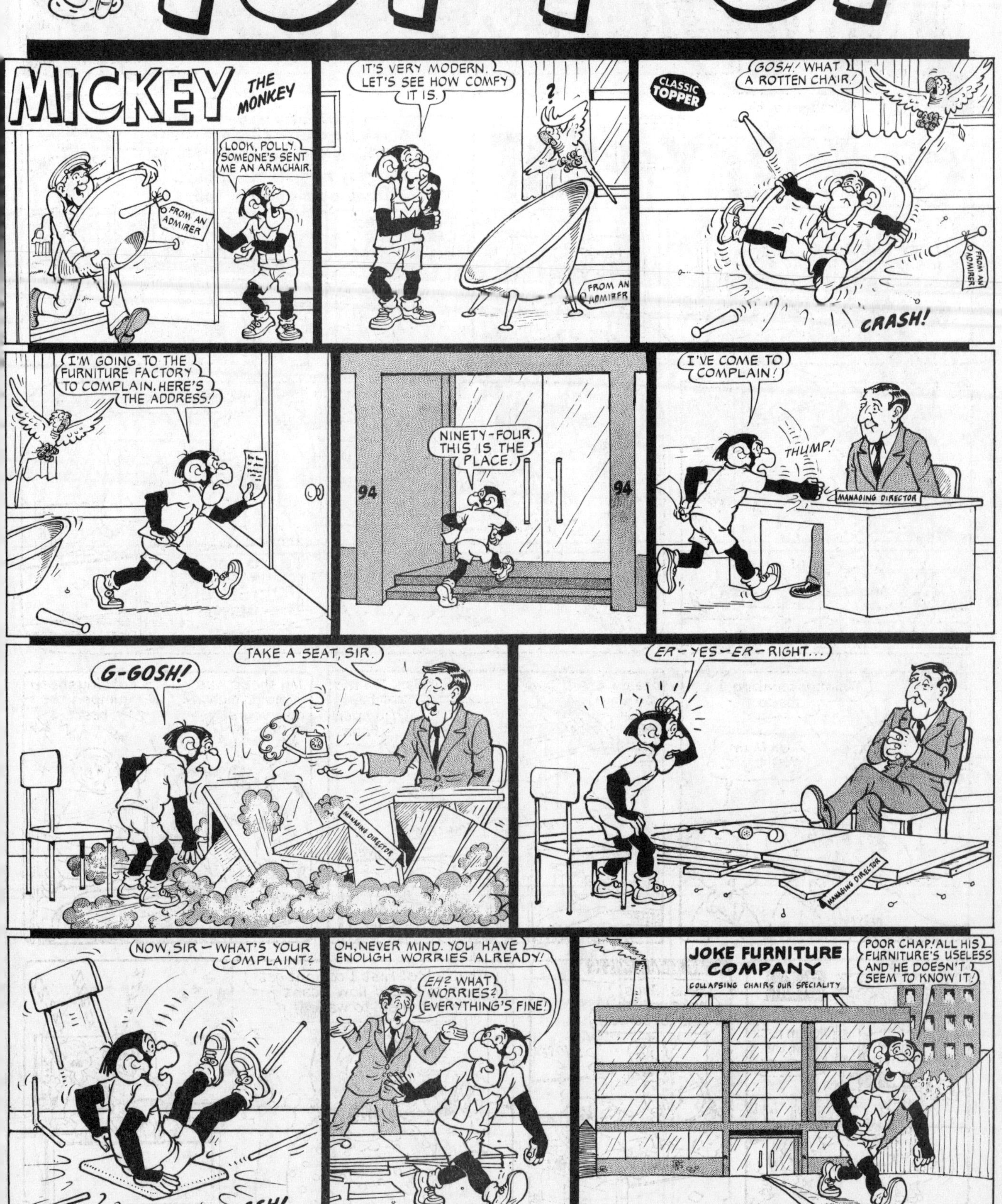

MICKEY THE MONKEY
LOOK, POLLY. SOMEONE'S SENT ME AN ARMCHAIR.
FROM AN ADMIRER
IT'S VERY MODERN. LET'S SEE HOW COMFY IT IS.
?
FROM AN ADMIRER
CLASSIC TOPPER
GOSH! WHAT A ROTTEN CHAIR!
FROM AN ADMIRER
CRASH!
I'M GOING TO THE FURNITURE FACTORY TO COMPLAIN. HERE'S THE ADDRESS!
NINETY-FOUR. THIS IS THE PLACE.
94
94
I'VE COME TO COMPLAIN!
THUMP!
MANAGING DIRECTOR
TAKE A SEAT, SIR.
G-GOSH!
MANAGING DIRECTOR
ER—YES—ER—RIGHT...
MANAGING DIRECTOR
NOW, SIR—WHAT'S YOUR COMPLAINT?
CRASH!
OH, NEVER MIND. YOU HAVE ENOUGH WORRIES ALREADY!
EH? WHAT WORRIES? EVERYTHING'S FINE!
JOKE FURNITURE COMPANY
COLLAPSING CHAIRS OUR SPECIALITY
POOR CHAP! ALL HIS FURNITURE'S USELESS AND HE DOESN'T SEEM TO KNOW IT!

# KORKY THE CAT

Korky's a crafty keeper
Who is sure to raise a laugh,
The way he gets his duties
Done by his animal staff!

!
JONAH
CLASSIC BEANO
THE JOLLOP BANK RADIO TELESCOPE IS PICKING UP STRANGE SIGNALS FROM OUTER SPACE....
PROFESSOR BULGEBRANE! QUICK!—IT'S THOSE NOISES AGAIN!
BLOOP! BLEEP! BLUP!
SOUNDS LIKE AN AMERICAN EARTH-SATELLITE BLOWING RASPBERRIES—IN RUSSIAN!
OR IT COULD BE CAUSED BY SOMETHING FIENDISHLY INHUMAN!
KAWK! KAWK!
THE ASSISTANT'S LAST GUESS WAS MORE ACCURATE.
BLOOP! BLEEP! BLUP!
JONAH IS ABOARD THE S.S. "ASTRAL"—FLOATING IN SPACE BECAUSE ITS CARGO, A SPACE-SHIP OWNED BY AN AMERICAN FILM PRODUCER, "SOMEHOW" GOT INFLATED!
BLOOP-BLEEP-BLUP!
MEANWHILE, IN THE CAPTAIN'S QUARTERS, THE CAPTAIN IS IN A TRANCE AND BELIEVES HIS SHIP IS STILL AFLOAT!
THIS SHIP SHALL NO' GO DOON!
I CAN'T MAKE HEAD NOR TAIL OF IT!
BLEEP! BLOOP! BLUP!
BLOOP! BLEEP! BLUP! IT'S ENOUGH TO DRIVE YOU UP THE WALL!
MEANWHILE, IN AMERICA, HERMAN SCHULTZ RECORDS A MESSAGE TO BE BROADCAST TO THE WORLD—
—THIS IS HERMAN SCHULTZ! PRODUCER OF FICTION FILMS LTD.! —I'VE BIN TOLD THAT THE S.S. "ASTRAL," WITH OUR BLOW-UP SPACE-SHIP ABOARD, HAS VANISHED INTO THIN AIR—HALF WAY ACROSS THE ATLANTIC!
WE CAN'T MAKE OUR FILM UNTIL IT'S RECOVERED! THE HOLD-UP IS COSTING US THOUSANDS OF DOLLARS! —SO I'M OFFERING A 5,000 DOLLAR REWARD FOR THE RECOVERY OF THAT SPACE-SHIP! I REPEAT,—
PRODUCER
A $5000 REWARD!
COO!
RADIO ROOM
HERE'S WHERE I GET RICH QUICK!
GALLEY
JONAH PULLS HIMSELF UP THE HOSE TO THE BELLY OF THE GAS-FILLED SPACE-SHIP, AND—
JAB
BANG!
WHOOO-OOSH
OH, HECK!
GRAVITATIONAL PULL
THIS SHIP SHALL NO' GO—
DOON
MEANWHILE, ON THE BANKS OF THE CLYDE, HISTORY IS IN THE MAKING—
IMPERISHABLE
B.B.C.
I NAME THIS SHIP "IMPERISHABLE".
TINKLE
—IN A FEW MOMENTS, THE WORLD'S FIRST ATOM-POWERED LINER WILL SLIDE GRACEFULLY DOWN THE SLIPWAY!
LADY DOOLITTLE HAS BROKEN THE BOTTLE OF CHAMPAGNE.
WOT'S THAT NOISE IN THE SKY, RON?
BBC
IT SOUNDS LIKE A DIVE-BOMBER!
—AND NOW SHE'S AFLOAT!
HOO-RAY! HOO-RAY! HOO-RAY!
I-IT'S GETTIN' LOUDER, RON! IT'S A REGULAR EAR-SPLITTIN' SHRIEK —!?!!—
EE-E-E-E
B.B.C.
SUFFERIN' COD-FISH!
EE-E-E-E-E
EE-E-E-E
S.S. ASTRAL
I'M SEEIN' THINGS!
BLIMEY!
AGH-H!
WHOOO-OOSH!
BOOM
£5,000,000
SO PERISHETH THE "IMPERISHABLE"!
COR! I ONLY HOPE THEY DON'T HAPPEN TO GLANCE UP HERE!
THIS SHIP SHALL NO' GO DOON!—
N W E S

We are the.....
LET ME SHOW YOU A GOOD SNAP!
It can't be true! The winner is...WHO?!?
SPARKY PEOPLE
LOOK AT THIS SUPER CAMERA I'VE GOT! IT GIVES YOU INSTANT PICTURES!
COO! YOU CAN TAKE ONE OF ME IF YOU LIKE!
AND ME!
CLASSIC SPARKY
GLEAM!
SOON—
I SAY! IT'S COME OUT RATHER WELL!
NEVER REALISED HOW HANDSOME I AM!
HUH! MAKES ME LOOK FAT!
SMILE, PLEASE!

SIR'S VOICE
WHAT'S GOING ON IN THERE? STOP GOSSIPING AND GET BACK TO WORK!
S-SORRY, SIR! I WAS JUST TAKING EVERYBODY'S PICTURE!

OH! IN THAT CASE YOU CAN TAKE ONE OF ME! I'M HANDSOME, I AM!
IT WILL BE AN HONOUR, SIR! SAY GORGONZOLA!
I THINK HE MEANS CHEESE!

LATER, AT TEA BREAK—
LOOK AT THIS! A FILM COMPANY IS HAVING A COMPETITION TO FIND A NEW STAR!
I FANCY BEING A FILM STAR!
LET'S SEND IN THESE PICTURES THAT I TOOK! MAYBE THEY'LL PICK ONE OF US!
BREAD AND DRIPPING

A WEEK LATER—
IS THIS THE SPARKY OFFICE? I'M FROM THE FILM COMPANY!
SPARKY
GOSH! ONE OF US MUST HAVE WON!

WHICH ONE OF US IS IT? H'MM?
OOH! SAY IT'S ME!
WAIT! I'LL SHOW YOU THE WINNER'S PHOTO!

THAT'S THE CHAP WE'RE INTERESTED IN!
IT CAN'T BE!
THAT'S SIR!

AHA! I HEARD THAT! COME INTO MY OFFICE MY GOOD MAN, AND WE'LL TALK ABOUT THIS!
YOU'LL BE GREAT IN THE PART!

WHAT? YOU WANT ME TO DO WHAT?
EDITOR
OO-ER!
SIR DOESN'T SOUND AT ALL PLEASED!

OUT! AND NEVER DARKEN MY OFFICE AGAIN!
BLAM!

EDITOR
SLAM!
HE'S NUTS! TURNED DOWN THE STAR PART IN OUR NEW FILM — THE THING FROM THE NIGHTMARE SWAMP!
HORROR FILMS, LTD.
HO! HO! HO!

MINNIE THE MINX
CLASSIC BEANO

CAN I HAVE SOME MONEY TO GO TO THE CINEMA, DEAREST DAD?
WELL, I MIGHT CONSIDER IT. BUT FIRST I WANT YOU TO GO AND FETCH OUR GRANDFATHER'S CLOCK...

BUT, MINNIE!
I'LL HAVE TO HURRY! THE BIG PICTURE STARTS IN HALF AN HOUR.
ZOOM!

HMM! NO SIGN OF GRANDPA. BUT THERE'S THE CLOCK. I'LL JUST TAKE IT.

I HAVEN'T GOT A MINUTE TO LOSE. I'LL SKATE ALONG INSIDE THE CLOCK.
I WONDER WHAT THE TIME IS, ETHEL?

IT'S FIVE MINUTES TO TWO, MADAM!
EEK!
SHRIEK!

LATER -
ZOOM!
HELP!

HILL TERRACE
JEWELLER
SALE OF TRAVELLING CLOCKS
TIME TO GET MY BEARINGS. GOOD! - I'LL SOON BE HOME!

JEWELLER
SALE OF TRAVELLING CLOCKS
HOW'S THIS FOR A TRAVELLING CLOCK, GENTS?

WHAT? - AARGH!
WHIZZ!

AH, ALMOST THERE!

HEH! HEH! THANK GOODNESS THE GATE WAS OPEN!

THUD!
OOYAH!

ER, HELLO, DAD! CAN I HAVE THAT MONEY FOR THE CINEMA, NOW?
CRASH!
THUMP!

GRR! THAT'S GRANDPA'S CLOCK! I MEANT YOU TO COLLECT OUR OWN GRANDFATHER'S CLOCK FROM THE JEWELLER, WHERE IT WAS BEING REPAIRED! HOW ARE WE GOING TO KNOW THE TIME NOW?
I KNOW WHAT THE TIME IS, DAD-

- IT'S TIME I WASN'T HERE!
GRR!

Splodge
THE LAST OF THE GOBLINS
CLASSIC TOPPER
OH, BOY! WE'RE GETTING LOTS OF PICNIC PARTIES IN THE FOREST THESE DAYS.
MARVELLOUS PLACE FOR A PICNIC, THIS. I'LL HAVE ANOTHER HAM SANDWICH, MOTHER!
AH, YES...
...THERE'S NO DOUBT ABOUT IT...
...THIS IS A WONDERFUL SPOT!
HEY! MY HAM— IT'S GONE!
GONE? DON'T BE RIDICULOUS, DAD. IT COULDN'T HAVE!
BUT IT HAS, I TELL YOU. LOOK!
HEH! HEH! I HOPE THERE'S A LITTLE MUSTARD ON IT!
MUNCH
I CAN GET AWAY WITH THINGS LIKE THAT 'COS NO HUMAN CAN SEE ME...
...ER...EXCEPT YOU READERS, OF COURSE.
HEY! DO YOU REALISE HOW LUCKY YOU ARE? YOU'RE THE ONLY HUMANS WHO CAN SEE ME!
I'M NOT SURE I LIKE BEING LOOKED AT, EITHER!
NO HAWKERS
SPLODGE
IN FACT I'M CERTAIN I DON'T!
SPLODGE
WHAT WE NEED IS A LITTLE PRIVACY AROUND HERE!
THERE—THAT'S BETTER! NOW I CAN SEE YOU BUT YOU CAN'T SEE ME!

The SMASHER
ARGH!
HO-HO! SHOWERY TODAY, EH?
GROO!
SWERVE!

ER... WE GOT SOAKED BY SMASHER, SARGE!
YOU'RE A USELESS PAIR! NOW YOU'LL HAVE TO GO HOME AND CHANGE!

POLICE STATION
I'LL TEACH THAT SMASHER A LESSON MYSELF!
CLASSIC DANDY
WANTED
REWARD
THE SERGEANT'S AFTER ME WITH A WATER PISTOL. WHAT A LAUGH!

COME HERE, YOU!
GOOD! HE'S CHASING ME!

AH! I'VE GOT HIM CORNERED—HE WENT INTO HIS GANG HUT!

AH! THE RASCAL'S RIGGED UP A BOOBY-TRAP!

I'M TOO SMART TO BE CAUGHT LIKE THAT. I'LL GO IN BY THE WINDOW!

HULLO, SARGE! YOU'VE GOT YOUR FEET WET!
ARGH!

BACK AT THE POLICE STATION
CALL YOURSELF A POLICEMAN? HUH! TRICKED BY A YOUNG SCAMP!
YES, INSPECTOR!

CORPORAL MALONE IS VISITING US FROM THE MOUNTIES. HE'LL CATCH SMASHER FOR US—HE'S AN EXPERT WITH A LASSO!
I'LL GET MY MAN!

PRESENTLY
GOT YOU!
WOW!

BUT—
OH, YEAH?
CUT!

HE DIDN'T GET HIS MAN THAT TIME! HO-HO!

I'LL SCRAMBLE THROUGH THIS HEDGE

I'M STUCK!
GOT YOU NOW!

GROO!
HO-HO! TRICKED YOU! I TIED THAT BUCKET TO THE END OF THE ROPE!
TUG!

YIPPEE! I'VE BEATEN THEM ALL!
OOH!
SQUIRT!

SOAK ME, WOULD YOU? YOU'RE UNDER ARREST!
POLICE STATIO
HE'S MET HIS MATCH AT LAST—A POLICEWOMAN! HOW WILL WE PUNISH HIM?
MAKE HIM HOSE DOWN THE CELLS —HE'S FOND OF WATER!

HECTOR the COLLECTOR

I like your tie, Sidney.
CLASSIC CRACKER
Why, thank you!
That's an idea! I'll start collecting ties!

There's Grandpa having a snooze! He won't mind if I borrow his tie!
Z

Oh, no! It's on elastic!
Z
S-T-R-E-T-C-H

YAAAARGH!
THWAK!
Oops! It's slipped out of my hand!

Come back, you rascal!
Eek! I'd better scram!

Ah! That man must be throwing out that tie!
JUNK

TUG!
JUNK
I'll take that old tie, mister!

Oh, no! It was the one he was wearing!
CLUNK!

Gurr! Just wait till I catch you!

BACK HOME—
Mustard . . . vinegar . . . lemonade—hee-hee! This will do the trick!

Here's a drink for you, Mr Brown!
Thanks, Hector!

Help! My throat's on fire!
He's loosening his tie—just as I planned!

Yippee! I got one at last!

BUT—
Not so fast, Hector! I want a word with you!
Eek! Grandpa!

So you've got Hector! Good! I've got some ties for him!

Ho-ho! He won't cause any trouble now!
Bah! They've TIED me up!

# Minnie the Minx

Splodge
THE LAST OF THE GOBLINS
CLASSIC TOPPER
WHEEEE
WHAT'S THAT NOISE—A JET PLANE?
WHOOOOSH
THUMP
A GOOD BATSMAN, OLD JOE.
AR! THAT WAS SOME HIT!
IT SURE WAS!

I'LL GET MY OWN BACK ON THOSE CRICKETERS. IT SHOULD BE EASY—HUMANS CAN'T SEE ME!

SNORT
BATSMEN—I HATE 'EM!
THIS BLOKE'S GOING TO BOWL!

I'LL BOWL 'IM A BOUNCER FOR STARTERS!
WATCH THIS, FOLKS!

? ? ?
R-RUMBLE

HO! HO! HO!
ULP!

BLUSH
ER—SORRY ABOUT THAT.

AND THE SAME AGAIN.

ERK! THEY'VE FALLEN AGAIN.
'ERE, WE CAN'T HAVE YOU HOLDING UP THE GAME LIKE THIS!

BOWL WITHOUT YOUR TROUSERS!

SPLODGE CLIMBS INTO THE UMPIRE'S POCKET...
HEY! THERE'S A COUPLE OF CRICKET BALLS IN HERE!
NOW IF I CHUCKED THEM ON TO THE PITCH...

HIT IT, JOE!
ARRR! BUT WHICH ONE?

SNICK
SWIPE
OWZAT?
SLASH

OUT THREE TIMES!
PAH! HE CHEATED! HE BOWLED THREE BALLS!
WHO ARE YOU CALLING A CHEAT?

THUMP
CLONK
WHOP
THUD
THWACK
THAT'LL TEACH 'EM NOT TO HIT ME WITH A CRICKET BALL!

THUMP
SQUASH

CLASSIC NUTTY
BLUBBA
AND THE BEAR

PERFECT! A NICE BIG ICE-BOX TO KEEP MY FISH IN!

I'VE A FEELING THIS IS MY LUCKY DAY!

HMM! BLUBBA'S LEFT HIS TOOLS. I WONDER...

GOT ONE! A BEAUTY!

IN YOU GO!

A LITTLE LATER...
GREAT! I'VE ENOUGH FISH FOR WEEKS!

THAT'S FUNNY. IT SOUNDS AS THOUGH...
ZZZZZZ

...SOMEONE'S SAWING THROUGH THE ICE! OH, NO!

YOU—YOU BEAR-FACED ROBBER, YOU!

DELICIOUS! THE BEST-TASTING FISH I EVER "SAWED"!
GRRRR!

# A GREAT BIG BUNDLE OF FUN!

# THE BEEZER

CLASSIC BEEZER

## POP, DICK and HARRY

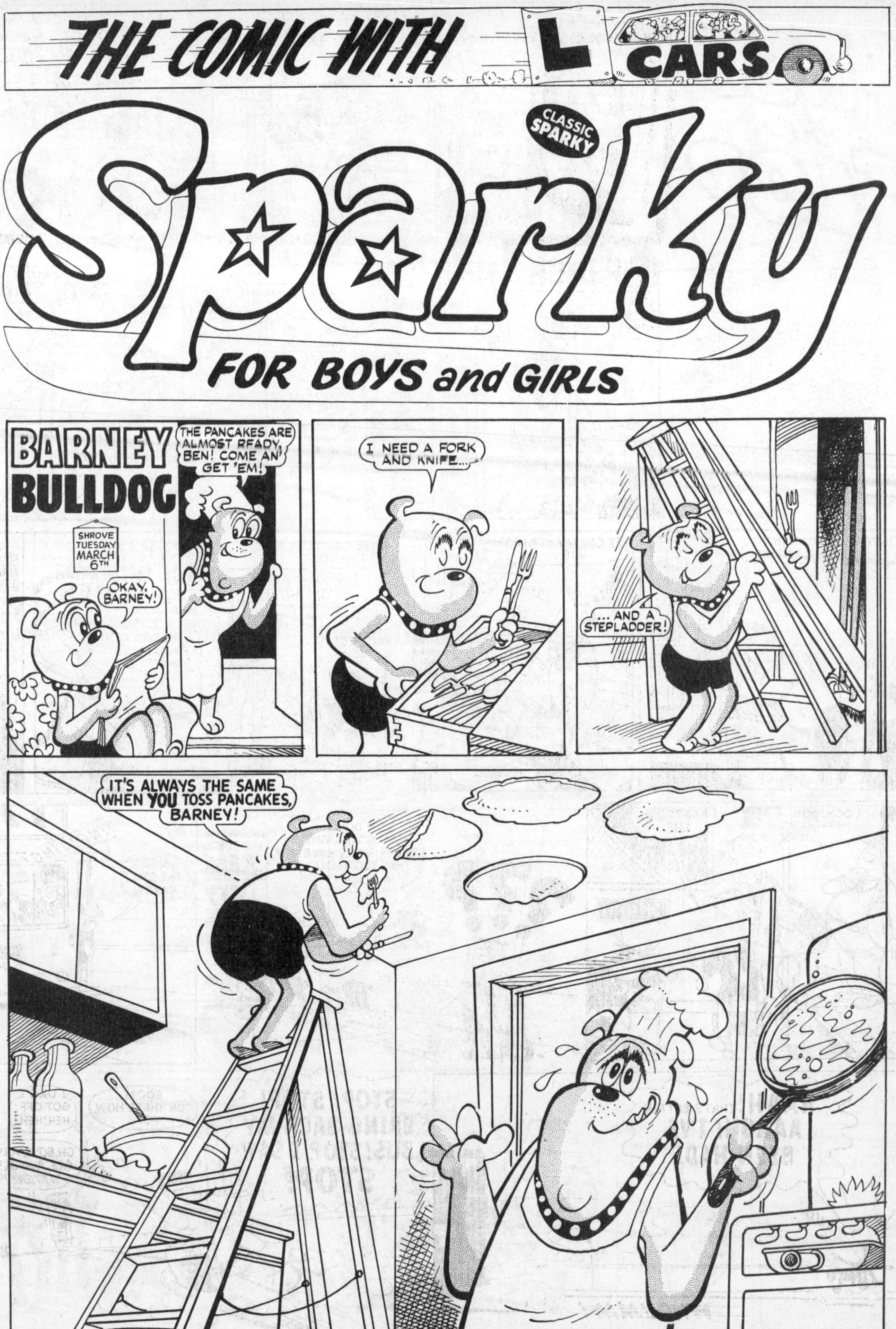

THE COMIC WITH L CARS

IT'S ALWAYS THE SAME WHEN **YOU** TOSS PANCAKES, BARNEY!

FRED the FLOP

. . . and you've won all these cups with your pedigree poodle?
Yes, a champion dog like this is worth a lot of money!
Hmm, is that so?

I've read that Lady Barking keeps pedigree poodles—so I'm going to try and pinch one.
CLASSIC BUZZ

What luck! One of the dogs is asleep at the window. All I have to do is grab it.

Oops! I didn't twig that was a wig!
Yikes!

Take that!
BONK!
Ow!

Help! Police! I've been attacked by a burglar!
Phew! I'm the one who was attacked!

Wow! I'll bet those racing greyhounds are worth a packet!

I'll take these!
SNATCH!

Oi! Come back!
Let's get outa here, doggies!
A cat! After it, fellahs!

Hey! Not so fast!

Oof!
THUD!
Perhaps that wasn't such a good idea!

LATER—
I've put two of our best dogs in the van. Sign here, please!
Righto!
PEDIGREE DOG KENNELS
Hear that?

I just have to pinch this van load of dogs and I'm in the money!
Stop!

AND SO—
Now, let's see what beauties we have here . . .

Hello there, Fred!
Eek!

Hard luck, Fred . . .these are two new police dogs! They just love catching crooks!
I know it!

NO FISHING

SURROUNDED? THAT'S WHAT THEY THINK! THEY DON'T KNOW HALF THE THINGS I CAN DO WITH A BROLLY!

!
CLASSIC BEANO
JONAH
THE S.S. "DARKHORSE" IS DUE TO SAIL ON A MYSTERY CRUISE.
HAW-HAW! JOLLY GOOD FUN — WHAT! I WONDER WHERE WE'RE BOUND FOR?
ALL PASSENGERS THIS WAY
MY GUESS IS THE ANTARCTIC, OLD BOY!
POPPYCOCK, LORD CASHBAGG! IT'S BOMBAY — OR ME NAME AIN'T COLONEL GRAPESHOTT!
AI COULDN'T CARE LESS, COLONEL!
ON ARRIVING AT OUR DESTINATION — AHEM! AI SHALL SIMPLY ABANDON THE ATTIRE THAT DOES NOT BE-FIT THE CLIMATIC CONDITIONS, OLD BOY!
SNIFF!
THUS, THE S.S. "DARKHORSE" SAILS FORTH ON HER VOYAGE OF MYSTERY —
—WHILE, ON THE UPPER DECK—
I SAY THERE! — MISTER MARINER! I'VE JUST THOUGHT OF A SIMPLY SPLENDID IDEA! BUT I'LL NEED YOUR HELP!
DISGUST
I'M GOING TO RUN A LOTTERY ON THE WHEREABOUTS OF OUR DESTINATION — AT A POUND A GUESS — AND I WANT YOU TO COLLECT THE MONEY FOR ME.
IT'S SILLY ASSES LIKE YOU WHO MAKE POOR PERISHERS LIKE ME HAVE TO SLAVE AS DECK-HANDS!
OF COURSE, YOU'LL BE SUITABLY REWARDED, MY GOOD MAN!
OH, WELL, ER — THAT'S DIFFERENT, — SIR!
ROLL UP, YOU LOT! WHO'S HAVIN' A BASH AT THE LOTTERY? A PAHND A GUESS!
— GUESS WHERE WE'RE A-GOIN' — OF AND WIN A PRIZE
AHEM! — COME NOW, CAPTAIN. HOW ABOUT DROPPING A LITTLE HINT?
TUT-TUT, M'LORD!
SURELY YOU WOULDN'T HAVE ME SPOIL ALL THE FUN!
DISGRUNTLED
COME ON, NOW! 'OW ABAHT YOU, MADAM?
Z-Z-Z Z-Z-Z Z-Z-Z
AGH-H!
Z-Z-Z
CAP'N! CAP'N! THE SHIP'S DESTINATION'S BEEN CHANGED! SHE'S GOING TO THE BOTTOM OF THE OCEAN!! JONAH'S ON BOARD!!
JONAH'S ABOARD! AGH-H-H! DOOMED! DONE FOR! SUNK!
FOLLOW ME!
AGH-H-H-H!
OUR VALUABLES! THEY'RE IN OUR CABINS BELOW, COLONEL!
M' TROPHIES!
MY WALLET!
LIFT
LIFT-MAN! TAKE US TO OUR CABINS — QUICK!
COR!
'ELP!
AGH-H!
THIS LIFT'S ONLY SUPPOSED TO HOLD EIGHT PEOPLE! —
— NOT EIGHTY!
GUG!
SNAP!
HELP!
WHOOSH!
ZOO-OO-OOM
AGH-H-H-H-H-H!
BOTTOM OF SHIP.
CRASH!
'ELP!
GLUB!
ERK!
GLURK!
S.O.S!
AND SO THE S.S. "DARKHORSE" GOES TO A DESTINATION NO ONE HAD THOUGHT ABOUT—
HIS-S-S!
BLOOP!
BLUP!
SH-S-S-S-S-S-S-S-S-S!
— THE WATERY DEPTHS —
PHOO-O-O-O-O!
— OF THE ATLANTIC OCEAN!
BLURB!
LOVELY AND COOL! A BREEZE MUST HAVE SPRUNG UP!
AND ONE WEEK LATER —
MY FRIENDS! ON THIS OCCASION, THERE IS NO MYSTERY AS TO WHERE I'M GOING!
WHERE, CAP'N?
'ELP!
I AM GOING GA-GA!
BOING!
HEH-HEH-HEH!!! WHO'S COMING WITH ME? — BLAH-H-H-H!

# SIR LAUGHALOT

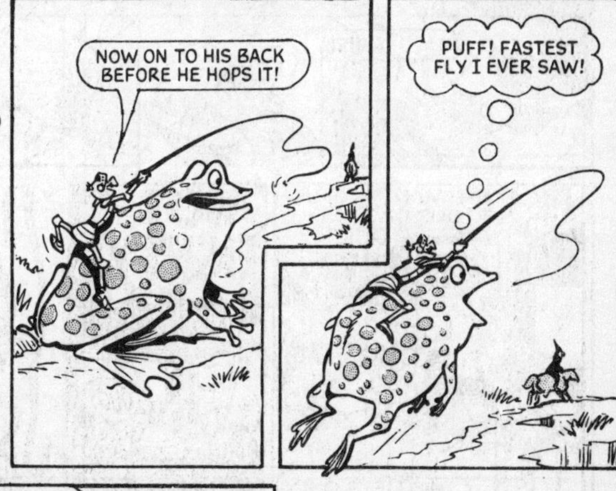

GNASHER
AND
GNIPPER

In the kitchen—
I LOVE MILK AND CORNFLAKES IN THE MORNING.
CLASSIC BEANO
MILK
MILK

BAH! BUT I CAN'T OPEN THESE MILK CARTONS.
MILK
MILK

PESKY CARTON.
JUMP
MILK

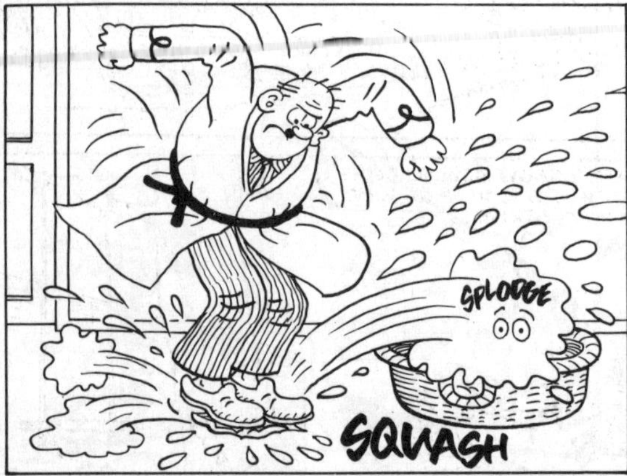
SPLODGE
SQUASH

HE'S HOPELESS.
DRIP
MILK

I'LL DO IT—DON'T WANT SQUIRTED AGAIN.
SNIP
MILK

TA, GNASHER.
I'LL TRY WHAT MY DAD DID.
MILK

JAB
MILK

CAN I BORROW SOME MILK FOR MY KITTY?
SPLODGE
SQUIRT
MILK

BAH! IT'S EMPTY.
SHAKE

ONLY ONE THING FOR IT.
GRAB

GNUMPH! THAT'S THE LAST TIME I HELP DAD.
WRING

# FOXY

HO! HO!
R LAUGHALOT GETS
ETTER EVERY
WEEK!

WISH I'D LIVED IN THE DAYS WHEN KNIGHTS WERE BOLD...

CLASSIC TOPPER
BUT WAIT... I CAN BE A MODERN KNIGHT!

AND WOE BETIDE ANY CHICKEN-HEARTED KNAVES WHO CROSS ME PATH!

WITH HIS TRUSTY STEED AN' A GOOD STOUT LANCE... SIR FOXALOT SETS OFF!
TO THE FARM

AHA! CHICKENS! HAVE AT THEE, FOWL KNAVES!

HO! HO! A FAIR CATCH, METHINKS! NOW FOR SOME MORE!

MEANWHILE...
HE'S GOT TO BE STOPPED!
YES, BUT HOW?

WAIT! I KNOW HOW TO DO IT! FETCH A BROOM AND SOME STRING!

THE CHICKS GET BUSY...
HAUL AWAY!

ONCE MORE SIR FOXALOT APPROACHES...
HAVE AT YOU, ME LITTLE CHICKADEES!
HERE HE COMES! RUN FOR IT!

RIGHT, MEN! PREPARE TO DO BATTLE WITH SIR FOXALOT!

CLUNK
TAKE THAT, SIR KNIGHT!

Billy the Kid
PETS' HAPPY SMILE CONTEST AT THE TOWN HALL 2 p.m. TODAY SUPER PRIZES
Guess who I'm going to enter for that contest . . . ?
...Pongo!
CLASSIC CRACKER
There's soppy Cyril Simpkins and his pet Cheshire cat.
My cat, Toothy, is sure to win the contest.

SWEETS
Heh-heh! My wicked mind is at work!
LIQUORICE MICE

SOON—
Is this a mouse I see before me?

Yum-yum! Liquorice!
MUNCH!
MUNCH!

Chortle! That's the main challenger out of the way.
Erk! Black teeth!

AT THE SHOW—
Attaboy! Get rid of their smiles, Pongo, pal!
GRR!
Help!

And the winner of our special prize is...

...Pongo the pup!
ROAR!
POLITE CLAP

And here's your super prize!
Toothpaste!
PET'S TOOTHPASTE

PONGO DOESN'T HAVE A VERY HAPPY SMILE NOW!
Snarl! Snort!

Mitey Joe
CLASSIC NUTTY
JOE IS DAYDREAMING ABOUT BEING TALL, AS USUAL—
SIGH!
WHEN SUDDENLY—
Greetings, Joe! I am your Fairy Godfather, and I've come to grant you a wish!
POP!
Huh?
WOW! FANTASTIC! I want you to increase my height by two feet!
No sooner said than done!

SHAZAM! There you are—two FOOTstools to make you two feet taller!
WH-WHAT?

GRR! That's not what I meant—I want you to make me GROW!
I see! I know just the stuff!

KABLAT! This smelly stuff makes my pansies grow a treat, so it should do wonders for a WEED like you!
POOH! Get me outta this!

LISTEN, YOU IMPISH CREEP! EITHER YOU MAKE ME TALLER NOW, OR I'LL SNAP YOUR LITTLE WAND IN TWO!
HMPH! So be it! DAWOOP!
POOP

This'll make you much taller—and teach you not to be rude to fairies!
GULP! Don't you think you're stretching the point a little too far?

AND—
AAACH!
HELP! HELP! . . .

. . . HELP! . . . Eh? OOYAH!
THUD

PHEW! It was all a bad dream. I'm not any taller than I was before!

I'm glad, really! Height isn't everything. Besides—being short GROWS on you! CHUCKLE!

# THE TRICKS of SCREWY DRIVER

CLASSIC DANDY

SO YOUR MUM AND GRANDAD ARE AWAY FROM HOME? WELL, YOU'LL HAVE TO LOOK AFTER YOUR FATHER. HE'S ILL. YOU'LL HAVE TO FEED HIM UP.

THIS IS KILLING ME. I'LL HAVE TO THINK OF SOME WAY TO DODGE IT.

WHAT ARE YOU DOING NOW?

I'M FIXING UP A WAY TO GET YOUR MEALS UP TO YOU.

RIGHT, DAD! HERE'S YOUR MEAL COMING UP ON MY QUICK SERVICE LIFT.

HOI! IT'S STOPPED AT THE WRONG PLACE! FIDO'S GOT IT, YOU IDIOT!

RIGHT! HERE'S MY DINNER. WE'LL TRY AGAIN.

IT'S GONE TOO FAR THIS TIME — STOP! YOW!

GET THIS INFERNAL THING OUT OF MY SIGHT!

CRASH!

YOW! MY NUT!

I PHONED THE DOCTOR — AND HE'S GETTING A NURSE TO DO THE COOKING — AT LEAST WE'LL GET SOME GOOD GRUB NOW.

MR DRIVER CAN HAVE EXTRA FOOD, NURSE — HE'S IMPROVING. BUT THIS BOY HAS A NASTY BUMP — NO FOOD FOR HIM FOR TWO DAYS!

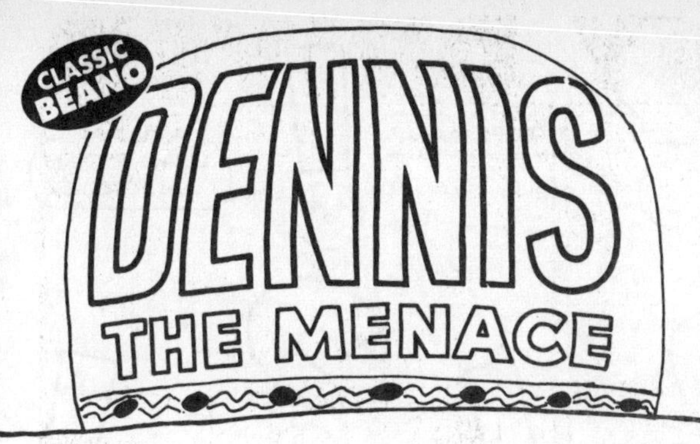
CLASSIC BEANO
DENNIS
THE MENACE

IN THE OFFICE, DAD'S BOSS IS FEELING THE HEAT—
PHEW! THESE HATS ARE NO USE IN THIS WEATHER. WHAT I NEED IS A LIGHT PANAMA HAT.
I'LL GIVE THE BOSS A PANAMA HAT AS A PRESENT AND I'M SURE TO GET PROMOTION!

SO LATER—
LOOK WHAT I'VE BOUGHT FOR THE BOSS!
HM! YOU'D BETTER PUT IT AWAY BEFORE DENNIS GETS HIS HANDS ON IT.

MEANWHILE—
THAT'S A SUPER COWBOY HAT YOU HAVE, CURLY.... I MUST GET ONE, TOO. I'LL BE BACK IN A JIFFY!

AT HOME—
LET'S SEE WHAT'S IN THIS WARDROBE.

AH! THIS'LL MAKE A SMASHING TEN-GALLON HAT. I'LL BORROW IT.

SO—
COME ON, CURLY! I RECKON IT'S ABOUT TIME I GAVE YOU A DEMONSTRATION OF BRONCO-BUSTING!
OH, YEAH?

NOBODY'S GOING TO BUST THIS BRONCO!
THUD!

HEE-HAW!
STAMP!
STAMP!
STEADY ON, NEDDY! I'VE GOT TO RETURN THAT HAT—IF THERE'S ANY OF IT LEFT!

NEXT MORNING—
ALLOW ME TO PRESENT YOU WITH A PANAMA HAT, BOSS!
HOW NICE!

GRR! IS THIS YOUR IDEA OF A JOKE?
EEK! PROMOTION? I'LL BE LUCKY IF I'M MADE OFFICE BOY AFTER THIS...
...BUT I KNOW WHO'S RESPONSIBLE ALL RIGHT!
SHIVER

I RECKON YOU'RE IN FOR A HIDING, YOU YOUNG COYOTE!
I RECKON I AM!

CLASSIC BUZZ
BUZZ
WHAT IS A NORSEMAN?
A MAN WHO RIDES AN 'ORSE!
WHAT DO SEA MONSTERS EAT?
FISH AND SHIPS!
WHAT WOULD YOU DO IF THE FORTH BRIDGE FELL DOWN?
BUILD A FIFTH ONE!
HOP, SKIP and JOCK
THIS WOULD BE A GREAT DAY TO GO CAMPING!
YEAH!
AYE! LET'S GET ALL THE LADS TOGETHER, AND GO!
HEIGH-HO! HEIGH-HO! IT'S OFF TO CAMP WE GO!
KEEP RIGHT ON TO THE END OF THE ROAD —
OOH! A SALMON'S NEST!
BOOT!
WOW! LOOK WHERE THE BALL'S GONE!
HOW DO YOU LIKE MY BELL TENT?
I LIKE TO LEAN OUT OF THE WINDOW TO SEE WHAT'S GOING ON!
I FANCY RABBIT STEW!
WELL, I DON'T!
THERE! THAT'S GOT RID OF THE MIDGES!
GLUG!
MOO!
RUN! IT'S A WILD MILK MACHINE!
NO CAMPING
I'M HENRYK ZABOROWSKI — I'M A TENT POLE!
AND I'M ONE OF THE TENT GUYS!
GIVE ME THE KETTLE! IT'LL BE LESS FOR YOU TO CARRY!
CHEEK! I DON'T WANT MY SON TO GROW UP HARD BOILED!
BOUNCE!
BONK!
I DON'T KNOW WHAT HOP'S GOT TO SMILE ABOUT!

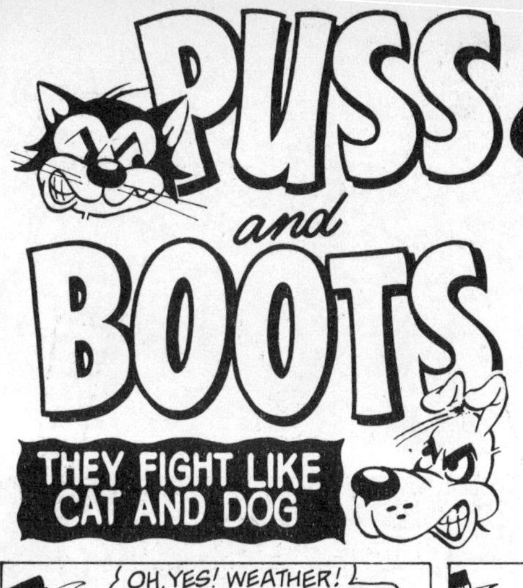
PUSS and BOOTS
CLASSIC SPARKY
THEY FIGHT LIKE CAT AND DOG

AND THAT PROGRAMME OF CHINESE PORRIDGE-TRAMPLING ENDS TONIGHT'S BROADCASTING ON NIRDLE NETWORK. BUT BEFORE CLOSE-DOWN HERE IS THE WEATHER FORECAST.
NTV

YES, THERE WILL BE WEATHER IN MOST PARTS OF THE COUNTRY TOMORROW! AND NOW, A LOOK AT TOMORROW'S CHARTS! THE DOSMOND SISTERS ARE STILL AT NUMBER ONE, AND...
THE WEATHER FORECAST, MAN! GET ON WITH IT!

OH, YES! WEATHER! UP HERE AT THE SCOTTISH ICE-CAP, THERE WILL BE A SUDDEN HEAVY SNOWFALL!

SNIGGER!

HARUMPHARUMPH! WELL, YOU CAN'T GET MUCH MORE SUDDEN THAN THAT! NOW, IN THE LAKE DISTRICT, THERE WILL BE HEAVY SHOWERS!

NERKLE! 'OODUNDAT?
HEM-HEM!
SPLASH!

SORRY ABOUT THAT, THEY'RE RECORDING AN INDIAN RAIN DANCE UPSTAIRS! OH, YES... THERE WILL BE STRONG WIND AT WINDERMERE!

GRAAGH!
BLAST!
HEE-HEE!
PLOP! PLOP!
COO! RIGHT THROUGH THE WALL!

HEE-HEE-HEE! I'M GLAD I GOT THIS JOB IN THE SPECIAL EFFECTS DEPARTMENT! I HAVEN'T HAD SO MUCH FUN SINCE I READ LAST WEEK'S SPARKY!
WHIRRR!

JUST A MINUTE, YOU WITH THE BASHED NOSE!
PARDING? I HAVEN'T GOT A BASHED...

...OOH-ME-NOSE!
TAKE THAT, AN' THAT, AN' THAT, AN' THAT, AN' THAT, AN' THAT...
BOP!
WHAM!
BANG!
CRUMP!

OW!
BANG!
OUCH!
BLAM!
OOYA!
WHAM!
AARGH!

HERE IS THE MOGGIE REPORT! AFTER TODAY'S BRIGHT IDEA, THE MOGGIE HAD BLOWS RAINED ON HIM AND IS NOW FEELING A MUGGY MOGGIE! IF HE TRIES ANY FUNNY BUSINESS TOMORROW HAIL BE THUMPED TILL HE HAS HAZY SPELLS THEN HE'LL BE A SMOGGY MOGGIE!
NTV
MIST AGAIN!
WHAT AN ARTISTE! DOES NOTHING PUT HIM OFF?

CAP'N HAND
and his
MERRY MUTINEERS
CLASSIC BEEZER

BEANS AGAIN! WISH I COULD HAVE SOME NICE FRESH EGGS FOR BREKKERS!

IN PORT
HAR! HAR! NOW I'LL GET FRESH EGGS!
SQUAWK!
CLUCK!
CLUCK!

WHERE ARE YOU GOIN' TO KEEP 'EM, CAPTING?
YOU'LL SEE! HAR! HAR!
SQUAWK!
CLUCK!

BED TIME— AND IN THE CREW'S QUARTERS...
THAT CAPTING'S GOT T'GO!
SCRATCHY
SQUAWK!
CLUCK!
BOSUN
EBENEZER
TUK! TUK!

4 O'CLOCK! YUS, THAT CAPTING AND HIS HENS HAVE GOT T'GO!
COCK-A-DOODLE-DOO!

BEANS? BEANS? WHAT'S HAPPENED TO MY EGGS?
HENS ARE HIDING IN THE HOLD, CAPTING!

HERE, CHOOK-CHOOKS! HERE, CHOOK-CHOOK-CHOOKS! COME TO YER CAPTING!
MAIN HATCH

AAIEE-E-E!
HAR! THEY'RE ALL GOIN' T'GO!
SHOVE!
MAIN HATCH

LATER, ON DECK.
RUN OUT A PLANK, LADS! THEY'RE GOIN' FOR A WALK!
MUTINOUS DOGS!

OOH! A WORM! TUK! TUK! LOVELY!
SHORT-SIGHTED HEN!

TUG!
PULL!
WHAT A STROKE OF LUCK! HAR! HAR!

FIVE MINUTES LATER . . .
HENS FIRST!

HAR! THEY'RE GOIN' T'GO!
SQUAWK!
CLUCK!
SLURP!

GET YOUR HANDS OFF THOSE HENS, YE SWABS!
!

BOOM!

UNTIE THOSE HENS! I'M CAP'N O' THIS HEN-COOP, AN' YE'D BETTER NOT F'RGET IT!

# BULLY BEEF AND CHIPS

CLASSIC BEANO
PUNCH AND JIMMY

I'm better at games than you!
Rubbish! I'm the best!
Oh, dear! What can I do to stop them fighting?

UP IN THE LOFT–
So they're keen on games, eh? These golf bags might come in handy.
BANG!
THUMP!
BASH!

SO–
Go and play golf~ and no fighting!
OK, Mum!

AT THE GOLF COURSE–
I'll beat you easily!
Never! I'm sure to win!

I'll have first hit~Oops!~ Missed!
SLOSH!
HACK!

PLEASE REPLACE THE TURF
Grr! I'll replace it ok~

~Right in your face!
UGH!

Agh! They're at it again!

Is there no way of keeping you two from scrapping?

THEN–
I've just had a great idea.
RATTLE!

In you go, Jimmy!
Oh, no!

Tee-hee! I knew these golf bags would come in handy!

# ROBINSON AND HIS DOG CRUSOE

CLASSIC SPARKY

# HUNGRY HORACE

**Horace wasn't warned... The beef-steak was horned!**

CALAMITY
JAMES
THE WORLD'S UNLUCKIEST BOY

BEWARE OF BIG SQUELCHY GREEN THINGS!
THOU SHALT NOT MAKE HORRIBLE RASPBERRY NOISES!
MD
NOSH
TRUDGE!
DO NOT SQUEEZE
CLASSIC BEANO
PLUMMET!
AAARGH!
WHAT AN UNLUCKY CHAP!

AW, I'M FED UP HAVING DISASTERS! WISH I COULD FORSEE DANGERS BEFORE I WALK INTO THEM!
REVOLVING TRICK WIG FACTORY
BEWARE! DIRTY GREAT SWEATY IRISH NAVVIES AT WORK!
SIGH!
GLOWER!
UNPRINTABLE GAELIC MUTTERINGS!

MADAME ZA-ZA! FORTUNE TELLER! SHE SEES ALL IN FUTURE! APPLY 12 NOSE LANE
LOOK, JAMES! HERE'S THE ANSWER!
SLOO!
WONDER LUMP REMOVER

At Nose Lane—
NOSE LANE
FORTUNES TOLD
11
12
COULD THIS BE THE PLACE?
WHAT A BRIGHT BOY YOU ARE!

But—
Off on a year's holiday to Tibet, you walking disaster! I could tell you were coming to see me! Ha-ha-ha!
SIGH! JUST MY LUCK!

WAIT — ANOTHER PLAN!
PUNY PEA-BRAIN PALPITATING AT FULL POWER!
OH, NO!

NEWSAGENT AND DENTURE POLISHER
MORNING NEWS
M.P. CRITICIZES PRIME MINISTER'S BIG NOSE!
EVENING NEWS
"AT LEAST MINE ISN'T SMOTHERED WITH PIMPLES" RETORTS P.M.
WAAA!
TRIP!
BOWSER

AND DENTURE POLISHER
I JUST REMEMBERED THEY PRINT HOROSCOPES IN NEWSPAPERS!
DAILY WAFFLE
STAGGER! LURCH!

HMM! TURN TO PAGE THIRTEEN ...
SILHOUETTE PIC AS USED BY OVERWORKED ARTISTS.
... HOWL!
SICKENING HOOTER-FRACTURING KRUNCH!
BLANG!

HERE IT IS, JAMES. 'AFTER BUYING THIS NEWSPAPER YOU WILL HAVE A NASTY ACCIDENT'! HA-HA-HA!
BLITHER! SLABBER!
PAGE 13 HOROSCOPES
DOH!
SEMI-CONSCIOUS SAMBA!

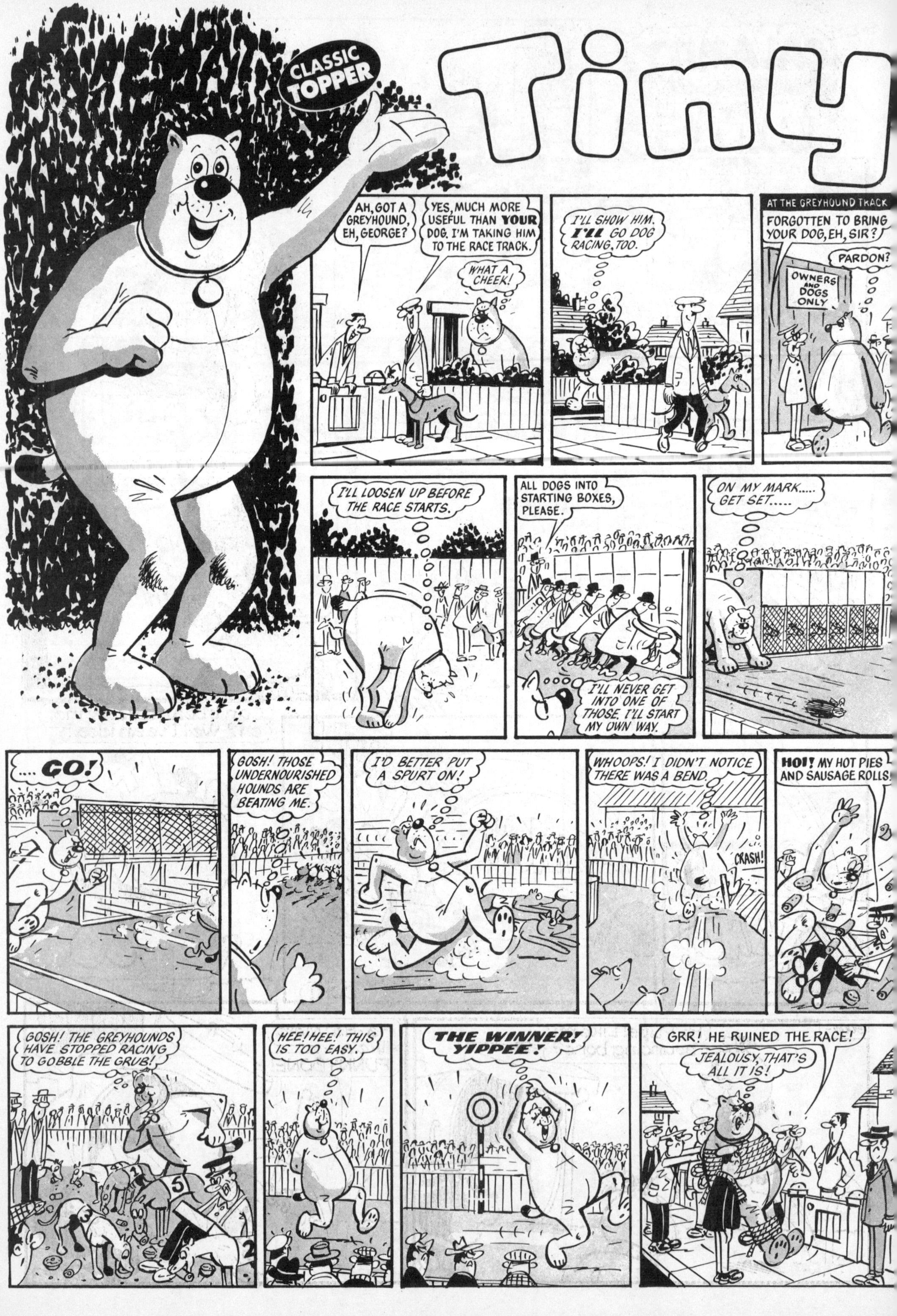

CLASSIC TOPPER

# Tiny

AH, GOT A GREYHOUND, EH, GEORGE?

YES, MUCH MORE USEFUL THAN **YOUR** DOG. I'M TAKING HIM TO THE RACE TRACK.

WHAT A CHEEK!

I'LL SHOW HIM. **I'LL** GO DOG RACING, TOO.

AT THE GREYHOUND TRACK

FORGOTTEN TO BRING YOUR DOG, EH, SIR?

PARDON?

OWNERS AND DOGS ONLY

I'LL LOOSEN UP BEFORE THE RACE STARTS.

ALL DOGS INTO STARTING BOXES, PLEASE.

I'LL NEVER GET INTO ONE OF THOSE. I'LL START MY OWN WAY.

ON MY MARK..... GET SET.....

PUP PARADE
with the BASH ST. PUPS
BONES
PEEPS
'ENRY
SNIFFY
TUBBY
SPOTTY
MANFRID
WIGGY
PUG
CLASSIC BEANO
Tum...tee...tum!
TRICK SHOP
Hmm! A bone!
I'll bury it like all of us good cats do!
Sniffy-dafter than daft
NNNGH!
PUSH
BEND
SUDDENLY—
Strange bone-I don't want it!
THROW
PYOING!
OOF!
THUD!
BUT—
YING!
THUD!
PYOING!
DOH!
Can't bear to leave me, eh? Well I've an idea!
SOON—
Hi, Pups! Like my bouncing bone?
Ha-Ha! More like a— FUNNYBONE!
BONG

# DOODLEBUG

CLASSIC NUTTY

# RUSTY

**The funny tale of the lad whose holiday togs–**

**Have gone to the dogs!**

# ROLY-POLY JOE

NO, NO, BO! GEESE CAN'T FLY!

# SPOOFER McGRAW

HE TELLS TALL TALES

CLASSIC TOPPER

# DESERT ISLAND DICK

The
CLASSIC BEANO
BASH STREET KIDS

YES, INDEED, SMIFFY IS A SOMEWHAT BACKWARD PUPIL.
YOU'RE NOT WRONG, HEADMASTER.
SCHOOL
WALKING BACKWARDS

SMIFFY, YOU'RE AN IDIOTIC IDIOT! YOU NEVER DO ANYTHING RIGHT!
WHACK!

SIT UP STRAIGHT, EVERYONE— BAH! SIT DOWN, SMIFFY, YOU DUNCE.... CLASS WILL FACE THE FRONT!

WAS THERE EVER SUCH A DOZY PUPIL?

SO—
BULL'S CHINA SHOP
SMIFFY, YOU'D BETTER STAY OUT HERE. WE DON'T WANT ANYTHING BROKEN!
KO!

CAN WE HAVE THE TEA-SET FOR TEACHER'S WIFE, PLEASE?

HERE IT IS. REMEMBER TO BE CAREFUL WITH IT.
CHINA
GO EASY!
WATCH IT!
DON'T THROW
NO THUDS!
GENTLY! GENTLY!
BUMP!
WE WILL— OUCH!

CRASH!

LATER, IN SCHOOL—
ER—TEACHER, SMIFFY'S DONE SOMETHING RIGHT AT LAST!
WHY, THAT'S WONDERFUL!

CLASS IIB –
GOOD MORNING, PUPILS.
GOOD MORNING, TEACHER.
TEACHER TRAP

BUT–
GOODNIGHT, TEACHER!

GOODNIGHT, SMIFFY! — EEK! BAH! FOOLISH CHILD! MUST YOU ALWAYS DO THINGS WRONG?

HANDS UP THOSE WHO HAVEN'T DONE THEIR HOMEWORK!

LUNCHTIME –
DANNY, IF YOU CAN GET SMIFFY TO DO SOMETHING RIGHT, I MIGHT GIVE YOU ALL A HALF-HOLIDAY!
OK, TEACHER WE'LL TRY.
PAT!

GOOD GRACIOUS! I NEARLY FORGOT — MY WIFE ASKED ME TO PICK UP A TEA-SET FROM THE CHINA SHOP THIS MORNING. NOW I HAVE AN INTERVIEW WITH THE HEADMASTER. WILL YOU COLLECT IT FOR ME?
CERTAINLY, TEACHER.

WHERE'S SMIFFY?
NICE PUSSY! PRETTY PUSSY!
GO EASY!
WATCH IT!
DON'T THROW!
NO THUDS!
GENTLY! GENTLY!

NO THUDS!
GENTLY! GENTLY!
TRIP
EEK!

WHAT'S WRONG, DANNY?
AARGH! NO!

THIS I MUST SEE! WHERE IS HE? IN THE CLASSROOM?

HE'S MADE A RIGHT MESS OF YOUR TEA-SET!
OH, NO!

CHOOL
GURR! I'LL MAKE A RIGHT MESS OF YOU LOT WHEN I CATCH YOU!
WHOOOSH!
ZOOM!

# SIMPLE SPYMAN

## KORKY the CAT

EXIT

HA! HA! SO THAT'S HOW HE DOES IT! GOOD OLD UNCLE KORKY!

# SNIP and SNAP

**Dearie dearie me... There'll be no egg for tea!**

# FIGARO!

LASSIC OPPER

HALLO, READERS! COME AN' JOIN US. WE'RE OFF TO ROB THE BANK.

KANVAS CITY

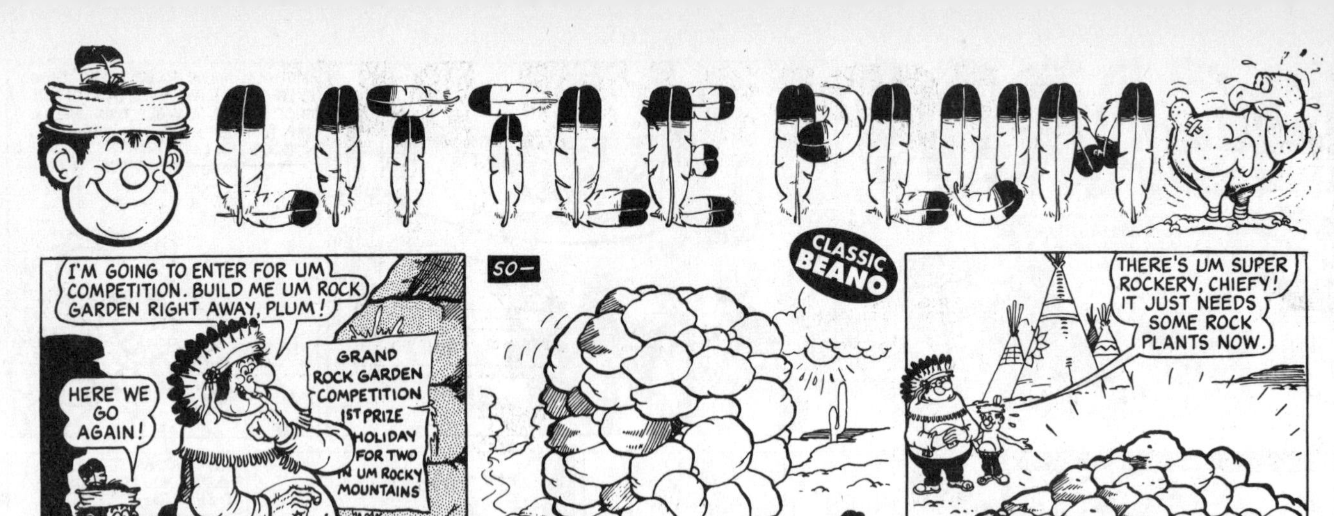
LITTLE PLUM
CLASSIC BEANO
I'M GOING TO ENTER FOR UM COMPETITION. BUILD ME UM ROCK GARDEN RIGHT AWAY, PLUM!
GRAND ROCK GARDEN COMPETITION 1ST PRIZE HOLIDAY FOR TWO IN UM ROCKY MOUNTAINS
HERE WE GO AGAIN!
SO—
RATTLE!
SWEAT
PUFF!
THERE'S UM SUPER ROCKERY, CHIEFY! IT JUST NEEDS SOME ROCK PLANTS NOW.

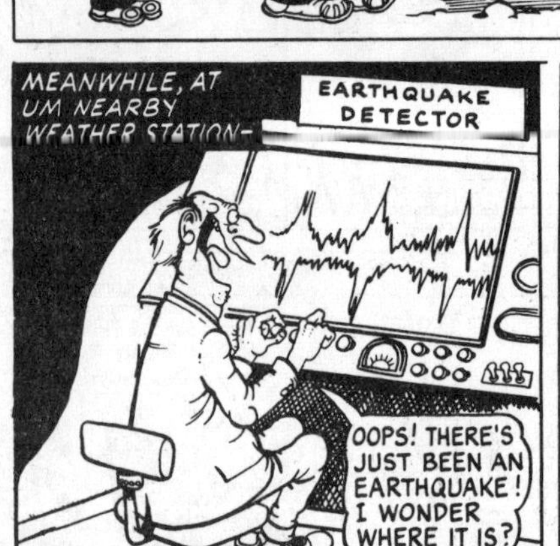
MEANWHILE, AT UM NEARBY WEATHER STATION—
EARTHQUAKE DETECTOR
OOPS! THERE'S JUST BEEN AN EARTHQUAKE! I WONDER WHERE IT IS?

IT'S HERE, AT UM SMELLYFOOT VILLAGE!
AARGH! UM ROCKERY'S VANISHED!
CRACK!
TREMBLE

SO—
SHIMMER
SHIMMER
I HAD TO—PUFF!—START ALL—PANT!—OVER AGAIN! GASP!

LATER—
UM ROCKERY'S FINISHED, CHIEFY. COME AND SEE IT.
ROCK PLANTS

YOU UM NIT! YOU'VE BUILT UM ROCKERY ON UM MARSH!
GULP!
DANGER
GURGLE!
GURGLE!
GURGLE!

SUDDENLY, UM SUPER IDEA STRIKES PLUM—
IDEA
THUMP!
UP IN UM MOUNTAINS ABOVE UM VILLAGE—
YAHOO!
2000 FT

PLUM'S YELL STARTS OFF UM AVALANCHE—
MA, ARE THOSE HAIL-STONES?

—AND UM ROCKS FINISH UP OUTSIDE CHIEFY'S WIGWAM!
WHAT UM SUPER ROCKERY!

CHIEFY WINS UM FIRST PRIZE.
I'VE GOT YOU TO THANK FOR THIS, PLUM, SO I'LL TAKE YOU WITH ME ON HOLIDAY!
CHEERS!
1ST PRIZE

# DESPERATE DAN

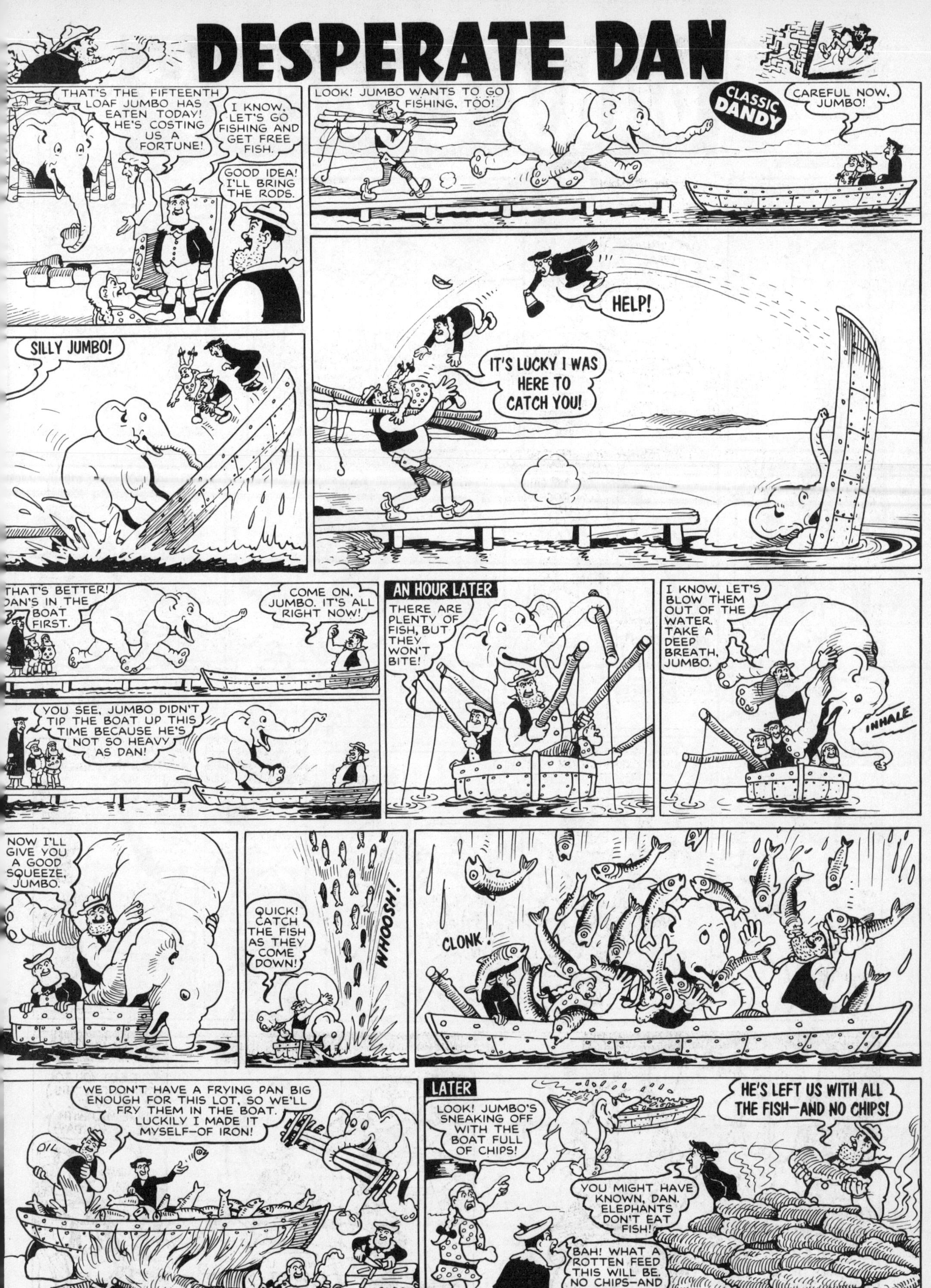

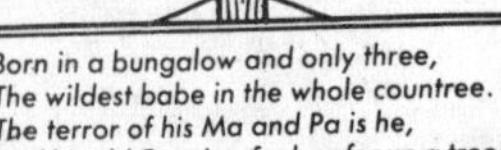

Born in a bungalow and only three,
The wildest babe in the whole countree.
The terror of his Ma and Pa is he,
And his old Gran'pa feels safer up a tree!
Baby—Baby Crockett—
King of the Familee!

baby Crockett

Mesgotacandyfloss!

CLASSIC BEEZER
Smashin!
Might as well get rid of this old pillow!

LOOK WHO'S COMING! IT'S COLONEL BLINK!
?

Goodness me! A parrot! Must be lost!

?
Hullo, Polly! Arf! You lost, eh? Arf! Arf!

C'mon with me–I'll soon find your owner!

AT BLINK'S HOUSE
Oho! A talking parrot, eh? Clever! Arf!
Me isn'taparrot! My name's Crockett-Baby...

Crockett, you say? I know the gentleman-you just wait there! Arf! Arf!
'Sno yoose!

Ah, the very man! I have something belonging to you, Crockett, old chap!
?

There! Your parrot! Found it in the street!
DAD!

Very fond of you, I see. Arf! Well, you might as well have this packet of seed I bought for it!
PARROT FOOD

G'bye, Crockett! G'bye, Polly! Arf! Arf!
Ho! Ho! C'mon home, POLLY!

CLASSIC BUZZ
NERO and ZERO

Oh! I hate guard duty! My feet are killing me!
We need a rest!

LATER
Ooh, thank the stars! It's knocking-off time at last!

Tomorrow, we're off to my villa in the hills for a few days' holiday!
Just what we need!

AND SO
Here's Caesar's coach! Off we go!

WOW!

There's no room in the coach, guards! You'll have to walk!
Walk?

TRAMP!
TRAMP!

MANY FOOTSTEPS LATER—
Here we are, guards!
We—we've made it, Zero!

We've arrived just in time for the grape harvest!
Oh, no—you know what that means!

We have to tramp the grapes!
TRAMP!
TRAMP!

LATER
That's enough—you can get out now!
Ooh! My poor feet!

Time for the washing now!
What? This is no holiday!

Enjoying your holiday?
No comment!
TRAMP!

Aw, listen to this: A note from my wife! I've to go home right away! The holiday's over!
Yippee!
THROB!

At least this makes a change!
Yeah! Now my feet and my hands are sore!

BILLY
WHIZZ
COOKING, SEWING, IRONING—PHEW!—I'M TIRED! AND NOW I HAVE TO BATH YOUNG ALFIE!
CLASSIC BEANO
I WONDER IF BILLY WOULD BATH ALFIE AND PUT HIM TO BED?
!
OK, MUM! I'LL BATH HIM!
IT'S BATH-TIME, ALFIE!
SNATCH
UP THE STAIRS WE GO!
BUMP!
BUMP!
ZOOOM!
BONK!
BASH!
BIFF!
THUD!
BANG!
BUMP!
I'LL FILL THE BATH.
CLUNK!
WON'T BE LONG NOW!
BUMP!
BUMP!
IN YOU GO!
SWISH!
OUT YOU COME!
ON WITH YOUR NIGHTIE...
...AND INTO BED! SWEET DREAMS, ALFIE!
WHEE!
ON SECOND THOUGHTS, PERHAPS I'D BETTER BATH ALFIE MYSELF!
PHEW!

# BERYL THE PERIL

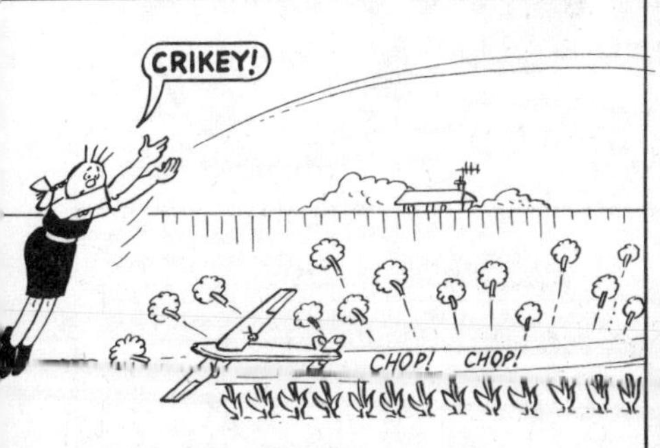

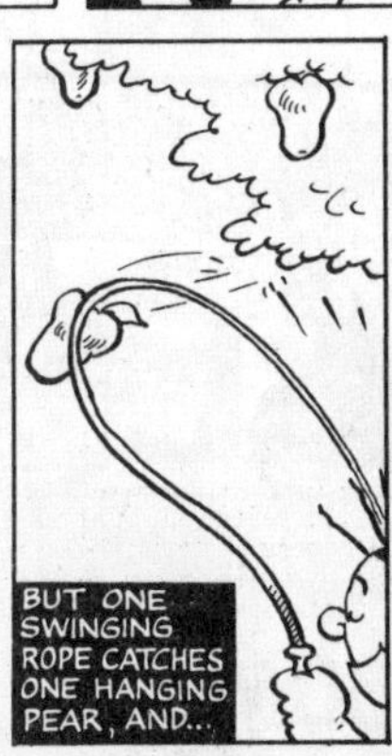

CAN FREDERIC BE...
L CARS
CLASSIC SPARKY

HO-HO-HO! SNIP AND SNAP REALLY MAKE ME LAUGH!
NOW LET ME SEE...
WHAT'S ALL THIS THEN?
Sparky
BRAIN POWER

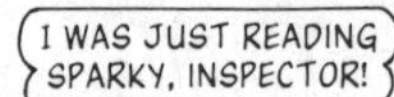

I WAS JUST READING SPARKY, INSPECTOR!
AND I'M READING HOW TO BE BRAINY 'COS I'M GOIN' TO ENTER FOR THE POLICE BRAIN OF BRITAIN CONTEST—
BRAIN POWER

BRAIN OF BRITAIN? HO-HO-HO! DON'T MAKE ME LAUGH! HA-HA-HA!
LET'S HAVE A REHEARSAL, FREDERIC. I'LL ASK YOU QUESTIONS ON GENERAL KNOWLEDGE...
WHO'S HE?
DRRING! DRRING!

YESSIR! RIGHT AWAY, SIR! AT ONCE, SIR! NOW, SIR!
OH-OH! THAT'S THE CHIEF CONSTABLE ON THE PHONE!
HOW DO YOU KNOW THAT, CEDRIC?

A CONVICT HAS JUST ESCAPED FROM WOODWORM SCRUBS PRISON! HE WAS LAST SEEN ON THE HEATH! GET GOING!
SIR!
ZOOOM!

AND TAKE THAT WITH YOU, BRAINY!
BONK!
OW!

THE BATTLE OF FLODDEN WAS FOUGHT IN 1513... MUTTER... MUTTER... $E=mc^2$ LIMA IS THE CAPITAL OF PERU... $C+H_2O=H_2+CO$...
COO! FREDERIC'S GONE ALL FUNNY!
THAT BUMP ON THE HEAD HAS MADE HIM BRILLIANT!

TAKE THE CAR TO THE MOORS, FREDERIC—AND QUICKLY!
YESSIR! AND BY THE WAY—THE SQUARE ON THE HYPOTENUSE...
YES! YES! NOW GET GOING!

LATER, ON THE MOORS...
THERE'S THE ESCAPED PRISONER—LOOK!
EXCUSE ME, SIR... $A^2+B^2$ MUTTER...MUTTER... $2\pi \times$ CUBIC DENSITY MUTTER...MUTTER...

WHAT ON EARTH ARE YOU DOING? HE'S GETTING AWAY—!
DON'T WORRY, SIR. EVERYTHING IS UNDER CONTROL!
WHAT'S HE UP TO?

# ...BRITAIN'S BRAINIEST P.C.?

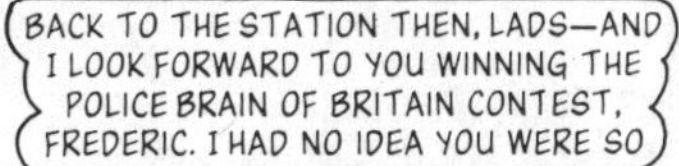

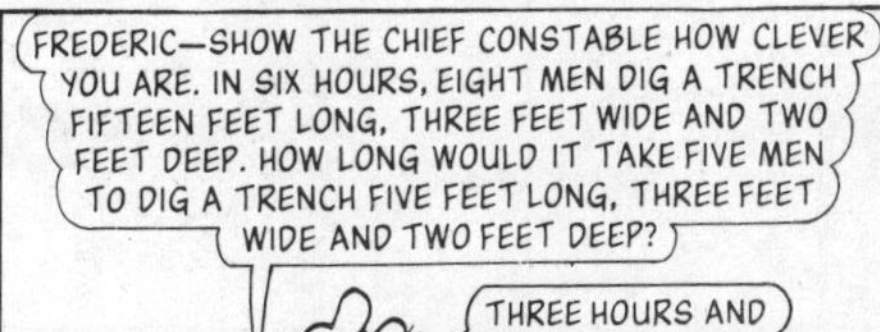

CLASSIC BEANO
BURP!
THE THREE BEARS

AAH! WELL DO I REMEMBER THE BLUEBERRY TURN-OVERS MY MA USED TO MAKE WHEN I WAS A CUB......

...AND HOW I USED TO FROLIC THROUGH THE LEAFY GLADES PICKING BLUEBERRIES....
TRALAH-TRALAH!

STAND BY THE STOVE, MA! I'M OFF TO PICK SOME BLUEBERRIES FOR BLUEBERRY TURNOVERS.

TRALAH! I FEEL LIKE A CUB AGAIN!
SOME CUB!

OO'ER! I'D FORGOTTEN ABOUT THIS HILL!
BLUEBERRY PATCH

PUFF!—I'M NOT AS FIT AS I USED TO BE!—PANT!

WHEEZE!—AH! AT LAST—BLUEBERRIES!

BUT—
LOOK OUT, PA!

TOO LATE!
AARGH!
SKID

OUCH! OOYAH! OW!

BACK HOME—
WHERE ARE THE BLUEBERRIES FOR THE TURNOVERS, PA?
DON'T MENTION "TURN-OVERS" TO ME! I'VE JUST DONE 200 OR SO!

MA MAKES APPLE TURNOVERS INSTEAD—
BUT NO PESKY TURNOVERS FOR ME! I'M HAVING CHEESE SANDWICHES.

THAT NIGHT—
POOR PA! THE CHEESE HAS GIVEN HIM A NIGHTMARE—AND HE'S STILL DOING "TURNOVERS"!
TURN
WHIRL
TWIST
TURN

CLASSIC NUTTY
SAMUEL CREEPS

TUM . . . TI . . . TUM . . .

I'm gonna flatten that little wimp, Samuel Creeps!

UH? He's stopped suddenly!
SCREECH!

YAAAH!
SWERVE!
Only my quick action prevented a disaster!

Poor little caterpillar! I almost squashed you!
OOOH!

SHORTLY—
Oh, golly-gosh! A hazard ahead!
DIETER'S DAILY
I'll ring my bell to warn him!

TRING!
YIKES! What was that?
LEAP

Strange! I was sure there was a fat man in my path!
I'll fix Creeps!

DIETER'S DAILY
NNNYAAGH!

SAMUEL RIDES ON—
Almost there . . .
I'll destroy Creeps!

I'm turning right! Must signal first!
WHUMP!
UMPH!

This is the place!
CYCLE SAFELY!

OOOH! He must be joking!
Here's your Road Safety award, Samuel!

# THE BEANO

THE COMIC WITH ROGER the DODGER

DENNIS the MENACE FAN CLUB

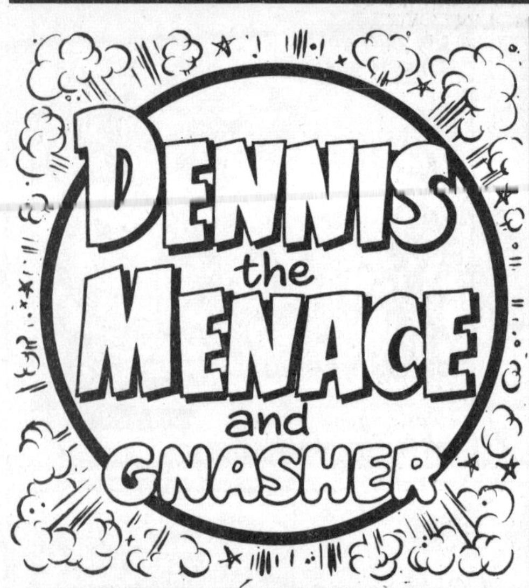

DENNIS the MENACE
AND GNASHER
YOU CAN'T GO IN THERE!
B-BUT I'VE TO DELIVER THIS!

BUT THIS IS A VERY DANGEROUS THING!
DANGEROUS?
SNATCH

YES—SOMEONE MIGHT DO THAT WITH IT!
CLASSIC BEANO
SPLUDGE!

HOLD IT! D'YOU HAVE A MACHINE GUN IN THERE?

IT'S ONLY A VIOLIN!
THAT'S YOUR STORY!

YOU COULD BE 'VIOLINT' WITH THIS!
OOH!
THWACK!
TWANG!

YOU MUST BE JOKING!
LADY MAUDE PYE
WHY CAN'T I PASS, YOU YOUNG RUFFIAN?

WALTER'S DOG, FOO-FOO
SNATCH
GASP!

YOU MIGHT DO THIS — GURR! GRUFF!
EEK! A WOLF!

BOO-HOO! IT'S ALL GOING DREADFULLY WRONG!
HEH-HEH!
TIP-TOE

TEE-HEE!
OW! OW!
PAT
PAT
I'LL BE THE BOUNCER NOW!
BOUNCE
BOUNCE

Colonel BLINK
CLASSIC BEEZER
ARF! ARF! JOLLY GOOD! ROVER—COME AN' SEE THIS FUNNY-LOOKIN' CHAP ON TH' TELLY!
THE KILLER STRIKES
RIGHT, MISTER! STICK 'EM UP!
!
RIGHT! HAND OVER YOUR MONEY! I KNOW IT'S IN THAT DRAWER!
MY SAVINGS! SOB! SNIFF!
DON'T LOOK ROUND! JUST HAND IT OVER!
?
NOW WALK OUT THE DOOR! AND REMEMBER—I'M RIGHT BEHIND YOU WITH THIS GUN!
JUST KEEP WALKIN'!
—TURN SHARP LEFT—
—AND SHARP LEFT.
I'M BEIN' KIDNAPPED!
KEEP MOVIN'—I'LL TELL YOU WHEN TO STOP!
BLINK! STOP!
I KNOW THAT VOICE!
CARTWRIGHT! TURNED TO CRIME!
?
YOU'VE SEEN THE ERROR OF YOUR WAYS, EH? WELL, HAND BACK MY MONEY AN' WE'LL SAY NO MORE ABOUT IT!
WHAT MONEY, BLINK?
SO THAT'S YOUR GAME! VERY WELL, I'M GOIN' TO 'PHONE THE POLICE!
OL' CARTWRIGHT A CROOK! WHO WOULD HAVE THOUGHT IT?
PUT DOWN THAT 'PHONE!
NO! NO! NO! DON'T SHOOT, CARTWRIGHT, I—I W-WON'T 'PHONE THE POLICE!
GET THOSE HANDS UP—AND START WALKIN'!
SPARE ME, OL' PAL!
KEEP WALKIN', AND REMEMBER, I'VE GOT THE GUN! ONE FALSE MOVE, AND—
?
?
CARTWRIGHT! YOU FOOL! YOU'LL GET A LIFE SENTENCE FOR THIS! CARTWRIGHT! ARE YOU LISTENIN'?

# WE ARE The SPARKY PEOPLE

**There's moaning and wailing... Life's not all "plane" sailing!**

THAT'S GOOD! WE'VE GOT ALL OUR WORK DONE FOR THIS WEEK!
SLURP! SLURP!
HUMM.... FOLD HERE... AND HERE....
OI! FEET!

CLASSIC SPARKY

A PAPER AEROPLANE, EH? I USED TO MAKE THEM!

HOW ABOUT THAT?
NOT BAD... LET'S SEE WHAT THE OTHERS CAN DO!

SOON—
WHEE!
MINES BEST!

HELLO ALL!
BLOW!
WHOOSH!
BLOW!
OH, NO! THAT DRAUGHTS BLOWN THEM OUT OF THE WINDOW!

HEY! THAT'S GREAT! BET THEY GO FOR MILES!

WAIT A MINUTE! DO YOU REALISE WHAT WE MADE THOSE AEROPLANES OUT OF?
AAARGH! NEXT WEEK'S STORIES!

GET THEM BACK!
RUN!
QUICK!
SPARKY
EEEEEEK!

GOT IT! ERK!
COME BACK!
OOH-ME-HEAD!

MUCH LATER—

The SMASHER
CLASSIC DANDY
HOLD IT!

BUT, MUM, I'M GOING TO THE PICTURES WITH WILLIE AND TOM!
CAN'T HELP THAT! YOU'LL GO TO THE SUPERMARKET FOR MY GROCERIES FIRST!

OH, NO! THERE'S A QUEUE WAITING TO GET IN!
SUPERMARKET

WHACK!
WELL, A QUEUE'S NOT GOING TO HOLD ME UP!
LOOK OUT-PAINT!
OOER!

ARGH! IT'S SPREAD ALL OVER THE PAVEMENT!
HO-HO! NOW I'M FIRST!
LEAP!

GARAGE
NOW TO CATCH A BUS HOME-GOSH! ANOTHER QUEUE!
BUS STOP
I'LL HAVE TO GET RID OF THEM!

GARAGE
I'LL BORROW THIS WATER HOSE FROM THE GARAGE AND FILL THE GUTTER BY THE BUS STOP!
BUS STOP

QUICK! OUT OF THE WAY OR WE'LL GET SPLASHED BY THE BUS!
BUS STOP
THAT'S SHIFTED THEM!

ONE ONLY!
THAT'S ME!

THERE'S YOUR GROCERIES, MUM—I'M OFF TO THE PICTURES NOW!
THANKS, SMASHER! CHEERIO!

YOU'RE LATE—LOOK AT THE QUEUE!
DON'T PANIC—I'LL SHIFT THEM!

QUICK! COME AND LOOK—A MAN-EATING FISH—IT'S HORRIBLE!

FISH RESTAURANT
WE'VE BEEN TRICKED —IT'S ONLY A MAN EATING A FISH!
HO! HO!

THERE HE GOES! THROW A STONE AT HIM!
QUEENS CINE
MISSED!
3/9
2/6

OOF!
WHUMP!

HO-HO! SMASHER'S BEEN STOPPED BY A Q AT LAST!
UEENS
HO-HO!
2/6

DUNDER ED
THE WONDER, BLUNDER, BOY!

ADMISSION FREE - I'LL POP IN HERE AND ENJOY MY LUNCH!
DAUBER'S HALL
ART EXHIBITION
ADMISSION FREE

CLASSIC CRACKER
NO CHAIRS. I'M NOT FUSSY - THIS'LL DO ME NICELY TO SIT ON.
NIAGARA FALLS
PRESS FIRE EXTINGU

OO-ER! WHAT'S HAPPENED? I ONLY SAT DOWN!
SPLOSH!
SQUIRT...
PRESS FIRE EXTINGU

LOOK WHAT YOU'VE DONE, YOU TWIT! GET OUT OF THIS ROOM!
HO! HO! IT SURE IS MOST REALISTIC!
HA-HA! FABULOUS!
OKAY, I'M OFF.

HERE'S A QUIET SPOT - SHOULD BE SAFE FROM TROUBLE HERE.

OH NO! NOT MORE TROUBLE!
LAUGHING CAV
CLUNK!

EEK! HE'S NO LAUGHING CAVALIER!
YOU AGAIN!
LAUGHING CAVALIER
KRASH!

OUT! AND STAY OUT!

LATER
I'LL TRY DRAWING A FEW FUNNY FACES.
ONLY GOT THIS CREAM BUN LEFT - OWK! ALL THE MIDDLE'S SQUASHED OUT!
ALL MY OWN WORK

JUST MY LUCK! WHAT A WASTE OF GOOD CREAM!
SPLAT!

WORK OF ART! THAT BEARD LOOKS JUST LIKE REAL!
IT REALLY STANDS OUT!
GENIUS!
THANKS, ED! SHARE THE TAKINGS!
CLINK! CLINK!
COO! TA!

# The Topper

Mickey
I'M A SPRINGBOARD-TESTER THIS WEEK.
ACE SPRINGBOARD COMPANY
ACE SPRINGBOARD COMPANY
CLASSIC TOPPER
CRACK!
COMPANY
I'LL FETCH ANOTHER BOARD. THAT ONE WAS TOO WEAK.
THUD!
SNAP!
HMM! THERE'S ANOTHER ONE THAT WAS TOO WEAK.
BONK!
TEST THIS FIBRE-GLASS ONE, MICKEY. IT'S OUR LATEST MODEL.
BEND
TWANG!
THAT ONE WAS TOO STRONG!

CLASSIC BEANO
MORE BACON AND EGGS
AUNT MAT'S LOOKING RATHER UNHAPPY JUST NOW. INSTEAD OF PLAYING TODAY, LET'S DO SOMETHING TO CHEER HER UP.
GOOD IDEA! I KNOW—WE'LL GATHER FLOWERS FOR HER.
LISTENING
MUNCHING
JOE
LORD SNOOTY AND HIS PALS
YES, ALL THE DIFFERENT WILD FLOWERS ARE IN BLOOM.
AUNT MAT WILL BE PLEASED!
I SAW THEM FIRST!
I CAN'T TAKE THAT FLOWER. THE BEE WOULDN'T LIKE IT!
NO, YOU DIDN'T! ANYWAY, I PICKED THEM!
IDIOT! NOW YOU'VE MADE ME PULL THE HEADS OFF!
LOOK, AUNT MAT—WE'VE BEEN PICKING WILD FLOWERS ALL FOR YOU. AREN'T THEY LOVELY?
OH, THANK YOU, CHILDREN!
HM! AUNT MAT STILL LOOKS RATHER WORRIED. I KNOW. WE'LL GIVE HER BREAKFAST IN BED TOMORROW.
SO, NEXT MORNING—
OH! I'VE LET THE TOAST BURN WHILE I WAS READING "THE BEANO"!
WATCH THOSE EGGS!
GOOD MORNING, AUNT! WE TOLD COOK WE'D MAKE YOUR BREAKFAST TO-DAY.
OH, THANK YOU! THIS IS SO GOOD OF YOU ALL.
AUNT MAT'S LOOKING MORE WORRIED THAN EVER! IT'S THE GARDENER'S DAY OFF TODAY. LET'S DO SOME GARDENING FOR AUNT MAT. SHE'S VERY FOND OF HER ROSES.
HA! HA! SNITCHY'S GETTING A FREE RIDE ON THE MOTOR MOWER!
PETROL
THE WATER PRESSURE'S AWFULLY LOW TODAY.
HELLO, AUNT MAT. WE THOUGHT WE'D DO SOME GARDENING FOR YOU.
INSECT KILLER
OH, THANK YOU, SNOOTY!
I'M AFRAID WE HAVEN'T MANAGED TO CHEER HER UP VERY MUCH!
IS THAT DOCTOR BROWN? WILL YOU PLEASE COME TO THE CASTLE AT ONCE—
OH! I MUST TELL THE OTHERS THAT AUNT MAT'S ILL!
COME QUICKLY! AUNT MAT'S ILL! SHE WAS PHONING THE DOCTOR. WE MUST GET HER TO BED.
ALL RIGHT, AUNT MAT—OFF TO BED WITH YOU! WE'LL LOOK AFTER YOU!
BUT—BUT—
SOON—
R-R-RING!
THAT'LL BE THE DOCTOR NOW. WELL, WE'VE GOT AUNT MAT TUCKED UP IN BED.
THE DOCTOR, M'LORD.
COME QUICKLY, DOCTOR! AUNT MAT'S VERY ILL!
AUNT MAT? BUT YOUR AUNT PHONED ME TO COME TO SEE YOU!
US?
YES, I SENT FOR THE DOCTOR BECAUSE YOU'VE ALL BEEN BEHAVING SO WELL LATELY, AND THIS WEEK YOU'VE BEEN EVEN BETTER, SO I THOUGHT YOU MUST BE ILL!
SWOON

YOUNG FOO
THE KUNG FU KID
AN AFTERNOON ON THE RIVER FOR GORSEDALE BOYS' SCHOOL
CLASSIC CRACKER
Now then, Basher! I want you to teach Young Foo how to row—it'll keep you both warm! It's rather chilly today!
I'll soon warm up the little squirt!
Most kind!
I'll climb in with the oars, Young Basher!
Allow me to help you aboard, Foo!
I've been waiting for a chance like this!
I'll have to stoop low to put these oars in!
SWOOSH!
Well, strike me! The little twit ducked!
SWIPE!
Most careless! It would seem that Young Basher has missed the boat!
SPLOOSH!
Gasp! Splutter! Gasp!
Hold tight and I'll fish you out!
Hullo? What's this?
A FLYING "FISH"?
AAAAAACH!
VAROOOOOM!
Tut! Most careless of me! I seem to have pulled too hard!
CRUNCH
Oh-oh! I fear Young Basher does not seem to have liked the way I fished him out—he's in one of his ugly moods!
You little squirt! I'll bash you one for that!
STAGGER STAGGER
(TRANSLATION) HAYAH!
SWIPE!
CHOP!
ZIP

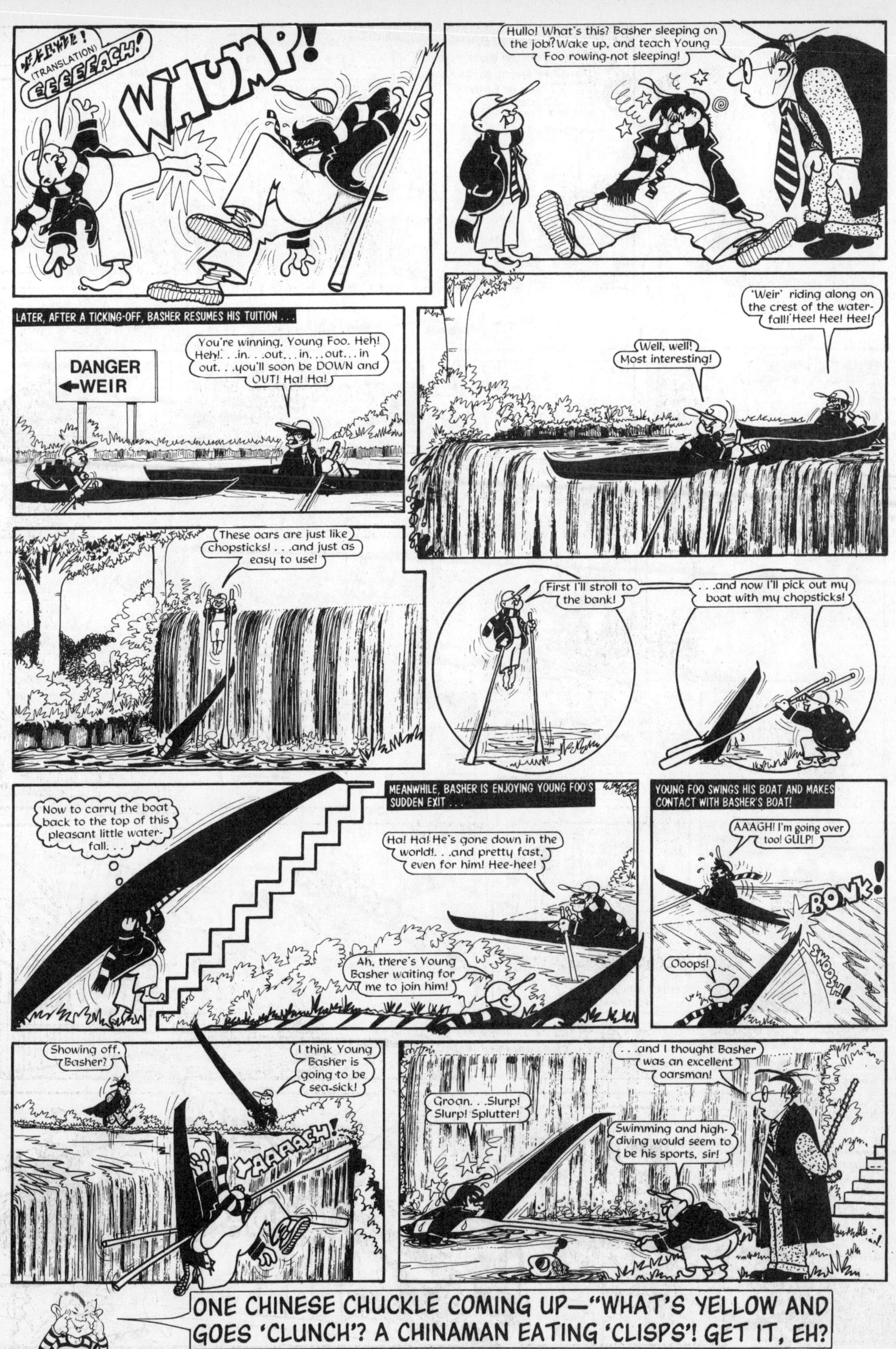
(TRANSLATION) EEEEEACH!
WHUMP!
Hullo! What's this? Basher sleeping on the job? Wake up, and teach Young Foo rowing-not sleeping!
LATER, AFTER A TICKING-OFF, BASHER RESUMES HIS TUITION . . .
DANGER
WEIR
You're winning, Young Foo. Heh! Heh! . . in. . .out. . . in. . .out. . . in out. . .you'll soon be DOWN and OUT! Ha! Ha!
Well, well! Most interesting!
'Weir' riding along on the crest of the waterfall! Hee! Hee! Hee!
These oars are just like chopsticks! . . .and just as easy to use!
First I'll stroll to the bank!
. . .and now I'll pick out my boat with my chopsticks!
Now to carry the boat back to the top of this pleasant little waterfall. . .
MEANWHILE, BASHER IS ENJOYING YOUNG FOO'S SUDDEN EXIT . . .
Ha! Ha! He's gone down in the world!. . .and pretty fast, even for him! Hee-hee!
Ah, there's Young Basher waiting for me to join him!
YOUNG FOO SWINGS HIS BOAT AND MAKES CONTACT WITH BASHER'S BOAT!
AAAGH! I'm going over too! GULP!
BONK!
Ooops!
SWOOSH!
Showing off, Basher?
I think Young Basher is going to be sea-sick!
YAAAACH!
. . .and I thought Basher was an excellent oarsman!
Groan. . .Slurp! Slurp! Splutter!
Swimming and high-diving would seem to be his sports, sir!
ONE CHINESE CHUCKLE COMING UP—"WHAT'S YELLOW AND GOES 'CLUNCH'? A CHINAMAN EATING 'CLISPS'! GET IT, EH?

ETHEL RED
CLASSIC NUTTY

This is the Crawlski Brothers, Dad! They want an escort boat for their swim across the Sea of Fog!
Not us! Too dangerous!

We know the way! We could guide you!
Sorry! I must think of the safety of my ship and crew!

We'd give you half the prize money!
Always ready to help sportsmen! We'll leave right away!

Straight ahead, for the moment!

THEN—
HARD TO STARBOARD!

Phew! Just as well we were warned about that rock!
Yes! That sailor wasn't so lucky!
ANYWHERE

SUDDENLY, THE FOG THICKENS . . .
Now we've lost the Brothers! We'll have to drop anchor!

BUT SOON—
The fog's clearing a little, and the Brothers are over there!
RAISE ANCHOR!

It's great to know we're safe with the Brothers around!

WE'VE HIT A ROCK! Why didn't they warn us?
CRUNCH!

Er—at least the Brothers will be able to bring back a rescue boat for us!

IDIOT!!! We were following a couple of walruses!
ULP!

Hey! Slow down! We're meant to be the swimming champs!
GRRR! RANT! RAGE!

# BIG HEAD AND THICK HEAD

CLASSIC DANDY

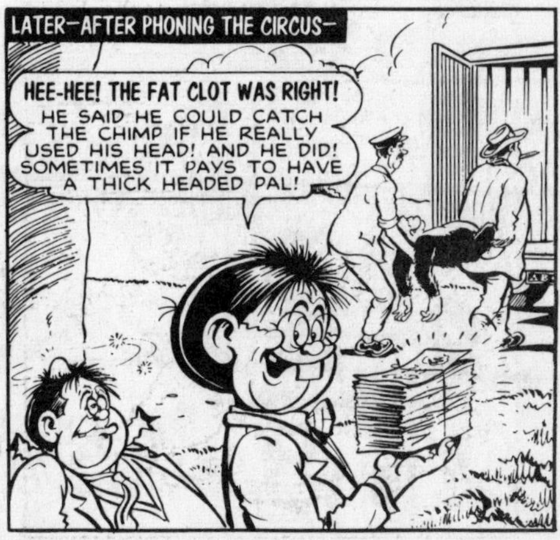

# BIG UGGY

CLASSIC TOPPER

# GINGER

CLASSIC BEEZER

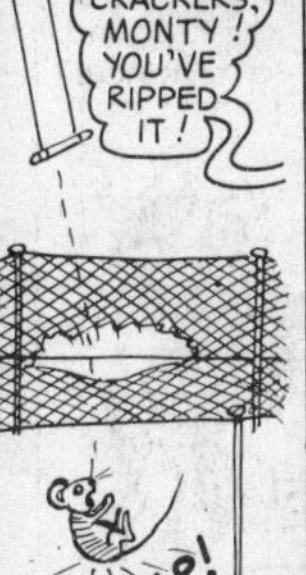

P.C. Big Ears
CLASSIC DANDY
OOOOH! MY POOR FEET! I'M FED UP POUNDING THE BEAT, SARGE! HOW ABOUT A TRANSFER?
I'LL SEE WHAT I CAN DO, BIG EARS.
NEXT DAY—
YIPPEE! THIS IS MORE LIKE IT! A PANDA CAR OF MY VERY OWN!
HELP! POLICE! I'VE BEEN ROBBED!
HA! I'LL SOON CATCH THE VILLAIN! HE'S ONLY GOT TWO WHEELS AND I'VE GOT FOUR!
HEE-HEE! I'M CATCHING UP ON HIM ALREADY.
ZOOM!
OO-ER! I TOOK THAT CORNER TOO FAST!
TOPPLE!
CRASH!
YEEARGH!
BONK!
OOYAH! WHAT HIT ME?
CAUGHT HIM! BUT I SEEM TO HAVE CAUSED A TRAFFIC JAM!
YOU'VE BLOCKED THE ROAD, YOU BUMBLING BOBBY!
GRR!
BLARE!
TOOT TOOT!
PEEP!
LATER—
OFF YOU GO, BIG EARS— AND MAKE SURE YOU BRING THAT CAR BACK IN ONE PIECE!
TEE-HEE! I WONDER IF THEY'VE GOT THAT TRAFFIC JAM CLEARED YET?
BANK
TR-R-RING!
BANK
I CAN HEAR A BELL RINGING IN THAT BANK. GOSH! IT'S A HOLD-UP!
HIS CAR'S FASTER THAN MINE BUT I'LL TAKE A SHORT-CUT UP THIS STREET.
ERK! IT'S A ONE-WAY STREET!
LOOK OUT, YOU CLOT!
ROAD HOG!
PHEW! THANK GOODNESS I DIDN'T HIT ANYTHING! NOW WHERE HAVE THOSE BANK ROBBERS GOT TO?
VROOOM!
ZOOM!
CRASH!
CRUNCH!
BACK AT THE POLICE STATION—
DON'T LET THAT WRECKER LOOSE ON THE ROADS AGAIN! HE'S TOO DANGEROUS!
I THINK I'VE GOT AN IDEA. GIVE ME A HAT AND WE'LL HAVE A WHIP ROUND.
I'LL DO ANYTHING— I'LL EVEN GO STRAIGHT FROM NOW ON, BUT PLEASE, SARGE, DON'T LET BIG EARS DRIVE ANOTHER CAR!
LATER—
BAH! THEY'VE TAKEN AWAY MY CAR AND GIVEN ME A PAIR OF ROLLER SKATES!
HA-HA! GET YOUR SKATES ON, BIG EARS!
HO-HO! BIG EARS HAS JOINED THE FLYING SQUAD!

THE
Dandy

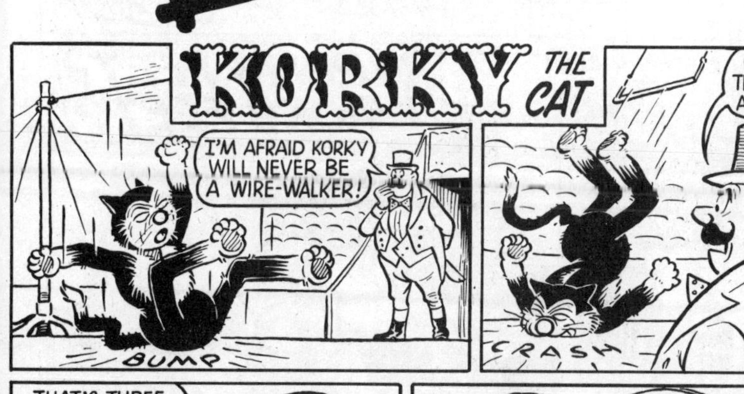
KORKY THE CAT
I'M AFRAID KORKY WILL NEVER BE A WIRE-WALKER!
BUMP
OR A TRAPEZE ARTIST!
CRASH

OR A BARE-BACK RIDER EITHER!
THUMP

THAT'S THREE ACCIDENTS YOU'VE HAD, KORKY. TRY SOMETHING SIMPLE. GO AND SEE MARVO.

THIS IS AN EASY JOB, KORKY. FIRST LET ME FASTEN YOU TO THE BOARD.

THEN ALL YOU HAVE TO DO IS STAND STILL!
OH, NO! MARVO IS AN AXE-THROWER!

GRAND CIRCUS
DARTS
SORRY, BOSS! I CAN'T RISK HAVING A REAL AXE-IDENT!

BRAINLESS
DID YOU HEAR WHY BRAINLESS PACKED IN HIS JOB AS A CIRCUS CLOWN?
YEAH! EVERBODY WAS LAFFIN' AT HIM!
BRAINLESS WON THE POOLS AND BOUGHT A BIG JAGUAR!
YEAA! AN' IT BIT HIM!
THESE SHOES ARE USELESS! I'LL TAKE 'EM BACK!—OUCH!!!
SHO
SHOES - SHOES -
THESE SHOES!!—ARE CRIPPLIN' ME!!!— CRIPPLIN'!!!!
H'MMM!
I'M NOT AT ALL SURPRISED SIR! YOU'VE GOT THEM ON THE WRONG FEET!!!!
EH?!
WRONG FEET? WRONG FEET?
YES!
BUT—THESE ARE THE ONLY FEET I'VE GOT!!
GASP!!!

Full Of FUN STARS

# DREAMY DANIEL

# DESPERATE DAN

# FOXY

FOXY
CLASSIC TOPPER
FOXES KEEP OUT.
I'LL LISTEN AT FARMER'S WINDOW. I MIGHT HEAR SOMETHING TO MY ADVANTAGE!

INSIDE...
YES, MOTHER... I'LL TURN THE CHICKS OUT INTO THE CORN-FIELD NOW IT'S BEEN HARVESTED... THEY CAN PICK UP THE SEEDS...

OH, JOY! I'LL REAP A FINE HARVEST MYSELF... A HARVEST OF CHICKENS!

POOR FOXY! HE DANCED AWAY TOO SOON- IF ONLY HE HAD WAITED ONE SECOND MORE TO HEAR THE REST OF WHAT FARMER WAS SAYING...
...AND JUST IN CASE FOXY IS THINKING OF PAYING US A VISIT, MA... I'LL BE READY FOR HIM, TOO!

AT DAWN...
THERE ARE SOME OLD SCARECROWS IN THE CORN-FIELD!
FOXES KEEP OUT

SO I'LL TAKE THE PLACE OF ONE OF THEM!

SOON AFTER...
COME AND GET IT, FELLAS!
HEH! HEH! HERE THEY ARE NOW!
FOXES KEEP OUT

POOR UNSUSPECTING LITTLE CHICKADEES...

I'LL EAT YOU FOR BREAKFAST-AND DINNER AND TEA AND SUPPER!

SQWAWK
SQWAWK
ONLY A FEW MORE TO COLLECT!

THE LAST ONE!

I THOUGHT YOU MIGHT TRY SOMETHING LIKE THIS...
EEK!
FARMER!

OUT!
HOW DOES HE DO IT? HE MUST BE A MIND-READER OR SOMETHING!
FOXES KEEP OUT

DUNDER ED
CLASSIC CRACKER
THE WONDER, BLUNDER, BOY!

HMM. I'LL HAVE A LOOK IN HERE.
KRUMBLING CASTLE OPEN TO THE PUBLIC

THIS IS A DUMMY OF SIR RICHARD IN CHAIN MAIL ARMOUR!
HUH - GETTIN' A BIT TATTY-LOOKING!
GUIDE
SIR RICHARD PYEKRUST

WE NOW MOVE ON, LADIES AND GENTS.
I'LL TIDY UP THIS LOOSE WIRE FOR THEM.
GUIDE

EEK! IT'S COMING UNRAVELLED LIKE KNITTING.
NO! STOP!

YOU CLOWN! THAT PRICELESS ARMOUR IS OVER 500 YEARS OLD!
NO NEED TO BE LIKE THAT! I WAS ONLY TRYING TO HELP!
GUIDE

HERE WE HAVE SOME ANCIENT WEAPONS.
MUST TAKE A CLOSER LOOK AT THAT OLD MUSKET.
Ye olde CANNON

OUCH! YEOWK!
OOER! SLIPPED ON THESE CANNON BALLS!
ZONK!

YOU AGAIN!
GUIDE

YOU'RE KEEN-I'LL SHOW YOU ANOTHER OLD RELIC.
COO, TA!

STEP IN, I'LL SHOW YOU HOW IT WORKS.

ROTTEN TRICK! LEMME OUT!
YE OLDE STOCKS
HA-HA!
THAT'LL KEEP YOU OUT OF TROUBLE FOR THE REST OF THE DAY!

A FEW DAYS LATER

PRISON SPORTS

ANY PRISONERS INTERESTED IN THE FOLLOWING EVENTS ARE ASKED TO ENTER THEIR NAMES HERE

100 YDS. SPRINT

120 YDS. HURDLES

LONG JUMP

POLE VAULT

1 MILE

RIGHT, LADS WE'RE ENTERIN'!

BUZZ
CLASSIC BUZZ
TODAY'S WEATHER
HIGH
HERE IS THE WEATHER FORECAST FOR BUZZLAND— LONG FUNNY PERIODS FOLLOWED BY GALES OF LAUGHTER!
HOP, SKIP and JOCK
LET'S GET THE FOOTBALL STRIPS OUT OF THE HUT, LADS!
OH, NO! THE MICE HAVE EATEN OUR STRIPS!
THEY'VE EATEN THE NUMBER OFF MY JERSEY! NOW I WON'T KNOW WHAT POSITION I'M PLAYING!
RUINED!
THESE MICE HAVE GOT T'GO!
PHEW! MY BREATH'S BEEN COMIN' IN SHORT PANTS SINCE I ATE THOSE SHORTS!
BEWARE OF MICE
GRR! THE MICE HAVE BEEN AT IT!
BAH! MISSED!
NO! NO! THAT'S MY PET MOUSE!
HURRY UP AND EAT THIS NET, BOYS, BEFORE HE CATCHES MICKEY.
CHOMP
MUNCH!
CHOMP!
AH'M NOT! THERE'S A MOOSE UP MY TROOSER LEG!
IDIOT! IT'S THE MICE YOU'RE MEANT TO LEAD AWAY, NOT THE CATS!
BEANS
JOCK! THIS IS NO TIME TO BE DOING THE HIGHLAND FLING!
I MUST BE NEAR A MOUSE — I CAN SNIFF HIM!
I'LL LURE 'EM OUT WITH CRUMBS OF CHEESE!
OUCH!
HURRAH! THE CATS ARE AWAY - LET'S PLAY!
GOT IT!
WELL FIELDED, MORTIMER!
CATCH!
MUNCH!
MUNCH!
LUNCH!
BOYNG!
HEY— THAT'S MY CLOCKWORK MOUSE!
PEAS
I ALWAYS HAD THE FEELING MORTIMER WAS A FIELD MOUSE!
I'M INNOCENT I TELL YOU! I'M INNOCENT!

# DOODLEBUG

Heh! Doodling portraits will make me a fortune.

SUDDENLY—
CLASSIC NUTTY
Portrait, sir? No problem.
FLASH
W-WOW!?!

SECONDS LATER—
There, ready in seconds. A photo beats a doodle any day, sir. That'll be 25p.
PULL
Coo! Thanks!
EH?

MUCH FLASHING LATER—
No! WAIT! My doodles are works of art!
I like it! I like it!
HO! HO! Tough luck, Doodlebug. Your doodles are no match for my instant photos.

I'm off to buy some more film for my camera. I'll soon have YOU out of business. HAR! HAR!
BOP!
OUCH! This is serious!

SOON—
Doodlebug, do another of your portraits of me. They're SO lifelike.
Oh, all right, Ugly Bug, but it'll probably be my last.

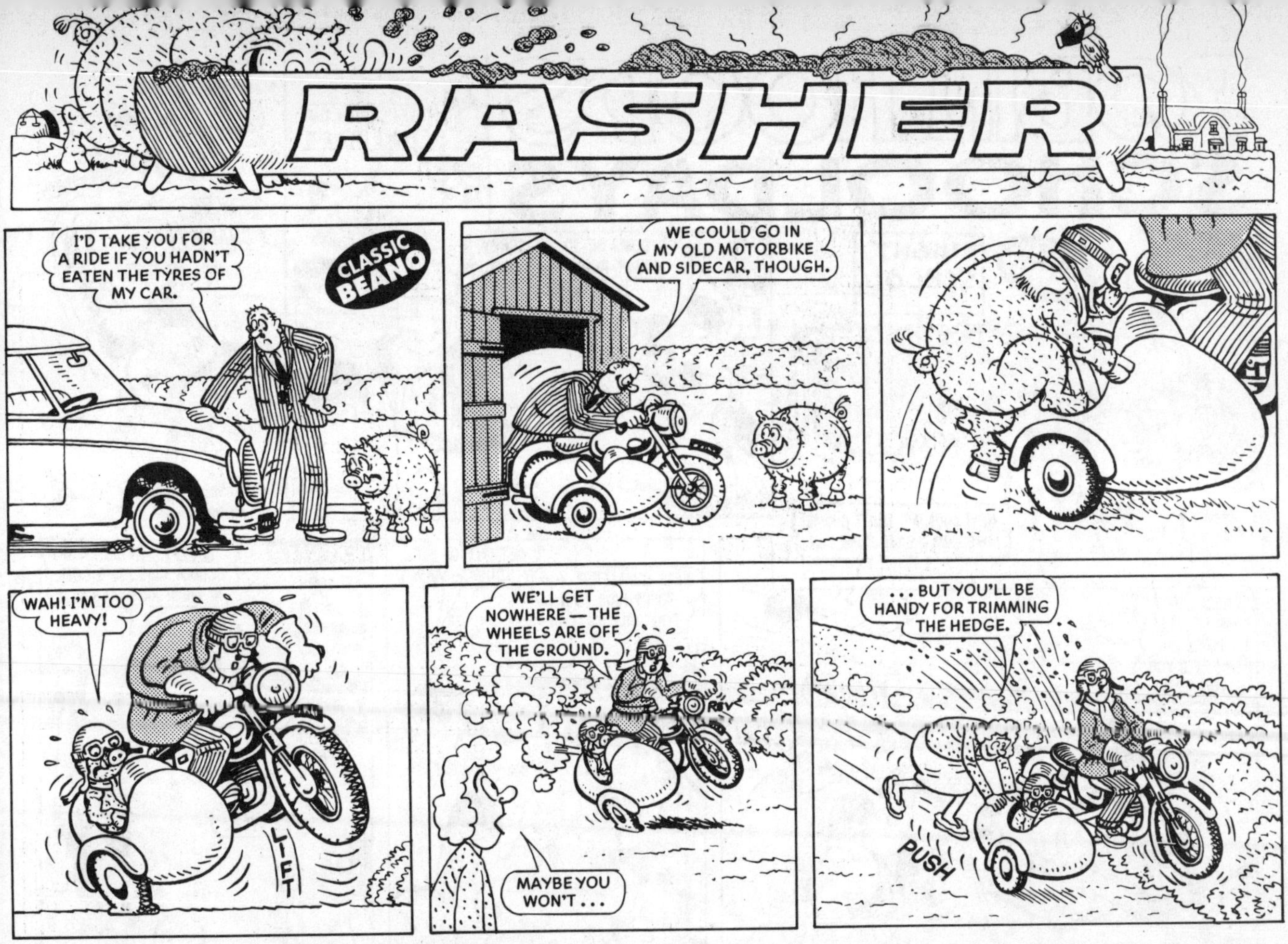

# RASHER

CLASSIC BEANO

I'D TAKE YOU FOR A RIDE IF YOU HADN'T EATEN THE TYRES OF MY CAR.

WE COULD GO IN MY OLD MOTORBIKE AND SIDECAR, THOUGH.

WAH! I'M TOO HEAVY!

LIFT

WE'LL GET NOWHERE — THE WHEELS ARE OFF THE GROUND.

REV

MAYBE YOU WON'T . . .

. . . BUT YOU'LL BE HANDY FOR TRIMMING THE HEDGE.

PUSH

# ROGER The DODGER'S DODGE CLINIC

HELEN HALE, OF STOURBRIDGE, HAS A MUM WHO MOANS ABOUT LOUD RECORDS!

DODGE CLINIC

BOOM! THUD!

TOO LOUD!

I DO TOO, HELEN!

CLASSIC BEANO

THIS COTTON WOOL WILL STOP HER HEARING MY RECORDS.

ZZZ!

ROBIN HOOD'S SCHOOLDAYS
CLASSIC DANDY
KNIGHT SCHOOL
HEY! LOOK AT THAT, CHUMS! WE COULD HAVE SOME FUN HERE!
DON'T BE SO ROUGH, RODNEY!
SORRY CECIL.
GENTLE PROD
LET'S LIVEN THE PLACE UP A BIT!
PUSH
RIGHT, PALS. CHARGE!
WHIZZ!
TAKE THAT! MAYBE IT'LL PUT SOME LIFE INTO YOU, YOU CISSY!
YEEOW!
ERK!
SOCK!
GET OUT OF HERE, YOU RUFFIANS!
WE'LL CHALLENGE YOU SOPPY KIDS TO A FOOTBALL MATCH.
SOB!
NEXT DAY—
GASP! THOSE KNIGHT SCHOOL KIDS HAVE COME IN THEIR ARMOUR SUITS!
TEE-HEE!
YEEOW!
ERK!
OH, DEAR! WHAT A ROUGH GAME!
SLAP!
BIFF!
JAB
CRUSH!
HAR-HAR! AN OPEN GOAL!
'TIS TIME I DID SOMETHING ABOUT THIS!
FIZZ!
HEY! WHAT'S HAPPENED?
STAB
TWANG
SEE THAT? JUST IN TIME!
TEACHER PRODUCES A NEW BALL—
OUTA MY WAY! I'M GOING TO SCORE!
WATCH THIS! MORE THAN ONE TEAM CAN PUT THE BOOT IN!
NOW FOR A CERTAIN GOAL!
OH, YEAH?
WHEE!
WHIZZ!
TWANG!
BUT THIS WILL BE A "BOOTIFUL" SHOT!

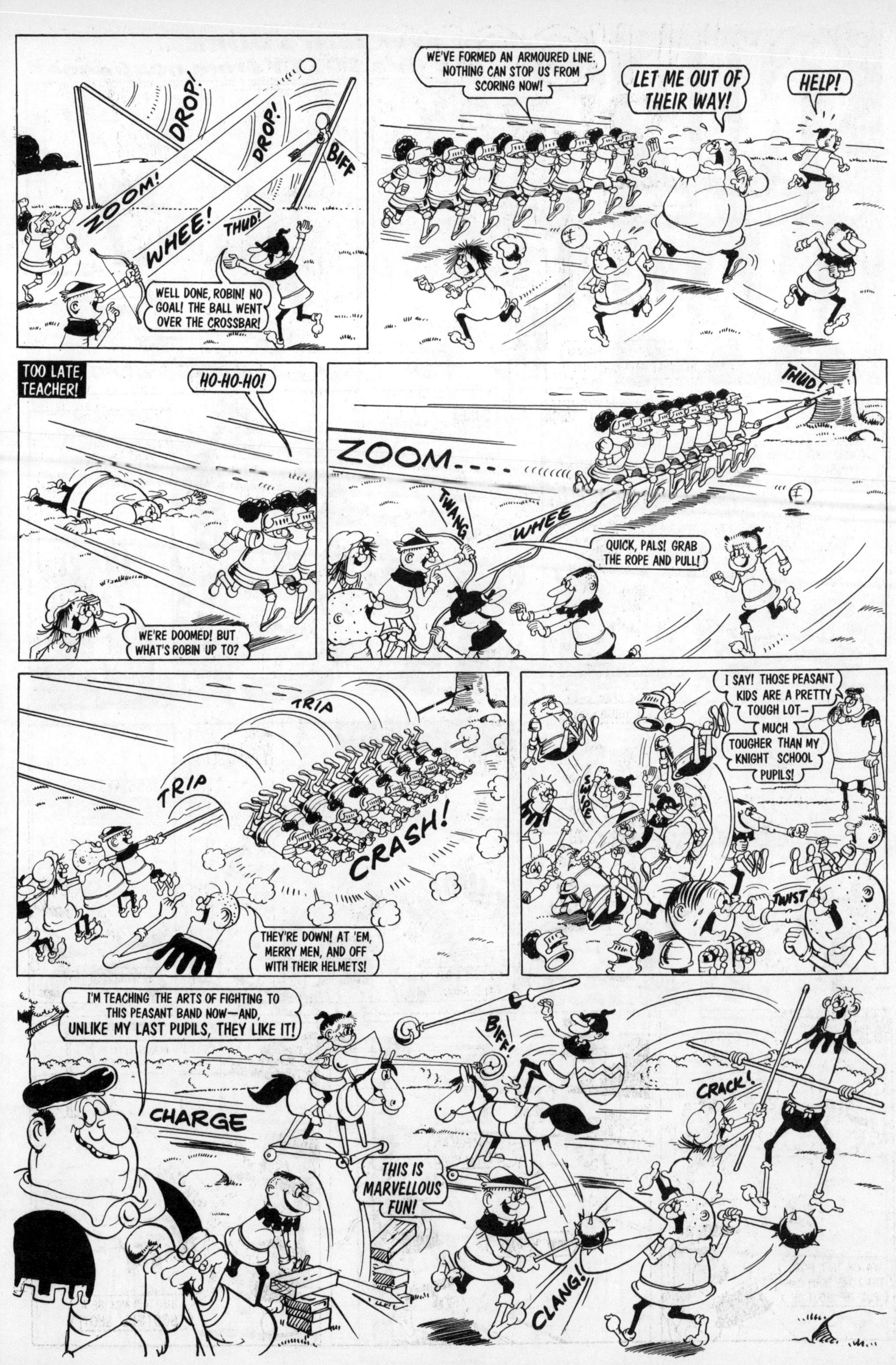
DROP!
DROP!
ZOOM!
BIFF
WHEE!
THUD!
WELL DONE, ROBIN! NO GOAL! THE BALL WENT OVER THE CROSSBAR!
WE'VE FORMED AN ARMOURED LINE. NOTHING CAN STOP US FROM SCORING NOW!
LET ME OUT OF THEIR WAY!
HELP!
TOO LATE, TEACHER!
HO-HO-HO!
WE'RE DOOMED! BUT WHAT'S ROBIN UP TO?
THUD!
ZOOM....
TWANG
WHEE
QUICK, PALS! GRAB THE ROPE AND PULL!
TRIP
TRIP
CRASH!
THEY'RE DOWN! AT 'EM, MERRY MEN, AND OFF WITH THEIR HELMETS!
I SAY! THOSE PEASANT KIDS ARE A PRETTY TOUGH LOT—MUCH TOUGHER THAN MY KNIGHT SCHOOL PUPILS!
TWIST
I'M TEACHING THE ARTS OF FIGHTING TO THIS PEASANT BAND NOW—AND, UNLIKE MY LAST PUPILS, THEY LIKE IT!
BIFF!
CHARGE
CRACK!
THIS IS MARVELLOUS FUN!
CLANG!

# SNIP and SNAP

**Was there ever such a BORE ...**
**As this SOFTY from next door?**

CLASSIC BEANO
CALAMITY JAMES
THE WORLD'S UNLUCKIEST BOY!
WE'RE GOING TO HAVE A GAMES DAY! KEEP JAMES'S MIND OFF HIS BAD LUCK!
YOU'RE NOT JOINING IN OUR GAMES, CLOUD!
RUMBLE!
James's pet — Alexander Lemming.
WAHEY!
THWANG!
IVAN LENTIL
PUFF! I CAN GET IT!
But the cloud drops and —
ORF!
PLOMPH!
CUMULO-NIMBUS MIRTH!
THUPOSE YOU THOUGHT THAT FUNNY, CLOUD?
TRYING HARD NOT TO TITTER!
GLARK!
WE'LL PLAY SOMETHING ELSE.
PWAARRP! FAARNNN! HONK!
TENNIS COURTS
SAXOPHONE TESTING WORKS
HIDE AND SEEK!
BLUEBOTTLE GOING TO SEE HIS GIRLFRIEND
MUCH MOOLAH
£100
But —
HUH! TRUST THAT CLOUD TO SPOIL OUR GAME!
BTHTHTHTH!
BEE WITH A LISP.
SIGH!
PORRIDGE PARLOUR
GLOWER!
FANCY A GAME OF CRICKET?
RAAASP! TOOT! BLAST!
HOVER!
WHOOPEE CUSHION FACTORY
HERE COMES A "LEMMING SPECIAL"!
TREMBLE! QUAKE!
DO NOT CHORTLE AT THE PARKY'S INCREDIBLY BIG CONK BY ORDER.
THUNDER!
WHOOSH!
POUR! LASH! TEEM!
GLUB!
BATTER!
HUMPH! WHAT BAD LUCK — RAIN STOPS PLAY!
CACKLE! GUFFAW!
LOOK OUT . . . I'M . . . GOING . . . TO . . . AAAA . . .
EAT MORE SPOTTED DICK!
SNUFFLE! SPLUTTER!
DRIP! SQUINGE!
SQUIDGE! SPLIDGE! SQUELCH!
OOO CHOOOO!
BLAST!
COO! HE'S BLOWN THE CLOUD APART!
SO, WE HAVE AN EVEN BETTER GAME NOW . . .
. . . JOIN THE CLOUD! A FLOATING JIG-SAW! HEH-HEH!

CLASSIC BEANO
The BASH STREET KIDS

WHY HAVE YOU GOT A DRESS ON, TEACHER?
ARTLESS PUPILS— THIS IS A PAINTER'S SMOCK!

A PRIZE TO WHOEVER CAN PAINT THEIR PARENTS BEST!
YAHOO!
CHOCS

THOSE ARE THE EYES . . .
SPLAT!

. . . NOW FOR THE NOSE . . .

WHY THE,CURTAINS ROUND THIS, PLUG?

MY DAD'S EVEN MORE HANDSOME THAN ME!
UGH!
SWOON!

HEY! YOU'RE COPYING ME!

Judging the contest—
THIS IS RATHER DIFFICULT . . .
'Erbert isn't very good at drawing faces!

Then—
AM I TOO LATE TO ENTER?
I SUPPOSE NOT, SMIFFY.

LET'S GET STARTED!
ART CUPBOARD
OLD MASTERS

WHY ARE YOU NOT DOING A PICTURE, BOY?
BUT I AM — WATCH!

. . THEN THE MOUTH!
IT'S REMARKABLE WHAT HE CAN DO WITH FOOD!

SOON FINISH MY ENTRY!
BLACK

THERE! JUST LIKE MY LOVELY MUM!
IT IS TOO!

I AM NOT — HE'S MY DAD AS WELL!

SPLATTER MY NOSE, WOULD YOU?

YOU TWO ARE DISQUALIFIED!
SPOT REMOVER

HERE!
GASP! WHAT'S THIS?

PROUD
I WIN! NOBODY PAINTED THEIR PARENTS BETTER THAN I DID!
Daft enough to let him!
GROAN! I GIVE UP!
HEH! HEH!

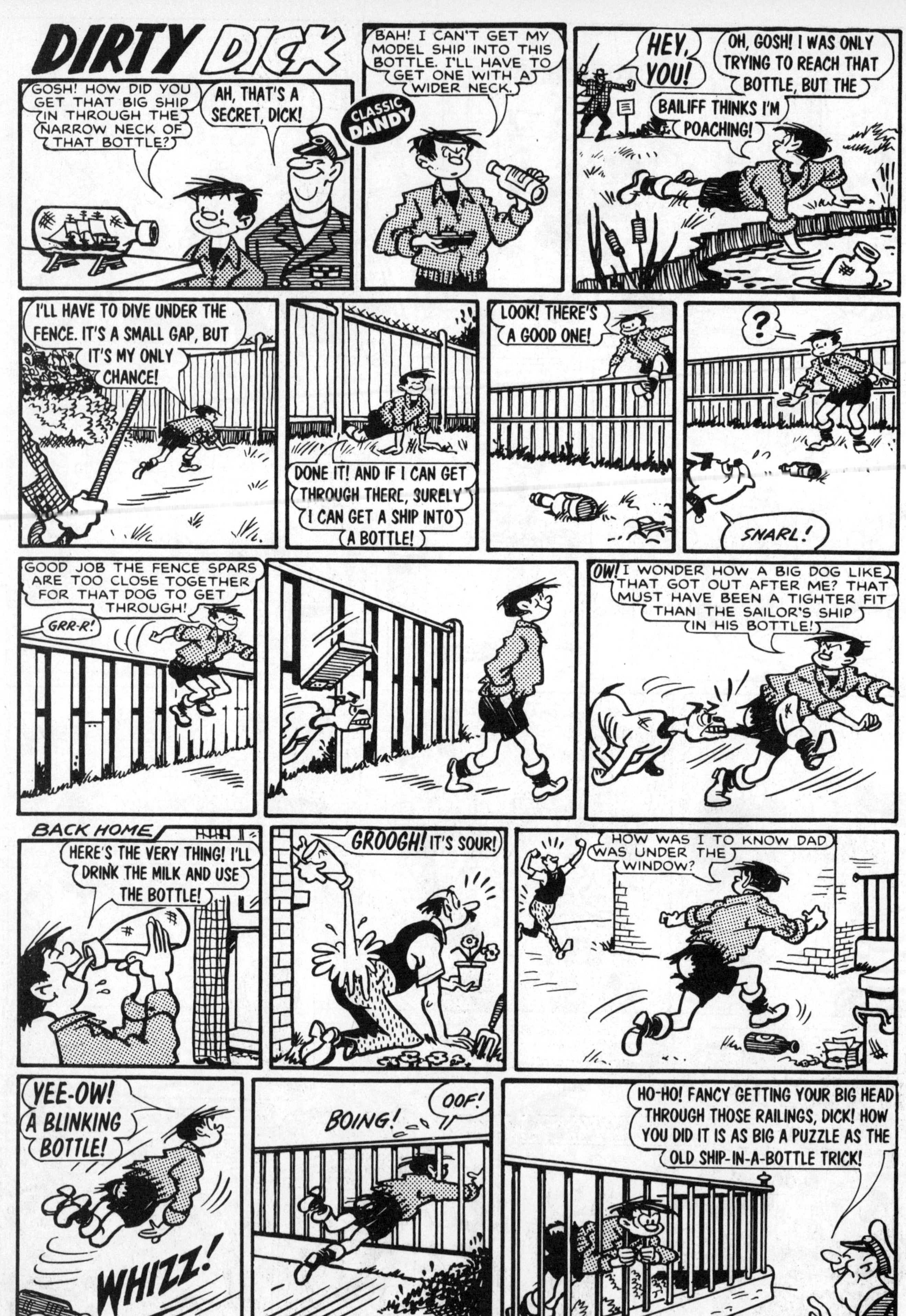

DIRTY DICK
GOSH! HOW DID YOU GET THAT BIG SHIP IN THROUGH THE NARROW NECK OF THAT BOTTLE?
AH, THAT'S A SECRET, DICK!
CLASSIC DANDY
BAH! I CAN'T GET MY MODEL SHIP INTO THIS BOTTLE. I'LL HAVE TO GET ONE WITH A WIDER NECK.
HEY, YOU!
OH, GOSH! I WAS ONLY TRYING TO REACH THAT BOTTLE, BUT THE BAILIFF THINKS I'M POACHING!
I'LL HAVE TO DIVE UNDER THE FENCE. IT'S A SMALL GAP, BUT IT'S MY ONLY CHANCE!
DONE IT! AND IF I CAN GET THROUGH THERE, SURELY I CAN GET A SHIP INTO A BOTTLE!
LOOK! THERE'S A GOOD ONE!
?
SNARL!
GOOD JOB THE FENCE SPARS ARE TOO CLOSE TOGETHER FOR THAT DOG TO GET THROUGH!
GRR-R!
OW! I WONDER HOW A BIG DOG LIKE THAT GOT OUT AFTER ME? THAT MUST HAVE BEEN A TIGHTER FIT THAN THE SAILOR'S SHIP IN HIS BOTTLE!
BACK HOME
HERE'S THE VERY THING! I'LL DRINK THE MILK AND USE THE BOTTLE!
GROOGH! IT'S SOUR!
HOW WAS I TO KNOW DAD WAS UNDER THE WINDOW?
YEE-OW! A BLINKING BOTTLE!
WHIZZ!
BOING!
OOF!
HO-HO! FANCY GETTING YOUR BIG HEAD THROUGH THOSE RAILINGS, DICK! HOW YOU DID IT IS AS BIG A PUZZLE AS THE OLD SHIP-IN-A-BOTTLE TRICK!

CLASSIC BEANO

# JONAH

JONAH HAS LANDED ABOARD THE S.S. "VULTURE", CAPTAINED BY JOCK McSCROOGE. JOCK SAILS THE SEVEN SEAS IN AN ANCIENT PADDLE-STEAMER, PICKING UP SURVIVORS OF SHIPS SUNK BY JONAH. HE HAS MADE HIS FORTUNE BY CHARGING THE SURVIVORS HUGE FEES FOR FOOD AND PASSAGE HOME!

YE'LL REMEMBER, CAP'N, THAT TIME WE PICKED UP A GOUT-RIDDEN GOAT WEARING HORN-RIMMED GLASSES—AND IT TURNED OUT TAE BE HIRAM S. SPHUNKENBLINKER, THE MULTI-MILLIONAIRE!

AYE!—BUT WHAT OF IT?

WELL, THIS CLOT MIGHT ALSO BE AN ECCENTRIC MILLIONAIRE.

I'LL LOOK HIM UP IN MY ILLUSTRATED COPY OF "WHO'S WHAT"—

—AND FIND OOT HOW MUCH HE'S WORTH!

WHO'S WHAT ILLUSTRATED

AGH-H!

WHO'S WHAT ILLUSTRATED

BEWARE GIRAFFES
UNFRIENDLY NATIVES
CAPTAIN CUTLER AND HIS BUTLER
NATIVE VILLAGE
BEWARE LIONS
CLASSIC SPARKY
CAPTAIN EGBERT CUTLER IS THE MAN WHO THOUGHT THAT THE HIGHLAND FLING WAS ANOTHER NAME FOR TOSSING THE CABER. HE CERTAINLY DIDN'T WIN ANY PRIZES FOR THE DANCE HE DID WHEN HE DROPPED THE CABER ON HIS FOOT! HE AND HIS AMAZING BUTLER, CRUMBS, ARE STILL SEARCHING FOR THE SOURCE OF THE RIVER BUNGO—
C-CRUMBS? WHAT ARE ALL THESE STRANGE PLANTS?
I SHALL INVESTIGATE THE MATTER, SIR.
UM...MACFOGELY'S EXCELLENT BOOK—POTTY PLANTS—SAYS THAT THE ONE BESIDE YOU IS A...OH, DEAR...
BURP!
BE CAREFUL, SIR, THAT'S A MAN-EATING IGGLE-FIGGLE PLANT...OH-DEAR-OH-DEAR...
ER... SIR? ARE YOU IN THERE, SIR?
POTTY PLANTS by
OF COURSE I'M IN HERE, CRUMBS! AND IT'S JOLLY UNCOMFORTABLE! HOW ARE YOU GONNA GET ME OUT?
MR MACFOGELY'S BOOK SAYS THAT AFTER SWALLOWING ITS VICTIM THE PLANT SLEEPS FOR TWENTY-FOUR HOURS BEFORE STARTING TO CHEW IT.
POTTY PLANTS by
WELL, HURRY UP! I'VE GOT ANTS IN MY PANTS, GNATS IN MY SPATS, AND FLEAS ON MY KNEES!
ER...MR SPARKY ARTIST, SIR. CAN YOU THINK OF A WAY TO GET CAPTAIN CUTLER OUT OF THE...ER...SPOT OF BOTHER HE'S IN?
SPARKY ARTISTS VOICE
POTTY PLANTS by MACFOGELY
'FRAID NOT, CRUMBS! I ONLY DRAW THIS! TRY THE SPARKY WRITER!
MR SPARKY WRITER, SIR?
NOPE! I ONLY PUT YOU DOWN AMONG THESE PLANTS! IF THE LITTLE TWIT WANTS TO GET HIMSELF SWALLOWED, THAT'S HIS BUSINESS!
WELL, CRUMBS? HAVE YOU GOT A PLAN TO PERSUADE THIS OVERGROWN BRUSSELS SPROUT TO COUGH ME UP AGAIN?
NO, SIR. AT LEAST... I MEAN YES, SIR.
MR ARTIST, SIR, I'VE DECIDED TO HAVE A CUP OF TEA, BUT HAVE RUN OUT OF SUGAR. COULD YOU PERHAPS DRAW SOME FOR ME?
H'MM. . .WELL, I SUPPOSE THAT'S OKAY . . . RIGHT! YOU SHALL HAVE YOUR SUGAR!
CRUMBS? YOU STILL THERE? SAY SOMETHING, CRUMBS!
I'M STILL HERE, SIR. AND I'M PUTTING MY PLAN INTO OPERATION...WITH YOUR PERMISSION, SIR.
FUNNY FELLOW! DRINKING TEA AT A TIME LIKE THIS! AH, WELL, THERE'S NO ACCOUNTING FOR BUTLERS!

THANK YOU, MR SPARKY ARTIST, SIR. THESE WILL DO SPLENDIDLY.
ER . . . THAT'S ALL RIGHT, CRUMBS! ER . . . ?

AND NOW, USING YOUR SPARE PAIR OF BRACES, SIR, I SHALL FILL THE PLANT WITH SUGAR, AND HOPE THAT IT HAS THE SAME EFFECT ON IT AS IT HAD ON ME WHEN I WAS A LITTLE PAGE-BOY.
PLUNK!
PLOP!
HUH?

CRUMBS! YOU'VE WOKEN THE PLANT UP! IT'S SHAKING! OOOOH! CRUMBS!

HIC! HIC!
HIC!
HIC!

I'M GOING UP!
WELL DONE, SIR. AND NOW, MR ARTIST, COULD YOU DRAW SOMETHING SOFT FOR THE CAPTAIN TO LAND ON?
HIC!
CERTAINLY, CRUMBS!

LOOK OUT! I'M COMING DOWN!
THERE! YOU WON'T GET MANY THINGS SOFTER THAN HIS HEAD!

OW—OOH—OW!
SOR-REE!
CRUMP!

BAH! STILL, I'M SAFE NOW! NO MORE WORRIES! NOTHING ELSE CAN HARM ME! NOPE!
WELL SIR...

CRUMBS! SOME OTHER POOR SOUL WAS TRAPPED IN THERE! WE MUST STOP AND HELP HIM!
I DON'T THINK THAT'S WISE, SIR...
HIC!

YAARGH!
INDEED, SIR.
ROAAR!

THERE, SIR. THAT SHOULD CONFUSE IT WHILE WE MAKE OUR GETAWAY.
COO!

GRRRR!
FASTER! LIONS DON'T CONFUSE THAT EASILY! RUN!
I'M RUNNING, SIR.

# BERYL THE PERIL

CLASSIC TOPPER

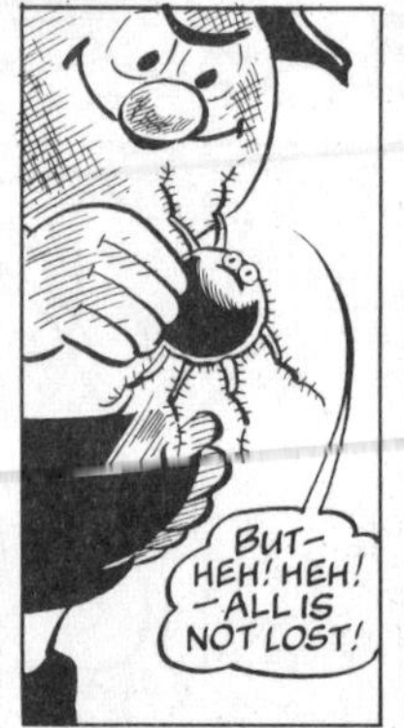

# SPOOKIE COOKIE

HE COOKS FOR THE SPOOKS

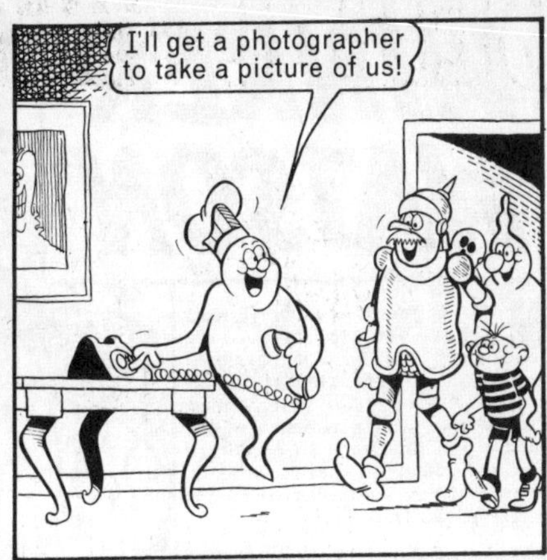

HERE'S A GHOSTLY GAG—"WHAT DO YOU CALL A SKELETON WHO DOESN'T WORK? LAZYBONES!" HAR-HAR!

The robber struggled for a moment and then lay still. He hadn't much choice with both boys sitting on top of him!

WELL DONE, LADS, AND NOW LET'S SEE WHAT THE SCOUNDREL LOOKS LIKE.

When Winker's handiwork was finished, he went to show off his invention to Creepy. He found the Master about to set off for the bank again.
HEY, MR CREEP, SIR, USE THIS CASE OF MINE—IT'S MUCH SAFER.
W.W

For once Winker didn't stop to think. He snatched the bag Creepy was carrying from the Master's hands.
I'LL TAKE YOURS, AND . . .
LET GO BEFORE SOMETHING SILLY HAPPENS, BOY . . .

At once Creepy snatched the brief-case back. And he shouldn't have done that! For it was the Master who got the full force of what happened next!
WHEEEEEE!

The piercing whistle given out by the brief-case brought a whole stream of bobbies running. Winker was amazed.
?
WHEEEEEEEE!

But the bobbies saw that it was a false alarm, and Creepy returned indoors to clean up.
THAT WAS A SPECIAL CASE THE SUPERINTENDENT GAVE ME, WATSON, AND THE RED DYE WON'T WASH OFF. WHAT'S MORE, I'M GOING TO MISS THE BANK NOW.
W.W

Creepy had to give up washing if he was to reach the bank before it closed. And Winker offered him the use of his invention.
YOU'VE STILL GOT TIME, SIR, IF YOU USE MY THIEF-PROOF BAG, AND WEAR A SCARF SO THAT THE DYE WON'T SHOW.

Creepy strode into the bank, all muffled up to hide his bright red face.
BANK
OPEN
W.W

He put the case on the bank counter, and started to feel in his pockets. That's when he made a nasty discovery.
OH, DEAR! I'VE FORGOTTEN THE KEY FOR THE HAND-CUFFS . . .
SHALL I TAKE THE CASE, SIR . . . ?

The bank teller got a nasty shock. For as he pulled the case towards him, he triggered off the tape recorder Winker had put inside, and out spoke a threatening voice. The teller thought it was Creepy who was talking!
DON'T MOVE ANOTHER MUSCLE. I'VE GOT YOU COVERED!
CLICK!

HELP! IT'S A BANK RAID!
BANK
OPEN
The teller's hands shot up, and his cries alerted a passing bobby. And with his scarf over his face, Creepy looked just like a bank robber!

Creepy tried to explain, but it was no use. The police sergeant dragged him off to a cell and locked him up!
POLICE NOTICE
NO SINGING OR WHISTLING IN THE CELLS
DON'T WORRY, SIR. OUR MONEY WILL BE SAFE ENOUGH IN THERE UNTIL TOMORROW!
HEE-HEE! AND SO WILL YOU BE, MR CREEP, SIR! TOO BAD THAT THEY'LL FIND OUT IN THE END THAT YOU'RE NOT REALLY A BOLD BANK ROBBER!
W.W

DENNIS the MENACE
CLASSIC BEANO
IT SAYS HERE THAT IT IS A GOOD THING TO HAVE A HEALTHY SUN-TAN.
GUIDE TO GOOD HEALTH
SO—
NOW TO START BASKING IN THE SUNSHINE!
AH! I FEEL HEALTHIER ALREADY!
SUDDENLY—
ERK! SOMETHING'S BLOTTING OUT THE SUN!
GO AWAY AND DO SOMETHING ELSE BOY!
SO DENNIS GOES TO PLAY WITH HIS PET RAT. WALTER, BUT—
POOR OLD WALTER'S GOT A CHILL.
SNIFFLE! SNIFFLE!
IT SAYS HERE THAT A SURE CURE FOR A CHILL IS A MUSTARD BATH.
GUIDE TO GOOD HEALTH
I'D BETTER PUT IN PLENTY OF MUSTARD. I WANT TO CURE WALTER QUICKLY.
EXTRA-HOT MUSTARD
BAH! I WISH I COULD BE FLYING MY KITE!
WATCH THAT FENCE, DENNIS!
VERY CONTENT
THEN—
OOPS!
STUMBLE
EEAAGH!
SIZZLE
NEXT DAY AT DAD'S OFFICE—
YOU'RE LOOKING RATHER UNCOMFORTABLE, OLD CHAP. WHAT'S WRONG?
ER—JUST A TOUCH OF 'SON'-BURN, BOSS!
WRIGGLE
SCRATCH
DENNIS IS FEELING UNCOMFORTABLE, TOO—BUT IT'S NOT SUN-BURN THAT'S BOTHERING HIM!

Splodge
THE LAST OF THE GOBLINS
CLASSIC TOPPER
SPLODGE'S LEANING TREE
WHAT A USELESS BUNCH YOU FAIRIES ARE. I NEVER SEE YOU DOING ANY MAGIC.

GO ON, YOU SOPPY LOT—TURN ME INTO A FROG!
STAY CALM, TINKLETOE. DO NOT BE PROVOKED BY A COMMON GOBLIN!

HAW-HAW! YOU CAN'T DO IT, CAN YOU?
COME ON, LET'S MEET THE OTHERS AT THE FAIRY RING.

SO—THEY'RE HAVING A MEETING, EH?

WONDER IF I CAN GET THERE FIRST?
WHOOOOOSH

GOOD-O! I'VE BEATEN THEM TO IT.

GLAD I KEPT THIS REEL OF THREAD—IT FELL FROM AN OLD LADY'S PICNIC BASKET.

HOPE THIS STUFF'S STRONG.

FINISHED JUST IN TIME. HERE THEY COME.

HOI, YOU LOT—LET'S SEE SOME MAGIC!
MAGIC ISN'T ALLOWED TO BE DONE WITHOUT GOOD REASON.

RIGHT! I'LL SHOW YOU SOME MAGIC, THEN—I'LL MAKE ALL YOUR TOADSTOOLS FALL DOWN.
RUBBISH! YOU CAN'T DO MAGIC.

YOU THINK SO? WATCH THIS.

HO! HO! IT WORKED!
YOU—YOU! I'VE A GOOD MIND TO KNOCK DOWN YOUR LEANING TREE BY MAGIC!

BUNKUM! I'M OFF TO HAVE A GOOD LEAN RIGHT NOW.

BUT—
YOU FAILED THE AXEMANSHIP TEST, I'M AFRAID, SMITH.

HULLO AGAIN—

I STILL SAY YOU CAN'T DO-ERK!
CREAK
SPLODGE'S LEANING TREE

KER-RASH
COO! SHE DID IT!
SPLODGE'S LEANING TREE

OK! OK! I BELIEVE YOU—NO MORE MAGIC! PLEASE!
WHAT'S GOT INTO HIM?

Jimmy Jinx
and WHAT HE THINKS
CLASSIC BUZZ

ZZZZZ!

Wake up, Jimmy!
It's too early—pretend to be still asleep!
No, that's naughty!

I'll soon get him up!

OLAY!
WHOOSH!

Tip him into a . . .

You can still pretend to be asleep on the floor, Jim, and Mum'll leave us in peace!

WOW!
SPLASH!

You win—even can't pretend t be asleep now

MUCH LATER
Time to . . .
Run, Jim!

Oh, no, you don't!

Grab hold of something, Jim!

It's no use—she's too strong for you!

Isn't my Mum funny? When I'm tired she makes me get up and . . .

. . . when I'm not tired at all, she makes me go to bed!

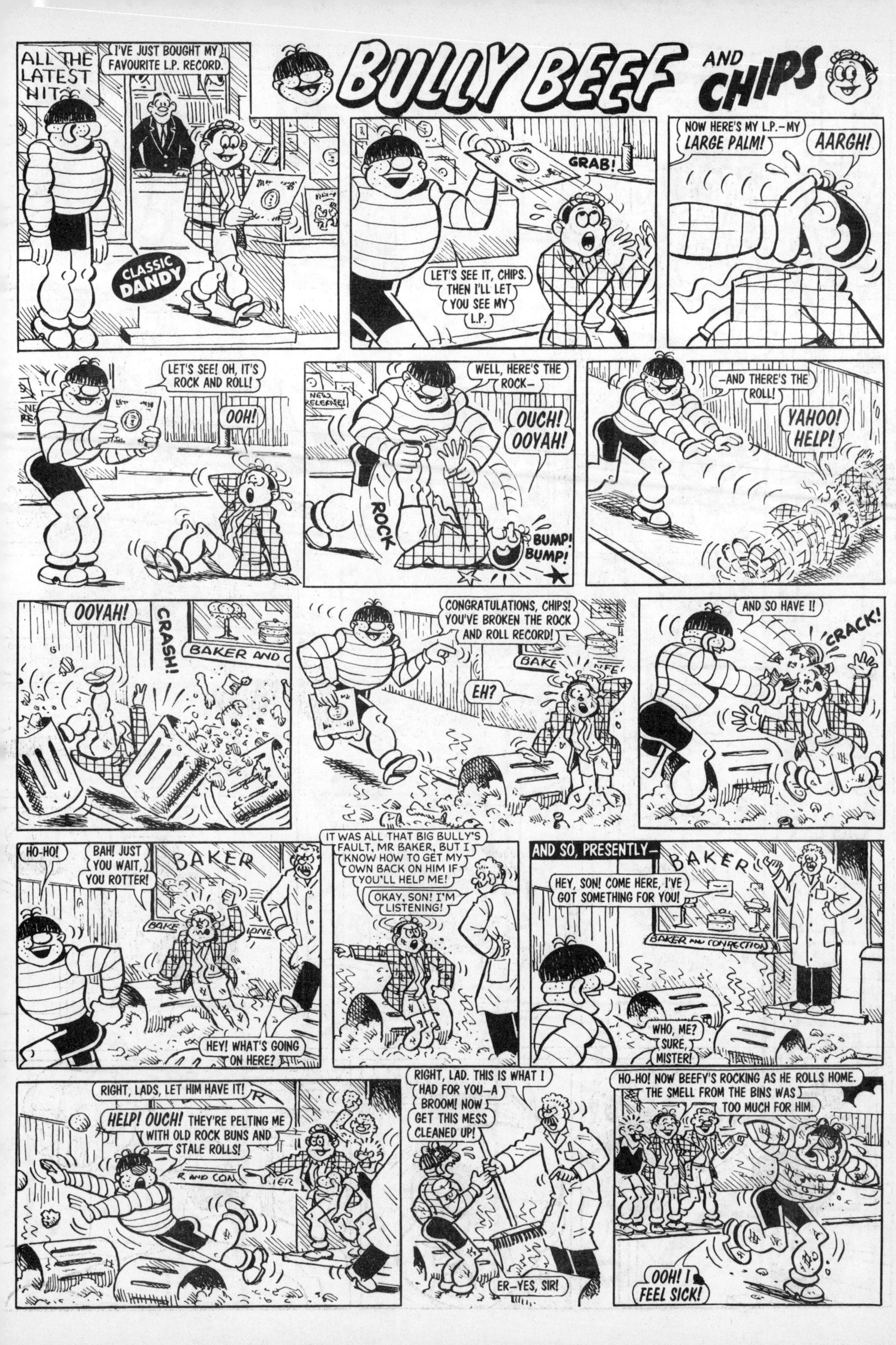
BULLY BEEF AND CHIPS
ALL THE LATEST HIT
I'VE JUST BOUGHT MY FAVOURITE L.P. RECORD.
CLASSIC DANDY
GRAB!
LET'S SEE IT, CHIPS. THEN I'LL LET YOU SEE MY L.P.
NOW HERE'S MY L.P.—MY LARGE PALM!
AARGH!
LET'S SEE! OH, IT'S ROCK AND ROLL!
OOH!
NEW RELEASE!
WELL, HERE'S THE ROCK—
OUCH! OOYAH!
ROCK
BUMP! BUMP!
—AND THERE'S THE ROLL!
YAHOO! HELP!
OOYAH!
CRASH!
BAKER AND C
CONGRATULATIONS, CHIPS! YOU'VE BROKEN THE ROCK AND ROLL RECORD!
EH?
AND SO HAVE I!
CRACK!
HO-HO!
BAH! JUST YOU WAIT, YOU ROTTER!
BAKER
HEY! WHAT'S GOING ON HERE?
IT WAS ALL THAT BIG BULLY'S FAULT, MR BAKER, BUT I KNOW HOW TO GET MY OWN BACK ON HIM IF YOU'LL HELP ME!
OKAY, SON! I'M LISTENING!
AND SO, PRESENTLY—
BAKER
HEY, SON! COME HERE, I'VE GOT SOMETHING FOR YOU!
BAKER AND CONFECTION
WHO, ME? SURE, MISTER!
RIGHT, LADS, LET HIM HAVE IT!
HELP! OUCH! THEY'RE PELTING ME WITH OLD ROCK BUNS AND STALE ROLLS!
R AND CON
RIGHT, LAD. THIS IS WHAT I HAD FOR YOU—A BROOM! NOW GET THIS MESS CLEANED UP!
ER—YES, SIR!
HO-HO! NOW BEEFY'S ROCKING AS HE ROLLS HOME. THE SMELL FROM THE BINS WAS TOO MUCH FOR HIM.
OOH! I FEEL SICK!

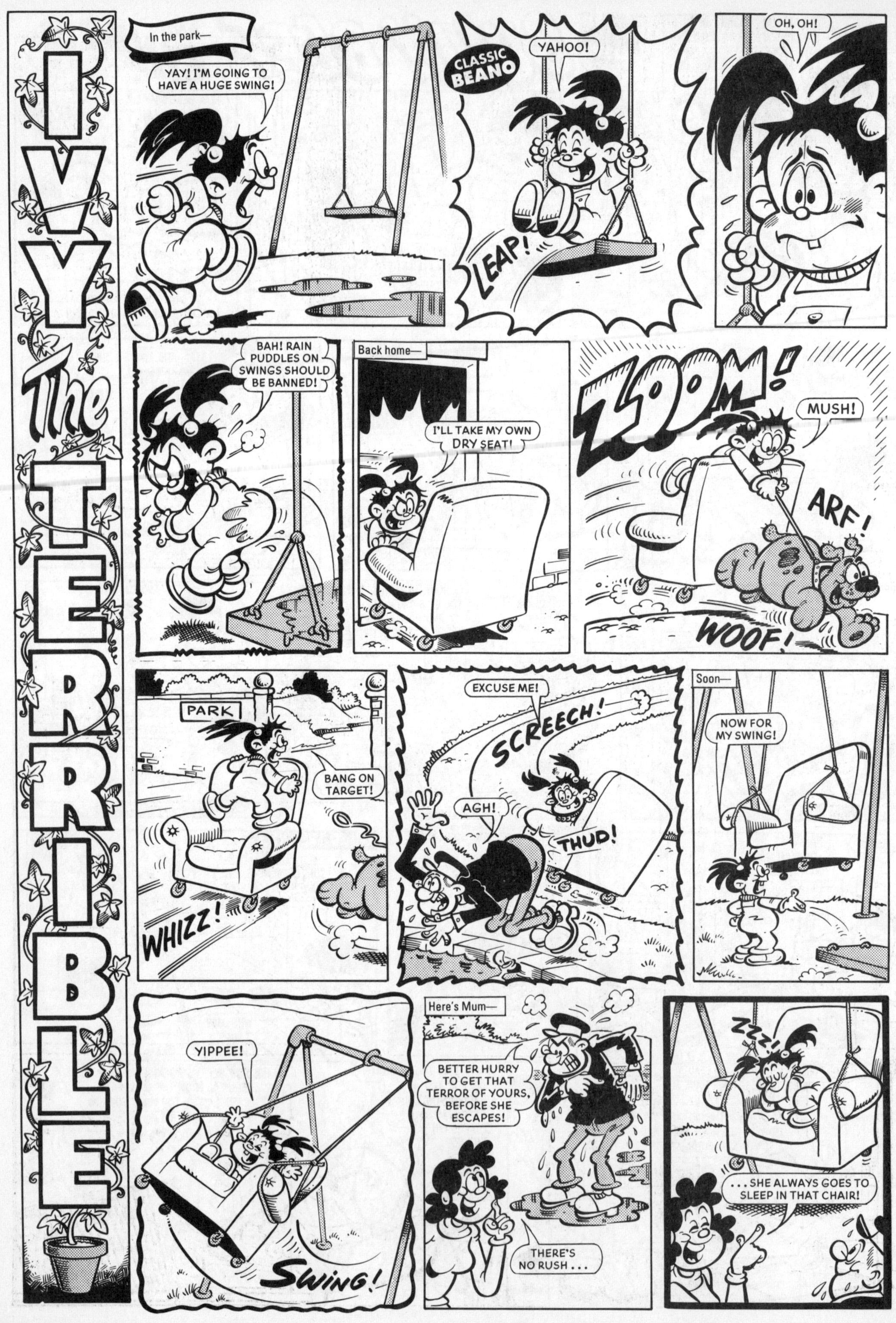

IVY The TERRIBLE
In the park—
YAY! I'M GOING TO HAVE A HUGE SWING!
CLASSIC BEANO
YAHOO!
LEAP!
OH, OH!
BAH! RAIN PUDDLES ON SWINGS SHOULD BE BANNED!
Back home—
I'LL TAKE MY OWN DRY SEAT!
ZOOM!
MUSH!
ARF!
WOOF!
PARK
BANG ON TARGET!
WHIZZ!
EXCUSE ME!
SCREECH!
AGH!
THUD!
Soon—
NOW FOR MY SWING!
YIPPEE!
SWING!
Here's Mum—
BETTER HURRY TO GET THAT TERROR OF YOURS, BEFORE SHE ESCAPES!
THERE'S NO RUSH . . .
ZZZ!
. . . SHE ALWAYS GOES TO SLEEP IN THAT CHAIR!

Colonel BLINK
CLASSIC BEEZER

GETTING DARK QUITE EARLY NOW, ROVER! HAVE T'FIND A HOBBY FOR THE LONG, DARK WINTER NIGHTS!
COAL

I KNOW! I'LL BUY A MUSICAL INSTRUMENT! MIGHT COMPOSE A SYMPHONY OR TWO! ARF! ARF!

OFFICE SUPPLIES
AN ACCORDION! TH' VERY THING!
TYPEWRITERS

HOW MUCH IS THAT DELIGHTFUL INSTRUMENT YOU HAVE IN THE WINDOW, SIR?
A MERE £25, SIR!

LATER, AT HOME
I'LL START OFF WITH A FEW BARS OF 'THE YEOMEN OF ENGLAND'S HEARTS OF OAK!' IT'S A CHA-CHA! ARF! ARF!

FUNNY! NO SOUND . . . IT'S NOT WORKIN'! IT'S A DUD!
PRESS! CLICK!
PRESS! CLICK!
PRESS! CLICK!

ONLY ONE NOTE PLAYS! IT'S DISGRACEFUL!
TING!
WHIZZ!

I'LL WRITE A STIFF LETTER TO THAT FIRM! WHERE'S MY PEN?
CIGARS

GOOD! HERE IT IS!
CIGARS

IT JUST ISN'T MY DAY, ROVER! NOW TH' PEN WON'T WRITE! IT'S TIME I HAD A TYPEWRITER!
CIGARS

. . . AN'THAT'S JUST WHAT I'LL GET!

LATER
I GOT ONE, ROVER BOY! IT'S A BEAUTY!

ARF! ARF! NOW, THEN! 'DEAR SIRS'. . .

# THE TRICKS *of* SCREWY DRIVER

# BING-BANG BENNY

CLASSIC BEANO
BALL BOY

I THINK IT'S TIME THIS PITCH WAS CUT.

WOULDN'T YOU SAY, TICH?
YES!
YANK!

SORRY, BOYS — MY MOWER'S UNDERGOING A VERY SERIOUS OPERATION.
SUPPA CUTTER
GROUNDSMAN
DAISY DUFFER
OIL

WE'LL BORROW SOME OF FARMER GRAY'S SHEEP!

So—
THESE MOWER'S DON'T NEED REPAIRING.
CHOMP! CHOMP!
CHOMP! CHOMP!

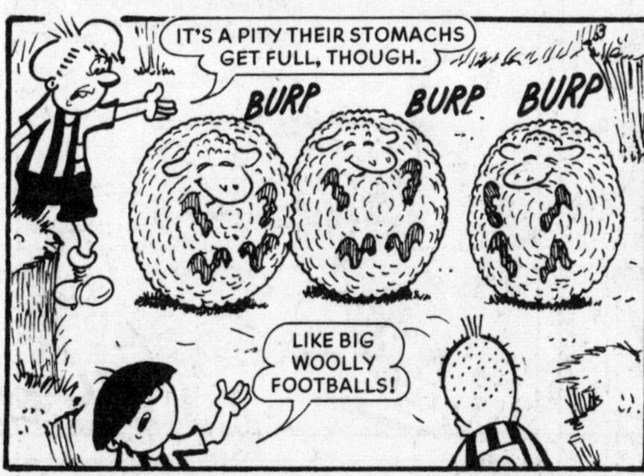
IT'S A PITY THEIR STOMACHS GET FULL, THOUGH.
BURP BURP BURP
LIKE BIG WOOLLY FOOTBALLS!

YOU COULD HELP US, CLAUDE.
BARBER'S
MOD STYLIST

THIS IS GOOD PRACTICE.
SNIP SNIP

LIKE IT?
RIDICULOUS! ONLY ONE THING FOR IT...

WANT TO TRAIN WITH US, CHOPPER?
OOER! HE'S THE DIRTIEST PLAYER IN THE LEAGUE.

I KNEW CHOPPER'S SCYTHING TACKLES WOULD DO THE TRICK.
SLICE
DODGE

THE
WILD
CLASSIC NUTTY
HUNK
MAGNUS PEEK
SINGH SONGH
PATCH
LADY

Now what appears to be the trouble?
Villy has a sore tummy, Doctor!

Up you get, Villy.
DOC
What's he up to?

Yes! It's a bad back you've got—not a bad stomach!

CRACK!
YOWCH! The bar's snapped!
THUNG!
WHANG!

It's the way you walk that gives you a strong back . . .

. . . Now walk this way, Villy!

You'll enjoy that grub. I've added plenty of curry powder!
GOBBLE!

See! It works! Your tummy is up already!

WATER!!!
OOF! How ungrateful can you get?
SLAM!

Where's Haggis gone?

THEN—
All your back needs is rest, Villy! Climb into this pipe!

You're a genius, Magnus! Now my back's supported!

# ROVERS

DOGSBODY
SILLY VILLY
TAFF
HAGGIS
BASIL CRUMB (DOG-CATCHER)

NUMBER 13
FIENDISH
BORIS DAD FRANKIE MUM GRAN TIDDLES
I'VE BORROWED ONE OF DAD'S OLD CLOAKS . . .
CLASSIC BEANO
. . . TO PUT UP A TENT IN THE GARDEN.
I'LL NEED TO TAKE A SNACK WITH ME . . .
. . . AND LOTS OF THINGS TO READ.
I'LL NEED A LIGHT TO READ MY "BEANOS" BY.
So—
YOU'LL DO!
GLOW WORM
GLOWWORMS ONLY
That night—
HOW BRAVE!
READER'S VOICE
Inside tent—
MOST PEOPLE IN TENTS GET SCARED AT NIGHT AND RUN BACK INTO THE HOUSE . . .
. . . BUT WHEN YOU'VE GOT A HOUSE LIKE OURS . . .
WAH!
. . . THE OPPOSITE HAPPENS!
SIGH! GOODNIGHT, READERS.

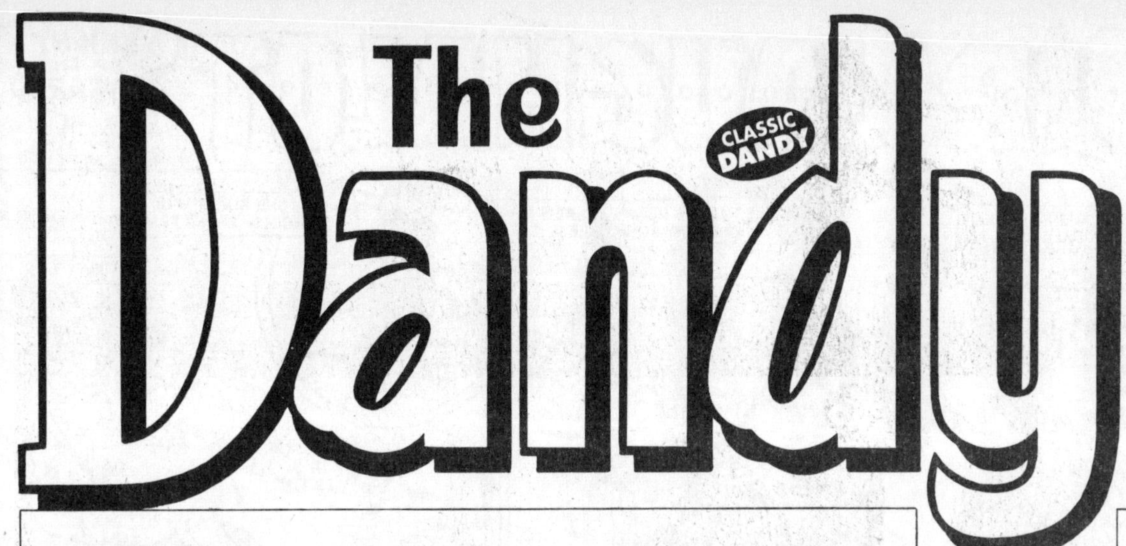
The Dandy
CLASSIC DANDY

KORKY THE CAT
COME AND LISTEN TO THE SOUND OF THE SEA IN THIS SHELL.

HEE-HEE-HEE! YOU CAN FEEL THE SEA AS WELL.
SLOSH!

BAH! I'LL HAVE TO GO HOME AND DRY OFF.

THIS WRINGER GIVES ME A GREAT IDEA!

I'VE GOT IT MOUNTED ON MY BOAT. NOW I'LL ROW OUT UNDER THE PIER.

GOOD! I'VE GOT HOLD OF HIS LINE!

NOW—A QUICK WHIRL OF THE WRINGER!
JERK!
HO! HO! HOW DO YOU LIKE THE SOUND OF WAVES IN YOUR EARS?

# SIR LAUGHALOT

# Minnie the Minx

ROTTEN EGGS

BEST PERFUMES SOLD HERE

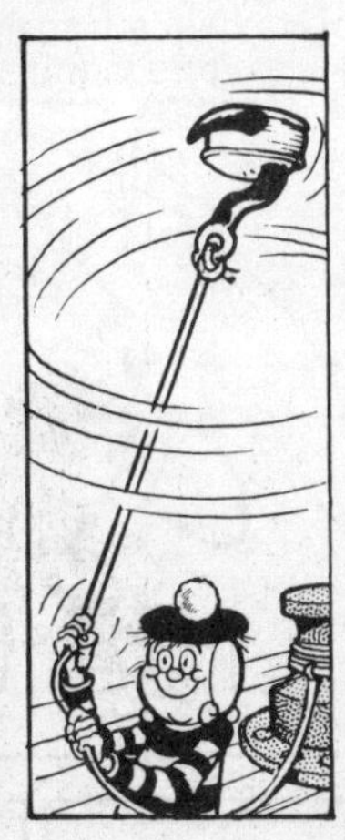

Billy the Kid
CLASSIC CRACKER
We've been watching a film about captives escaping from a prisoner of war camp!

We'll pretend we're in a prisoner of war camp and we're tunnelling our way out.

That's the way, Pongo!

Hoi! My prize pansies!

GERROUTOFIT!

We'll escape over the fence!

OOPS!
CRASH!
CRUNCH!
TINKLE!

SNARL!
The prison commandant is angry!

I'll use this grappling hook to help me scale the prison walls!

MEANWHILE FRED SPLURGE, THE BINMAN, IS PASSING –

Splutter!
YANK!

I've been hearing bad things about you, lad!
ANGRY NOISES!

We've been put into solitary confinement!
SLAM!
CLICK!

Calamity Kate
CLASSIC BUZZ
I'll try out my new catapult!
CLUNK!
Bull's-eye!
Ouch!
!
Golly! Whassat noise?
MUFFLED ROAR!
Gulp! It's Dad! And he's looking a trifle—er—pail!
Kate! I'll take that before you do any more damage!
SNATCH!
Super-duper! Just what I need!
Now I'll borrow Dad's braces . . .
Oh, no! Look at the size of that catapult!
I'll soon put a stop to . . . HELP!
Ooer! Dad's not going to like that!
TRIP!
WHUMP!
Old meanie! Took that catapult, too! I might as well go for a stroll!
Ah, Kate—I'd like you to do a job for me . . .
Okay, Mr Murphy!
LATER—
I—I don't believe it! She's going to make an even bigger catapult!
No more catapults, understand? Not one more!
B-but, Dad . . .
STAMP! CRUNCH!
I've just been collecting the last letter for Mr Murphy's new shop sign!
J. MURPH
ELECTRICAL SUPPLIES
Bah! That silly twit has spoilt my sign!
I've got a job for you!
J. MURPH
ELECTRICAL SUPPLIES
HO-HO!
You'll stay there until I can get a new letter 'Y'

GASP! THOSE NEW MEN ARE SWIMMING IN THE LAKE! I'D BETTER WARN THEM OF THE DANGER!
CUZ
CLASSIC DANDY
CORPORA
CLOT

OUCH! EEYAARGH! GET THIS OFF ME! ITS TEETH ARE SHARP!

GOOD JOB THIS PIKE'S NO LONGER HUNGRY, SIR!
OUCH! CAREFUL, CLOTT! THOSE TEETH ARE LIKE RAZORS!

SO YOU'VE SPOTTED OLD DEVIL HAVE YOU, CLOTT? I'LL CATCH BRUTE THIS TIME, AS SOON AS GET SOME BAIT!
HE'S BEEN A TERROR FOR YEARS AND HE MUST WEIGH HALF A HUNDRED-WEIGHT BY NOW!

YEEAARGH! GLUG!
THUD!

GROOGH! STAND BACK WHILE I WASH THIS SMELLY BAIT OFF!
WOW!

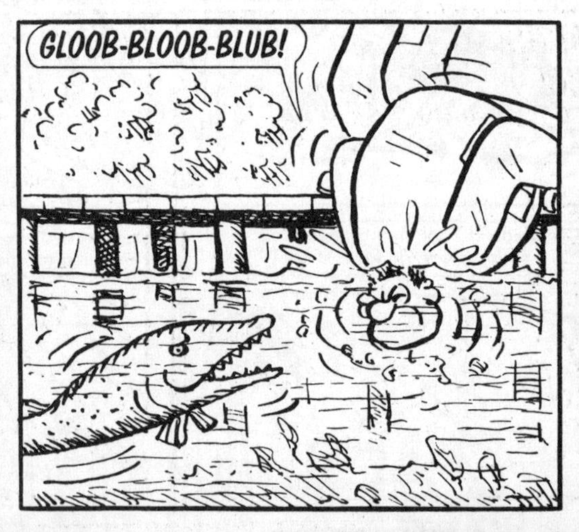
GLOOB-BLOOB-BLUB!

GET READY TO CATCH HIM IN THE NET, SIR, AS SOON AS HE GETS HOLD OF THE MEAT!
OKAY, CLOTT!

SNAP!
NOW'S YOUR CHANCE, SIR! GET THE NET UNDER HIM!

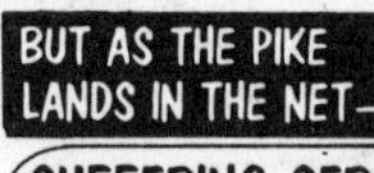
BUT AS THE PIKE LANDS IN THE NET—

SUFFERING SERG
THE WEIGHT OF THE
PLUS THE PIKE WA
MUCH FOR THE BR

OH, DEAR! I'M TOO LATE! I MUST TELL COLONEL GRUMBLY ABOUT THIS!
YEOWW! HELP!
EEK! THERE'S A MONSTER PIKE IN THE LAKE!
WOW!

THIS WILL LOOK GOOD UP HERE—
COLONEL, SIR! I'VE URGENT NEWS FOR YOU—

PRESENTLY—
I DON'T KNOW WHERE THE COLONEL'S GONE—
I THOUGHT HE'D HAVE BEEN HERE AHEAD OF ME!

OH, BOY! A BITE!
I'VE GOT PLENTY OF BAIT, ANYWAY!

YAHOO!
SLIDE!

JEEPERS! THE PIKE'S GOT HIM!

BRISTLING BRIGADIERS! THAT WAS A CLOSE ONE! I JUST MANAGED TO ESCAPE!
R-R-RIP!

A LITTLE LATER—
THIS JOINT OF SMELLY MEAT GIVES ME AN IDEA!

SNAP!

LATER—
I'LL HAVE A SWIM MYSELF BEFORE TRYING TO CATCH THAT PIKE AGAIN—AND NEXT TIME IT SHOULD BE EASY!

WAHH! HELP! I DON'T LIKE BEING BAIT!
CHUCKLE! CLOTT'S KEEPING OLD DEVIL EYES AWAY FROM THE MEN AND HE'S TIRING THE BRUTE OUT FOR ME TO CATCH LATER! HO-HO!
SNAP!

GNASHER
AND
GNIPPER

At the fair —
CLASSIC BEANO
GNIPPEE!

GOT YOU, CAT.

THIS IS GREAT FUN.

OFF! NO DOGS!
THUD
NEVER MIND, SON — I'LL GET YOU ANOTHER ROUNDABOUT.

WHIRR!
SPIN
HOW'S THIS?

HOI! THAT'S A CLEAN SHEET — OUT!
REVOLVE

So —
TRY THIS.
CLICK!

But —
MUST HEAR THE NEW DINMAKERS RECORD.

SORRY, GNIPPER!
THWACK!
PTCHEE!
CLICK!

BATH-TIME, GNIPPER.
GRAB
GNAHA!

GNISPER WHISPER!
HEH-HEH! THAT'S A GOOD IDEA!

SPIN
SPIN
HANDY THING A LAWN SPRINKLER — A SHOWER AND A ROUNDABOUT AT THE SAME TIME.

# The Topper

CLASSIC TOPPER

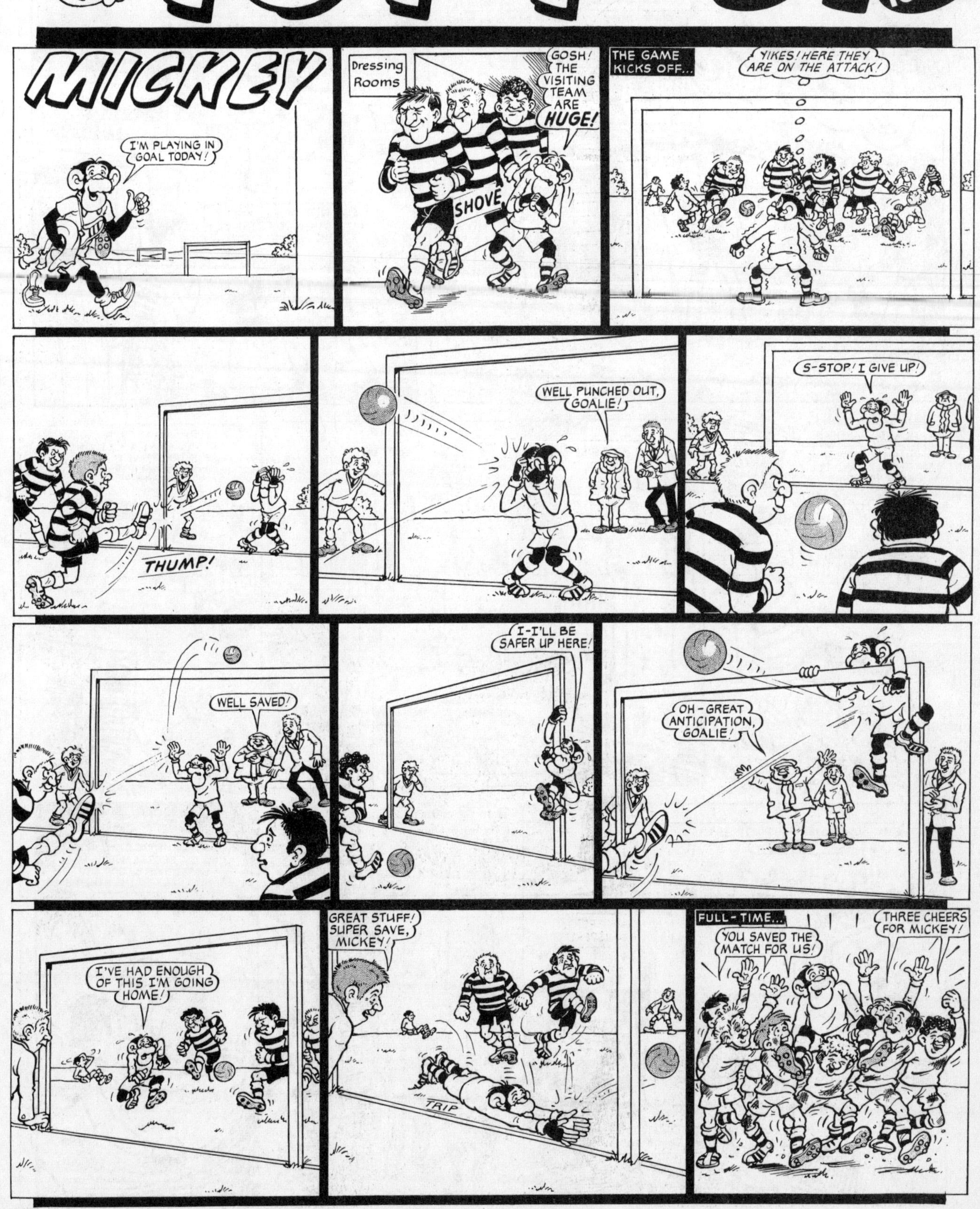

CLASSIC SPARKY
MR BUBBLES
HI THERE! MY NAME'S MR BUBBLES AND I'M A BUBBLE IMP! I LIVE IN A PLASTIC BOTTLE AND EVERY TIME SOMEONE SQUEEZES IT I POP OUT AND GRANT THEM THREE WISHES!
Robbie and his pals had built a club house on a piece of waste land—
COME ON, EVERYONE—INTO THE CLUBHOUSE FOR A MEETING!
RIGHT, THIS IS WHERE THE OFFICE BLOCK IS GOING. START CLEARING THE SITE.
OH, NO! THEY'LL KNOCK DOWN OUR DEN!
Then Robbie found Mr Bubbles' bottle—
HI THERE, ROBBIE! I'M MR BUBBLES AND I'LL GRANT YOU THREE WISHES!
SMASHING! I WISH OUR DEN WAS A FORTRESS!
HAUL UP THE DRAWBRIDGE AND DROP THE PORTCULLIS! PREPARE TO WITHSTAND A SIEGE!
HEY! WHAT'S THIS?
NOBODY SAID ANYTHING ABOUT DEMOLISHING A BLOOMING FORTRESS! WE'LL NEED HELP!
COME ON NOW, BOYS! THIS FORTRESS HAS TO COME DOWN!
NEVER! WE'LL DEFEND IT TO THE LAST MAN!
Then the chums made an unhappy discovery—
THERE'S NOTHING TO EAT HERE! WE'LL DIE OF STARVATION!
I WISH THERE WAS A TUNNEL FROM HERE TO MY HOUSE!
SECOND WISH, ROBBIE!
COME ON, GEORGE! WE'LL FILL A BASKET WITH FOOD AND BRING IT BACK TO THE OTHERS!

THIS LOT SHOULD KEEP US GOING!
SMASHING!

GET BACK, SPOT! YOU CAN'T COME!
COME ON, ROBBIE!

THIS IS GREAT, ROBBIE!
PASS ANOTHER CAKE, PLEASE!

Outside, a council of war was being held—
KNOCK IT DOWN, I SAY!
IT'S A MAGNIFICENT BUILDING. WE SHOULD TURN IT INTO A MUSEUM!
WE MUST GET THOSE KIDS OUT!

THEY'RE BRINGING UP LADDERS!
QUICK! TO THE BATTLEMENTS! WE MUST BE READY TO PUSH BACK THE LADDERS!

A HELICOPTER! THAT'S NOT FAIR!

ROBBIE! WHAT'S ALL THIS NONSENSE—AND WHO'S BEEN PINCHING ALL MY FOOD?
GOSH! SPOT'S BROUGHT MUM!
I WISH I'D WISHED FOR A SECRET DEN IN THE WOODS—INSTEAD OF A FORTRESS!
LAST WISH, ROBBIE!

THIS IS GREAT, GANG! NO-ONE WILL EVER FIND US HERE!
BUT SOMEONE WILL FIND ME NEXT WEEK! 'BYE FOR NOW!

# LITTLE PLUM

CLASSIC BEANO

TINY
CLASSIC TOPPER

HMM! TINY NEEDS SOME EXERCISE.
SUPER BONE THIS! M-M-M!
GNASH! GNAW!

HERE, TINY! LOOK, BOY!
EH?

GO ON! FETCH IT, TINY!
HE MUST BE JOKING! I'D GET ALL WET.
SPLASH!

GO ON, YOU LAZY HOUND! FETCH IT!
NOT LIKELY!

RIGHT, THEN! I KNOW YOU'LL GO IN AFTER THIS.
HOI!

SOME THINGS ARE WORTH GETTING WET FOR - HERE GOES!
SPLASH!

HO-HO-HO!
GLUB! UBBLE! GLUB! I MUST GET MY BONE BACK BEFORE SOME PESKY FISH EATS IT!

HO-HO-HO! HA-HA!
GRRR! WHAT A ROTTEN TRICK!

WELL DONE, TINY. GOOD BOY!

AH! I KNOW YOU'LL GO IN AFTER THIS
MY WALLET!

FETCH IT, BOY!
AGH! MY MONEY!

HO-HO-HO! HA-HA-HA!
GRR! WHAT A ROTTEN TRICK!

WELL DONE, MASTER! GOOD BOY!
PAH!

# BILLY WHIZZ

CLASSIC BEANO

CLASSIC NUTTY
SAMUEL CREEPS
OOH! This week's NUTTY is soopah, but Bananaman's a bit rough!
What NUTTY needs . . .
COSTUMES
. . . Is a nice, softy super-hero . . . like me!
I'm Supersofty, and I'm off to deal with a hold-up.
Is that so, Samuel?
Well, that costume of yours is certainly causing a traffic HOLD-UP!
What a funny sight!
CHEEK!
He looks ridiculous!
BUT THEN—
BANK
He's going into a bank! There must really be a hold-up!
GUFFAW! He's holding-up the bank teller's wool!
You're a sweet boy, Samuel!
SHORTLY—
. . . And then . . . CHUCKLE! . . Samuel held up her wool . . .
HAR-HAR!
I'll teach those louts not to laugh at Supersofty!
HANDS UP!!!
SAMUEL PUTTING ON A DEEP VOICE!
SAMUEL'S FLOWER-ARRANGING SCISSORS!
YIKES! A HOLD-UP!
SNIP!
SNIP!
SNIP!
GASP! OUR PANTS!
Supersofty snips again!
Well, what do you think of that HOLD-UP, boys?
GURR! I'd belt 'im one, if I didn't have to hold up my trousers!

the BASH STREET KIDS
ROCK ROCK ROCK ROCK ROCK

CLASSIC BEANO
TEACHERS' WASH ROOM
I'LL PUT THIS TRICK SOAP IN HERE!

GRR! THIS IS THE LAST STRAW. I'M GOING TO SEE THE HEAD AND HAVE YOU EXPELLED!
TEECHIR IS A FOOL

HEAD'S STUDY
YOU'RE ALL EXPELLED! THAT MEANS YOU CAN'T COME BACK TO SCHOOL!
YIPPEE!

SO NEXT MORNING THE KIDS HAVE A LONG LIE.

SMASHIN' JUST LYIN' HERE IN BED SHOOTIN' DOWN BLUEBOTTLES FROM THE CEILING~
~BETTER'N HAVING TO GET UP FOR SCHOOL!

AFTERNOON
THIS IS MUCH BETTER THAN SCHOOL!
FLOUR

AFTER THREE DAYS, THE MUMS ARE NERVOUS WRECKS.

SO~
HEADMASTER! TAKE THE BASH STREET KIDS BACK TO SCHOOL!
TAKE 'EM BACK

I'M SORRY, LADIES! BUT I WILL NOT HAVE THOSE LITTLE SAVAGES BACK HERE!
WHISPER
WHISPER

SO-NEXT MORNING AT 11 A.M.
WHERE ARE YOU, MUM~WHAT'S FOR BREAKFAST~HUH?
Here's the frying pan. Make your own breakfast. I've gone to school - Mum

IN SCHOOL
THAT WAS A CRAFTY PLAN. THE KIDS AREN'T ALLOWED IN HERE SO WE'RE SAFE FROM THEM!

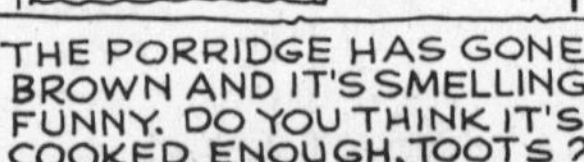
MEANWHILE
THE PORRIDGE HAS GONE BROWN AND IT'S SMELLING FUNNY. DO YOU THINK IT'S COOKED ENOUGH, TOOTS?

TEA

AND SO~AFTER 2 DAYS OF MAKING THEIR OWN MEALS, WASHING UP DISHES AND WASHING THEIR CLOTHES—
SO YOU WANT TO COME BACK, EH? WELL, YOU'LL ALL HAVE TO SIGN THIS FIRST!
PLEASE CAN WE COME BACK?
WE PROMISE NOT TO PLAY TRICKS ON TEACHER
WE PROMISE NOT TO FIGHT IN CLASS
WE PROMISE NOT TO DIG ELEPHANT TRAPS FOR JANITOR
SIGN HERE

THEY'RE WELL BEHAVED NOW BUT I WONDER HOW LONG IT WILL LAST!
HANDSOM TEECHIR
TEECHIR IS A NICE FOOL

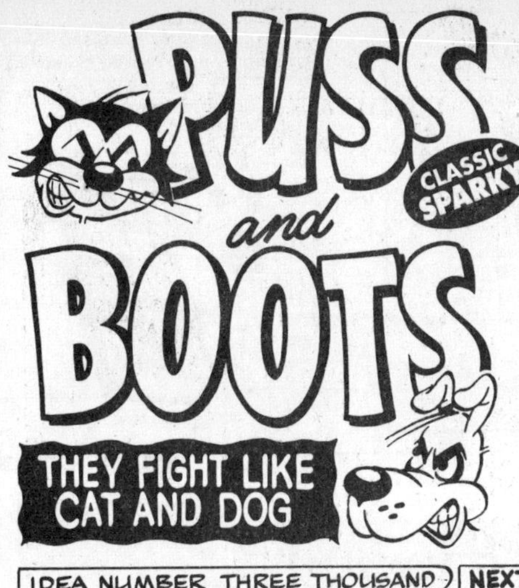
PUSS and BOOTS
CLASSIC SPARKY
THEY FIGHT LIKE CAT AND DOG

ONE NIGHT, IN A CERTAIN TWO BEDROOMS, A CERTAIN TWO SWORN ENEMIES ARE WIDE AWAKE —
BAH! MUTTER-- MUTTER... THIS CAN'T GO ON, I TELL ME! I'VE GOT TO GET SOME SLEEP!
YAWN... I'LL TRY COUNTING SHEEP... TICH, NIP OUT AND GET SOME SHEEP...
BAGGLE... ZZZ...

I COULD GIVE HIM A HAIR-CUT WITH A HARVESTER... A SHAVE WITH A SHEARS... OR A CLIP WITH A CUTLASS! I JUST CAN'T SLEEP FOR THINKING ABOUT WAYS TO SMASH THAT MUTT!

IDEA NUMBER THREE THOUSAND "STAY AT HOME AND HOPE THAT THE MOGGIE TRIPS OVER SOMETHING!" DEAR-OH-DEAR! THIS BLOKE'S MOGGIE-MASHING WAYS ARE WORSE THAN MINE!
MOGGIE BASHING VOL 73 BY DOUG THE PUG

NEXT DAY —
CHEMIST
OLD BOTTLES FOR SALE
I'LL SEE IF THIS BLOKE HAS ANYTHING TO HELP ME SLEEP!
YAWN!

OF COURSE, YOUR MOGGIE-SHIP! I'VE JUST SOLD A BOTTLE OF THE SAME STUFF TO AN ORANGE GENTLE-MUTT WITH RED EYES!

THAT NIGHT —
IT'S WORKING! I'M GETTING DROWSY! ANY MINUTE NOW I'M GOING TO FALL ASZZZ!
ZZUB-ZZUB! MOGGIES? I'VE NEVER EVEN SEEN A MOGGIE! BLOIKLE!
ZZZ!
ZZZ!
SNORE!

ZZZZ!
ZZZZ!

MUMBLE... ZZZ... MOGGIE... WHAT'S A MOGGIE? I'M NOT EVEN THINKING ABOUT MOGGIES... MUMBLE... ZZZ!
ZZZ... EVEN IF I'D HEARD OF DOGS WHICH I HAVEN'T, I PROBABLY WOULDN'T FIND THEM TOO BAD... ZZZ... MUTTER...

ZZZZ!
ZZZZ!
BASH!
WHAM!
BAM!
BOOP!
THUMP!
CRUMP!
CLOMP!

TWO HOURS LATER —
ZZZZ!
ZZZZ!

NEXT MORNING —
AH-ME! THAT WAS THE BEST NIGHT'S SLEEP I'VE HAD IN YEARS! I DIDN'T EVEN DREAM ABOUT THAT MUTT, LET ALONE THINK ABOUT HIM...

IDDLE-I-FO! MORNING ALREADY! I DON'T BELIEVE I MOVED ALL NIGHT! HEH! I BET THAT MOGGIE'S WISHING HE'D BOUGHT SOME SLEEPING-MIXTURE!

?
?
?
?

# HARUM SCAREM

CLASSIC BUZZ

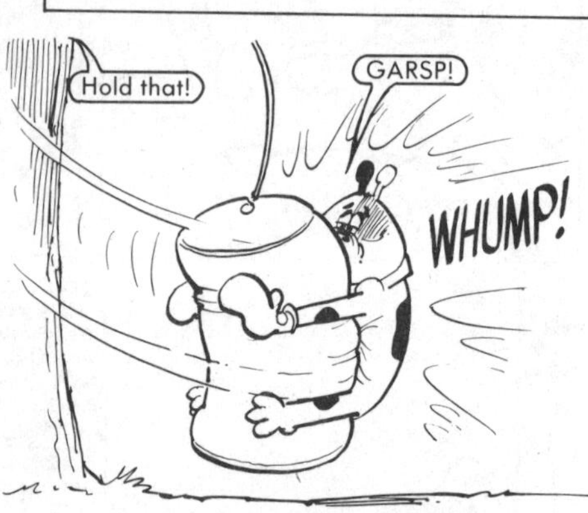

DESPERATE DAWG
CLASSIC DANDY
WANTED
BILLY THE KIT, ALIAS MIKE MOGGY CAT BURGLAR
OHO! I'D BETTER HURRY HOME AND LOCK UP!
HULLO? WHAT ARE THOSE SCRATCH MARKS DOING UP THE SIDE OF MY HOUSE?
THE PLACE HAS BEEN RANSACKED BY THAT CAT BURGLAR! HE'S SCOFFED ALL MY GRUB!
I'LL SET A TRAP FOR THAT BILLY THE KIT, BUT I'LL NEED TO CATCH SOME FISH FOR IT.
TO THE RIVER
BAH! THAT GRIZZLY BEAR IS FISHING IN MY FAVOURITE SPOT!
HEY! SCRAM, YOU! I WANT TO FISH HERE!
THE GRIZZLY DON'T TAKE KINDLY TO BEING PUSHED AROUND—
BIFF!
WHAM!
AT LEAST THAT GRIZZLY SHOWED ME A GOOD WAY TO CATCH FISH!
BUT—
YUMMY! THAT DESPERATE DAWG GUY SURE IS A SMART FISHERMAN!
CHOMP!
MUNCH!
DAWGGONE! THAT PESKY CAT BURGLAR MUST HAVE BEEN HERE TOO! HE'S SCOEFED ALL MY FISH!
TAILOR
HURRY UP AND FINISH THAT COSTUME FOR ME, TAILOR!
LATER—
!
WOWEE! WHAT A DOLL!
HI-YAH, BEAUTIFUL!
WHO'S BEAUTIFUL? GURR!
YOWEE! IT'S DESPERATE DAWG!
TAKE THAT!
MEEOWCH!
WHUMP!
NOW I CAN BUY PLENTY OF GRUB WITH ALL THIS REWARD MONEY!
MIND THEY DON'T SELL YOU CATS' FOOD BY MISTAKE, DAWG! HAW-HAW!
JAIL

THE
HILLYS
CLASSIC BEEZER
AND THE
BILLYS
DOWN IN HAPPY VALLEY, PAPPY BILLY IS SCHEMING AGAINST THE HILLYS.
C'MON OUTSIDE, LADS! AH'VE GOT SUMP'N T'SHOW YOU!
SURPRISE! SURPRISE!
HERE'S MAH LATEST PRESENT TO THEM HILLYS!
A BIG ROCK!
YEAH, A DUMMY ROCK—CRAM' FULL O' US BILLYS! HO! HO!
YORE A GENI PAPPY!
LATER
. . . I TELL YOU, THERE'S SOMETHIN' AFOOT! IT'S TOO QUIET, AN' THERE AIN'T NO SIGN O' THEM BILLYS!
PHOW!
WHEEE!
ZING!
BANG! BANG! BANG!
ZIP!
WHEE!
WHEEE!
BILLYS!
WHEEE!
TAKE COVER, FELLAHS!
S'FUNNY—I CAN'T SEE A SOUL! WHERE CAN THEY BE HIDIN'?
WHEEE
ZING!
CRACK!
HEY, PAW—THAT LOOKS MIGHTY LIKE RIFLE SMOKE A-COMIN' FROM THAT BIG ROCK!
H'MM! SO THAT'S IT, EH! A DUMMY BOULDER!
AFTER 'EM!
OF ALL TH' DOGGONE LUCK—THEY SPOTTED OUR GUNSMOKE! RUN, FELLAHS!
THERE THEY ARE! JUMP ON 'EM, LADS!
THUD!
WHAM!
WHUMP!
NOW AIN'T IT A SHAME THEY PICKED THE WRONG BOULDER! HEH! HEH!
NOW WE CAN REALLY FOOL 'EM! THEY'LL NEVER SPOT US AMONG ALL THE ROCKS IN TH' QUARRY!
ROCK QUARRY
SORRY—YOU CAN'T ENTER TH' QUARRY. WE'RE GOIN' T' BE BLASTIN'!
ROCK QUARRY
BLASTING IN PROGRESS
BAH! AN' WE SAW 'EM GO IN THERE!
INSIDE THE QUARRY
HERE'S A HEFTY BOULDER NEEDS BREAKING UP!
HEY, YOU BILLYS! THAT WAS A MIGHTY FINE DISGUISE—IT EVEN FOOLED TH' ROCK BREAKERS! HEH! HEH!
YEOW!
BOOM!

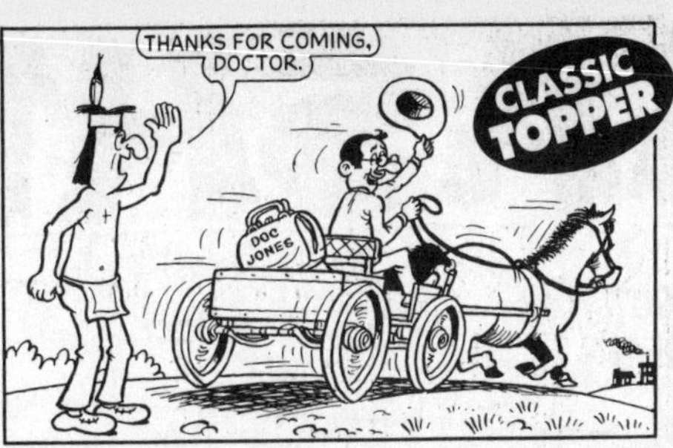

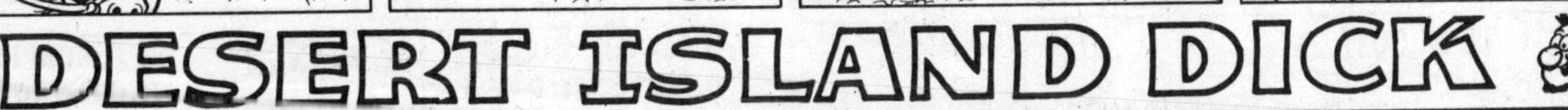

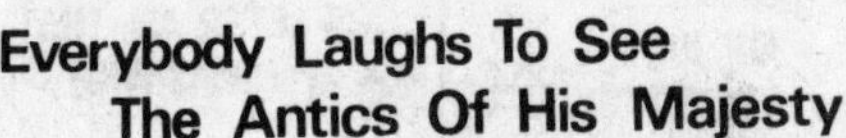


Everybody Laughs To See The Antics Of His Majesty

# THE SMASHER

GOLLY! THESE TYRES ARE HEAVY! I'LL NEVER GET THEM TO McCLUSKY'S GARAGE.
CLASSIC DANDY

AH! I'VE GOT AN IDEA!

WHY DIDN'T I THINK OF THIS BEFORE? NOW I CAN RIDE TO THE GARAGE!

WOW! A PAINTER AHEAD! —AND I FORGOT TO FIX A HORN!

LOOK OUT!
WHITE PAINT

WELL DONE, SMASHER!— YOU'VE SAVED ME A BACK-BREAKING JOB!
?

FURTHER ON
WOW! I'M GOING TO RUN INTO THAT FACTORY!
TIN TACK CO

GOOD FOR YOU, SMASHER! YOUR TYRES ARE PICKING UP ALL THE OLD TIN TACKS FROM THE FLOOR!
POP

TIN TACK CO. LTD.
GOSH! A THOUSAND PUNCTURES! NEVER MIND—I'LL FILL THE TYRES UP WITH CLAY!

OFF AGAIN—
WOW! THERE'S THE GARAGE AND I'VE GOT NO BRAKES!
McCLUSKY'S GARAGE

CRASH

GARAGE
HE'S KNOCKED A HOLE IN THE GARAGE WALL JUST WHERE WE NEED IT FOR FITTING THAT NEW DOOR.
AND HE'S DRIVEN THOSE OLD TYRES STRAIGHT ON TO THE BONFIRE WHERE THEY WERE MEANT TO GO!

A WORD WITH YOU, SMASHER!
AH! JUST THE BOY I WANT TO SEE!
AH! THERE YOU ARE!
TIN TACK CO.
OH, DEAR!

WONDER WHAT I'VE BEEN REWARDED FOR AFTER ALL THAT SMASHING?

# THE TOPS IN FUN!

# THE BEEZER

## POP, DICK and HARRY

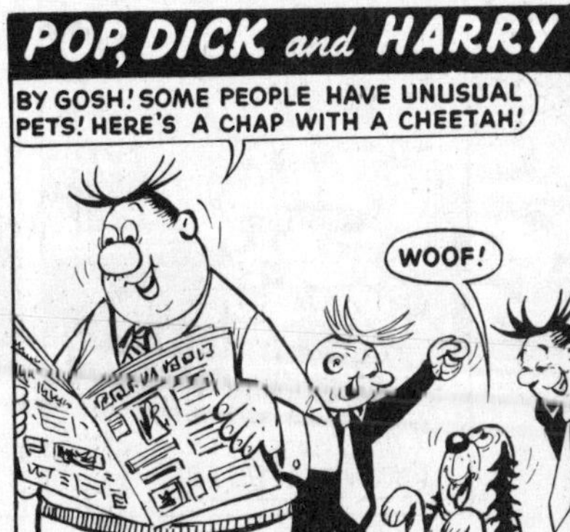

MONKEY BIZNESS
CLASSIC DANDY
ZIP-A-TEE DOODAH!
HERE COMES THE BOSS! GOSH! HE'S FULL OF BEANS THIS MORNING!
BEANS, EH? WELL, HERE ARE SOME MORE FOR HIM!
BONK!
OOYAH!
HEE-HEE!
TRIP!
GRR! I'LL TEACH YOU NOT TO—OO-ER!
TITTER! HE GOT EVEN MORE BEANS THAN WE BARGAINED FOR!
CRASH!
GROAN! PILE UP THOSE CANS, SAM. SUSIE, YOU CAN GRIND SOME BEANS AND MAKE ME A CUP OF COFFEE.
HEH-HEH! GRIND SOME BEANS, HE SAID! AND I'LL GRIND ALL KINDS OF BEANS!
HERE'S YOUR CUPPA, BOSS!
AH, SPLENDID!
GROOGH! I'VE BEEN POISONED!
BAH! YOU THICK HEADS ARE TOO FULL OF TRICKS! GET SOME WORK DONE!
BIFF!
LATER—
PHEW! ALL THAT HARD WORK HAS GIVEN ME AN APPETITE!
LET'S HAVE A FRY-UP THEN.
HEE-EE! WE'RE GOING TO BE FULL OF BEANS TOO NOW—AND SAUSAGE, EGG AND CHIPS!
SO—HAVING A BEANFEAST, ARE YOU? I'VE HAD ENOUGH OF YOU TWO TODAY AND THIS IS THE LAST STRAW!
OO-ER!
GRR! COME BACK AND I'LL SPIFFLICATE YOU!
GROAN! I HOPE THOSE WERE RUNNER BEANS WE ATE!
SHUT UP AND KEEP RUNNING—OR WE'LL GET BEANED!

HECTOR the COLLECTOR
CLASSIC CRACKER
Hmm! What'll I collect today? Ah! A bus ticket–I'll collect tickets!
BUS STOP
Here comes a bus I'm bound to find some tickets here!
All aboard!
Oh boy! Here's plenty!
DRING!
Hey! Wait! I wanted to ask if you've got any spare...
...tickets! Gosh!
ZOOM
SNAP!
Aw! That's torn it! I only got one!
STATION
Never mind! I'll collect some train tickets instead.
Excuse me! Can I have some...
Hey, little lad! Come back!
I was only going to ask if you had any old tickets!
A likely story! You were trying to sneak past without paying!
Hey! I wonder what these pieces of paper are?
Airline tickets! Super!
Boysoboys–It's a ticket for the cup-tie–I'm not going to keep this one!
My airline tickets– thank goodness! I've been hunting high and low for them!
AW!
Here, Sonny– take this for finding my tickets!
?
Another ticket?

# THE BEANO

THE COMIC WITH Minnie the Minx

DENNIS the MENACE FAN CLUB

CLASSIC BEANO

## DENNIS the MENACE and GNASHER

IT'S ABOUT TIME YOU DID SOMETHING ABOUT THAT HAIR!

DAD'S RIGHT—SO I'M WASHING IT—WITH PLENTY STARCH TO MAKE IT STIFF!

STARCH

TEE-HEE! THIS IS FUN!

WALTER, A WELL-KNOWN SOFTY.

RUB

JUST RIGHT FOR A SPOT OF MENACING!

DENNIS the MENACE
AND GNASHER

I'VE GOT A NEW GAME THAT DENNIS CAN'T SPOIL...
I HOPE IT'S NOT ROUGH!

I'VE SCORED THREE!
CHARGE!
COTTON WOOL DARTS

AND I'VE SCORED ONE THOUSAND AND EIGHTY! SNIGGER!
PRANG!
EEK!
BUMP!
ZOOM!
BUMP!
DONK!

WE'RE GOING INDOORS— IT'S POURING!
I'M A TOUGH MENACE— I DON'T MIND A FEW...

... SPOTS?

GRR! THAT RAIN REALLY RUINED MY FUN— NOT TO MENTION MY HAIR!
SMIRK

I JUST LOVE SNIFFING FLOWERS AFTER THE RAIN!
SNIFF!

HAVEN'T SEEN THIS PLANT BEFORE!

BOO!
TOPPLE
SPLASH!

SNIVEL! I'M ALL WET, MUMSIE!
YOU ALWAYS WERE!
GRAB
COME TO DADDY, LADDY!

In the barber's—
THIS IS WHAT I MEANT WHEN I SAID YOU SHOULD DO SOMETHING WITH YOUR HAIR!

SORRY, GNASHER, BUT YOU'LL HAVE TO STAY THERE TILL MY HAIR GROWS — OR NONE OF "THE BEANO" FANS WILL RECOGNISE ME!
LOWER

I'LL JUST RUN UP THAT WALL...
SPOOFER McGRAW
HE TELLS TALL TALES.
HE'S HEADING FOR A FALL!
CLASSIC SPARKY
BO, OL' SON, WHAT ON EARTH ARE YOU DOIN'?
MAKING PANCAKES! IT'S SHROVE TUESDAY, Y'KNOW!
YOU'VE GOT IT WRONG, BO! IT'S NOT SHROVE TUESDAY, IT'S SIR OVE TUESDAY!
SIR OVE? WHO WAS HE THEN? I'VE NEVER HEARD OF HIM!
HE WAS THE MOST FAMOUS PANCAKE-EATER OF ALL TIME, BO. EVERY TUESDAY WITHOUT FAIL, HE HAD PANCAKES FOR TEA! NOW, YOU MAY NOT THINK THAT'S UNUSUAL, BO...
BUT HE HAD HUNDREDS OF 'EM...
CHOMP! GOBBLE! SLURP! MUNCH! BURP!
WHICH ANNOYED OL' KING 'ENERY NO END...
CHOMP! MUNCH! BURP!
GAAH! WHO'S THAT SPOILING MY KINGLY AFTERNOON STROLL?
ER... IT'S SIR OVE, SIRE. IT'S TUESDAY AGAIN, SIRE!
AN' ROTTEN OL' 'ENERY HAD SIR OVE LOCKED UP IN TH' TOWER...
WAIL!
HA! NOW PERHAPS WE'LL GET SOME PEACE AND QUIET!
BUT COOKIE, SIR OVE'S FAITHFUL PANCAKE-COOKER WASN'T GONNA SEE HIS MASTER GOIN' WITHOUT HIS TUESDAY PANCAKES, BO!
OH? WHAT DID HE DO?
WHY, HE KINDLED A FIRE OUTSIDE THE PALACE, AND STARTED COOKING...
COO, THEY SMELL GOOD, COOKIE! ER... HOW ARE YOU GOING TO SEND 'EM UP?
ONE MOMENT, SIR...
LIKE THAT, SIR!
FLIP!
BRILLIANT! STOUT FELLOW, COOKIE!
AN' SIR OVE WAS GOBBLIN' AWAY, WHEN....
HMM! WONDER HOW THAT FLY MANAGES TO WALK UP WALLS?
THEN IT STRUCK HIM...
OF COURSE! BIG, FLAT, STICKY FEET-JUS' LIKE PANCAKES, IN FACT!
AND SIX-AND-A-HALF SECONDS LATER....
PLOP!
HI, COOKIE!
PLOP!
COO!
AN' THAT'S WHAT SIR OVE TUESDAY'S ALL ABOUT! CELEBRATIN' HIS ESCAPE, BO! BO...?
JUS' WATCH THIS, SPOOFER!
IF SIR OVE COULD WALK ON WALLS, SO CAN I!
SNIGGER!
HO-HO! TSK! P'RAPS YOU DIDN'T COOK YOUR PANCAKES LONG ENOUGH, BO! HEE-HEE-HEE!
WAAH!
THUD!

CLASSIC DANDY
BULLY BEEF and CHIPS
IN THE MARKET-PLACE—
THERE'S YOUR HOT DOG, SON.
THANKS, MISTER.
OFFEE
FRESH FRUIT
HOT DOGS
OO! I LOVE HOT DOGS!
I LIKE LOTS OF TOMATO KETCHUP ON A HOT DOG.
SQUEEZE
HOT DOGS
I'M GONNA ENJOY THIS!
NO, YOU'RE NOT, CHIPS! I AM!
SNATCH
EH?
HOT DOGS
CHOMP!
GIMME THAT BACK!
HOT DOGS
COFF
NO FEAR! BUT YOU CAN HAVE SOME MORE KETCHUP—
YAHOO!
SLIP!
THAT WAS LOVELY!
GURR! I'M GONNA BASH YOU!
HOT DOGS
PEE
IES
DON'T BE SAUCY, CHIPS! HERE, HAVE ANOTHER SQUEEZE OF KETCHUP!
SQUEEZE
GLOOB!
HO-HO! TA-TA, CHIPS!
HEY! COME BACK WITH MY BIKE, YOU ROTTER!
TAKE THAT!
GOODO! THE BOTTLE HAS CAUGHT IN THE SPOKES!
YAHOO! HELP!
EEK! MY TOMATOES!
FRUIT
HO-HO! BEEFY HAD BETTER NOT LET THAT BARROW BOY "KETCHUP" WITH HIM!
TO THE MARKET
GURR! TAKE THAT, YOU CLUMSY OAF!
HELP!
SPLAT!

WHY CAN'T BRAINLESS IRON CURTAINS?
'COS!-'COS HE KEEPS FALLIN' OFF THE LADDER!
BRAINLESS
BRAINLESS WANTED TO GO WATER SKI-ING BUT HE COULD'NT FIND A LAKE WITH A SLOPE ON IT!!!
HOW'S THAT NEW CHAP GETTING ON?— THE ONE I STARTED THIS MORNING?
I'M A BIT WORRIED ABOUT HIM, BOSS!- I THINK HE'S A BIT WELL- ODD!!!!
ODD? WHY DO YOU THINK HE'S ODD??
WELL, JUST LOOK AT HIM!- OVER THERE......
THROWIN' BREAD!— TO THE HELICOPTERS!!!
COME ON, BIRDIES!!!!

# KORKY THE CAT

Korky built up his muscles
To give a bully the boot—
But then he found that these muscles
Were unsuitable for his new suit!

WE ARE...
THE SPARKY PEOPLE!
It's all happening...
...thanks to pencil sharpening!
CLASSIC SPARKY
TCHA! ANOTHER PENCIL BROKEN! I'M FED UP SHARPENING PENCILS ALL DAY!
I'VE GOT A SHARPENING MACHINE SOMEWHERE!
SNAP!
ALL YOU HAVE TO DO IS SCREW IT TO THE WALL!
GREAT! GOT ANY SCREWS?
NOPE!
HELLO? JOHNSON THE JOINER? CAN YOU SEND A MAN TO FIX A PENCIL-SHARPENER?
SOON-
THERE! ALMOST DONE!
MOUSE AHOY!
SQUEAK!
WHAT'S THAT...? OH!
SMASH!
MISSED!
OH, NO! THE WINDOW!
HELLO? GILBERT THE GLAZIER? YES, SEND A MAN ROUND!
SOON-
LET'S ALL GET BACK A BIT AND KEEP OUT OF THE GLAZIER'S WAY!
OOH-ME-CORN!
TRAMPLE!
OH, NO! INK ALL OVER THE WALL!
HELLO? PETER THE PAINTER? SPARKY OFFICE... A WALL... YES, SEND A MAN ROUND!
SOON-
HERE COMES THE PAINTER'S VAN NOW! OH, NO! HE'S SKIDDED ON THE INK THAT WENT THROUGH THE WINDOW!
CRASH!
RUN!
HELLO? BERT THE BUILDER? OH, YOU HEARD THE CRASH! THE MEN ARE ON THEIR WAY? OH... JOLLY GOOD!
TEN MINUTES LATER-
SIR's BEWILDERED WAIL
THROGMORTON! I'VE JUST COME IN! WHAT ON EARTH IS HAPPENING?
OH... JUST SHARPENING MY PENCIL, SIR... GULP!
GLARE!
GASP!
SHULP-SHLOP!
TUM-TE-TUM!
TRA-LA-LA!

Minnie the Minx
GET THE HOSE GOING OVER THE PLANTS, MINNIE!
HUH! WATERING'S BORING! I COULD THINK OF A BETTER USE FOR A HOSE THAN THIS.
MY OLD ENEMIES, THE STATION ROAD GANG, ARE PLAYING FOOTBALL OVER THE WAY. I KNOW HOW I'LL RUIN THEIR GAME.

CLASSIC BEANO
THIS IS A BETTER USE FOR A HOSE.
RUN FOR IT, LADS! MINNIE'S BOMBARDING US WITH SOOT BOMBS!
BOOMF
WHANG
SOOT BOMB
SOOT BOMB
SOOT BOMB
AMMO TRAIN

LATER
I'LL USE THE HOSE TO BEND THE MAN-NEXT-DOOR'S APPLE TREE OVER THE FENCE.

NOW TO GIVE IT A GOOD SHAKE.

FANCY THAT! ALL THESE TASTY APPLES FELL OFF IN MY GARDEN! THEY BELONG TO ME NOW—THAT'S WHAT THE LAW SAYS!

LATER
TOOL SHED
I'LL HAVE MORE FUN WITH THIS HOSE.

SHAKE
A-A-AGH! A SNAKE!
RUN, ALFIE! IT MUST HAVE ESCAPED FROM THE ZOO!

HEH-HEH! FANCY PEOPLE THROWING SWEETS AWAY. I MIGHT AS WELL HAVE THEM IF THEY DON'T WANT THEM.

BUT ROUND THE CORNER
BOOMF

S-SORRY, MISTER! BUT THERE'S A BIG SNAKE BACK THERE. IT'S AFTER US!
SNAKE? A LIKELY STORY!

SNAKE, MY FOOT! THIS IS A HOSE PIPE!

YANK
THERE'S THE ONLY SNAKE AROUND HERE—THAT LITTLE REPTILE ON THE END OF THE HOSE!

THIS HORRIBLE LITTLE ANIMAL WAS RESPONSIBLE FOR MY RECORDS BEING SMASHED! THEY COST 42/-, SO PAY UP.

THIS IS ONE USE FOR A HOSE MINNIE HADN'T THOUGHT OF.

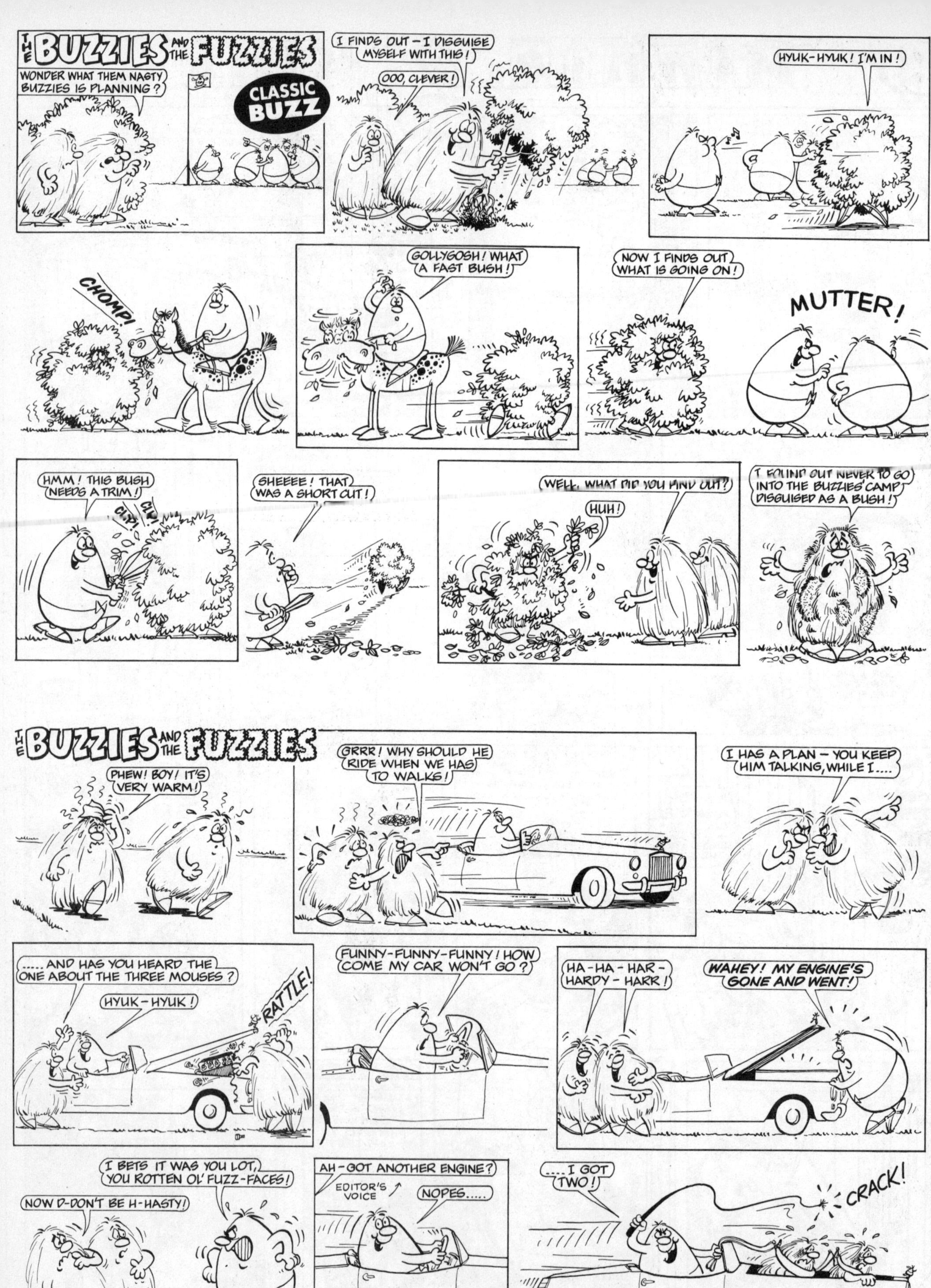

THE BUZZIES AND THE FUZZIES
WONDER WHAT THEM NASTY BUZZIES IS PLANNING?
CLASSIC BUZZ
I FINDS OUT – I DISGUISE MYSELF WITH THIS!
OOO, CLEVER!
HYUK-HYUK! I'M IN!
CHOMP!
GOLLYGOSH! WHAT A FAST BUSH!
NOW I FINDS OUT WHAT IS GOING ON!
MUTTER!
HMM! THIS BUSH NEEDS A TRIM!
SHEEEE! THAT WAS A SHORT CUT!
WELL, WHAT DID YOU FIND OUT?
HUH!
I FOUND OUT NEVER TO GO INTO THE BUZZIES' CAMP DISGUISED AS A BUSH!
THE BUZZIES AND THE FUZZIES
PHEW! BOY! IT'S VERY WARM!
GRRR! WHY SHOULD HE RIDE WHEN WE HAS TO WALKS!
I HAS A PLAN – YOU KEEP HIM TALKING, WHILE I....
..... AND HAS YOU HEARD THE ONE ABOUT THE THREE MOUSES?
HYUK-HYUK!
RATTLE!
FUNNY-FUNNY-FUNNY! HOW COME MY CAR WON'T GO?
HA-HA-HAR-HARDY-HARR!
WAHEY! MY ENGINE'S GONE AND WENT!
I BETS IT WAS YOU LOT, YOU ROTTEN OL' FUZZ-FACES!
NOW D-DON'T BE H-HASTY!
AH-GOT ANOTHER ENGINE?
EDITOR'S VOICE
NOPES.....
.... I GOT TWO!
CRACK!

BERYL THE Peril
GRRRR!
OOOH! WH-WHAT'S THAT?

EEK!
CLASSIC TOPPER
A TIGER—HUH!

HO! HO! DID I GIVE YOU A FRIGHT? NEVER MIND, MUM— THIS OLD TIGER-SKIN I PICKED UP AT THE SALEROOM WAS A REAL BARGAIN!
YOU DIDN'T SCARE ME! THAT'S AN' OLD TRICK.

VERY NICE, EH?
IT LOOKS FINE, DAD!
SILLY TIGER-SKIN! I'M OFF OUT TO FLY MY GLIDER.

STAND BY! TAKE-OFF!

NOT THAT WAY! COME BACK HERE, GLIDER!

BEWARE OF THE DOG
OH-OH!

SNARL! TRESPASSERS WILL BE TORN APART!

GRR!
RASP!

BACK IN BERYL'S HOUSE...
THIS IS WHAT I NEED TO HELP ME GET MY GLIDER. A BERYL-TIGER WILL SCARE THAT DOG!

SO—
YELP! AN ESCAPED TIGER!

BUT, OH-OH! BERYL'S DISGUISE HAS CAUGHT ON THAT PRICKLY BUSH...
OHO!

YOICKS!
GURRR!

HAVE A TIGER-SKIN —MAYBE THAT'LL STOP YOU....

...LONG ENOUGH—PUFF!—FOR ME TO RACE YOU BACK HOME.
WOOF! WOOF!

SLAM!
UH! FOILED!

HO! HO! BERYL'S TRYING TO SCARE ME!
WHAT A HOPE—A TIGER-SKIN DOESN'T FRIGHTEN ME, BERYL!
GRRRR!

NO, DAD—BUT THE DOG UNDER IT SEEMS TO! HO! HO!
WOOF! SNARL!

BANANAMAN
CLASSIC NUTTY
I'm taking the day off today to do a spot of sun-worshipping!
TO SPAIN AN' ALL THAT
SOON, IN SPAIN-UPON-SEA—
Ah! This is the life!
COSTA DEL ROSA
BUT—
Hello—what's happened to the sun?
AND, SECONDS LATER—
HUH! Would you believe it—it's raining!
QUACKIN' IN THE RAIN...
Well, I'll soon take care of those rain clouds with a blast of super-breath!
BLAST!
That's got rid of them—now for a nice tan!
BANANACRAB?
HOURS LATER—
YAWN! Well it's about time I was on me bike back home!
AND SO—
Heh! Poor old Britain's covered in cloud. It must be raining cats and dogs!
AND—
ZOINKS! Everywhere's flooded!
Thank goodness you're back, Bananaman! We need your help!
While you were away, a freak wind blew all the rain clouds from Europe over the British Isles!
GULP! Really?... er...
Don't you DARE let on, readers!
What a hero!
WATER IS WET!

THE BADD LADS
CLASSIC BEEZER
KINGS OF THE BLUNDERWORLD
THIS OLD HIDEOUT IS BEGINNING TO LEAN DANGEROUSLY TO ONE SIDE!
I WOULDN'T BE SURPRISED IF A GUST OF WIND CAME ONE DAY . . .

. . . AND . . .
WHUFF!

. . . BROUGHT IT DOWN ABOUT OUR EARS!

YOU'RE THE ONLY FIT ONE, KNUCK! SEE IF YOU CAN PINCH A LORRY-LOAD OF BRICKS! WE'LL BUILD A REAL SOLID HIDEOUT THIS TIME!
OKAY, BOSS!

LATER
THIS IS THE LATEST BRICK-MAKING MACHINE, SIR! JUST POUR THE MIXTURE IN ONE END AND OUT COME THE BRICKS FROM THE OTHER END!
SUPER ICE CREAM BRICK Co.
OFFICE
SOUNDS WONDERFUL! WE'LL GO FOR LUNCH FIRST THEN YOU CAN GIVE ME A DEMONSTRATION!
OH, BOY! MY LUCK'S IN!
SPECIAL SUPER BRICK MIX
SPECIAL SUPER BRICK MIX

PITY KNUCK WAS TOO BUSY PINCHING THE LORRY TO NOTICE THIS SIGN
SUPER ICE CREAM BRICK Co.
OFFICE

ALL THROUGH THE NIGHT THE LADS WORK
THERE'S SOMETHING QUEER ABOUT THESE BRICKS! THEY'RE AWFULLY COLD!
BRRR! MY HANDS ARE FROZEN!
PROBABLY JUST A NEW TYPE OF BRICK, BOSS!
SPECIAL SUPER BRICK MIX

WELL, COME WIND, RAIN OR SHINE, WE'VE GOT A SOLID HIDEOUT NOW!

10 MINUTES LATER

ICE-SLURP!-CREAM!

MEANWHILE, AT A LARGE NURSERY SCHOOL NEARBY!
SORRY, CHILDREN! NO ICE CREAM TODAY! THE BADD LADS HAVE STOLEN THE MACHINE THAT MAKES IT!
SO! C'MON, EVERYBODY! LET'S GO AN' GET 'EM!

KEEP FIRING, KIDS! MORE AMMO COMIN' UP!
STEAL OUR ICE CREAM, WOULD YOU?
BONK!

OK! LET'S TAKE THIS MACHINE BACK TO THE ICE CREAM FACTORY!

ANYWAY, WE'VE FINALLY GOT OUR BRICK HIDEOUT!

YOUNG FOO
CLASSIC CRACKER
THE KUNG FU KID
THE HEADMASTER OF GORSEDALE SCHOOL HAS HAD A DISAGREEMENT WITH THE SCHOOL COOK—
HUMPH
BULLY BASHER AND NEW BOY, YOUNG FOO, ARRIVE—
Yes, we had a slight difference of opinion—he's resigned, in fact!
Trouble with cook, Sir?
He always comes back, but what will we do about the cooking in the meantime?
Please, sir, I can cook!
What a noble gesture, Young Foo! You can start right away. Basher will assist you!
Very good, sir!
LATER...
Gurr! You landed me this horrible job, you little squirt!
Control yourself, Young Basher! We must prepare lunch!
All right, but I'll get you later!
Most kind!
Now what shall I cook for lunch? Hmmmm, I think I will make Chinese egg and chips!
He must be Chinese crackers!
First, I collect a basket of peeled potatoes!
POTATO PEELER
ON
OFF
...and then I throw them high into the air, like so...
YOUNG FOO ADOPTS A FIGHTING POSITION—
AND AS THE POTATOES FALL—
THWOP!
TWAK!
SHOOM!
HE MAKES THEM INTO CHIPS!
ENGLISH TRANSLATION
Hai-ho!

Humph! I suppose you think that was clever, Young Foo?
CLASSIC CRACKER
Oh, no! Young Basher, any fool could do it...even YOU.. with practice!
CLOSE-UP OF A SCHOOL BULLY ABOUT TO EXPLODE!
AND DURING THE EXPLOSION!
YOUNG FOO PREPARES TO DEFEND HIMSELF...
Take that, squirt! Eh..?
VAROOM!
BASHER!
Cheerio, Basher! Must get on with my cooking!
Mmmm! Chips smell good!
LOOK OUT, YOUNG FOO! HERE COMES BASHER FOR ANOTHER HELPING!
You've had your chips this time, you crazy cook!
TWOP!
EEEOW!
Pass me the frying pan please, Young Basher! I must fry eggs!
One frying pan coming up...and down!
AAACH!
KICK!
...and now to fry eggs!
GREAT PAIN
MORE PAIN
UP GO THE EGGS—
WOOSH!
YOUNG FOO CHOPS THEM OPEN—
SHOOM!
CRACK!
CRACK!
CRACK!
This looks delicious, Young Foo! This is the very first time I've had Chinese egg and chips!
Young Basher gave me a hand— I mean TWO hands, sir!

School Report
DENNIS the MENACE
CLASSIC BEANO
YOU HAVE MY SYMPATHIES, DENNIS. IT IS WITH GREAT SORROW THAT—
— I GIVE YOU YOUR REPORT CARD FOR YOUR FATHER TO SIGN.
GULP!
REPORT CARD
IT'S NOT ALL THAT BAD!— BUT YOU KNOW HOW DAD WILL CARRY-ON!
CLOUD OF GLOOM
I'LL TRY FORGING DAD'S SIGNATURE AFTER I'VE HAD SOME PRACTICE WRITING LETTERS IN HIS STYLE!
BUZZ OFF, YOU VANDAL!
REPORT CARD
GO ON! BURN IT!
IT WAS AN ACCIDENT, DAD. IT JUST SLIPPED OUT OF MY HAND, AND........
REPORT CARD
OH, WHAT'S THE USE? DAD WOULD ONLY ASK TEACHER FOR ANOTHER ONE.
REPORT CARD
LATER—
AHA! SCARED TO SHOW ME YOUR REPORT CARD, EH?
REPORT CARD
'SCUSE ME WHILE I GET MY SLIPPER READY!
JUST LISTEN TO THIS, MUM! 'ENGLISH — AWFUL — MATHS — DREADFUL —
REPORT CARD
— HISTORY — TOO THICK TO LEARN. CONDUCT — INDESCRIBABLE!' THIS IS SHOCKING!
SWISH
REPORT CARD
WHAT A DISGRACE! AREN'T YOU ASHAMED OF THIS REPORT?
YES, DAD! I'M THOROUGHLY ASHAMED OF YOU! IT'S ONE OF YOUR OLD REPORT CARDS! I FOUND IT IN A TRUNK UPSTAIRS!
REPORT CARD
THIS IS TO SHOW HOW DAD IS FEELING — PRETTY SMALL!
HO! HO! HO!
SIGN MY CARD, DAD, AND WE'LL NOT SAY ANOTHER WORD!

Splodge
THE LAST OF THE GOBLINS

CLONK

CLASSIC TOPPER
GRR! A HORSE CHESTNUT! THIS IS A DANGEROUS TIME IN THE FOREST. YOU'D THINK AFTER ALL THOSE YEARS NATURE WOULD HAVE FITTED CHESTNUT TREES WITH SAFETY NETS.

NEVER MIND. I'LL GET SOME FUN OUT OF THIS—THERE'S OLD BADGER DEEP IN THOUGHT!

I'LL SHAKE A FEW NUTS DOWN ON HIS NUT! HEE! HEE!

BAH! NOT A NUT FELL!

CLUNK

THUMP

UP TO YOUR TRICKS AGAIN, SPLODGE?
ER—IN A WAY, BADGER—BUT THAT WASN'T ONE OF THEM.
BOOT

I'LL MAKE SURE SOME NUTS FALL OFF THIS TIME.

BONK

THUMP
CLONK

BIT OF A LET-DOWN, EH, SPLODGE?
SPLATT

OH, NO! NOW WHAT?
CHUG!
CHUG!
OI NEVER COULD GET THE HANG O' THESE CONTRAPTIONS. WHOA, THERE!

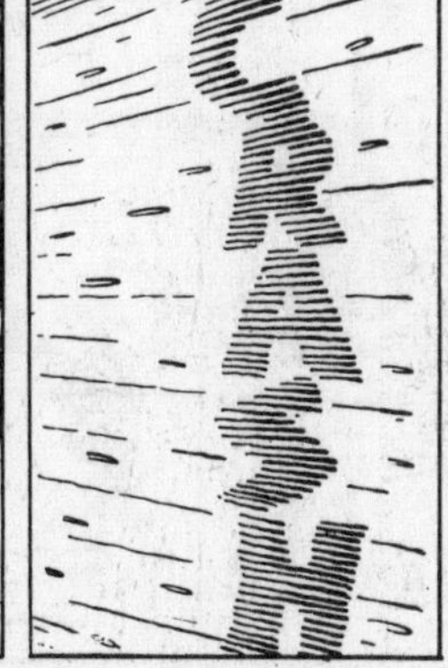
CRASH

WHOOSH
THUMP
DONG
BONG
WELL...LOOKING ON THE BRIGHT SIDE—THAT'S ALL THIS YEAR'S DANGER PAST IN ONE GO!

DREAMY DANIEL

CLASSIC SPARKY

BAXTALL THEATRE
PRESENTS
FRANKLY VAIN
I'M JUST A POVERTY-STRICKEN ENTERTAINER, BUT I KNOW THAT ONE OF THESE DAYS I'LL BE A STAR!

HEAD MASTER
I MUST PRACTISE MY DANCE STEPS SO THAT I'LL BE PERFECT WHEN MY BIG BREAK COMES!
BOY!
CLICK
TAP! TAP!
TAP!

HOW DARE YOU DANCE IN THE CORRIDOR—TAKE A THOUSAND LINES!
YES, I WILL LEARN THE LINES OF YOUR NEW PLAY, MISTER DIRECTOR!

IN CLASS—
THIS IS MR DICK CRIMBLEBY—HE'S HERE TO MAKE A FILM OF OUR SCIENCE LESSON TO BE SHOWN ON TV!
HI!
WOW! A SCREEN TEST FOR A FAMOUS HOLLYWOOD FILM COMPANY! THIS IS IT!

THIS TERM WE HAVE BEEN DOING EXPERIMENTS TO FIND OUT WHY THINGS DECAY...
BAH! HE'S HOPELESS!

NOW JOHN WILL TELL YOU ABOUT SOME OF OUR RESULTS!
WELL, WE LEFT THESE BITS OF ORANGE PEEL FOR A WEEK. YOU'LL NOTICE HOW MOULDY THEY'VE BECOME...
TSK! HE'S EVEN WORSE! HE SHOULD PUT MORE FEELING INTO HIS WORDS!

NOW DANIEL WILL TELL YOU ABOUT HIS EXPERIMENT!
AT LAST! NOW I'LL SHOW THEM HOW A REAL STAR PERFORMS!

TWIRL!
GIVE-A-ME THE MOONLIGHT
GASP!

STOP THIS NONSENSE AND TELL US ABOUT THESE BITS OF ROTTEN POTATO!
OH, SORRY! I DIDN'T KNOW IT WAS DRAMA YOU WANTED! I'LL DO SOME SHAKESPEARE...

DANIEL IS IN CLASS 2B, AND...
2B OR NOT 2B... THAT IS THE QUESTION.
MUFFLED MIRTH

HOWEVER—
PHEW! FINISHED AT LAST...NO THANKS TO HIM!
I'M FAMOUS AT LAST! THE CROWDS CHEER AS I LEAVE THE THEATRE . . .

PESKY WEEDS!
THE ADORING FANS SHOWER ME WITH FLOWERS . . .

. . . AND OF COURSE, THE AUTOGRAPH HUNTERS MILL AROUND ME . . .
WOULD YOU SIGN OUR PETITION? WE'RE TRYING TO GET THE COUNCIL TO PUT UP MORE BENCHES!

BUT THE GREATEST THRILL IS SEEING MY NAME UP IN LIGHTS OVER THE THEATRE ENTRANCE!
DANIELS' PORK SAUSAGES

CALAMITY JAMES
CLASSIC BEANO
THE WORLD'S UNLUCKIEST BOY!
GERM FACTORY
WICKED CLOUD
SIZZLE!
Alexander Lemming
SIGH! WONDER WHAT DISASTER WILL BEFALL ME TODAY?
Suddenly, there's a break-out from the Germ Factory—
LOOK, CLARENCE — A VICTIM!
LET'S GET HIM, CECIL!
An instant later—
AARGH! WHAT'S HAPPENING TO ME? MUST SEE A DOCTOR.
SNIGGER!
FESTER POP!
So—
PUT THIS IN YOUR GOB!
IS IT CATCHING, DOCTOR?
DOC
PILLS
I'LL SAY IT IS! LOOK AT THE THERMOMETER!
GO STRAIGHT HOME TO BED, YOU GERM-RIDDEN PERSON!
PROD!
PATIENT PRODDER (GIANT ECONOMY SIZE)
UNCLEAN! UNCLEAN!
WHAT LUCK! A BUS!
NOT GOING ON A BUS WITH THAT ILL YOUTH.
(INFECTED) BUS STOP
I'LL HAVE THE BUS TO MYSELF! HEH-HEH!
TOO TRUE! WE'RE NOT STAYING ON EITHER!
COWARDLY DRIVER
CONDUCTRESS
GROAN! CAN'T GET HOME NOW.
LOOKS LIKE I'LL BE ILL FOR AGES.
GLOOM!
FESTER!
But—
WOW! I'M OK! THE GERMS HAVE GONE! BUT WHY?
ZZT!
ZAP!
COS WE'VE CAUGHT JAMESITIS, THAT'S WHY! PESKY CLOUDS!

Sir Coward de Custard
CLASSIC DANDY
CHA-A-A-RGE!
BY HARRY! SIR COWARD'S GOT HIS DANDER UP THIS MORNING! I'VE NEVER SEEN HIM LOOKING SO WARLIKE!
HEE-HEE! I'VE LANCED A LOT!
ORCHARD
GADZOOKS! HE'S PINCHING THE FARMER'S APPLES!
HA-HA! BRAVELY DONE, SIRE! YE SKEWERED THOSE APPLES AS EASY AS WINKING!
YUM-YUM!
BUT—
ARREST THE VILLAINS, OFFICER!
OO-ER! HERE COMES TROUBLE!
DON'T WORRY, SIRE. I'LL HIDE THE EVIDENCE IN HERE.
THAT MIGHT BE THE ROGUE! I DIDN'T GET A PROPER LOOK AT HIM BECAUSE HIS FACE WAS HIDDEN BY HIS HELMET!
THERE'S NO SIGN OF APPLES THOUGH.
TAKE COVER! THE OUTLAWS ARE RAIDING THE VILLAGE!
QUICK! FIRE THE CANNON!
I CAN'T! THERE ARE NO CANNON BALLS!
OO-ER! I'M OFF! HERE'S YOUR PIPE, FARMER.
OOPS!
TRIP!
THE GLOWING ASH FROM THE FARMER'S PIPE FALLS DOWN THE TOUCH-HOLE OF THE CANNON.
FSSSSSS
OOYAH!
BOOM!
YAHOO!
BIFF!
OUCH!
SMACK!
ERK!
THUMP!
YEEARGH!
LOOKS LIKE MY APPLES KNOCKED THOSE VARLETS OVER! BUT, SIR KNIGHT, YE HAVE DONE US A GOOD TURN AND I'LL DO YE ONE IN RETURN.
GROAN!
HA-HA! AN APPLE A DAY KEEPS THE OUTLAWS AWAY. EH, WHAT? TUCK IN, MEN!
APPLE PIE
CIDER

MY MASTER'S TAKEN ME CAMPING – BUT HE MAKES ME SLEEP OUTSIDE THE TENT!
CLASSIC TOPPER

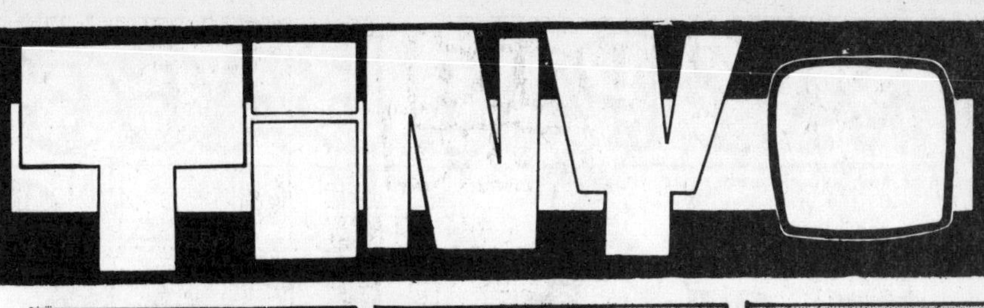
TINY

HUH! RAIN!

I'LL SHELTER IN THE TENT. MASTER ISN'T AROUND!

HMM! I WAS AFRAID THAT MIGHT HAPPEN!

G-GOSH! HE'S COMING BACK!
HMM! THE RAIN'S GETTING HEAVY, BUT I'LL SOON BE SNUG INSIDE MY TENT!

I MUST DISTRACT HIS ATTENTION!
HULLO, TINY!

FEELING HAPPY IN THE RAIN, EH?
YES – AS LONG AS WE KEEP DANCING.

WELL, I'D BE HAPPIER UNDER COVER. I'M GOING INTO THE TENT!
OO, CRUMBS!

TINY! THIS IS NO TIME FOR GAMES!
THAT'S WHAT YOU THINK!

I GATHER YOU WISH TO GO FOR A WALK. WELL, I DON'T!
TO CLIFF WALK

TINY! IF YOU DON'T STOP AT ONCE I'LL CANCEL YOUR "TOPPER"!
OH, NO – ANYTHING BUT THAT!

NOW, NO MORE NONSENSE – I'M GOING BACK TO THE TENT!
THEN THIS IS THE END!

OOH! STUPID COW! IT'S KNOCKED DOWN MY TENT!
OH, BOY – SAVED!

SHOO! SHOO!
HO! HO! GOOD OLD COW! I'LL GIVE IT ONE OF MY BONES NEXT TIME I SEE IT!

# MY PAL, BAGGY PANTS

FRED the FLOP
CLASSIC BUZZ
Heh-heh! I'm going to rob this bank messenger, and this nylon stocking is going to help me!
Mut lub bour yands . . .
Pardon? Sorry! Hmm! Must be a foreigner . . .
. . . or an idiot! I can't understand a word he's saying!
This stocking's too tight! Bah! I can't get it off now!
Hope this works!
I'll tie the end on this branch and jump off the wall—it should pull off easily.
STRETCH!
THUD!
TWANG!
AAGH!
Huh! I'd better get off the streets before I'm seen!
Ah-ha! A villain!
Caught you in the act, eh?
EEK!
Gug!
STRETCH!
Changed your mind and come back, eh?
TWANG!
Right! Take off the mask!
I'll do it, sarge!
MUMBLE!
Erk! It's stuck!
I'll help you!
Yahh!
Gasp!
Pull, lads! It'll come off this time!
Eek!
STRETCH!
WHAM!
Ouch!
We must get his mask off and find out who he is! Tie him to this chair!
Tie this thread to the end of your motorbike and drive up the hill!
Ho-ho! It's working! The chair's spinning and the nylon thread is unwinding!
VROOM!
Why, it's Fred the Flop!
You can speak now, Fred! What were you up to?
SPEECHLESS!

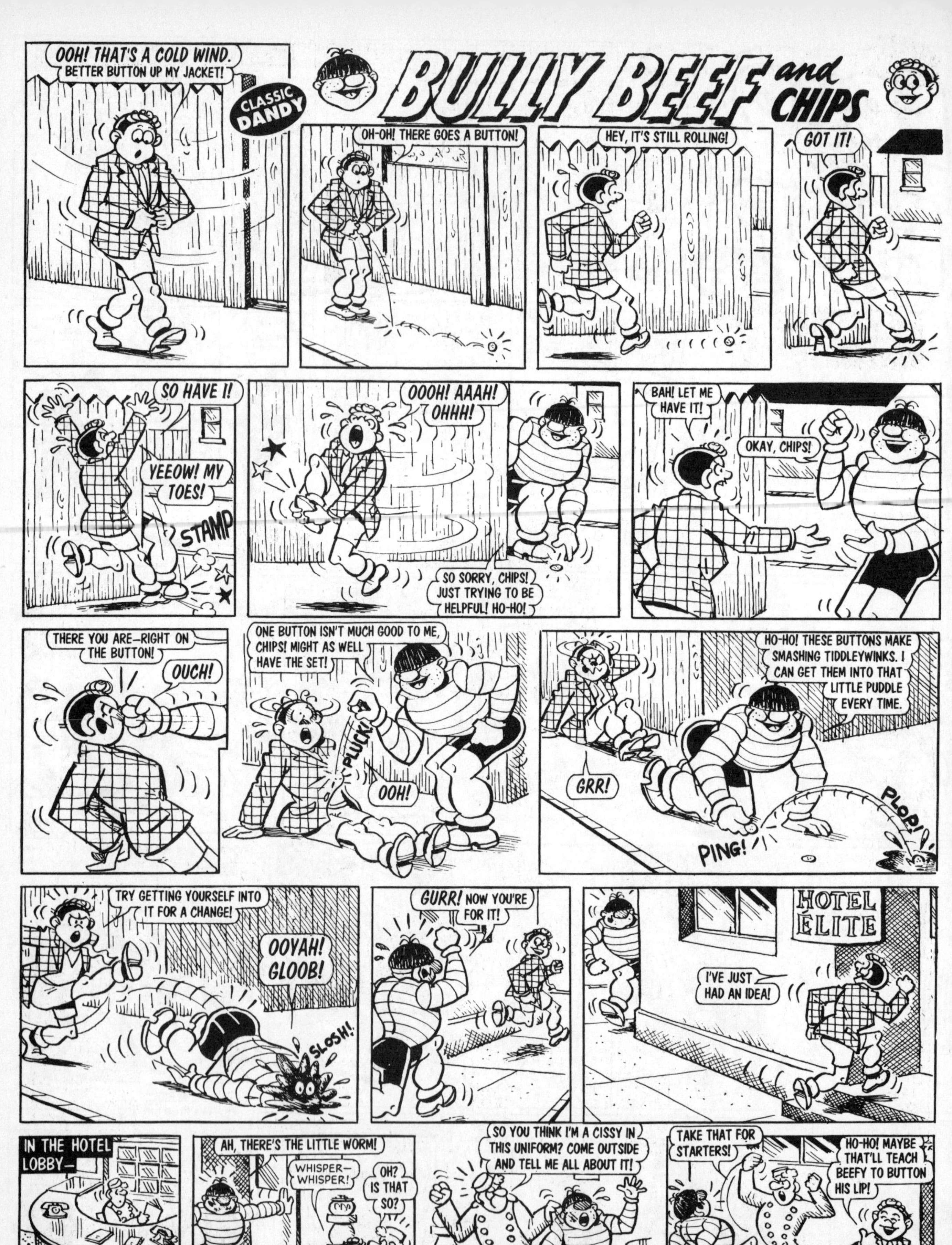
CLASSIC DANDY
BULLY BEEF and CHIPS
OOH! THAT'S A COLD WIND. BETTER BUTTON UP MY JACKET!
OH-OH! THERE GOES A BUTTON!
HEY, IT'S STILL ROLLING!
GOT IT!
SO HAVE I!
YEEOW! MY TOES!
STAMP
OOOH! AAAH! OHHH!
SO SORRY, CHIPS! JUST TRYING TO BE HELPFUL! HO-HO!
BAH! LET ME HAVE IT!
OKAY, CHIPS!
THERE YOU ARE—RIGHT ON THE BUTTON!
OUCH!
ONE BUTTON ISN'T MUCH GOOD TO ME, CHIPS! MIGHT AS WELL HAVE THE SET!
PLUCK!
OOH!
HO-HO! THESE BUTTONS MAKE SMASHING TIDDLEYWINKS. I CAN GET THEM INTO THAT LITTLE PUDDLE EVERY TIME.
GRR!
PING!
PLOP!
TRY GETTING YOURSELF INTO IT FOR A CHANGE!
OOYAH! GLOOB!
SLOSH!
GURR! NOW YOU'RE FOR IT!
HOTEL ELITE
I'VE JUST HAD AN IDEA!
IN THE HOTEL LOBBY—
HEY! I WANT A WORD WITH YOU!
AH, THERE'S THE LITTLE WORM!
WHISPER—WHISPER!
OH? IS THAT SO?
SO YOU THINK I'M A CISSY IN THIS UNIFORM? COME OUTSIDE AND TELL ME ALL ABOUT IT!
EH? WHAT?
TAKE THAT FOR STARTERS!
HO-HO! MAYBE THAT'LL TEACH BEEFY TO BUTTON HIS LIP!
BUT—OOYAH!

CLASSIC SPARKY
PUSS and BOOTS
THEY FIGHT LIKE CAT AND DOG

GOOD-NESS! WHAT HAVE WE HERE? YE HISTORY OF SQUIRE PUSS VERSUS BARON BOOTS!
JUNK SHOP
"BIGGEST LOAD OF JUNK IN TOWN"
AHA! A VICTIM... ER... CUSTOMER!

IT'S A VERY RARE VOLUME, YOUR MAJESTY! THE MUSEUM AND THE COUNCIL CLEANSING DEPARTMENT ARE BOTH AFTER IT!
1 GROAT
RIGHT! I'LL GIVE YOU A PAIR OF BRACES AND AN ALMOST NEW BOILED CABBAGE FOR IT!

ONE DAY, IN YE YEAR OF NIRDLE-NOCKY-NOO, SQUIRE PUSS OF MOGGIE MANSION DECIDED TO GO FOR A STROLL IN YE COUNTRY..."
IT'S GREAT BEING A SQUIRE—YOU DON'T HALF FEEL POSH!

YE OLDE OOPS! METHINKS ME HAS LOST MY WAY IN YE TREE-TYPE WOODS!

YE OLDE SUDDENLEE—
OI! GET YOUR DISGUSTING PAWS OFF MY NICE CLEAN MUD! CAN'T YOU READ?
NO MOGGIES!
UGH! BARON BOOTS, NEWLY RETURNED FROM DESERTING FROM OUR SIDE IN THE BATTLE OF BANANA!

THAT'S A LIE! I THOUGHT I'D LEFT THE TELLY ON, AND WAS JUST POPPING HOME TO CHECK!
GLURK!
BAM!

OO-AR!
OO-AAR!
I AM GOING TO SCARE YOU WITHIN AN ERG OF YOUR GLONK!
YOU? YOU COULDN'T BARKLE A GRUMMIT IF IT WAS SNURKED ON A PANCAKE!
ANCIENT BRITISH INSULTS
Z-Z-Z-Z
OOO?
OO-AAR!
OOO-AAR!

YE TIME PASSED—
HEY! I ENJOYED THAT! I'M GONNA TAKE UP POOCH-PUNCHIN' AS A HOBBY!
YEAH! AN' I'M GONNA DEVOTE MY LIFE TO MOGGIE-MASHING!
OO-AR!
OO-AAR!

SO EACH YEAR ON YE THIRTY-SECOND OF FEBROOBARB, SQUIRE PUSS AND BARON BOOTS MET—
THUMP!
WALLOP!
BASH!
CRUNCH!
BOP!
WHAM!
OO-AR!
Ye Annual GOB-THUMP FAIR
OO-AR?

WHAT A QUAINT LITTLE TALE... OI!
GIMME THAT! STOP PRETENDIN' THAT YOU'VE LEARNED TO READ!
SNATCH!

I'M GONNA BUY THIS BOOK! IT'LL BE PERFECT FOR MY NEW BOOK-CASE—TO PROP UP THE WOBBLY LEG!
OH, YEAH? LOOK AT THE DATE!
32nd FEB

SOON—
HAPPY THIRTY-SECOND OF FEBROOBARB, MOGGIE! I HOPE YOU ENJOY BEIN' BASHED AS MUCH AS I ENJOY DOIN' IT!
YOWCH! I'VE WON MORE OF THE ANNUAL GOB-THUMP FIGHTS THAN YOU! TAKE THAT!
I DO LIKE IT WHEN OLD TRADITIONS ARE KEPT UP! OOO-AAR!
CRUMP!
THUMP!
BASH!
WHAM!
CRUNCH!
BOP!
OO-AAR!
OO-AR!
OOO-AAR!

LITTLE PLUM
CLASSIC BEANO
LOOK AT THIS UM LAUNDRY! ALL UM BUTTONS OFF AGAIN! IN FUTURE YOU CAN DO UM WASHING, PLUM!
UM TRIBAL LAUNDRY
THAT'S THAT DONE! NOW I CAN HAVE UM FORTY WINKS!
BUT, WHILE PLUM HAS A SNOOZE—

YAWN—WHAT WAS THAT THAT WENT BY—? AWLK! UM HERD OF BUFFALO HAS RUN ALL OVER UM WASHING!
I'LL HAVE TO DO IT ALL AGAIN!

1 HOUR LATER
WASH HOUSE
SKID
SOAP!
THAT DIDN'T TAKE LONG! NOW TO FINISH MY SLEEP!

POST OFFICE
UM WASHING WILL SOON DRY THERE!

FIVE MINUTES LATER
WHAT'S UP?

GET UM WASHING OUT OF THERE, PLUM! I'VE GOT TO SEND UM TELEGRAM.
IT'S UM POSTMAN! UM SMOKE'S MADE UM WASHING ALL BLACK AGAIN!

HO-HO! I'VE GOT A GOOD IDEA THIS TIME!
TO HOT SPRINGS

WHY DIDN'T I THINK OF THIS IN UM FIRST PLACE?
SUDSO SOAP POWDER

UM WIRE BASKET FROM UM TRIBAL CHIP-SHOP COMES IN HANDY.

WHOOSH

WOW! UM GEYSER'S SPOUTED ALL UM CLOTHES IN UM AIR!

AND THE WIND BLOWS THE WASHING INTO CHIEFY'S GOAT-PEN.

LATER—WHEN PLUM GETS RID OF THE GOATS
WOW! THEY'VE EATEN ALL UM CLOTHES AND LEFT UM BUTTONS!

LAST TIME IT WAS SHIRTS WITHOUT BUTTONS! THIS TIME IT'S BUTTONS WITHOUT UM SHIRTS! I'LL SKIN THAT LAUNDRY BOY ALIVE, PLUM!
LAUNDRY

# CAP'N HAND

## and his MERRY MUTINEERS

# WILLIE GETAWAY

OR WILL HE NOT?

CLASSIC BEANO
RASHER

DINNER!
OINKSLURP!
TUMBLE!

SACRE BLEU! ZIZ IS AN OUTRAGE.
WHAT?

I AM PIERRE LE PONG FROM THE INSTITUTE OF TURNEEP CUISINE — ZIS IS DISGUSTING!
EH?

A TURNEEP SHOULD BE CARRIED ON A SILVER TRAY.

DON'T EVER USE A WHEELBARROW AGAIN, EENGLEESHMAN.
SMACK!

IT SHOULD BE PEELED CAREFULLY.
CARVE!

SEE — VERY PRETTY!

AH! ZEE WONDERFUL AROMA!
SNIFF! SNIFF!

SOME CAVIARE WILL FEENEESH IT PERFECTLY.
SLURP!
CAVIARE
PLOP!

ZIS IS HOW TO DO IT — NOT HOW YOU DEED EET.

I PREFERRED IT THE OLD WAY . . .

. . . AT LEAST I GOT TO EAT SOME!
GO AWAY, PEEGEE. ZIS IS TOO GOOD FOR YOU!
MUNCH!

STEEVIE STAR
CLASSIC NUTTY
AS
BULLIUS CAESAR
IN
"ROMAN IN THE GLOAMIN"
IN ANCIENT ROME, ONCE A WEEK, THE COLOSSEUM WOULD ECHO TO THE INFAMOUS CHANTS OF . . .
NEXT WEEK'S VISITORS YORK CITY K.O. 3—P.M.
BLOCK A
HAIL, CAESAR!
HAIL, CAESAR!
HAIL? Nonsense! According to my weather report, it's going to be sunny all day . . .
WEATHER
. . . SO LET THE GAMES COMMENCE!
AND SO, ENTER THE SLAVES—
Bring on the opposition—we'll SLAUGHTER 'em!
SWEEPER
Tear 'em to pieces, we will!
BUT—
YORK CITY K.O. 3—P.M.
GULP! Then again . . .
GROWL! LEAP
Mummy!
TWO MINUTES LATER— LIONS—4 SLAVES—0.
Huh! That didn't last long. What's next?
GROAN!
BLEH!
THEY EVEN CHEWED HIS LEG-IRON!
AND—
OH, NO! Not Ericus and Ernio again!?!
Bring me sunshine . . .
LUTON
SUM OF THE JOKES AND PLAYS I'VE WRIT
SKIP!
I say! I say! I say! What d'you call a cannibal who eats his mother-in-law?
WINCE!
A GLADIATOR! Get it? "Glad 'e ate 'er"! Heh!
We are not amused! Feed them to the crocodiles! No, perhaps not—they won't go down well with them either!
DRAG!
Aha! Chariot racing next, I see. Always lots of action in that!
BUT—
OH, NO! A KIDDIES' RACE!

CLASSIC NUTTY
YAWN! This entertainment's terrible. Wish they'd hurry up and invent T V !
SO..
I've had enough of all this!
GASP! HE'S GOING TO JUMP!
GULP!
FLOAT!
I'm going to provide the entertainment myself!
HOORAY!
AND SO—
Right, you lot, this is what I want you to do . . . WHISPER! . . .
AND SHORTLY—
YAHOO! Just call me Eddius Kiddus!
GALLOP!
GULP!
WAHEY!
ZOOOM!
I can't look
PHEW!
BUT!
HOORAH! Well done, Caesar!
I thank you!
OH-OH! LOOK OUT, BULLIUS!
SWERVE!
OH, DEAR!
CRASH!
AND SO IT WAS, THAT FOR ONE BRIEF MOMENT IN HISTORY, THE INFAMOUS ROMAN CHANT WAS ALTERED EVER SO SLIGHTLY . . .
RUMBLE! CRUMBLE!
CRAACK!
SPLIT!
Not to mention the Colosseum!
. . . TO—
NAIL, CAESAR! NAIL, CAESAR! SNORT!
BOP!

COLONEL BLINK
CLASSIC BEEZER
AH, YES! I'M AFRAID I NEED A NEW PAIR OF SHOES, ROVER!
THESE ARE FULL OF HOLES—THE TOPS HAVE PERISHED! ARF!
. . . SHOULD GET A DECENT PAIR HERE!
SHOES
H'MM! THAT MUST BE THE GENTS' DEPARTMENT UP THERE! ARF! ARF!
I'D LIKE A NICE PAIR OF SHOES, SIR!
MY! WHAT A FUNNY LITTLE MAN!
AHEM! SEE TO SIR HERE, WILL YOU, CHARLES?
THIS WAY, SIR!
I'LL LEAVE THIS PAIR FOR YOU TO TRY, SIR!
SHOES, MADAM? IF YOU'LL TAKE A SEAT . . .
NOW! WHERE'S THAT PAIR HE SAID HE'D LEAVE . . .
I'LL JUST PUT MY OWN PAIR HERE FOR NOW!
SILLY OL' ME! HERE THEY ARE! ARF! ARF!
MADAM FEELS THEY'RE A LITTLE ON THE TIGHT SIDE? I'LL BRING ANOTHER PAIR!
PERFECT! SMART—SNAPPY—AND JUST MY SIZE! ARF!
I SAY! SALESMAN! I'LL TAKE THIS PAIR, SIR!
THANK YOU, SIR! A WISE CHOICE! I'LL JUST PARCEL THEM UP FOR SIR!
MUSTN'T FORGET MY BROLLY! ARF!
SEND YOUR ACCOUNT TO ME, SIR! I'LL KEEP THEM ON!
I KNOW THOSE SHOES!???
ARF! QUITE A STEEP HILL, THIS! DIDN'T NOTICE IT BEFORE!
STOP!
GIVE ME THOSE SHOES, YOU CAD!
ARF! HARD LUCK, SIR! I SPOTTED 'EM FIRST!

# DESPERATE DAN

CLASSIC DANDY

HELP! FIRE! AND I'M AFRAID TO JUMP!
LOOK, JUMBO! THERE'S A FIRE THAT MUST BE PUT OUT!

CLASSIC BEANO
The BASH STREET KIDS

IIB
WHAT HAVE YOU UNTIDY LOT GOT IN YOUR POCKETS?

GOOD GRIEF! WERE YOU GOING TO EAT ALL THAT AT LUNCHTIME, FATTY?

. . . SAND IN THIS ONE . . .
SO I SEE!

. . . AND THIS! IF YOU PUT IT TO YOUR EAR, YOU CAN HEAR THE SEA!
LET ME TRY.

Outside —
WINDOW CLEANING TIME AGAIN!

WELL, I'VE GOT READING SPECS, WRITING SPECS, SLEEPING SPECS, EATING SPECS, JOGGING SPECS . . .
YOU'RE ALWAYS MAKING A SPECTACLE OF YOURSELF!

YOUR POCKETS ARE ALL IN A DREADFUL STATE — YOU'VE GOT EVERYTHING BUT THE KITCHEN SINK IN THEM!
I'VE GOT THAT . . .

. . . ME! GIGGLE! WHAT A WIT I AM!
THAT'S NOT FAIR!
BOO!

Outside again —
I FOOLED THEM AT LAST! CHORTLE! CACKLE! CHUCKLE!
LAUGHING LIKE THAT COULD BE DANGEROUS . . .

. . . IN AN OLD BANGER LIKE THAT!

OF COURSE NOT . . .

. . . THAT'S MY PLAYTIME SNACK! THIS IS FOR LUNCHTIME!
GLUTTON!

WHAT ABOUT YOUR POCKETS, DANIEL? WHAT'S IN THEM?
SOUVENIRS OF MY HOLIDAY . . .

PITY THAT ONE'S OPEN, THOUGH!
SPLOOSH!

HEY! YOU DON'T ONLY HEAR THE SEA—YOU CAN FEEL IT AS WELL!

GROAN! 'ERBERT, YOU'RE NEXT.

. . . ALONG WITH THE REST OF THE FURNITURE FROM MY DOLL'S HOUSE!

I'VE AN IDEA—THE PERSON WITH THE NEATEST POCKETS CAN GO HOME NOW.

WELL, THERE'S NO DOUBT WHO THE WINNER IS . . .

DRAT! I'VE LAUGHED IT TO BITS!

Soon—
AND HE HAD THE CHEEK TO COMPLAIN ABOUT OUR POCKETS!

GROAN! THIS IS THE ONLY WAY I CAN GET MY MOTOR CAR HOME!

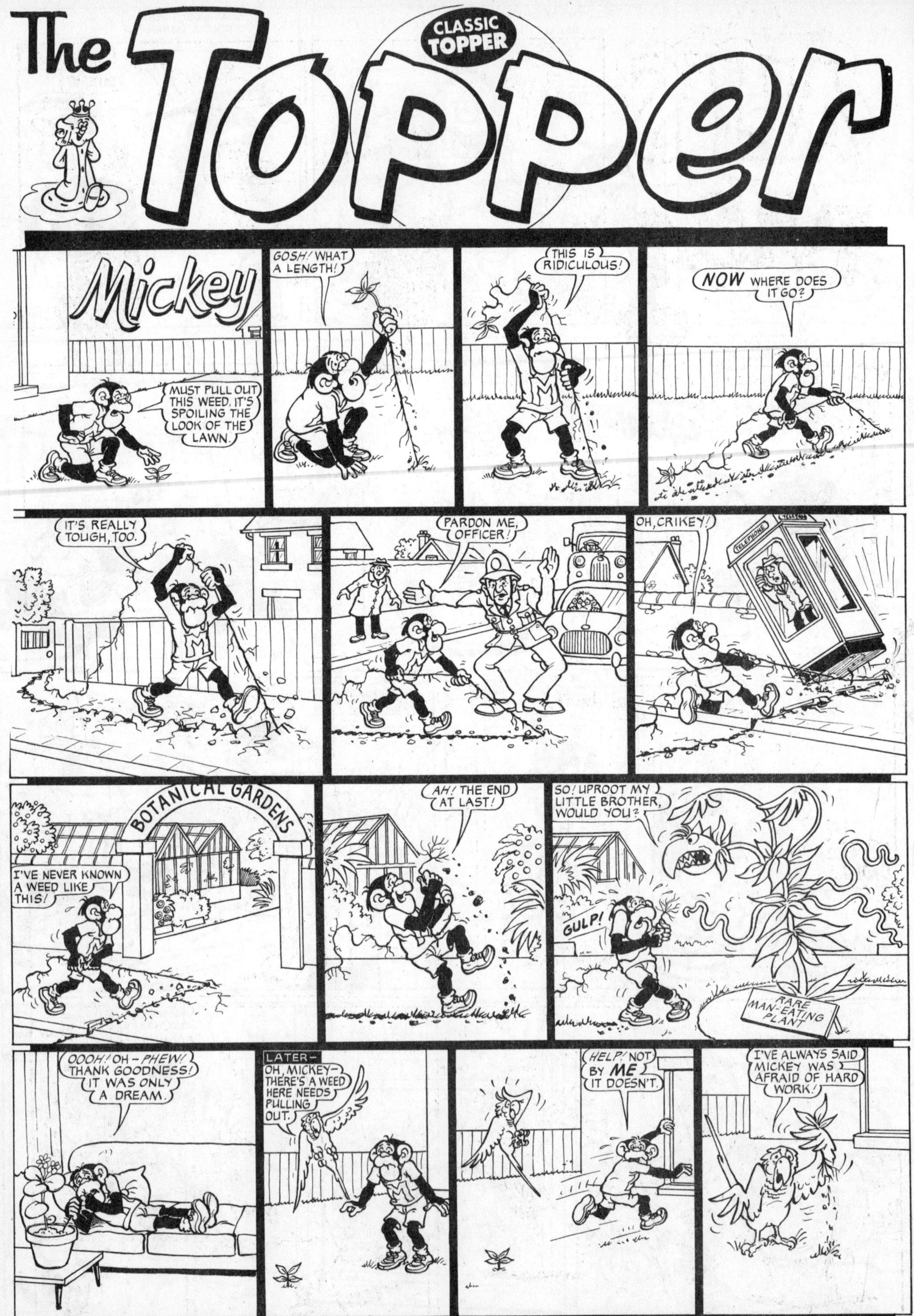
The Topper
CLASSIC TOPPER
Mickey
MUST PULL OUT THIS WEED. IT'S SPOILING THE LOOK OF THE LAWN.
GOSH! WHAT A LENGTH!
THIS IS RIDICULOUS!
NOW WHERE DOES IT GO?
IT'S REALLY TOUGH, TOO.
PARDON ME, OFFICER!
OH, CRIKEY!
TELEPHONE
BOTANICAL GARDENS
I'VE NEVER KNOWN A WEED LIKE THIS!
AH! THE END AT LAST!
SO! UPROOT MY LITTLE BROTHER, WOULD YOU?
GULP!
RARE MAN-EATING PLANT
OOOH! OH-PHEW! THANK GOODNESS! IT WAS ONLY A DREAM.
LATER—
OH, MICKEY—THERE'S A WEED HERE NEEDS PULLING OUT.
HELP! NOT BY ME IT DOESN'T.
I'VE ALWAYS SAID MICKEY WAS AFRAID OF HARD WORK!

ALI'S
BABA
CLASSIC SPARKY
ERK!
BABA GOT HOOPLA SET! BABA GONNA PLAY WITH IT ALL DAY!
PHEW! SAVED IT!
AW! MISSED!
THEN—
OH, NO! NOW HE'S AIMING FOR MRS CLARK'S CONK!
HOOPLA!
PHEW! JUST IN TIME!
AW! MISSED AGAIN!
LATER—
YIKE! IT'LL PECK HIM!
BABA HOOPLA PARROT ON STAND NOW! HOOPLA!
PET SHOP
WHAM!
PECK!
GOT IT . . . YOW!
HUH! BABA GETTIN' FED UP WITH THIS!
GRR! OUCH! OWF!
AHA! NOW THERE'S AN IDEA!
THE ZOO! WHAT'S HE DOING IN THERE?
ZOO
HOOPLA!
YIPES!
HOOPLA! BABA GOOD NOW!
NOT AT ALL CHUFFED
H'MM...HOW CAN BABA GET HOOPS BACK?
I'D BETTER GET THEM BEFORE THERE'S TROUBLE!
GRR!
OOH! OW! WOW! OOH!
BOUNCE!
BUCK!
COO! RHINO THROW BABA'S HOOPS BACK!
TOSS!
OOF!
THUD!
THANKS, MR RHINO! BABA COME AND PLAY AGAIN SOON!
OOH! MOAN!

CLASSIC BEANO
JONAH
YOU'VE GOT A NERVE – BOARDING HERE, MATE! THIS HOME IS RESERVED FOR SEAMEN WHO'VE HAD A BREAKDOWN AFTER BEING SUNK BY YOU!
I'M A SAM-PAN!
SAILORS' REST
WHAT ORDERS, CAP'N NELSON?
LATER, THAT NIGHT—
HELLO! SOMEONE'S SMUGGLED IN FISH-AND-CHIPS FROM SAM'S PLACE!
THIS TORN NEWSPAPER REEKS OF SOUR VINEGAR AND STALE CODFISH! — COO! LOOK AT THIS!
WANTED. – ONE VOLUNTEER TO MAN NEW SHIP.
THERE'S A WORD MISSING HERE.
"UNLESS THE NAVY FINDS A VOLUNTEER TO MAN THEIR NEW SHIP QUICKLY, THE LAUNCHING WILL HAVE TO BE POSTPONED FOR A MONTH!"
GIVE THAT COCOA TO SIR FRANCIS DRAKE, MATE! I'M JUST OFF TO TAKE COMMAND OF MY NEW BATTLESHIP!
!
SNIFF
MEANWHILE, AT NAVAL H.Q.—
GENTLEMEN! THE LAUNCHING IS SCHEDULED FOR NOON TODAY. UNLESS SOME HUMAN VOLUNTEERS, WE'LL HAVE TO PUT JOE IN COMMAND!
MATES! YOUR WORRIES ARE OVER! I'M HERE!
JONAH!
IT'S 'IM!
QUICK! GRAB HIM! HE'S OUR ONLY HOPE! GET A MEDICAL REPORT ON HIM AT ONCE!
WHIMPER!
AND SO—
Medical Report on JONAH.
WE HAVE REACHED THE UNANIMOUS DECISION THAT THE SUBJECT WAS ACCIDENTALLY DROPPED HEAD-FIRST FROM A GREAT HEIGHT AT AN EARLY AGE — AND THAT HIS FALL TERMINATED ON A THREE-TON SLAB OF REINFORCED CONCRETE. SIGNED—
Doctors { L. Probe. U. Vaddit.
—IN OTHER WORDS, HE'S JUST THE LAD FOR THE JOB!
HALF AN HOUR LATER, AT PORTSMOUTH—
FULL SPEED AHEAD TO OUR SECRET RENDEZVOUS, CAPTAIN!
PREPARE THE SPECIMEN FOR LAUNCHING!
COO!
THEY'RE PUTTING ME IN CHARGE OF AN AIRCRAFT-CARRIER. WHEN DO I TAKE OVER, MATES?
AT NOON, DEAR BOY!
JUST BEFORE NOON.
M'BOY! YOU'RE PRIVILEGED TO BE PRESENT AT THE LAUNCHING OF BRITAIN'S FIRST SPACE-SHIP — CONTAINING A LIVING BIOLOGICAL SPECIMEN! — YOU!
EH?!
UP ROCKET!
WHIRR-R-R!
ORIGINALLY WE WERE GOING TO SEND UP A BABOON CALLED JOE, BUT 50,000 ANIMAL LOVERS PROTESTED! HOWEVER, IN YOUR CASE, WE'VE ONLY HAD ONE PROTEST — FROM JOE!
AWLK! NO!
NO! I PROTEST! I RESIGN!
AGH-H-H-H!
CLANG!
POSITION THE PROJECTILE ON THE SPECIALLY CONSTRUCTED LAUNCHING PLATFORM, GENTLEMEN!
NO! PUT ME DOWN!
I DON'T WANT TO VISIT THE MOON! I'VE BOOKED MY HOLIDAYS FOR BLACKPOOL THIS YEAR!
OVER A BIT!
AGH-H-H! WHICH OF THESE BUTTONS OPENS THE DOOR?
PRESS
JAB
FINGER-CONTROL FIRING-BUTTON
AGH!
HE'S PRESSED THE LAUNCHING BUTTON BEFORE THE ROCKET'S ON THE FIREPROOF PLATFORM!
RUN FOR IT!
THE EXHAUST WILL BURN THROUGH THE FLIGHT-DECK LIKE AN ACETYLENE CUTTER!
IT DOES! — AND TEN MINUTES LATER—
IT'S CUT THROUGH EVERY DECK AGH-H-H-H! ABANDON SHIP!
HISS-S-S
ZOOM
BLOOP
HELP! I'M GOING UP!
HELP! WE'RE GOING DOWN!
AT PRECISELY NOON—
GONE

CLASSIC BEANO
JONAH
DUE TO A GOVERNMENT BLUNDER, JONAH HAS BEEN LAUNCHED IN A ROCKET BOUND FOR THE MOON—
HELP!
WHILE BACK ON MOTHER EARTH—
GENTLEMEN! I CAN ASSURE YOU THAT EVERYTHING POSSIBLE IS BEING DONE TO RECTIFY THIS GRAVE ERROR! THE ENTIRE NAVY IS SEARCHING FOR THE ROCKET AND THE AIRCRAFT-CARRIER THAT LAUNCHED IT.
QUESTIONS ARE BEING ASKED IN THE "HOUSE."
MEANWHILE, ANOTHER GOVERNMENT IS DEBATING THE SUBJECT WITH EQUAL FERVOUR.
IT HAS BEEN FIRMLY ESTABLISHED, THAT THE EARTH ROCKET, POSSIBLY CONTAINING AN EARTH-CREATURE, WILL BY-PASS THE MOON AND ALIGHT ON OUR PLANET!—
GLUK!
GLOILK!
—AND SO, FELLOW MARTIANS, WE MAY, AT LONG LAST, BE PRIVILEGED TO SEE ONE OF THE NOBLE INHABITANTS OF THE PLANET EARTH!
A RACE, WE BELIEVE, OF CIVILISED, INTELLIGENT BEINGS.
MARTIANS! MARTIANS! THE ROCKET HAS JUST LANDED INTACT IN CANAL Nº 437 —AND SOMETHING INSIDE IT IS MAKING QUEER GLAWKING NOISES!
TO CANAL 437!
TWO MILLION MARTIANS LATER—
MARTIANS! THIS IS AN EPOCH-MAKING MOMENT IN THE HISTORY OF OUR PLANET!
CANAL 437
WHAT YOU ARE ABOUT TO SEE, REPRESENTS THE HUMAN RACE!
OILK! GUG! GLEWP!!
GASP
AGH-H!
AGH-H-H! THEY'RE WORSE THAN WE ARE!
IT'S HORRIBLE! IT'S GHASTLY! TO THINK THAT SUCH THINGS EXIST!! SHUT THE LID—QUICK!—AND FIRE IT BACK TO EARTH!
DOH-H!
10,000,000,000 GALLONS OF ROCKET-FUEL LATER—
TO EARTH
WE WILL NOW SPEND THE REST OF TODAY HUMBLY THANKING OUR LUCKY STARS FOR WHAT WE ARE!
YOU ARE NOW APPROACHING MARS.
PLEASE GLIDE CAREFULLY
BOOM
WELCOME TO MARS
MEANWHILE, ON EARTH, A VAST SEA-OPERATION IS IN PROGRESS. OPERATION "FIND-THE-GOON".
THIS IS THE BIGGEST THING SINCE D-DAY, BLENKINSOP! FIFTY DESTROYERS STRUNG OUT IN A LINE—ALL LOOKING FOR A MOON-ROCKET CONTAINING JONAH!
IF YOU SEE ANYTHING THAT LOOKS LIKE AN EXHAUSTED BLUEBOTTLE BLOWN OFF ITS COURSE—BLAST IT OUT OF THE WATER IN CASE IT TURNS OUT TO BE 'IM!
AYE-AYE, SIR!
JONAH ALARM
BUT JONAH RETURNS TO EARTH 300 MILES AWAY—AT AN ANGLE OF FORTY-FIVE DEGREES—
WHOOOOOOSH-H-H-H-H
AWLK!
—WITH ENOUGH ROCKET-FUEL LEFT TO PROPEL HIM ANOTHER 600 MILES AT A SPEED OF 300 MILES PER SECOND.
ERK!
HISS-S-S-S-S
—SO, A SECOND LATER—
CAP'N, LOOK!
TH-THERE'S A THING LIKE AN EIGHTY-FOOT-LONG-TORPEDO APPROACHING US AT A SPEED FASTER THAN SOUND!
AGH-H-H! IT'S JONAH'S MOON-ROCKET! BLOW IT TO SMITHEREENS! ERK! TOO LATE!
CHUNG
ZIP
CHUNG
ZIP
CHUNG
AND SO—FIFTY DESTROYERS AND THE LONEROCK LIGHTHOUSE LATER—GREAT BRITAIN'S FIRST ATTEMPT TO MASTER THE MOON ENDS LIKE THIS—
ONE-OUT! TWO-OUT! THREE-OUT!
HELP!
MAYDAY!
S.O.S!
START BALING!

# SNIP and SNAP

**Postie, look below... And watch out for your TOE!**

DESPERATE DAWG
WHAT ARE YOU TRYING TO DO WITH THE TIN LIZZIE, SHERIFF?

AH'VE GOT AWFUL TOOTHACHE, DAWG, AN' AH'VE GOTTA DRIVE INTO THE NEXT TOWN TO SEE THE DENTIST. BUT I CAN'T START THE CAR.
CLASSIC DANDY
MAYBE IF YOU COULD GIVE IT A GOOD TURN OVER, DAWG, YOU COULD START IT?
STOP, DAWG! YOU'RE TURNING OVER THE WHOLE CAR!
TWIRL!

PERHAPS IT WOULD BE SAFER IF YOU GAVE THE CAR A PUSH.

HOW'S THAT?
TOO HARD! YOWEE!
WHIZZ!

SPLOSH!

DO SOMETHING, DAWG! I'M DRIFTING DOWNRIVER!

THIS IS AN EMERGENCY! I'LL NEED THAT PICK-AXE, AND A ROPE!
ROAD WORKS

OOF!
CLUNK!

A GOOD HARD TUG, NOW!

OH, CORKS! A BIT TOO HARD!
CRASH!

ALL RIGHT, DAWG! THERE'S NO NEED TO START THE CAR NOW. YOU KNOCKED OUT MY BAD TOOTH WHEN YOU HIT ME WITH THE PICK-AXE!
AH, WELL! ALL'S WELL THAT ENDS WELL!

# HUNGRY HORACE

**Horace's had enough... Of that green boiled stuff!**

CLASSIC SPARKY

I GOTTA GET ME A CHICK. BUT HOW? HOW? THAT IS THE QUESTION...

CLASSIC TOPPER
FOXY

BUT, WAIT...
SNAP

...I GOT IT, FOLKS. JUST YOU WATCH!

AT THE FARM...
CLUCK, CLUCK, SQUAWK, SQUAWK! TUCK!
!?!
HEH! HEH! HOW DO YOU LIKE MY FOWL IMPERSONATIONS, FOLKS?

CLUCK! CLUCK!
THAT'LL BE FOXY AFTER THE...PUFF... CHICKENS...PANT!

HEH-HEH! NOW I GIVE HIM THE RUN-A-ROUND!

FUNNY...NOTHING HERE!
CLUCK, CLUCK! SQUAWK!

PUFF...GASP...SOUNDS LIKE HE'S OVER BEHIND THE BARN SOMEWHERE... PANT...NOW.
CLUCK! CLUCK!

NOTHING AGAIN! THERE'S SOMETHING FUNNY GOING ON...

...AND I THINK I KNOW WHAT!

CLUCK! TUCK! CLUCK!

CLUCK! CLUCK!
PUFF!
GASP!
PANT!
HEH-HEH! POOR OLD CHAP...HE'S WORN OUT WITH ALL THE DASHING ABOUT!

GASP-PUFF!
HO-HO! JUST AS I THOUGHT... HE'S TOO EXHAUSTED TO GO ON!

PANT-GASP!
THAT LEAVES THE COAST CLEAR FOR ME TO PICK UP A CHICK OR TWO!

BUT AT THE CHICKEN-RUN...
SO!
FUF-FARMER... B-B-BUT-

YEOW!
BANG!

HO-HO! WELL DONE, MA...FOXY'S NOT THE ONLY ONE WHO CAN DO IMPERSONATIONS!
?????

# ONE BIG LONG LAUGH!

# THE TRICKS of SCREWY DRIVER

# CURLY'S COMMANDOS

CLASSIC CRACKER

HELLO, FOLKS! I'M CURLY! MEET THE GANG!

HAMISH

TITCH

PODGE

WHERE'S HERBERT? HE'S LATE FOR PARADE AGAIN!

HE'S AT THE LOCAL BARRACKS WATCHING A PARADE....

...AND THIS IS CLARENCE... THE REGIMENTAL GOAT!

COO! WHAT A SUPER MASCOT!

AND JUST THEN...
AAAH!
THAT'S NO REASON—ERK! OR IS IT?
CHOO!
CLASSIC CRACKER
ERK!
ARGH!
CRIKEY! I'D BETTER GET OUT OF HERE! I'M OFF HOME!
WE NEVER HAD THIS TROUBLE WITH TOWSER!
PLEASE TAKE YOUR OLD JOB BACK, PLEASE!
READ MY DEMANDS CAREFULLY, THEN SIGN ON THE DOTTED LINE, LAD!
DEMANDS
I'LL FETCH YOU ANOTHER PILLOW, TOWSER, SIR!
WOULD YOU CARE FOR A NICE JUICY BONE?
MORE BANGERS AND MASH, SIR?
THIS IS WHAT'S KNOWN AS A DOG'S LIFE!
TALKIN' OF ELEPHANTS, I ONCE SAW AN ELEPHANT FLY! HE WAS IN A JUMBO JET!

# The Dandy

CLASSIC
DANDY

KORKY THE CAT
FISHING CONTEST
THANKS FOR BRINGING THE SCALES, KORKY.

YOU'LL BE IN CHARGE OF THE WEIGHING.

THE FIRST MAN'S CATCH—
THAT ONE WEIGHS FIVE POUNDS, MISTER!
IT DOES?

THE SECOND MAN'S CATCH—
ER—THAT ONE WEIGHS SEVEN OUNCES.
RUBBISH!

THAT MACHINE IS USELESS—LIKE YOU! CHUCK IT IN THE RIVER OR I'LL CHUCK YOU IN!
ULP! Y-Y-YES, SIR!

AT ONCE, SIR!
HEAVE!
SPLASH!

SPLOOSH!
HA-HA! NO DOUBT ABOUT WHO WON. KORKY CAUGHT THE BIGGEST FISH!
FISHING CONTEST

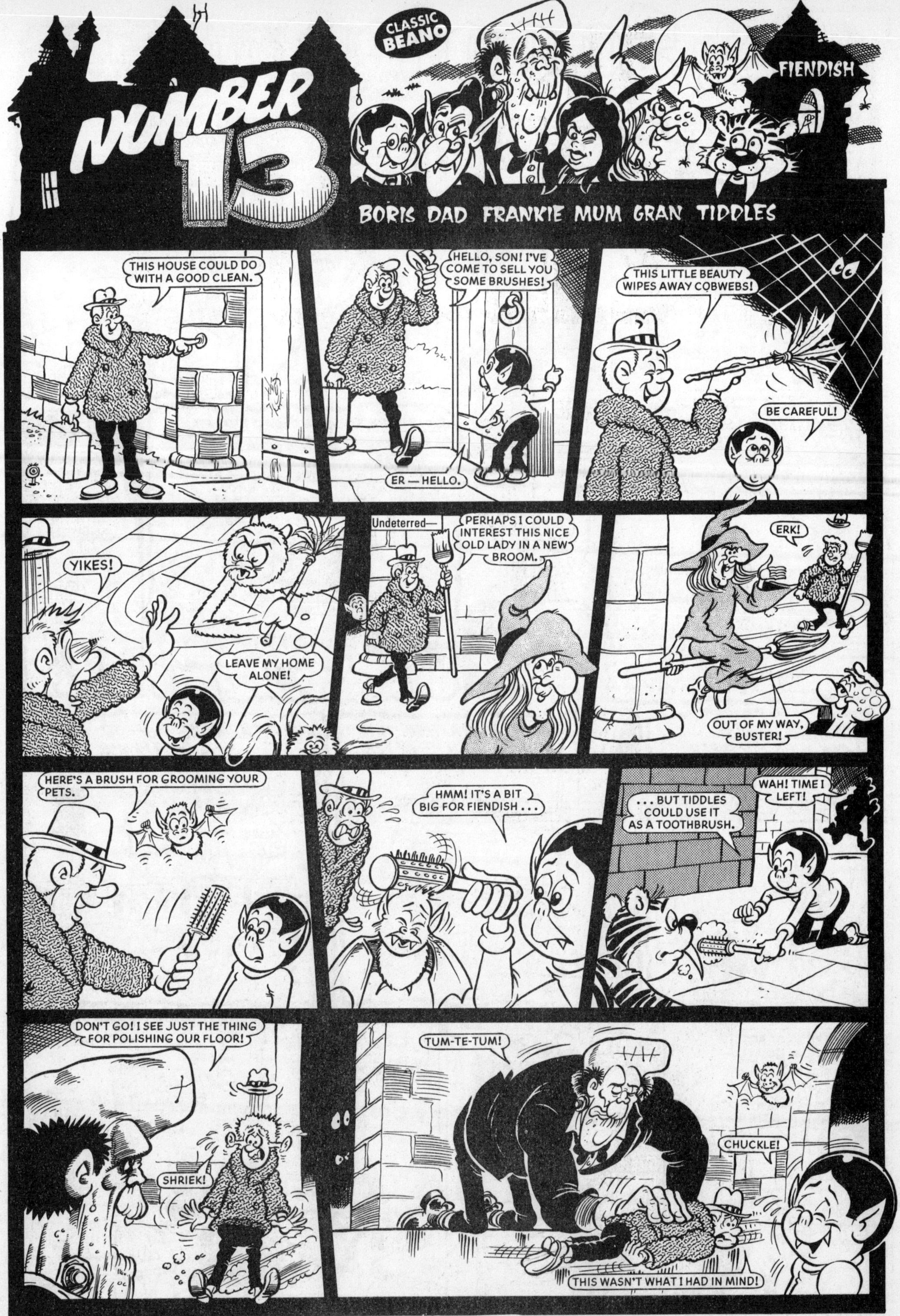

CLASSIC BEANO
NUMBER 13
FIENDISH
BORIS DAD FRANKIE MUM GRAN TIDDLES
THIS HOUSE COULD DO WITH A GOOD CLEAN.
HELLO, SON! I'VE COME TO SELL YOU SOME BRUSHES!
ER — HELLO.
THIS LITTLE BEAUTY WIPES AWAY COBWEBS!
BE CAREFUL!
YIKES!
LEAVE MY HOME ALONE!
Undeterred—
PERHAPS I COULD INTEREST THIS NICE OLD LADY IN A NEW BROOM.
ERK!
OUT OF MY WAY, BUSTER!
HERE'S A BRUSH FOR GROOMING YOUR PETS.
HMM! IT'S A BIT BIG FOR FIENDISH . . .
. . . BUT TIDDLES COULD USE IT AS A TOOTHBRUSH.
WAH! TIME I LEFT!
DON'T GO! I SEE JUST THE THING FOR POLISHING OUR FLOOR!
SHRIEK!
TUM-TE-TUM!
CHUCKLE!
THIS WASN'T WHAT I HAD IN MIND!

THE KNIGHT OF THE YEAR SHOW?
Spoofer
McGRAW
HE TELLS TALL TALES.
THEY COULDN'T MISS THAT, BO!
IN THE MUSEUM–
CLASSIC SPARKY
COO! LOOK AT THAT ARMOUR! MAKES YOU WONDER HOW KNIGHTS USED T'MANAGE T'WALK ABOUT, EH, SPOOFER?
KNIGHTS DIDN'T WEAR ARMOUR, BO!
OOH! THEY DID SO! EVERYONE KNOWS THAT!
EVERYONE IS WRONG, BO! SHUT UP, AND I'LL LET YOU INTO A SECRET...
A-A-SECRET?
YES, BO–THE TRUTH ABOUT ARMOUR! Y'SEE, IT ALL STARTED BACK IN KING ARTHUR'S TIME....
POOR OL' ARTHUR... WHAT A MEMORY HE HAD....
CRUMBS! IS THAT YE TIME? I'VE GOT A WAR IN YE HOLY LAND ON SATURDAY!
JANUARY 4
SIR LAFFALOT
SIR PRIZE
SIR CUS
SO HE CALLED HIS ARMY TOGETHER AN' TOLD 'EM TO GET READY....
WE LEAVE ON FRIDAY NIGHT!
MOAN!
COMPLAIN!
GRUMBLE!
BOO!
THE ARMY WASN'T AT ALL HAPPY, I CAN TELL YOU...
WHY WAS THAT, SPOOFER?
WELL... FRIDAY NIGHT WAS THE FINAL OF THE "KNIGHT OF THE YEAR" CONTEST....
WE'LL HAVE TO TELL HIM WE JUST CAN'T GO!
WHAT? AND GET OUR HEADS CHOPPED OFF?
NO FEAR!
GONE TO LUNCH
5
BUT LUCKILY FOR THEM, MERLIN THE MAGICIAN CAME UP WITH THE ANSWER!
WHAT WAS THAT?
ROBOTS, BO–GIANT CLOCKWORK SOLDIERS...
...SO THAT'S IT! WE MAKE A FEW DOZEN AND SEND THEM OFF TO THE WAR!
GREAT!
AN' POOR OL' KING ARTHUR WAS SO SHORT-SIGHTED HE NEVER KNEW THE DIFFERENCE....
FORWARD, MEN–TO YE HOLY-LAND!
HO-HO HO!
CLANK!
CLANK!
AND THE ARMY WENT OFF TO THEIR FINALS...
BRRR!
COLDEST KNIGHT OF YE YEAR
HOTTEST KNIGHT OF YE YEAR
SHORTEST KNIGHT OF YE YEAR
LONGEST KNIGHT OF YE YEAR
HOORAY!
WHOOPEE!
YAHOO!
KNIGHT OF YE YEAR FINALS
AND THIS LOT ARE JUST RUN-DOWN ROBOTS, BO!
COO! JUS' FANCY THAT! ROBOTS, EH?
I'LL GIVE THIS ONE A SHOVE AND SEE IF I CAN GET IT TO GO!
NO! STOP...
HOI!
DON'T WORRY, MISTER! JUST LEAVE IT AND IT'LL COME BACK UP BY ITSELF!
GRRR! I'LL DO YOU, SO I WILL!
OH-OH! TIME-T'GO-TIME!

# the BASH STREET KIDS

LOOK, CORPORAL CLOTT! THEY'RE HOLDING A VIKING DAY AT THE VILLAGE. AND THERE'S A PRIZE FOR THE BEST BATTERING RAM TEAM.
THAT SOUNDS WORTH ENTERING, COLONEL GRUMBLY, SIR!
VIKING DAY
PRIZE FOR THE BEST BATTERING RAM TEAM
CORPORAL
CLOTT
CLASSIC DANDY

IN THE WOODS
THAT TREE WILL M
A GOOD BATTERING
CLOTT! CHOP IT D
RIGHTO

OUT YOU COME, SIR!
GURR! THE LORRY'S A WRITE-OFF! YOU'D BETTER FETCH SOMETHING ELSE TO CARRY THE BATTERING RAM!

SOON
THERE YOU ARE, SIR. I'VE TIED IT SECURELY TO THE BACK SEATS OF THE JEEP!

GOOD JOB IT'S A WIDE ROAD ALL THE WAY BACK TO CAMP!

AT THE VIKING FESTIVAL
THERE'S YOUR TARGET, MEN! THE WINNING TEAM WILL BE THE ONE TO KNOCK DOWN THAT HEAVY DOOR WITH THE LEAST NUMBER OF BLOWS!

LOOK, CLOTT, ONE OF THE HORNS HAS COME OFF MY HELMET!
OH, DEAR! LUCKY WE'VE GOT A FEW MINUTES TO SPARE!

I'VE MANAGED TO BORROW THIS WATCHMA BRAZIER! WE'LL WELD THE HORN BACK O
COME ON, CLOTT! WE'R TO GO! THIS THING'S GETT

SNORT!
EEK! IT ISN'T CLOTT! IT'S A MAD BULL!

AYEE! HELP!
POOR COLONEL GRUMBLY! THE BULL'S CHASING HIM ON TO THE FESTIVAL FIELD!

EEYULK!
HELP!
WOW!

OOYAH!
OOPS! A FLYING SPLINTER! SORRY, SIR!
PING!

BAH! I'M STAYING IN HERE, WHERE IT'S SAFE!
LOOK OUT, SIR-TIMBER-R-!

CRUNCH!
AARGH!

EEAARGH!
CAMP ENTRANCE
OH, DEAR! THE ENTRANCE WASN'T AS WIDE AS I THOUGHT!
BAH! YOU IDIOT, CLOTT!

RIGHT, MEN, COLLECT YOUR VIKING HELMETS HERE!
THANK YOU, SIR!

HELP! THE BATTERING RAM'S ON FIRE!
WOW!
CRUMBS! TIME FOR ME TO GO!
GURR! NOW WE'VE NO BATTERING RAM!

SNARL! I SAW THAT IDIOT COME THIS WAY. AH! THERE HE IS HIDING BEHIND THOSE BUSHES!

TAKE THAT, CLOTT!
GRUNT!
BONK!

CRASH!

COLONEL GRUMBLY WINS THE TROPHY FOR THE BEST BATTERING MACHINE!
THREE CHEERS FOR COLONEL GRUMBLY!
HOORAY!
EH? WHAT HAPPENED?
WELL DONE!

# DOODLEBUG

CLASSIC NUTTY

HOWL! WAIL!

It must be terrible putting up with a howling Buglet all day. I'm glad I can just sit here doodling.

Doodlebug, be a sweet and mind little Peregrine for an hour.

Me? But . . .

GOO! GOO!

And my Tyrone's no bother!

And my Humphrey's an angel!

GAA! GAA!

I can't continue with these Buglets bothering me—IT'S IMPOSSIBLE!

GURGLE!

GRR! GET OFF! BEHAVE YOURSELVES!

YELL!

BOO! HOO!

SECONDS LATER—

GOO! GOO!

Pencil super fun!

WHUMP!

GNNGH!

Nice Doodlebug take us walkies!

GROAN! Walkies?!? Oh, no!

BIG UGGY
BIG UGGY AND DOPEYDOKUS SAIL DOWN A RIVER IN STONE-AGE FRANCE, PURSUED BY STONE-AGE FRENCHMEN, WHO ARE VERY ANGRY BECAUSE DOPEY-QUITE BY ACCIDENT-KNOCKED DOWN THE EYEFUL TOWER...
Keep paddling, Dopey. We've got them beaten for speed.
Vandals!

They won't catch us now.
Ah! There's a good sign. We're homeward bound.
TO SEA AND STONE-AGE BRITAIN
CLASSIC TOPPER

BUT...
Heave to! If you're leaving France, you must stop at this Customs Post! Have you anything to declare?
Yes—I declare that we want to pass in a hurry!

Are you taking out that fur?
Why, of course—it belongs to me!

The duty payable is two feet of log.
SAW!

And are you exporting that Dopeydokus?
Yes—he's my friend!

That'll cost you another three feet.

Are you exporting that log?
What's left of it!

Two more feet!

Huh! Left with hardly a foot to stand on!

Lucky we can both swim—or we'd be sunk!

IN MID-CHANNEL
There's nobody chasing us now. We've got clean away.
But there's a boat ahead!

You're not in the race, then? All right. Hop in!
Can we come aboard?
CROSS CHANNEL SWIM

Gosh—you look all-in!
No—I'm only HALF in!

Stop your chum panting! He's blowing a half-gale, and my swimmer can't keep up!
Wait for me! Wait for me!
WHOOOSH!
CROSS CHANNEL SWIM
Eh? I haven't even the breath to stop MYSELF panting!

L CARS
CLASSIC SPARKY

ON THE NIGHT SHIFT . . .
YOU SCRUFFY OAFS—YOU'RE A DISGRACE! SMARTEN YOURSELF UP! HAVE YOU SEEN YOURSELVES IN THE MIRROR? GO ON—TAKE A LOOK!
YES, SIR!
SIR!

OH, WE'RE NOT TOO BAD, INSPECTOR, SIR!
NOT BAD— NO! DISGRACEFUL!
DRRING! DRRING!

YES...OF COURSE, SIR! RIGHT AWAY, SIR! IMMEDIATELY, SIR!
THAT SOUNDS IMPORTANT...
YEAH!

A LARGE NUMBER OF SPOTLAMPS HAVE BEEN STOLEN FROM THE JALOPY CAR FACTORY. YOU TWO WILL INVESTIGATE!
SIR!
SIR!

OW!
AAH!
WHUMP!

TO THE FACTORY, FREDERIC!
OKAY!
VAROOOM!

JALOPY CARS
SO! THEY BROKE IN HERE, EH?
AND NO CLUES AROUND. WE BETTER GO TELL THE INSPECTOR.

JUST THEN—
WHAT'S GOING ON AT THE JEWELLER'S DOWN THERE?
HELP! I'M DAZZLED!
YEEK! I CAN'T SEE!
EXCUSE ME! TA!

HELP! I CAN'T SEE!
OOH! NEITHER CAN I!

JEWELLER
OOH!
OW!
CRASH!
HAR-HAR! THE BOBBY DAZZLER GANG STRIKES AGAIN!

BACK AT THE STATION—
CLASSIC SPARKY
...THEY DAZZLED US, SIR...
WELL, WEAR DARK GLASSES!
YES, SIR!

AND SMARTEN UP! LOOK IN THIS MIRROR!

LATER . . .
LOOK OUT! THERE THEY ARE!
GLASSES ON!

SMASHIN' THAT BLACK PAINT WE PUT ON THE GLASSES MAKES THEM REAL DARK! THEY WON'T DAZZLE US NOW! HEH-HEH! I CAN'T SEE A THING!
NEITHER CAN I!
DAZZLE!

HO-HO! ANOTHER VICTORY FOR THE BOBBY DAZZLER GANG!
CRASH!
UH?
OOPS!
WHOOOOM!
LET'S GO AND DAZZLE ANOTHER JEWELLER'S!

AND SO, BACK AT THE STATION AGAIN—
TWITS! YOU LET THEM GET AWAY—AND LOOK AT THE STATE YOU'RE IN NOW!

I'VE GOT IT, SIR!

BANG! THUMP! CRASH!
OOPS!
CAR GARAGE
PRIVATE! KEEP OUT!
OUCH!

THAT'S THE MIRRORS ALL FIXED! NOW WE'RE SURE TO CATCH THEM!
YIPPEE!

Jewellers
THERE THEY ARE! READY?
READY!

AAAH!
MIRRORS! OH, NO!
DAZZLE!
DAZZLE!

CRASH!
HAR-HAR! GOT THEM, CEDRIC!

INTO THE CAR, IF YOU PLEASE—
C'MON!

LATER . . .
GREAT IDEA, LADS! YOU MAY NOT LOOK SMART. BUT YOU'VE GOT REALLY SMART BRAINS!
YES, SIR!
TA, SIR!

THE
HILLYS
AND THE
BILLYS
THE HOT LEAD'S SINGING IN HAPPY VALLEY—AND EVERYBODY'S HAPPY!
SMASHIN' FEUD!
BANG!
BANG!
WHEE!
BANG!
ZIP!
PHOW!
HEY, PAW! QUIT THAT STOOPID FEUDIN' AN' RUN AN ERRAND F'R ME! TAKE THIS NOTE TO TH' STORES IN TOWN!
CLASSIC BEEZER
AW, SHUCKS! AN' I WUZ ENJOYIN' MYSELF, MAW!
JES' MY LUCK T' MISS ALL TH' FUN!
HMM! PARACHUTISTS IN TRAININ'!
I'VE GOT IT! PARACHUTISTS! WE COULD BE PARACHUTISTS! AN' KICK OUT THEM PESKY BILLYS!
I AIN'T GOT NO TIME T' GO INTO TOWN! I'M GOIN' T' PUT MY CLEVER PLAN INTO OPERATION RIGHT AWAY!
ZOOM!
HERE! GRAB THESE SHEETS! WE'RE GONNA BECOME PARACHUTISTS!
WE'RE ALL GOIN T' HAVE A NICE AIR TRIP!
BUT, PAW! IT COSTS THREE DOLLARS EACH.
DEADVILLE AIRPORT
WE'LL PAY WHEN TH' PLANE LANDS—'CEPT WE WON'T BE IN IT THEN. HEH! HEH!
HAW! HAW!
WOULD YOU TAKE US FOR A FLIP OVER HAPPY VALLEY?
CERTAINLY! HOP IN!
THIS SURE IS GOIN' T' BE A PLEASURE TRIP! HO-HO!
PLEASURE TRIPS THREE DOLLARS EACH PERSON
A FEW MINUTES LATER
HERE WE ARE, GEN'LEMEN—RIGHT OVER HAPPY VALLEY!
AN' THAT'S THE BILLYS' PLACE!
JUMP, FELLAHS!
WOW! MY SHEET'S FULL O' HOLES!
HELP!
SO'S MINE! HELP!
HEY, PAPPY! IT'S RAININ' HILLYS!
SURE IS! HO! HO!
WHUMP!
WHAM!
WHERE HAVE YOU BEEN, PAW HILLY? YOU DIDN'T GET MY MOTH BALLS FROM TH' STORES AND TH' MOTHS ARE RUININ' ALL MAH SHEETS!

The Whiteys and the Stripeys
They're stranded on two islands,
Just a yard or two apart.
Whenever they come face to face—
Wow! Watch the fighting start!
CLASSIC BUZZ
Not many fish about today!
CRUMBLE!
Help!
Wow!
Glub!
Glug!
Our new jetty will be much safer for fishing!
NAILS
That's it finished, Capting!
Good! Let's get our fishing rods!
Plenty fish here!
BUT, ON STRIPEY ISLAND —
Listen, men! We're pirates, ain't we, so we should attack them Whiteys by boat!
That's it, lads—build me a boat!
Har! It's good to get command of me own ship again. Splice me timbers and shiver the mainbrace!
MEANWHILE
That was a good day's fishing! We'll go and have a feed now!
Wait a minute! We've no knives or forks to eat with!
Don't worry! I've an idea!
I know just the thing to use!
A MINUTE OR TWO LATER
Look! Nails! We can use them to eat with!
Great idea, Dopey!
By the way, where did you get the nails?
That's a secret, Capting!
MEANWHILE AT THE WHITEYS' JETTY
They've built a jetty! We'll use it to go ashore!
Now to give them Whiteys a shock!
SMACK!
WHAP!
SMACK!
Ho-ho! So that's where Dopey got the nails from!

 DESERT ISLAND DICK 

Hey! That's MY money ...

It's MINE now, sonny!

# PETER PIPER

CLASSIC SPARKY

HERE YOU ARE, PETER. OFF YOU GO TO THE SHOPS FOR ME!

AW, AGAIN? RIGHTO, MUM. *SIGH!*

LIST

BUT—

I'LL HAVE THAT!

HEY!

*I'LL FIX HIM! I'LL BRING THE THINGS ON THE COINS TO LIFE WITH MY MAGIC PIPES...*

YEOW! WH-WHAT'S HAPPENING?

HA!

DON' THE GREE

BITE!

ROAR!

PROD!

NIP!

RIP!

*I'LL HAVE TO BE QUICK! I'LL BRING THIS POLICEMAN TO LIFE!*

BAH! GET OFF!

DON'T FORGET THE GREEN CROSS CODE

HELLO, HELLO, HELLO. WHAT'S ALL THIS THEN?

C'MERE YOU! ERK!

HELLO! YOU'RE NEW AND YOU'VE NICKED VIV THE SPIV—WELL DONE, LAD!

IT WAS NOTHING, SARGE!

THAT TAKES CARE OF THAT—NOW TO GET ON WITH THE SHOPPING!

NO holiday for the boys of Greytowers School! Mr Creep had laid down the law and the only hope of any pupil getting outside was to sneak out unseen. Keen-witted Winker Watson at once saw possibilities of profit in this situation. But he wasn't the only one. His young bother Wallie was a cunning little wangler, too!

Winker borrowed a ladder to assist escapers over the school wall. It was cheap at a penny a climb, but Watson Major got no customers. And why was that?

Winker Watson was thunderstruck. His kid brother had borrowed a trampoline from the gym. A leap and a bound—and every breaker-out was over the wall, at no charge at all!

That "free" business puzzled Winker, but Wallie silenced him by offering him the same chance.

Winker took the offer. Up he soared, heading for freedom—just as his own Form master appeared.

Wallie was left to face the music. But Winker hadn't forgotten that Dad Watson had made him promise to keep Wallie out of trouble.

Down from the tree hurtled the wangler. And poor Mr Creep happened to be standing below.

So Wallie was saved once more and Winker now looked after Creepy's welfare.

As soon as the Form Master was in sick bay, Winker would be able to sneak out and see what tricks his kid brother was playing now.

LATER ~~
The wily Wallie was up to tricks sure enough. He had pinched Winker's ladder and was making very profitable use of it!
HEY, WINKER, WALLIE'S PINCHED YOUR LADDER AND NOW HE WANTS A TANNER EACH TO GET US BACK OVER THE WALL!
CLASSIC DANDY

OO-ER! UP AND OVER I GO — AND THE LADDER GOES WITH ME!
HEY, COME BACK WITH MY LADDER, YOU PERISHING PROFITEER, WALLIE!
That was why the little stinker had helped everyone out, so that he could sting them getting in! Winker was wild. Wallie scampered hastily to safety and he took a pocketful of sixpences with him.

Winker was outside with the others—but no one would catch him paying sixpence to get in!
NOW DON'T WORRY, CHAPS, I'LL GET YOU BACK OVER THE WALL — AND I'LL GET YOUNG WALLIE, TOO!

NOW, LISTEN, CHAPS, HERE COMES A LORRY — I'LL WAVE IT DOWN AS THOUGH I WANT A LIFT AND YOU ALL KEEP OUT OF SIGHT AND.....
Winker's brain-box was working furiously.

OVER WE GO, BOYS!
GIVE YOU A LIFT TO THE VILLAGE, SON? DON'T BE DAFT, I'VE JUST COME FROM THERE! BE OFF WITH YOU!
TRANSPORT COMPANY
A little cross-talk with the lorry driver was enough. Under cover of it, the boys used his lorry to scale the wall.

Now it was Winker's turn and he made it before the lorry driver could think of a way of stopping him!
OKAY, THEN, GUV'NOR, THANKS ALL THE SAME!
HEY! HOW DARE YOU USE MY LORRY AS A STEP-LADDER!

I'VE GOT WALLIE, CHAPS! PUT THE LADDER UP AGAINST THE WALL AGAIN!
RIGHT, WINKER!
WHAT'S THE BIG IDEA, WINKER?
When Winker caught his profiteering brother, he hauled him to the wall.

?
HUP AND OVER THE WALL, WALLIE, ME LAD!
Wallie was gently "helped" over. In two twos he was out of school without permission, even though he was only just outside.

L-LEMME BACK IN, WINKER!
OKAY, THEN, WALLIE, BUT IT'LL COST YOU EVERY TANNER YOU TWISTED OUT OF THE CHAPS!
Either way, Willie was due for a big drop. If he didn't fork out the dough, he would get a whale of a hiding for breaking bounds. He was forced to pay, and the price was every unlawful tanner the boys had been fleeced out of!

LATER ~~
WALLIE'S, ER, TREATING US TO THIS LITTLE LOT, CHAPS, AND IF THERE'S ANY GRUB LEFT OVER I'VE PROMISED HIM HE CAN LICK THE PLATES!
YUM-YUM!
GRR! BIG BROTHERS — BAH!
ICES
The TUCK SHOP PRICES
HOT PIES
TEAS
COLD DRINKS
So Wallie the business man had the "pleasure" of seeing his profit eaten up by Winker's gang—but he took no pleasure in it!

**A BIG DRAW! – Well over a hundred funny pictures!**

## BIFFO the Bear

BUDDA BA DUB

WHOOOOO

IN THE TUNNEL

NOW FOR A BITE OF MY LOLLIPOP!

OUT OF THE TUNNEL

'S FUNNY! I'M SURE I ONLY TOOK ONE BITE!

I'LL HAVE ANOTHER LOLLIPOP!

BIFFO

ANOTHER TUNNEL

JUST ONE BITE! THAT'S ALL I'LL TAKE!

SO! ONE OF THESE BOYS IS STEALING BITES OUT OF MY LOLLIES!

AH, WELL! I'LL JUST HAVE TO EAT MY LAST ONE!

BIFFO

ANOTHER TUNNEL

I WON'T TAKE A BITE THIS TIME!

ANY MINUTE NOW!

SOAP

SPLUTTER!

THE LAST TUNNEL

THUMP!

THAT'LL TEACH HIM!

HARUM SCAREM
Time for a bit of fishing!
CLASSIC BUZZ

This'll get Scarem out of the way while I pinch some grub!

He's rising to the bait!
A bone!

Have a close look at this hammer! Ho-ho!
CRUNCH!

LATER–
Oooh! Wh-what hit me? Oh . . . now I remember–Harum! He fooled me again!

TEA-TIME–
The same old trick won't fool Scarem, so I'll try this . . .

Aye-aye! What's this?

Perfect!
He won't fool me twice! I'll reach up and grab him!

Gotcha! That'll keep you out of my way for a while!
CLICK!

GRR!
Lovely fresh vegetables! I do like the carrots here! Mmmm!

I'll try a simple trick this time! It always works!
KNOCK! KNOCK! KNOCK!

BUT–
Heh-heh! Now it's my turn to win!
CREAK!

He doesn't know about my new back door!
Yoohoo! Scarem!

WOW!
BOO!

CRUMP!

Aah! He even knocks himself out now! What a helpful pooch he is! Sweet dreams, Scarem!
NNNNH!
CARROTS

Minnie the Minx
CLASSIC BEANO
WHAT A USELESS CAT CHESTER IS!

HOI! SAP! YOU'RE MEANT TO CHASE MICE — NOT PLAY WITH THEM.
BONK!

NO! WON'T TOUCH HIM — HE'S MY PAL.

AH, WELL — IF CHESTER WON'T BE THE CAT IN THIS HOUSE . . .

. . . I'LL HAVE TO DO IT MYSELF.

YOU CAN BE MINNIE FOR TODAY.

Soon—
AH! I'LL USE CHESTER'S TAIL TO DRY MYSELF.

SQUEAK-TI-TUM.
RUB! RUB!

HOI! MOUSE! WHAT ARE YOU DOING WITH MY TAIL?

SQUEAK! THIS ISN'T THE CHESTER I KNOW AND LOVE.

AT LEAST I'M SAFE IN HERE.

CRASH!

CLASSIC BEANO
MY WALL!
CLATTER!

MINX! PEST!

I'LL DO WHAT CHESTER DOES WHEN HE'S CHASED — CLIMB CURTAINS.
GRAB!

R-R-RIP!
WAH! I'M HEAVIER THAN CHESTER.

AH, WELL AT LEAST WE CATS ALWAYS LAND ON OUR FEET . . .

. . . OR SOMEONE ELSES,
WHUMP!

OH-OH! DAD IS NOT TOO HAPPY.

TIME TO GO!
PSSST.

IN HERE, MINNIE.

I TAKE BACK WHAT I SAID ABOUT CATS HAVING TO CHASE MICE.

STOMP!
MICE ARE VERY HANDY PEOPLE TO KNOW.

# THE SMASHER

CLASSIC DANDY

WELL— 'OW LONG WILL IT GO IF YOU DO WIND IT??

GLURK! SHEESH!!!

CRASH!

TWOINKLE

PY-YOING!

PLGING!

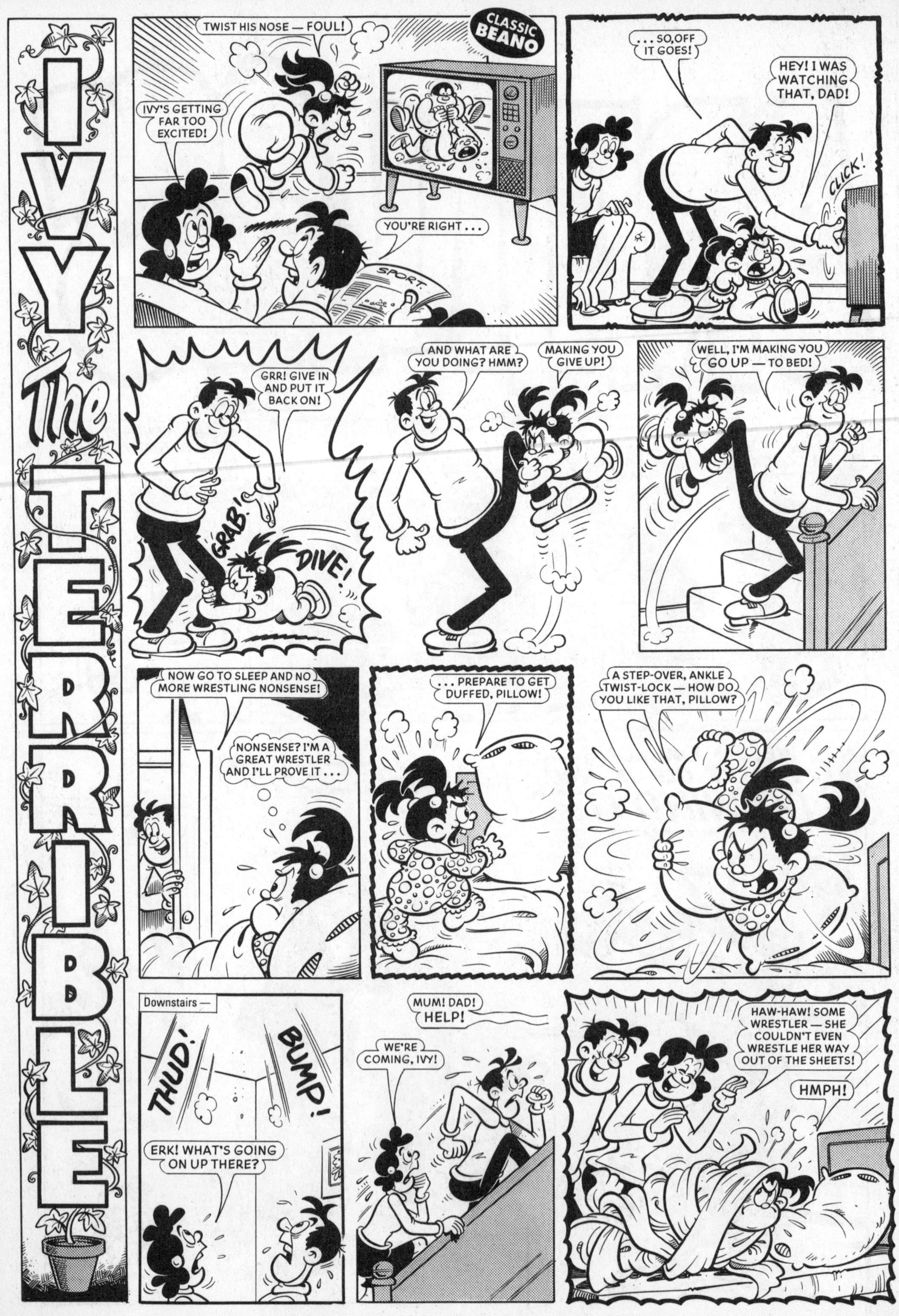
IVY The TERRIBLE
CLASSIC BEANO
TWIST HIS NOSE — FOUL!
IVY'S GETTING FAR TOO EXCITED!
YOU'RE RIGHT . . .
SPORT
. . . SO, OFF IT GOES!
HEY! I WAS WATCHING THAT, DAD!
CLICK!
GRR! GIVE IN AND PUT IT BACK ON!
GRAB!
DIVE!
AND WHAT ARE YOU DOING? HMM?
MAKING YOU GIVE UP!
WELL, I'M MAKING YOU GO UP — TO BED!
NOW GO TO SLEEP AND NO MORE WRESTLING NONSENSE!
NONSENSE? I'M A GREAT WRESTLER AND I'LL PROVE IT . . .
. . . PREPARE TO GET DUFFED, PILLOW!
A STEP-OVER, ANKLE TWIST-LOCK — HOW DO YOU LIKE THAT, PILLOW?
Downstairs —
THUD!
BUMP!
ERK! WHAT'S GOING ON UP THERE?
MUM! DAD! HELP!
WE'RE COMING, IVY!
HAW-HAW! SOME WRESTLER — SHE COULDN'T EVEN WRESTLE HER WAY OUT OF THE SHEETS!
HMPH!